9/94 7c
7/95 9c

D0408233

AGAINST ALL HOPE

AGAINST

The Prison Memoirs of

ALL HOPE

Armando Valladares

Translated by Andrew Hurley

Alfred A. Knopf New York 1986

THIS IS A BORZOI BOOK
PUBLISHED BY ALFRED A. KNOPF, INC.

Copyright © 1986 by Alfred A. Knopf, Inc.

All rights reserved under International and Pan-American Copyright Conventions. Published in the United States by Alfred A. Knopf, Inc., New York, and simultaneously in Canada by Random House of Canada Limited, Toronto. Distributed by Random House, Inc., New York. Originally published in Spain as *Contra Toda Esperanza* by Plaza & Janes Editores, S.A., Barcelona. Copyright © 1985 by Armando Valladares

Library of Congress Cataloging-in-Publication Data

Valladares, Armando.
  Against all hope.

  Translation of: Contra toda esperanza.
  I. Valladares, Armando.   2. Political prisoners—Cuba—Biography.   3. Cuba—Politics and government—1959–   .   I. Title.
HV9557.5.V35A3813   1986   365'.45'0924 [B]   85-81503
ISBN 0-394-53425-5

Manufactured in the United States of America
Published May 9, 1986
Reprinted Once
Third Printing, August 1986

*To the memory of my companions
tortured and murdered in Fidel Castro's jails,
and to the thousands of prisoners
still suffering in them.*

Who against hope believed in hope . . .

—ROM. IV: 18

Man is Nature's most wonderful creature.
Torturing him, crushing him, murdering him
for his beliefs and ideas is more than a
violation of human rights—it is a
crime against all humanity.

A.V.

Contents

Photographs follow page 336.

Introduction

This book is my personal account of the twenty-two years I spent in the political prisons of Cuba, solely for having espoused and expressed principles distinct from those of the regime of Fidel Castro.

In my country there is a fact which not even the most fervent defenders of the Cuban Revolution can deny—a dictatorship has existed there for more than a quarter of a century. And no dictatorship can remain in power for so long without violating human rights, without persecutions, without political prisoners, without political prisons.

In Cuba at this very moment there are more than two hundred penal installations, ranging from maximum-security prisons to concentration camps to so-called farms and "open fronts," where prisoners do forced labor. In every one of these two hundred or so prisons there is material for dozens of books, which means that these pages are the merest sketch of the terrible reality of Cuban prisons.

Someday, when the history of all of them is known in detail, mankind will feel the revulsion it felt when the crimes of Stalin were brought to light.

In its latest reports, Amnesty International has denounced the executions of dozens of political opponents of the regime, the physical mistreatment and abuse, the beatings. And when it appealed to the Cuban government to abolish the death penalty, the Vice-President of Cuba, Carlos Rafael Rodríguez, who had been a minister in the Batista government as well, answered that the death penalty was necessary in Cuba. Rodríguez was also quoted in an interview published in Madrid's *Diario 16* on October 10, 1983, as saying, in answer to the interviewer's question whether groups struggling for labor-union freedom and for human rights existed in Cuba, that indeed people holding such idyllic ideas as the freedom to organize into labor unions and the protection of human rights did exist, but that he predicted a future of ridicule for them.

.   .   .

For me, this book represents the long night I have left behind me, but for the thousands of my countrymen still held in the jails, for my comrades, some of whom have already spent twenty-five years in prison, it represents daily reality. They have been held longer than any other political prisoners in Latin America, perhaps in the world. The violence, repression, and beatings, the torture, the lack of mail, news, and visits, and the solitary confinement are facts of life for them. Today, at this very moment, hundreds of political prisoners are naked, sleeping on the floors of cells whose windows and doors have been sealed. They never see the light of day, or for that matter artificial light. They are denied medical care and visits, and all because they refused to enter the Political Rehabilitation Program.

Photographs of some of the people I talk about in this book are included here, as evidence that those people really existed, really exist, that they are people with faces. Those who are still alive reside now in the United States, Venezuela, and other countries.

I feel I should say that in my terrible pilgrimage from prison to prison I did meet military men and women and civilian officials of great humaneness, men and women who helped us as much as they could—and in so doing risked going to prison themselves. In order to protect them, their names and the favors they did us cannot be revealed.

I do not want to conclude without recalling those to whom I owe my freedom, and reiterating my gratitude to them. Their names are not written here because the list would grow much too long for a brief introduction, and also because there are people whose names I do not even know, people whose thoughts were with me, who anonymously worked to free me, help me, who did things for me I perhaps am not even aware of. To all of these I send, with this book, my best—the best from my memory, the best from my heart.

ARMANDO VALLADARES
Madrid, 1984

AGAINST ALL HOPE

1 / Detention

My eyes flew open. The cold muzzle of a machine gun held to my temple had shocked me awake. I was confused and frightened. Three armed men were standing around my bed, and one of them was shoving my head into the pillow with his machine gun.

"Where's the pistol?"

As the man with the machine gun kept my head immobile, another slid his hand under it to check for that purely imaginary pistol I was supposed to be armed with. Then the oldest of them, a thin man with graying hair, spoke to me again. He brusquely told me to get dressed, I had to go with them.

These were agents of Castro's Political Police. I was to learn later that the older man, the one doing the talking, had been an agent in the Batista regime as well. There was a fourth agent in the living room keeping watch on my mother and sister.

I hadn't heard them come in. When they knocked at the front door, it was my mother who had gone to open it. I was in a deep sleep in the last bedroom down the hall, with blankets piled on me to keep out the cold.

The three agents made me get dressed in front of them. I reached to open the closet, but one of them cut me off. He opened the door himself and slid the hangers to one side, one by one, and then he gave a quick glance around at the rest of the things in the closet. I began to dress, while they stood around me and watched me carefully. But they seemed more relaxed now, less nervous. When these agents are sent out to detain some citizen, they are not told who he is or why he is being arrested. They *are* told, though, as a matter of course, that he is armed and extremely dangerous. Now they knew that I wasn't armed and I didn't seem particularly dangerous; in fact, I never had been either.

When I had gotten my clothes on, they began the search of the house. The search was thorough, painstaking, long. They spent almost four hours going through everything. There was not one inch of the house they didn't go over with a fine-tooth comb. They opened jars and bottles, they went through the books page by page, they emptied toothpaste tubes, they looked at the motor of the refrigerator, at the mattresses.

I tried to reassure my mother and sister. I told them this had to be some sort of mistake, since I hadn't done anything that warranted my being arrested. I kept up a conversation with my mother, who was terribly nervous and upset by this middle-of-the-night violation of the peace of our home, but as we spoke I tried to think who might have reported that I had weapons. It seemed obvious to me that it must have been someone who wanted to see me detained for a while, see me harassed on some trumped-up charge. Of course, sooner or later it would all be straightened out. I figured the denunciation must have come from someone in my office.

At that time I had a good job in the Caja Postal de Ahorros, which might be termed the Postal Savings Bank, an office attached to the Ministry of Communications in the Revolutionary Government. I had received several promotions, thanks largely to the fact that I was a university student. Some of the people I worked with there, I knew, were out to get me.

A few weeks before, one of the directors, a man I had developed a close friendship with, called me in to warn me that the Political Police had been around asking questions about me. I had had some friction in the office because I had frequently spoken out against Communism as a political system because it went against my religious beliefs and some of my more idealistic notions of the world.

In those days, several things had happened which could be seen as signaling the radicalization of the internal structure of the Ministry of Communications. The Minister, Enrique Oltuski, a professional engineer, had been removed from office, and replaced by Raúl Curbelo, who had fought with Castro in the anti-Batista guerrillas. The only thing Curbelo knew anything about was cows; he told me so himself a few days after he had been appointed, when he came around to introduce himself in my department.

"Listen, Valladares, I don't know anything about any of this. I was in the Agrarian Reform Institute, but Fidel sent me here to take charge of this Ministry. The only thing I know anything about is cows, so I'm counting on all of you to pitch in and help me make this work."

And he wasn't kidding. The only thing he knew anything about was cows —but he was a man Castro could trust.

The subdirector of the Postal Savings Bank was replaced by another Communist, as was the treasurer, by an old Party militant from Camagüey province. That was when they fired one of my best friends and co-workers, Israel Abreu, because of his anti-Marxist statements. Israel had been a member of the underground groups struggling against Batista's dictatorship, so the new Minister's decision to fire him caused a great deal of discontent among all of us. I personally spoke out against the measure. I called it an abuse of authority and a violation of freedom of expression, which had been one of the basic tenets for which Castro's revolution had supposedly been fought.

It wasn't surprising, then, that I had been marked as an anti-Communist. One of my last outbursts was brought on by a slogan which was being spread throughout the country by the government propaganda apparatus. By that time Castro was accused of being a Communist, so they circulated the slogan "If Fidel is a Communist, then put me on the list. *He's* got the right idea." This slogan was printed on decals and bumper stickers and on little tin plaques to be displayed on the doors of private homes; it was published daily in the newspapers; it was blazoned on posters pasted up on the walls of schools, police stations, factories, shops, and government offices. The purpose of all this was quite clear and simple: Castro was presented to the country as a messiah, a savior, the man who would return the country to freedom, prosperity, happiness. Castro could never be linked to anything evil, to anything bad at all. Whatever Castro was, or might be, was good by definition. Therefore, if he was a Communist, then put me on the list.

That was the kind of reasoning the propaganda specialists of the Party had used. The great majority of the Cuban people didn't know much about Communism. They weren't really politically aware, and it was difficult for them to believe the bad things people were saying about Marxism. The Party was using the slogan to prepare the masses, gradually get them used to the idea of a Communist government.

The Communists in the Ministry came in one day to set a card with that slogan on my worktable. I refused to let them. They were surprised and a little perplexed, because even though they knew I was opposed to Marxism, they thought I wouldn't reject the card, the slogan, since that would be tantamount to rejecting Fidel. They asked me if I had anything against Castro. I answered that if he was a Communist I did. And that I wouldn't be on that list. That set off an argument.

Every day I felt more and more out of place, more and more conspicuous. And I was very naive—I had assumed that the worst they would do to me would be fire me from my job, as they had Israel. It never occurred to me they would do anything more drastic; it never occurred to me that because I expressed my opinions, because I spoke out against Marxism, they would drag me off to jail. Moreover, the government still hadn't declared itself Marxist. Castro would do that only some months later.

Within the ranks of the revolutionaries who had fought against Batista, there were thousands of people who would not allow themselves to think that Castro was a Communist. They admitted that it was true that Communists were gradually moving into certain areas, that dreadful things were happening, but it was all behind Fidel's back. When he found out about it, he'd put a stop to it. How naive they were! I understood their dilemma— many of them seemed almost willfully unable to come to grips with the fact that Castro had tricked them, used them, gotten them to fight, manipulated them for his own ends. They held to their beliefs by arguing from declarations Castro had made at the very beginning of the Revolution, the statements he had made in Cuba, in Latin American countries, before leaders of the Foreign Relations Committee of the United States, and in numerous press conferences. He had held one press conference on April 17, 1959, in Washington, D.C., where he had been invited to speak before the Newspaper Editors' Association at a meeting in the Statler-Hilton Hotel. There he stated, "I have said that we are not Communists."

That same day Charles Porter, Congressman from Oregon, pointedly asked Castro if his brother Raúl was indoctrinating the soldiers in Communism, to which the Leader of the Revolution, "indignant," responded, "Do you really believe that I would permit the Communists to destroy the army that I have built?"

Two days later, on April 19, 1959, Fidel Castro appeared as a guest on the famous program *Meet the Press,* and there in the NBC studios he responded to the journalists' questions. One of them, Lawrence Spivak, asked Castro point-blank: "I want to know where your heart lies in the struggle between Communism and democracy. Whose side, where is your heart and where are your feelings?" Castro immediately responded, "Democracy is my ideal, really. . . . I am not Communist. I am not agreed with Communism. . . . There is no doubt for me between democracy and Communism."

These, then, were the statements always appealed to by those who did not want, or did not dare, to accept the fact of the deception. They were judging Castro by their own system of values, by their own ethical principles.

Dr. Raúl Roa, Cuba's ambassador to the United Nations, also lashed out against Communism, calling it "an inhumane theory, because it enslaves mankind." Saying that they were not Communists, that they never lied, that they would hold free elections, that they would respect human rights, was no more than a smokescreen, a tactic in the struggle. Therefore, the revolutionaries who insisted on believing that Fidel would put an end to the growing power of the Communists were incapable of admitting to themselves that although the government had still not declared itself Marxist, practices were being carried out which were indisputably Marxist in character—forcible expropriation of private property, land takeovers, nationalization, the transfer of the privately held means of production to the State, and the constant preaching of hate and praising of the class struggle.

The Political Police officers continued the search. They finished in the bedrooms, the bathroom, the kitchen, and they came into the living room. They examined all the pictures on the walls and all the porcelain figurines. Suddenly they seemed to pounce on one of the figurines—they had discovered something inside. One of them fished out a piece of paper with the end of a ballpoint pen. It was a piece of shredded paper, the kind used to pack glassware. He opened it, but when he realized that I was smiling sardonically at his absurdity, he crumpled it and threw it out the window. They made us lift up the couch; they turned it over and examined it carefully. The search finally ended, and no weapons or explosives or propaganda or lists had turned up. Nothing, absolutely nothing. They had to leave empty-handed. Or almost empty-handed—they took *me* with them. Although they hadn't found anything, there were some routine questions I had to answer. My mother argued with them. She said I hadn't done anything, there was no reason to take me away. They told her not to worry, I'd be right back. They'd bring me back home themselves.

The return would take more than twenty years.

We went out into the street. It was four o'clock in the morning; the night was very cold and there was a stiff wind blowing in from the bay. They put me into a gray Volkswagen and an agent sat on either side of me. They handcuffed me. Another car joined us at the corner. Not one word was spoken, though from time to time the radio crackled out a message incomprehensible to me. One of the transmissions was for the car I was in. The driver picked up the receiver and responded with a short phrase—a coded countersign, I assume.

We came to Fifth Avenue and Calle 14 in the Miramar section of Havana. That was then the location of the main headquarters of the Political Police, the Cuban Lubyanka. Several residences which had been taken over by the government formed the G-2 complex, which was what they called State Security in the beginning.

A white-helmeted soldier armed with a rifle opened the main gate. At the entrance of an office there was a bench. They told me to sit down. About half an hour later they led me to the back part of the building, where they had constructed a block of cells. They took off my handcuffs and put me into the first cell. There were already other prisoners in that small dungeon. In one corner, behind a wall, was the toilet. Three tiers of beds were attached to the walls. Some of the prisoners, from up on their perches, stuck out their heads to see the new boarder.

I was called out and taken to the second floor, the records office. They took my fingerprints and photographed me with a sign that read "COUNTER-REVOLUTIONARY."

That same afternoon I was subjected to my first interrogation. It was held in a small office before a one-way mirror of dark-green glass. A group of agents were waiting for me, but only one officer was sitting down, and he was the one who spoke to me. He told me they knew about everything; they knew I was a counterrevolutionary, an enemy of the Revolution. He said they were going to see to it, too, that I was punished for that. I told him in return that I hadn't committed any crime whatsoever, that they had

searched my house from top to bottom and seen for themselves that there
was nothing in my possession which could make them even remotely consider me a traitor or an enemy of the Revolution.

"But we know about the remarks you've made in your office—we know
you've been attacking the Revolution."

I defended myself. I said that I had not attacked the Revolution as an
institution.

"But you *have* attacked Communism."

I didn't deny that. I couldn't, nor did I want to.

"Yes, that's true," I said. "I think that Communism is a worse dictatorship than the one we Cubans have just overthrown. And if Communist rule
is established in Cuba, then Cuba will be just like Russia, going from czarism
to the dictatorship of the proletariat."

"We didn't fight this revolution for just more of the same privilege and
exploitation. Yankee imperialist exploitation is finished in Cuba, and we're
not going to allow people like you, in the service of capitalist interests, to
interrupt the march of revolutionary progress."

That, then, was my first interrogation. It hardly lasted ten minutes. That
same afternoon, they took me along with a group of other prisoners, including one woman, into a small room. They ordered us to sit down on a wooden
bench. They turned on spotlights set up around the room, and photographers and cameramen began to take pictures and movies of us. The next day
we appeared in the newspapers as a band of terrorists, CIA agents captured
by State Security. I didn't know any of those people; I had never even seen
any of them before. It was only there that I first came in contact with Nestor
Piñango, Alfredo Carrión, and Carlos Alberto Montaner, all three university students. I also met Richard Heredia there, who had been one of the
leaders of the 26th of July Movement in Oriente province. He had fought
in both the Sierra Maestra and the underground, and when the Revolution
triumphed he became the first governor of Santiago de Cuba. When they
arrested him, they forced him to put on one of the uniforms of the defeated
Batista army; they photographed him in it and published a picture of what
they called a "recruit of dictatorship" in all the newspapers.

The next day I went through my second interrogation. Each day they
would give us the official newspaper, the daily *Revolución,* which was calling
us terrorists. In the interrogation I protested against that. The officer told
me they were sure that I was an enemy of the people.

"You studied in a school run by priests," he said to me.

"Yes, in Escolapius. What difference does that make?"

"A big difference. Priests are counterrevolutionary, and the fact that you
went to that school is one more piece of evidence against you."

"But Fidel Castro studied in a school taught by Jesuits. He went to
Belén."

"Yes, but Fidel is a revolutionary. You, on the other hand, are a counterrevolutionary, tied to priests and capitalists, and so we are going to sentence you to jail."

"There isn't a shred of evidence against me. You have discovered nothing that incriminates me in any way."

"It's true—we have no proof, or rather no concrete proof, against you. But we do have the conviction that you are a potential enemy of the Revolution. For us, that is enough."

When I came out of the interrogation, I heard people shouting and automobile horns blowing. A march had been staged in front of the buildings, along Fifth Avenue, and the people were calling out, "Firing squad! Firing squad!" for the "CIA terrorists." The Communists had organized not only that demonstration but another one in front of the Presidential Palace as well. That one called for our execution too.

That night, they took Richard Heredia and me out of the cell, into a room where they made a movie of us for the newsreels. One of the reporters said under his breath that it seemed a shame for such a young man to be shot. He was talking about me. The campaign organized by the Communists had reached such vast proportions that it made me begin to fear very seriously for my life. By now, faced with what I was going through, I had discarded my assumption that the worst that could happen to me was being fired from my job. It might actually be the firing squad instead.

The next morning very early I was taken to my last interrogation. It almost had the flavor of a farewell.

"We know that you have connections to elements that are conspiring against the State, that you are friendly with some of them. If you cooperate with us, we can give you your freedom and send you back to your job."

"I don't know any of those people. I don't have any contact with conspirators."

"This is the last chance you have to get yourself out of this."

"I don't know anything. You people can't send me to jail, you can't find me guilty, because I haven't done *anything*. There's no proof against me. You have no evidence to show."

"Our conviction is enough for us. We know that you are a potential enemy of the Revolution. Look!" And he tossed several afternoon newspapers at me. In big letters on the front page was written "FIRING SQUAD FOR TERRORISTS."

"They want an example made of you, so . . ." He left the threat hanging in the air.

That night Carlos Alberto, Richard, and I took a can opener and began to make a hole in the wall behind the toilet. We were going to try to escape. It wasn't easy; we had to chip off the stucco that covered the wall before we could even start taking out the cement blocks.

The day after my arrest, my sister went to the police station nearest our house to try to find out what had happened to me. They told her they didn't know anything about me. She went to Fifth Avenue and Calle 14, where I was being held at the time, and there too they told her they didn't have me in custody. When the newspaper stories about me and the others came out, the vigilance committees* in my neighborhood, led by several plainclothes agents from the Political Police, organized a march in the street. They stoned the doors and windows of my house. The inflamed mob cried, "Firing squad! Shoot them!" My mother was terrified. She collapsed to the floor senseless. My sister ran out of the house crying for a doctor.

Later, she tried once more to find out where I was, and that time they did not deny that I was at the headquarters of the Political Police. They ordered her to sit down. After a while, they sent her into an office and began to interrogate her, accusing her too of being a counterrevolutionary. Their hatred for my whole family was such that they not only forced her to undergo the interrogation, and the accusations they flung at her, but also photographed her, as they had me, with a sign reading "COUNTERREVOLU-TIONARY." They would not allow her to see me.

Carlos Alberto, Richard, and I took turns trying to make our hole in the wall. We knew we were risking reprisals, but we felt we had to try to escape. We didn't manage to finish the job, however; they took us away before we could. We never knew whether it was a coincidence or whether one of the many prisoners held there was an informer or an agent of the Political Police.

In the interior patio, a car was waiting. There was another prisoner already in it—Zoila, the same woman I had seen when they had taken our photographs. They warned us not to speak.

Those were the first days of 1961. All along the shore in Havana, there were cannons pointed toward the north. The United States had broken off relations with Cuba, and the government was concerned about the threat of an invasion. The wind raised great waves that leaped over the wall of the Malecón, the seawall that runs along the coast of Havana. The car sped down the shore road and went through the tunnel across the bay, and we entered the fortress of La Cabaña. In front of the high fence, its gate opening onto the medieval-looking main entrance of the prison-fortress, they ordered us out of the car. They turned some papers over to the soldier posted at the gate, and the car went on toward the women's prison, the other passenger's destination.

---

*Committees for the Defense of the Revolution (CDRs), organized by city blocks; lowest Party instrumentality in the hierarchy. —Trans.

2 / La Cabaña

The fortress of La Cabaña was built by the Spaniards two hundred years ago to protect the entrance to the port of Havana. When the English took the port in 1762, the first thing they did was secure this fortress. Because of its location, it was said, "Whoever holds La Cabaña holds the key to the city." Since the triumph of the Revolution, it had been converted into a political prison, and in its deep moats, now dry if they had ever been filled with water, the executions by firing squad were carried out.

La Cabaña sat atop a hill on the opposite side of the bay from Havana. It was very isolated. Great parade grounds, firing ranges, and open land surrounded it. The artillery school was located there.

They opened a small metal door and ordered me inside. Now at the entrance to the fortress, I could see the prison yard in front of the *galeras,* large rooms which had served the many purposes of a colonial fortress— barracks, storerooms, ammunition magazines, and so on—and which now were barred and used as large cells for the prisoners held there. There were hundreds of prisoners looking out curiously at us, the new arrivals. I went first into a small apartment, where they registered me and gave me a card, and then to the storehouse. There they stripped off the clothing I wore, a new suit, and gave me the prison uniform, which had a large black *P* stenciled on the back. They promised to give the suit to my family the first time they came to visit me, but they never did. The head of the storeroom had been a member of Castro's rebel guerrillas; he was now in prison for the crime of armed robbery. These "delinquents," common criminals, lived in a *galera* which opened off the main gate outside the central patio, intentionally kept separate from the political prisoners. They still wore the olive-green uniform, and this one wore his hair in a ponytail in imitation of Raúl Castro. He hated political prisoners, and never missed an opportunity to show it.

I left the storeroom and found myself suddenly in the prison yard, in the midst of that multitude of prisoners. I didn't know a soul. They had assigned me to *galera* 12, so I went to look for it.

At the door, a young prisoner stood watching me. Behind his sunglasses his bright eyes sparkled with intelligence and bottled-up energy. He smiled affably and extended his hand. He was Pedro Luis Boitel, a leader of the Student Movement at the University. He had fought against Batista in the underground and later had managed to flee to Venezuela, but he had returned when the dictator fell. He had recognized me from the photographs that had appeared in the newspapers. He was the first person I met there, and we became great friends, as close as brothers. Boitel lived toward the center of the gallery, on a high bunk. All the beds were taken. There were too many prisoners.

The *galeras* were vaulted galleries—that is, shaped like rural mailboxes, or tunnels, open at both ends. One end of all of them faced the moat that circumscribed the fortress. At that outward-facing end of the *galeras* they were secured by not one but two iron gratings of thick bars. The walls were about three feet thick, so the gratings, which were on the exterior and interior faces of the walls, wound up spaced about a yard apart. There were two masonry observation posts, called *garitas,* at the top of the wall around the prison yard, from which guards with machine guns always kept the prison yard, the prisoners, and the iron bars of the cells under surveillance.

That afternoon some of the prisoners who had been with me at Political Police Headquarters arrived—Carlos Alberto Montaner, Alfredo Carrión, Nestor Piñango, and some others. They all knew Boitel from the University, and they were also sent to our gallery.

The first night we had to sleep on the floor between the beds and in the passages between the rows. Since one end of all the cells opened to the north, the cold wind blew fiercely through the barred window arches. There were not enough blankets to go around, and we almost froze. The next day we got word out to our families that they would be permitted to visit us.

Two men, cousins, Ulises and Julio Antonio Yebra, had been arrested the same morning I had. They had appeared in the newspaper photographs too. Julio Antonio was a doctor, and a brave man, brave almost to the point of rashness, in fact. In the search of his house they had discovered an old .22 rifle. That was all. The Political Police deduced that if he possessed a rifle, it must be that he intended to use it against someone, and since Julio Antonio was well connected in the Revolutionary Government, since he was a professional, he couldn't intend to use it against some rank-and-file soldier, some simple unknown militiaman. The someone had to be someone important, a leader of the Revolution, and who more important than Fidel Castro? That was the reasoning which led to Julio Antonio's being accused of possessing a weapon intended for use in an attempt on Fidel Castro's life. He was sentenced to death.

During the Batista years, Armando Hart, one of the leaders of the 26th of July Movement and current Minister of Culture in Cuba, had been jailed. So had his wife, Haydée Santamaría, at that time the third-highest-ranking woman in the regime, director of Casa de las Américas. (Years later, on a now-symbolic 26th of July, 1982, disillusioned by the system which she had helped to implement, Haydée committed suicide.) Julio Antonio had pulled off a courageous and daring coup by helping to rescue Armando Hart from the hands of Batista's police when Armando was being tried in the Audiencia building in Havana. Now the situations were reversed—Julio Antonio was the one in prison. So Julio Antonio's mother knocked on Armando Hart and Haydée Santamaría's door. It was a time for loyalty, a time to acknowledge the debts of friendship, but they flatly refused to intercede for the man who had saved their lives. Worse even that that, Haydée wrote a letter alleging that Julio Antonio had participated in anti-Castro demonstrations. The letter went on to say that he had never really been a completely trustworthy person.

Julio Antonio was tried under Article No. 5 of 1961. This law took effect five days after his arrest; they applied the law to him retroactively. His trial began early in the morning. At noon the next day, a two-hour recess was called. Julio returned to his cell and said to one of the men there, "Do me a favor—open that can of pears you've been saving and give me a glass of milk. That's the last thing I'll ever eat, since tonight I'll be far away from here, close to God."

Many of the men tried to reassure him with words of sympathy and comfort, but he merely repeated gently and calmly, "Yes, tonight I'll be with God."

He wrote several letters. At two o'clock that afternoon they took him back to the trial. Julio Antonio didn't return to the cell this time after he left the trial. He was left in one of the small chapels in the fortress which were now reserved for prisoners sentenced to death. Men who were there say that he behaved with the same strength and valor during the trial that he had always lived by.

At nine o'clock we were in the habit of gathering into groups and praying in all the *galeras*—faith in difficult times. The sound of a motor was heard. Total silence fell. It was the truck carrying the coffin for the corpse. Then we heard the motor of a jeep that was carrying the prisoner, and some voices. There was a long stairway leading down into the moat. A few yards from the wall stood the wooden stake to which the prisoner was tied. Before they tied him up, Julio Antonio shook hands with each one of the soldiers on the firing squad and told them that he forgave them.

"Firing squad . . . attention!"

"Ready! . . . Aim! . . . Fire!"

The discharge was ragged; the platoon fired in disorder, not at all in unison.

"Down with Commun—!" Julio Antonio's cry was never finished.

Then there came the dry crack of the *coup de grace* behind the ear. I will never forget that single mortal sound.

Within the prison the silence was dense and charged with suspense, until it was broken by the sound of the hammers nailing the lid on the rough pine box. From our *galera* there was nothing to be seen, but we could hear everything. I imagined the scene: the prisoner tied to the stake, the marksmen, then the fall of the dying body, its breast ripped by the bullets. "May God receive him in His arms," someone cried, and Ulises, unable to contain himself any longer, began to cry for his cousin.

The next day Pedro Luis Villanueva and some other prisoners declared a hunger strike to protest the shootings. They were taken out of the yard and carried to the chapels. Clodomiro Miranda, former commander of Fidel Castro's army, was also being held in that improvised death row. Clodomiro had joined the rebels in the mountains of the province of Pinar del Río, the most westerly province of Cuba. He had fought with great courage defending liberty and finally rose to the rank of commander.* Though he was not a man of great political consciousness, he could see clearly enough that the Revolution was not taking the course that Fidel had promised for it. So when he realized that the ideals of the Revolution had been betrayed, Clodomiro Miranda took up his weapon again and went off once more into the mountains. Castro ordered him hunted down, and thousands of militia were sent out to find him. He was wounded in a skirmish. When they captured him later, his legs had been completely destroyed by bullets, and there were other shells lodged in one arm and one side of his chest. He was carried into his trial on a stretcher. When they sentenced him to death he was taken out of the military hospital and locked up in one of those horrific cells without a bed. Clodomiro was unable to stand up, so he had to drag himself along the filthy floor. His unattended wounds became infected; then they filled with maggots. That is how Pedro Luis and Manuel Villanueva found him. They were the last prisoners to speak with him.

It was also on a stretcher that they took Clodomiro down into the moat to the firing squad. The stairway which descends into the moat hangs from the wall on one side. On the other side there is just space—not even a handrail. The two-hundred-year-old stone steps, worn down by generations of slaves and prisoners, can be seen even from the end of the galleries. The file of guards which carried Clodomiro descended unsteadily. Almost at the bottom of the stairs, one of the guards stumbled. He let go of the stretcher as he groped to steady himself, and Clodomiro fell onto his wounded legs and tumbled down the last steps. One of the guards told us that they tried

Comandante, here and throughout. —Trans.

to tie him to the post, but he simply couldn't stay erect. They had to shoot him as he lay on the ground. When they shot him, he too cried, "Down with Communism!"

Clodomiro was perhaps the only man ever executed who was being devoured by worms even before he died.

3 / Life and the Terrors
of Death at La Cabaña

The first visit we had with our families took place in the morning. Men were not allowed to visit the prisoners; only women were allowed inside. Even so, the searches they performed were humiliating. They stripped all the women, with no respect even for the elderly. Among the women guards who performed the searches, there were two who always caused problems—one was called La China and the other was named Mirta. Both of them were lesbians, and they made the most of the situation. However much my mother and sister tried to hide from me the shame and indignation they suffered when they were searched, I saw through it. I begged them not to come again.

Every night there were firing squads. When I heard the discharges of the rifles, I would be seized with horror, and I embraced Christ in desperation. I had come to prison with some religious feeling; my beliefs were genuine but no doubt superficial at that time, since they had never been submitted to hard trial. I held to the religion I had learned at home and at school, but it was very much like a man who has acquired good manners or who carries along the lessons of the things he first learns to read, without examining them. But very quickly I began to experience a substantial change in the nature of my beliefs. At first no doubt I embraced Christ out of the fear of losing my life—since I was certainly in danger of being shot at any time. But that path I took in approaching Him, however human it was, still seemed unsatisfactory and incomplete, merely utilitarian, to me. There came a moment when, seeing those young men full of courage depart to die before the firing squad and shout *"Viva Cristo Rey!"* at the fateful instant, I not only understood instantly, as though by a sudden revelation, that Christ was indeed there for me at the moments when I prayed not to be killed, but realized as well that He served to give my life, and my death if it came to that, ethical meaning. Both my life and my death would be dignified by my belief in Him. It was at that moment, I am sure, and not before, that

Christianity became, more than a religious faith, a way of life for me. Because of my situation, it seemed my life would necessarily be a life of resistance, but I would be sustained in it by a soul filled with love and hope.

Those cries of the executed patriots—"Long live Christ the King! Down with Communism!"—had wakened me to a new life as they echoed through the two-hundred-year-old moats of the fortress. The cries became such a potent and stirring symbol that by 1963 the men condemned to death were gagged before being carried down to be shot. The jailers feared those shouts. They could not afford to allow even that last courageous cry from those about to die. That rebellious, defiant gesture at the supreme moment, that show of bravery and integrity by those who were about to die, could easily become a bad example for the soldiers. It might even make them think about what they were doing.

The recruits who made up the platoons of the firing squads received five pesos and three days' leave for each man executed. At least in western countries it is customary for a soldier in a firing squad never to be certain that he is the one who killed that other man, for of the six rifles, one is loaded with blanks. The soldiers pick up their guns at random, so they never know whether their cartridge is real or a blank. This method affords relief for the soldiers' consciences. But that is not the method employed in Cuba. All the rifles are loaded with lead bullets.

Balbino Díaz and Robertico Cruz were very young. They had been accused of shooting at José Pardo Llada, the spokesman for the government at the time. At their trial, nothing could be proved; no one could identify them. At one point in the proceedings, the defense attorney approached the prosecutor, Flores Ibarra, a man everyone knew by the nickname Bloodbath, and asked him to reduce the sentence he was requesting, since it was obvious that he had not been able to prove the accused men were guilty. He responded, "I have received orders to have them shot, no matter what, as a means of social prophylaxis. If we didn't go through with that, all those other counterrevolutionaries that think they're tough would unleash a wave of attempts on the lives of the leaders of the Revolution."

Two militiamen who were members of the tribunal, Sergio Arenas and Alejandro Meneses, stamped their fingerprints on the sentence. They were illiterate; they didn't even know how to sign their names. Balbino and Robertico were immediately executed.

The lawyer for the defense, Dr. Acosta Mir, was detained at the end of the trial; he was set free later only after he was warned not to defend any more counterrevolutionaries.

Commander Jesús Carreras was one of the leaders of the guerrilla army that had fought against the dictatorship of Batista. He had operated in El Escambray, a mountainous region in the central part of the island. His bravery in the battles there had made him a legendary hero in those parts, and certainly Commander Carreras had not fought so bravely just to see established a dictatorship which was a thousand times more vicious than the one he had helped to topple. So Castro sent him to jail, as he did so many other officers. But for the high-ranking officers Castro bore a special, almost sadistic, hatred. Moreover, Castro had a personal grudge against Carreras. Carreras had had a falling-out with Castro in the middle of the war because Carreras was unalterably opposed to Castro's appointment of a Communist, Ché Guevara, as head of the guerrilla front in El Escambray. When Ché penetrated into the rebel zone that Carreras controlled, Carreras was ready to kill him. Neither Castro nor Ché ever forgot that. Carreras and I talked frequently, because we lived in the same group of cots, and he told me he was certain he'd be sentenced to death for what had happened. Sure enough, Carreras was the next high-ranking officer shot after Commander Clodomiro Miranda.

Then they shot William Morgan. The leader of the firing squad was so angry with Morgan that he gave him several *coups de grace.* Even before that, but in Las Villas province, another commander of the guerrilla forces had fallen before the firing squad. This one, Porfirio Ramírez, president of the Student Federation of Central University, had fought right beside Castro.

Because of the constant firing squads the prison at La Cabaña had become the most terrible of all the jails. But added to that terror of death came another—the terror inspired in us by the early-morning "inspections."

Captain Herman F. Marks, an American whom Fidel Castro had appointed head of the garrison of La Cabaña and official executioner, was the man who fired those *coups de grace* and carried out the inspections. When he was drunk, which he was very frequently, Marks would order the garrison to form up in full military gear and attack the prisoners. He called the prison his "private hunting reserve." Another of his amusements was to stroll through the *galeras* and call out to those who were to be tried for offenses which carried the death penalty; he would ask them behind which ear they wanted the *coup de grace.* He had a dog he took with him to the executions so the dog could lap up the dead men's blood. Years later he returned to the United States.

For the inspections the platoon of soldiers, armed with wooden truncheons, chains, bayonets, and anything else they could use to beat us with, would erupt into the *galeras* shouting and striking out blindly. The order was that we prisoners were to come out of the cells the instant the cell doors were opened. But when the cell doors would be opened, the angry mob of soldiers would rush in like a whirlwind, meting out blows at random. Prisoners, also like a whirlwind, would be trying to get out into the prison yard, and so a knot of prisoners and guards beating them would form at the door, since we couldn't all fit through the door at the same time. We were always in mortal terror of those inspections. We would be gripped by panic, desperation, and, worst of all, confusion—we would try to escape unharmed, but that was virtually impossible, since outside in the patio a double file of guards armed with rifles and fixed bayonets made sure that no one failed to receive his quota of blows and kicks.

Hundreds of prisoners ran or staggered out in all states of dress and undress, some even naked. When we were all out, they rushed us and began beating us with even more ferocity. The more the guards flailed and yelled at us, the more furious they became, their faces growing more and more horrible and deformed with hatred and sadism. Up on the roof a line of soldiers, including women, their rifles cradled in their arms, contemplated the spectacle. Among the soldiers up there was always a group of officers and civilians from the Political Police, and, of course, conspicuous, Captain Marks.

About three o'clock one morning in the days after my trial, which I will talk about in a moment, the cry of "Inspection!" woke us all up. Men were shouting the terrifying word from the *galeras* nearest the main gate. Almost instantly the prison yard filled with guards, but they didn't open the cell doors. That was strange—soldiers were just standing there before the bars. But when they opened the doors and gave the order to come out, on the double, the blows began. They did not go inside the *galeras*. They beat us outside. One of us, a seventy-eight-year-old man named Goicochea who could hardly walk, was pushed, fell to the ground, and fractured his thigh. But no one picked Goicochea up; no one even stopped to help him.

We ran around him, trying at the same time to dodge the soldiers' blows and not to trample him. We ran toward the front wall, where we always formed up under the yells of the guards armed with rifles and fixed bayonets waiting for us there. At that inspection, as at some others, platoons were present from the National Revolutionary Police, which collaborated with the garrison at La Cabaña. This time the inspection had a special purpose. Months before, the Revolutionary Government had begun a campaign to collect money to buy arms. Castro's own slogan at the beginning of 1959— "Arms? For what?"—had been utterly forgotten, and now the rage to arm Cuba was spreading over the land. The government had asked the people to contribute money and jewelry—rings, pendants, gold chains—to the defense coffers.

Because of the terror, anguish, and blind panic the inspections always gave me, I had forgotten to grab my watch when I ran out. I always hid it inside a shoe when I went to bed, but like everyone who possessed a watch I always took it out with me during these inspections. It was a matter of prudence—if you left it the soldiers would find it and "confiscate" it for sure. And if you dared to report the "loss," the soldiers invariably took it as an accusation of thievery against themselves; the consequences to the prisoner are easily imagined. As I had run out of my cell I had realized that I had left the watch. No doubt about it, I had thought, I might as well give it up for lost. It had been a gift from my father.

But now all the prisoners were being stripped of their watches, pendants, chains, and wedding rings anyway. One by one, as we entered the *galeras,* completely naked, they took our jewelry. The officers shouted, egging on the pillaging by the soldiers, "Let's go! You people have to contribute to buying weapons and airplanes just like everybody else!" If one of us dared not to turn over a piece of jewelry he was beaten even worse.

All the jewelry was dumped into a canvas bag. When we returned to the *galeras* there was a huge mess of clothing and personal articles strewn down the passageway. Now that we were safe, out of reach of the guards, the prisoners began to rage against them, accusing them of being thieves and robbers. When I picked up my shoes under the cot, I was amazed to find my watch, which had escaped the search. What should I do now? Suddenly I was frightened, frightened to have in my possession my own watch. What if the garrison troops saw it and jumped to the conclusion I'd hidden it from them? They might feel I had intentionally mocked or tricked them, even defied them. Good Lord, what to do? I stood there dazed and bewildered, holding the watch, while some of the prisoners around me looked at it incredulously and asked, "How did you manage to sneak that one by?"

I was now paralyzed with worry. I would have to hide the watch as though I had stolen it. I toyed with the idea of going to the door, calling the guard over, and very politely turning it over to him. I would explain what had happened. That way I would avoid reprisals, but that seemed a weak and even cowardly thing to do. I decided not to do that, and I think that somehow that decision was what determined all my future conduct. I would always act according to my own set of values, because reprisals would be more bearable than the reproaches and censures of my own conscience.

Every morning at sunrise La Cabaña awoke to the same question—"Who will they shoot today?"

After the morning headcount they opened the cells and we congregated in the prison yard and waited in the interminable line for breakfast. The youngest member of our particular group was Carlos Alberto, who was underage, although he was taller than any of us. Carlos Alberto had married very young, and his wife, Linda, had brought their daughter, Gina, to the last visit, when she was only a few months old. Carlos and I had made our attempt to escape from the jail at Political Police Headquarters, so the possibility, or rather virtual certainty, of our being executed always hung over our heads. Because of that and because of his age, Carlos Alberto's family had requested that he be transferred to a jail for minors.

A few days after his trial he was called to the main gate with his belongings. He was being sent to a prison outside Havana. Within a few weeks, somehow supplied with a hacksaw, he cut through the bars of his cell and escaped. He managed to enter the Venezuelan embassy, and after months of pressure the Cuban government allowed him to leave the country.

Carrión, Piñango, Boitel, and I were jubilant at Carlos Alberto's escape —one man fewer in that hell! When days before I had thought of Linda and the months-old baby girl, I couldn't help being overwhelmed by grief for them. I remembered Juan José and Pedrito, and I thought about their little children, whom I had played with during the visit, and who a week afterward had been left fatherless. Gina, at least, would not be an orphan.

The authorities did not bother to notify the families of the men they had executed, so that quite often the mothers, wives, and children of executed men appeared at visiting time asking to see them. A wrenching silence would fall. The prisoners would look at one another, as though saying, "You tell them." Sometimes the family interpreted that silence perfectly, and they would open their eyes wide in pain and shock and break into tears.

When Julio Antonio Yebra's mother found out about her son's execution, she exclaimed with extraordinary self-possession and integrity, "If the death of my son were the last blood shed by these firing squads, I would accept his death without another word."

But he would not be the last. Thousands and thousands more would follow Julio Antonio.

4 / The Trial

Less than two weeks after my detention I was taken to trial. It was a cold morning, so I borrowed a sweater from Manolito Villanueva. As I went out the front gate my guards handcuffed me and two soldiers armed with Czech submachine guns stepped in to flank me. The gusty north wind whirled pieces of paper around my feet.

"March!"

And we began to march. The road that begins outside the gate is made of slate paving stones brought from Spain during the colonial period and laid by Negro slaves. The soldiers' boots were heavy on those blocks worn down by two centuries of iniquity. A slow drizzle started to fall. As we crossed the moats and left the prison behind I turned my head and gazed at the old lichen-covered walls and the bars of the *galeras*. To my left I saw the firing-squad post, a rough wooden stake, and behind it a wall of sandbags, some with holes made by the bullets as they passed completely through the bodies. At the foot of the stake were bloodstains and a few hens pecking around, probably at the remains of the brains of a man executed last night.

We came to the last guardpost after crossing through a promenade of leafy laurel trees, and then we entered the wide cleared area where platoons of guards paraded. In one of the old officers' quarters buildings, the revolutionary tribunals sat. We went in, and I was motioned into a little room to the right, which was furnished only with two green couches and a Coca-Cola machine. Later two women dressed in prison garb were also ushered in. Zoila was one of them; the other, whom I had never laid eyes on before, was Inés María, a nurse they had detained when she helped Oliver Obregón reach the mountains of Escambray to join the *alzados,* a group of anti-Castro guerrillas. We were to be tried as a group. Originally the Political Police had planned to bring the same charge against everyone detained that early morning of December 28, 1960, but later they changed their mind and grouped us under five different charges.

Obregón was also tried in our group.

Then two other prisoners were brought in to be tried as well. These were the Bayolo brothers, two campesinos, poor countryfolk, accused of having made off with dynamite sticks from the quarries near their hometown. The Bayolos didn't have a defense attorney; they hadn't been allowed to make contact with anyone. I promised them that if my lawyer came I'd speak to him about representing them—but what could he do? How could he help them? He didn't even know anything about the case, so how could he possibly organize a criminal defense for men that he would see for the first time only minutes before their trial? The lawyer I was waiting for didn't come until later, though, when the Bayolo brothers had already been sentenced to death and carried out of the courtroom.

After about an hour they decided that our trial would not be held in that building, but in another one, the Officers' Club. We got up to leave as the trial of three telephone company employees was coming to a close. The only one whose life was spared was Armando Rodríguez Vizcaíno; the other two were executed the next morning. The pregnant wife of one of them cried inconsolably when the sentence was handed down. That was the last scene I saw as I left the improvised courtroom.

Thirteen days had passed since the morning I had been taken from my home and carried to the Ministry to be asked a few questions. In that short time, the Political Police had prepared the whole case. Of course, in twelve or thirteen days it was physically impossible to conduct an investigation, but that's the way the trials were. I was not allowed to talk privately with the lawyer defending me, nor did they allow him access to the list of charges.

In the second courtroom we found a wooden platform with a long table set up on it. At the table the members of the tribunal were sitting talking among themselves, laughing, and smoking cigars, which they held on one side of their mouths, chomping on them in Pancho Villa style. They all wore military uniforms. This, then, was one of those typical tribunals, made up of anybody at hand. This one was composed of laborers and campesinos. At the start of the trial, the president of the tribunal, Mario Taglé, put his feet up on the table, crossed one boot over the other, and leaned back in his chair and opened a comic book. From time to time he turned to the men on each side of him and showed them some tidbit that had struck him as particularly funny. They'd all laugh. And the sad truth was that paying any attention to the proceedings, even out of courtesy, was utterly unnecessary, and they knew it. The sentences had already been decided on and written out at Political Police Headquarters. Say what one would, do what one would, the sentence was not to be changed.

The prosecutor began the examination with Obregón, accusing him of being an enemy of the people. Then he asked him whether he had ever known me, or run into me at work, in meetings, or "casually." Obregón answered that he had not. He asked Zoila the same question. He received the same answer. No one knew me; none of them accused me of anything at all. The prosecutor called up the leader of the police squad that had arrested me in my house.

"It was you who made the arrest of the accused?"

"Yes, sir, and we searched his house thoroughly, but we didn't find anything."

"Quiet! Don't answer unless I ask you!" the prosecutor shouted at him, visibly angered by the agent's spontaneous declaration. Not that it mattered in any material way, but that exchange of words was beneficial to me in the eyes of the few spectators present—all military men, since relatives were forbidden to attend the trial, even had they known that it was being conducted. We had already been told by Obregón's defense attorney, Dr. Aramis Taboada, who had connections inside State Security and who often defended political prisoners in the early '6os, that there were not to be any death sentences handed down at our trial. One can imagine what a relief that was to all of us. Still, one wanted the trial to go well, whatever that might mean under the circumstances.

The prosecutor asked me two or three questions, largely related to my religious beliefs.

"Then you agree with those priests that are always preaching and writing counterrevolutionary sermons?"

"I have nothing to do with any of that."

"But our investigations indicate that you have many connections among the priests, and that you went to a Catholic school."

But the prosecutor could not bring forward any evidence against me, so he began a long monotonous speech about Cuba before Castro. He lashed out against Yankee exploitation, he spoke about prostitution, and he ended by saying that all of us accused in that courtroom wanted to return to the ignominious past of the capitalist exploiter.

He then turned to the president of the tribunal and told him that I was an enemy of the Revolution who had committed the crimes of public destruction and sabotage. Public destruction is the name they give the ravages caused by a bomb, arson, or any other act of sabotage. He recited a number of laws which supposedly determined the punishment I merited.

But neither then nor later—because for twenty years I kept asking—could any of the authorities tell me where I had committed an act of public destruction. Such a crime, one would think, is concrete, visible, palpable. I asked the prosecuting lawyer where—in which factory, in what business, on what date—I was supposed to have caused this damage. He was unable to answer, because I had, of course, never done anything of the kind. It was like a murder trial in which the district attorney, asked who has been killed, says he doesn't know; and asked about the corpse, says there is no corpse. Imagine killing a figment of someone's imagination.

No tribunal in a more rightist regime could have found me guilty. There was not one witness to accuse me, there was no one to identify me, there was not a single piece of evidence against me. I was found guilty, simply out of the mistaken "conviction" held by the Political Police.

And sadly, my case was no exception. Dr. Taboada, Obregón's defense attorney, had been one of Castro's fellow students at the University, and after they graduated they had worked for the same law firm. On one occasion, Castro asked Taboada to write a book about those years. It was, one assumes, to be an apologia for the dictator, a work meant to swell the already extensive corpus of memoirs, biographies, and accounts which documented Castro's cult of personality. Taboada kept putting off the request, until one day he wound up in the political jails. Years later he was given a reprieve, but only for a while. In 1983 he was imprisoned again, charged with being one of those responsible for a report which generated an international protest campaign: News was leaked to the outside world that five young syndicate members had been shot before a firing squad for having tried to organize an independent union modeled on Solidarity.

Another of the best-known cases was that of Dr. Rivero Caro, a lawyer like Taboada and a practicing journalist as well. He says he has never forgotten the words of Idelfonso Canales, the Political Police interrogator, who was frustrated and visibly angry at not being able to extract a confession from his detainee, even under torture, and who finally told him straight out, "Do you know what has you so balled up? That lawyer mentality of yours, that's what. You're seeing your situation with that mentality, a lawyer's mentality, but you're wrong to take that point of view. You see, what you say at the trial doesn't matter; whatever proof you may be able to bring forward doesn't matter either; what your lawyer says, what he alleges or proposes, doesn't matter; what the prosecuting attorney says, the proofs he presents, don't matter; what the president of the tribunal thinks doesn't matter. Here the *only* thing that matters is what G-2 says."

In a case in 1961, in which Jorge Gutiérrez was brought to trial, his court-appointed attorneys got access to the summary of charges two hours before the trial. The prosecutor knew that there were to be two death sentences at the trial. Because of the short time he had, one of the lawyers found it physically impossible to read the documents, and so he asked the prosecutor before the trial began whether there wasn't some chance of reducing the demand for the death penalty. The prosecuting attorney told him that there was no chance at all, since the order to have them shot at nine o'clock the next morning had already been given. He added that the defense attorney should probably start doing the paperwork for the appeal, at least for form's sake.

As when Dr. Taboada had found out that I was not to be given the death penalty, there were occasions when prisoners—those whose lawyers had contacts among the Political Police leaders—might find out before the trial was held what sentence was to be handed down by the tribunal. It was that sort of contact which allowed Commander Humberto Sorí Marín's aged mother to discover that her son, one of the men closest to Castro, was to be found guilty of conspiracy and executed by firing squad.

Ironically enough, Sorí Marín had been the author of a notorious law under which dozens of Batista's followers had been shot during the first months of 1959, at the beginning of the Revolution. So the morning Sorí Marín entered the prison yard of La Cabaña was perhaps the most difficult moment of his life. There was a *galera* full of men there waiting to be shot because of the law he had written. He had personally asked for the death penalty for many of them. And of course many men had already been executed under the provisions of the law. Therefore he was shocked beyond belief when one of those prisoners who had been sentenced to death put out his hand and said, "Doctor, this side of those iron bars, we're all in the same boat. So take a seat here among friends."

The man speaking was ex-Commander Mirabal, the old head of Military Intelligence and one of the participants in Batista's *coup d'état* on March 10, 1952. He took Sorí Marín to the *galera,* found him a bed, offered him one of his best cigars, and said to him simply, "God have mercy on us all, Doctor."

Sorí Marín had been one of Castro's closest advisers and collaborators. He had fought next to him in the mountains and had been a member of his staff. He wrote and signed the Agrarian Reform Act. In the first months after the Revolution had come to power, his ties to Castro grew even closer. Castro was even in the habit of having lunch from time to time at Sorí Marín's house, since Sorí's mother was an excellent cook. Naturally, then, Señora Marín went to see Castro the minute she discovered that her son was to be executed. She was grief-stricken. The meeting with Castro was very moving. The old lady cried as she clutched the Revolutionary Leader and pleaded with him.

"Fidel, I beg you, don't let them kill my son. Please, for my sake . . . "

Castro stroked her head gently. "Don't worry. Nothing will happen to Humberto, I promise you."

So Sorí Marín's mother, beside herself with happiness, her eyes still brimming with tears, kissed Fidel and ran off to tell the family the good news. She had hoped that her son would be pardoned—Humberto and Fidel had gone through so much together, so much danger, so many hard times and so much anguish! Surely that shared past couldn't simply be forgotten, just like that.

The next night, at Castro's express order, Humberto Sorí Marín was shot by firing squad.

In *galeras* 11, 12, and 14 of La Cabaña were collected the most dissimilar types—officers in Batista's army and revolutionaries who had defeated them were all thrown in there together. Many of the former Castro supporters were, like Sorí Marín, to die under the same laws they had cited in executing their enemies. David Salvador was there, the leader of the 26th of July

Movement and former Secretary-General of the Federation of Cuban Workers. He was one of the most radical and fervent young Communists. In fact, it was he who grabbed the microphone away from the former President of Costa Rica, José Figueres, while Figueres was speaking at a meeting once. It seems that Figueres declared that if an armed conflict arose between the United States and the Soviet Union, Latin America would take the side of the Americans. Salvador was incensed by Figueres' words; Fidel Castro, who was sitting on the dais too, smiled in sympathy with Salvador. Nevertheless a few months later David Salvador was sentenced to thirty years in prison as a counterrevolutionary.

Another of the prisoners in those *galeras* was Guillermo Díaz Lanz. He was the brother of the first commander of the Revolutionary Air Force. His brother had escaped to the United States within a few months of the Revolution's takeover and was combatting Castro from there. It was literally a crime for Guillermo to have such a brother—he was found guilty of being the brother of the "traitor" Pedro Luis Díaz Lanz. And that was *all* he was found guilty of.

The machinery of the Revolution was not to be halted, and like Saturn it devoured its own children. But within the prison population, there was a moving sense of camaraderie. There might have been isolated incidents of anger and resentment when a revolutionary arrived who had been a man's arresting officer or the prosecuting attorney against a prisoner held there now under sentence of death, but those incidents happened very rarely. There were bankers, students, ex-soldiers from both sides in the recent civil war, workers, campesinos. But they shared a single identity, or a principle of identity, more powerful than old differences. Everyone bore the black *P* stenciled on the back of his uniform, and the same bayonets prodded and wounded them all, and the same bullets awaited them, the same firing squad.

The men who fought alongside Castro to establish democracy had been tricked; some fled the country, others took up arms again or formed conspiracies against him. The army officers, police agents, and officials of the deposed regime who had been charged with crimes—unproven in many instances—had already been shot. But Castro had found a new enemy—the enemy within—and no one was safe from this threat of "instant justice."

It was during those months that a group of women dressed in black would come into the *galeras,* peering intently, scrutinizing every face. All it took was for one of those women to lift a finger and point: "That one! That's the one who killed my son!" The man stood accused. That testimony, without any other corroboration, was enough. The prisoner was shot. This situation lent itself, obviously, to personal vendetta; it didn't necessarily require any real criminal action. The execution was often carried out without any trial, in fact.

The men who had been in La Cabaña since the beginning of 1959 say that whenever one of those delegations of women appeared at the prison gate some prisoners would hide under the beds. One case was notorious. A mother pointed out the supposed murderer of her son, and the man was executed within a few hours. But the next day her son, safe and sound, arrived from Venezuela, where he had fled without his mother's knowledge. He showed up at the prison, horrified that an innocent man had been killed.

5 / The Year of the Firing Squad

Early in 1959, on January 21, to be exact, Castro gave a speech in front of the Presidential Palace in which he declared, "There will not be more than about four hundred henchmen and conspirators against the Revolution that we will execute." But many more than that had already fallen before the firing squads in those days of barbarity and death.

On January 12, on a firing range located in a small valley called San Juan, at the end of the island in the province of Oriente, hundreds of soldiers from the defeated army of Batista had been lined up in a trench knee-deep and more than fifty yards long. Their hands were tied behind their backs, and they were machine-gunned there where they stood. Then with bulldozers the trenches were turned into mass graves. There had been no trial of any kind for those men. Many of them were hardly more than boys, who had joined the army because money and food were scarce at home. The mass execution was ordered by Raúl Castro and attended by him personally. Nor was it an isolated instance; other officers in Castro's guerrilla forces shot ex-soldiers en masse without a trial, without any charges of any kind lodged against them, simply as an act of reprisal against the defeated army.

By 1961 the Cuban people's struggle against the growing strength of Communism was becoming more determined every day. Flames devoured large warehouses and stores in Havana. Hundreds, thousands of acres planted with sugar cane were fodder for the flames; the Cuban nights were illuminated by those bonfires. Bombs destroyed telephone and electric lines and derailed trains. Armed confrontations in both the mountains and the cities constantly broke out between the patriots and the repressive forces.

And government terror tactics grew in step with the resistance. Guilty and innocent alike fell before the firing squads. In the mountains when government troops captured some of the *alzados,* the *alzados* would be shot down where they were captured, and doctors of forensic medicine would cut open their abdomens to try to find the rest of the guerrilla groups by seeing what the contents of the dead men's stomachs were and determining where such food might be found.

Castro had declared in the auditorium of the Federation of Cuban Workers building, "We will answer violence with violence. We may not have God on our side, but we do have an infantry—and it's the finest in the world."

Juan Carlos Alvarez Aballí had the bad luck to be detained at his home in the middle of that period of violence. He was told only that there were some things he had to clear up at Political Police Headquarters. He was in his shirtsleeves; when he started to put on a jacket and tie, the soldiers told him he'd be back in less than an hour, he didn't have to get all dressed up. He kissed his wife and children. He was calm and confident; after all, he knew he had done nothing wrong. One of the agents, the oldest one, even had a few words for his wife: "Don't worry, ma'am, in an hour at most I'll bring him back myself."

Alvarez Aballí's brother-in-law, Juan Maristany, had been involved in conspiratorial activities, a weapons-theft plot, and seeking to evade capture by Castro's forces, he had taken asylum in a neutral embassy. That was the only reason that Alvarez Aballí was arrested now. Since the authorities couldn't get their hands on Maristany in the embassy, at least they'd have Alvarez. So there he was, in the prison yard, awaiting a trial on charges that had no substance to them—a trial at which, he thought, he'd be found innocent and walk out a free man. That, at least, is what he thought until he heard the prosecutor's statement of the charges. Alvarez was accused of conspiring with his brother-in-law, and the prosecutor was asking for the death penalty. When the prosecutor read him the statement, Alvarez Aballí collapsed weeping and repeating his protestations of innocence.

By the afternoon they called him to trial he was serene; he had placed his trust in God. Firmly, sincerely, movingly, he related to the tribunal the story of his entire life. He had dedicated it wholly to his work and his family; it was the furthest life imaginable from a life of political activism. His defense attorney even dared—and it was an act of true courage—to present in evidence a letter from Maristany himself, certified by the ambassador, in which Maristany stated that he and he alone was guilty of the arms theft and explained in detail certain facts which proved that Alvarez Aballí was innocent. The tribunal rejected the letter as evidence, although they did suggest that if Maristany left the embassy and turned himself in to the authorities they would change Alvarez' verdict.

The day after the trial had ended, Alvarez Aballí was led to the cells for those condemned to death. With him went another prisoner who had better luck—he was removed from the cells moments before Alvarez Aballí was carried to the firing squad. This man told us that Alvarez Aballí became somehow larger, grander when he was faced with the fact of his own death, and spent all his time praying. He embraced his friend in farewell when the time came, but not a single tear rose to his eyes.

When they took him out and led him toward the moat, he passed in front of the portraits of Fidel and Raúl Castro. He paused a moment and then exclaimed, "And to think that because of those two wretches there are about to be five orphans!" Angrily he turned toward Lieutenant Manolito, head of the prison, and said to him, "Come on. Let's get this over with."

Throughout the whole extent of the island, the firing squads were carrying out their executions. It was during those days that Captain Antonio Nuñez Jiménez declared that from that moment on, the year 1961, officially designated the Year of Education, would be called the Year of the Firing Squad. And his prediction came true.

Men who had been sentenced to death did not return to the *galeras* after their trial. They were led to tiny cells located down at the end of *galera* 22, alongside the cells for Revolutionary Army soldiers sentenced to prison terms for robbery, drug abuse, and so forth—"common crimes" as opposed to "political crimes." The prisoners sentenced to death would have to walk down the entire length of the *galera* of those common prisoners. The common prisoners were kept separate from us political prisoners by the little yard surrounded with high fences just at the main gate. We could see them from our yard, but there was no chance of physical contact with them.

It might have been that they thought they could score some points with the prison guards, or it might have been that they were actually channeling their hatred of those who stood up against the Revolution that many of them had supported, and still supported. For whatever reason, all through that walk, those common prisoners, "delinquents," really criminals, would harass the men sentenced to death, who would have their hands tied behind their backs and be led by guards; they would insult them, spit at them, throw things at them, push them. And it was not solely those few moments of walking down the *galera* which were exploited by the common criminals to harass the political prisoners. There were even some who would follow them to their cells on that improvised Death Row, to which the common prisoners had access, and keep on insulting them, screaming at them there, denying them in their last hours the peace and seclusion that would have allowed them to pray, meditate over their lives, be still.

The guards did nothing about the harassment. The authorities did not even deign to disguise their approval of those proceedings. On the contrary, whenever there were political prisoners on Death Row, the authorities would pass out liquor to the common criminals to get them drunk so they'd sing the "Internationale" and crow about the triumphs of the Revolution and the beating the counterrevolutionaries had taken and were taking.

Some of the prisoners spoke to the authorities and requested them to put a stop to the delinquents' standing in front of their cells insulting them and yelling at them. But the authorities had not an iota of compassion for them. From the moment the condemned men came out of the tribunal trials with their hands tied behind their backs and began walking to the cells of that Death Row, their escorts pushed and shoved them, mocked and laughed at them. The guards even stripped them of their shoes and threw them to the common prisoners, who fought over them like vultures.

And when the platoon of guards led them to the firing squad, the farewell the political prisoners received from the common prisoners in *galera* 22 was cries of *"Viva Fidel Castro! Viva la Revolución!"*

When the van with the members of the firing squad passed through the entrance which opened into the moats, the unmistakable sound of its motor would be heard throughout the *galeras* and of course in Death Row, where the men knew the decisive moment was at hand. Throughout the *galeras* the murmur of voices in prayer would begin. Otherwise we prisoners, lying on our cots, kept an oppressive, painful silence, a silence made even more painful by our absolute impotence to prevent the death of one who until a few hours before had shared with us his hopes, his dreams, his troubles. A throng of images and thoughts whirled through our heads during those moments: his fatherless children, his widow, his mother prostrate with grief. And the thought too, which made us shiver, that the man the firing squad awaited could well be any one of us. Often I would suddenly see myself with my hands tied, gagged, led into the moat . . . descending those steps to the wooden stake before the wall of sandbags, the spotlights trained on it . . . officers shoving me against it and pulling a piece of rope tight around my waist . . . the soldiers raising their rifles and deafening thunder echoing all along the moats. . . . That could happen to me; I expected it. Every night I rehearsed that journey. I could see every inch of it in my mind. I knew the route by memory—every step, the wooden stake. . . .

There were nights when there would be ten or twelve executions. You would hear the bars of the man's cell door and someone coming to the bars to see his friend and cry out to him the last goodbye. There was no way to sleep in the *galeras.* That was when God began to become a constant companion of mine, and when death became a door into the true life, a step from the shadows into eternal light.

The blows of the hammers nailing together the wooden coffin would echo from the stone walls of the moats. The corpse was not given over to the relatives so they could hold a wake and funeral or accompany it to the holy ground of a cemetery. Instead, a van with INRA (National Institute of Agrarian Reform) painted on its side took the body to Colón Cemetery, where it was buried in a common grave, in a plot reserved for that purpose by the Ministry of the Interior. In the van would be an officer from the Political Police and several soldiers. The body was buried without a marker or headstone or anything else to identify it. The family did not even have the sad privilege of knowing where their loved one was buried.

But it was not only corpses that disappeared; some detainees were secretly subjected to interrogations and, when the authorities had finished, taken directly from Political Police Headquarters to the firing squad. We could see that happen sometimes from our *galeras*. Once when I was in the prison yard with a group of my friends, I saw them take down a gagged man with his hands tied behind his back. He was dressed in olive green. They shot him hurriedly. He had not come out of that prison; no one knew who he was. And that happened many times—men were executed and buried secretly.

6 / Isla de Pinos

When the guards had something they wanted to announce to the prisoners they would broadcast it over two loudspeakers installed in the prison yard. One afternoon at the end of the headcount the loudspeakers began to blare out a list of prisoners who were to get all their belongings together immediately. These prisoners were being transferred.

While the names on the list were being called out in groups, a total silence reigned throughout the jail. Every man strained to hear whether his name was called. The loudspeakers went on chanting their litany for what seemed a very long time; the names were all called out twice.

I heard my name called, and I left the cell door to go get my things ready. In front of me Pedro Luis Boitel and beside me Alfredo Carrión were also getting their bags together. The men in my *galera* whose names had been called had already begun to throw their possessions into canvas sacks. There was a kind of anguish in the air; the authorities had never said where we were being transferred. But we could guess—leaving La Cabaña, and such large numbers of men, could only mean one destination: Isla de Pinos.

The transfer to that prison, which was located on an island south of Cuba, was a terrible blow to our spirits. Horror stories were told of what went on there. We all knew that visits had been suspended there, and that just a few days before a man named Monteiras had been kicked to death. Terror reigned on Isla de Pinos.

But even more daunting to us than the treatment we might get—I'm sure the stories didn't seem quite real to us—was being taken so far away from our families, being cut off from news and visits. At least in La Cabaña news of our families came sometimes as often as twice a week.

That prisoner transfer was one of the largest ever carried out. More than three hundred prisoners' names had been called.

Prisoner transfers are always a frantic rush. Before the echoes from the lists of names had faded away, platoons of soldiers were already formed up in front of the cells, ordering the men whose names had been called to get moving. Anxiously we were throwing our few belongings together, any old way, into the canvas sacks which all prisoners were provided with. Our families usually brought them to us.

"Let's go! Get a move on!" the guards were mechanically calling out. They looked tired. Reserves, soldiers that had just come off guard duty—everyone had to turn out and help during the transfers; they couldn't sleep. And so they were all in a bad mood—but it was always the prisoners who paid the consequences.

The first prisoners, who had come out of *galeras* 8, 9, and 10, were gathering in the prison yard. They were loaded down. They all had to carry their sacks and other bags if they had them; aluminum cups and spoons hung from their belts, and towels were draped around their necks; many of them had toothbrush and toothpaste sticking out of the pockets of their prison shirts.

"Let's go, everybody out!"

As the guards hurried the prisoners into the prison yard, there were moving scenes inside the cells. The men staying at La Cabaña clasped the hands of their departing comrades and friends. Cries of "Good luck at your trial!" were called constantly. All of us, those of us staying and those of us leaving, were virtually certain that we'd never see anyone from the other group alive again, so there was really very little we could say in those moments. You embraced your friend in farewell, but it was almost like embracing a dead man—so few of us felt we had any chance of survival. There were no words for that—the eyes had to speak, and the prayer sprang up silently in our hearts.

Almost two hundred prisoners with their sacks were finally standing in the prison yard. A group of lieutenants carrying lists began to call out names, and the prisoners nearest the soldiers would turn and repeat the names so the men in back could hear. So we started filing out and forming up at the main gate, two by two. When there was a group of about fifty, they were taken out; then followed another, and another. Many hours passed in this roll call.

Our group was one of the very last. We were herded out into the street, Boitel straggling along. Boitel was a "ninety-seven-pound weakling." He had been a sickly child. From the time he was a little boy, he had had to work, though, helping one of his uncles in a coffee home-delivery business. And by dint of his parents' efforts and his own will to overcome his weak constitution, he had managed to go to the University, where he studied electrical engineering. He was a popular student; other students admired him for his strength of character, his uprightness, and his dedication. But he left college to join the action groups fighting against Batista. He was almost caught, but he got away to Venezuela, from where he went on aiding Castro. It was in Caracas that the news of the fall of the dictator reached him; he returned to Cuba in January 1959. He went back to the University and was nominated for student president by the other students. During his campaign he had worn a large crucifix which a Catholic priest had given him. But Boitel had to resign his candidacy and leave the University, since he had become an active anti-Communist and Castro had threatened him personally; Boitel went into hiding, living underground for months before he was finally tracked down and captured.

We were standing with our bags and bundles in the street outside the main gate, that same street I had been on when they took me to my trial, but now it was full of guards coming and going constantly, in battle dress with helmets and fixed bayonets.

"Let's go! Double file!" It was a fat black sergeant that I had never seen before. We began to form up. The sergeant went down the line counting. He checked the count against some lists he was carrying and gave the order to move out.

At the end of the first tunnel, a little beyond the portcullis-like main entrance to the prison, buses were waiting. They were English Leylands, painted white; they had originally belonged to a private busline and had been expropriated by the government. The rear seat was taken up by six escorts with submachine guns. I got in. Carrión sat beside me; Boitel had plumped down with his load on the first seat. When all the seats were full, other guards were posted at the doors and behind the driver, and a lieutenant came in and warned us not to so much as dare to stand up, let alone try to escape. The caravan of buses, escorted by National Police patrol cars and Political Police unmarked vehicles, pulled out.

I had hidden my watch since the day of the search. I was sure that when we got to Isla de Pinos it would be discovered, so I thought I might as well put it on my wrist. But not now; I'd do it when we were closer to the other prison. It might be that I could get it through, there, without any terrible consequences.

The caravan of buses drew away from the fortress, came to the Vía Monumental, turned right, and entered the tunnel into Havana, headed toward the Columbia Military Camp, from which we prisoners, loaded into planes, would depart for Isla de Pinos.

Doubts and questions always plague the prisoner when he is transferred —hundreds of questions. They arise, one after another, but they always go unanswered. There is intense mental activity going on in every man, even as silence descends and not a single voice is to be heard. Many men, perhaps, passed by their own houses, since we were crossing the city. All of us were assailed by a rush of memories. How many times had I walked down those avenues a free man, never even remotely suspecting that one day I would be driven through them a prisoner!

We came to the military camp and rolled to a stop before hangars and other Air Force installations. High fences and lookouts with rifles protected the airport. A little farther on, the office buildings and barracks, gray runways, and silhouettes of transport planes were blurred shapes in the gloomy night.

We got out of the buses in front of a barracks. There were guards everywhere, coming and going like ants. There was the sound of hammering; they were finishing the job of boarding up the barracks windows. Inside, there was a large room full of bunks made of wood and covered with heavy canvas; there were no pillows. Outside, orders were still being shouted back and forth. They were stationing soldiers on guard all around the building. One soldier dragged a chair over in front of the only door and sat down.

Boitel, Carrión, Ulises, Piñango, and I took some of the last bunks. Prisoners were already beginning to adapt to this new situation. Some of them asked the guard where the latrines were, but they had to wait until he could consult his superiors. When the answer finally came, he let us go in groups of four. Boitel and I went more to look the place over than out of any physical urgency; we thought we should explore every possibility of escape. But there was only one window set very high in the wall, next to the ceiling, and it opened onto the side of the building where a large group of soldiers was posted. We went back and lay down on the bunks, some to sleep, some to meditate, trying to see into the future that awaited us.

Around that time there was tremendous optimism about the possibility of the fall of the regime. Only a few weeks before, the United States had broken off relations with Cuba, and President Eisenhower had stated that "the Communist penetration into Cuba is real, and it constitutes a grave threat to the Western world." At that time many Cubans believed that a Marxist regime would not be tolerated in the Americas; analysts argued, on the basis of OAS treaties and Cuba's geographic proximity to the United States, that the United States would have to take action. People were saying with complete assurance that Castro would not last many more weeks in power. And at the same time, there was hope—and this was indeed more reasonable—that the Resistance in Cuba, which was becoming more and more powerful, could pull off a coup.

"On your feet! Headcount formation here!" Very early, before it was light, a group of officers came in to get us up.

Sleepily we started lining up, wrapped in blankets—even though the barracks was completely closed up, it was cold.

They brought in a big aluminum drum and gave us a piece of bread and a sip of coffee. They ordered us to get our things together, then took us out of the barracks and headed us to the transfer point. The sky was still gray and dense, and clouds were running low before the north wind.

We crossed one of the runways. Battalions of militia wearing green berets were marching and singing revolutionary anthems, among them the "Internationale." It was from this camp that Batista had escaped Cuba, early on the morning of January 1, barely two years ago. Now the militia was parading and hundreds of political prisoners were awaiting an uncertain destiny.

The names of the first transfer group were called off from lists which had already been made up at the prison in Havana. The plane, an old C-46, taxied up. The guards shouted and threatened the men getting on; it was a means they used to keep us frightened—even more frightened, that is.

When the plane turned for takeoff, a cloud of dust, dirty paper, and trash enveloped us. They had us off to one side of the runway, in a field of dry yellow weeds. The rest of us were going to have to wait for the plane to return before another contingent was transported. So the transfer was slow, but then it was suspended altogether because the plane was commandeered to carry a herd of cows to Camagüey province. It was already nightfall. We hoped they would take us back to the barracks, but it was not to be. The militia received reinforcements and staked out a cordon of guards around us. We had to stay there on the side of the runway through the night.

The wind and cold rattled our bones. We took the blankets out of our sacks and huddled together as close as we could, to await the next day. Explosions were heard off and on.

Early in the morning the temperature fell considerably, and there was no way we could sleep anymore. We were shivering with cold. When above the houses and treetops on the other side of the fences it began to grow light, they brought us a little coffee and some bread. The wind swept across the grayish asphalt runway, bending the weeds and grass and scudding paper across the ground. I carefully took out my watch and put it on. I pulled the sleeve of my uniform down over it, and I also wrapped a handkerchief around it, to make sure it was completely covered. I might be able to use it in the other prison.

There was only a small group of us left. Platoons of militia stood in formation in front of the hangars and began their drills. They marched by within a few yards of us and looked at us out of the corners of their eyes. Many of those men, who at that time were ready to fight in defense of the Revolution, would fall fighting against it or go to the political jails years later for standing up to it; but at that moment they could not imagine what the country would become when Communism took over completely. So they couldn't imagine our opposition, either.

At last our group was called. Boitel was taken aside for a moment to be handcuffed; other men were handcuffed in pairs. It was done not for security but out of simple cruelty. As we neared the boarding steps of the plane, the soldiers began to shout and yell and grow fiercer and more and more enraged. The transport plane had no seats, and they hadn't cleaned it out at all after they had used it to transport the cattle, so the floor was covered with cow manure. A rope divided the plane in half lengthwise—we were crammed into one side and the guards were stationed on the other.

"Everybody on the floor! Down!" A murmur of protest swelled; were we going to have to sit in that cowshit all over the floor? But the guards began to push and shout like madmen. "Hurry it up! Everybody down! On the floor!" Boitel, handcuffed, tried to drag along one of his bags. Carrión was carrying the other one for him. They stuck a rifle butt into Guillermo's back and shoved him violently. His feet tangled in his duffel and he fell flat on his face.

The metallic noise of the bolts of the machine guns was heard, and some orders were cried. No one moved. I was terrified.

"Now listen." It was a lieutenant speaking. "We have orders to shoot any man that disobeys. No one is allowed to look out the windows or even raise your head. Anyone that does will pay the consequences. . . . And another thing. Complete silence. No one will be permitted to speak during the trip. Is that understood?"

The aim of all those repressive measures was to discourage us from any attempt to take over the plane. After all, there were men of action in our group that had shown their courage on plenty of occasions—in the mountains fighting with the guerrillas as well as in the city and in underground groups.

The pilot was escorted on board by guards who shut themselves up with him in the cockpit. In Cuba this was not a measure taken only for transporting prisoners. Even at that early time in the Revolution all Cuban flights carried two guards, and the cockpit door and its peephole were armorplated. Until the plane touched down, the cockpit could not be opened, no matter what happened. This procedure is still being followed today.

With our heads lowered, unspeaking, we made the voyage.

The plane set down at the little airport of Nueva Gerona, the capital of Isla de Pinos. It bumped several times, as though the runway had ended and we were rolling across uneven ground. And so we were. The plane turned to the left toward the soldiers of the presidio, our reception committee, who were waiting for us with several military trucks. The door of the plane opened. Outside, high grass came up above the knees of the dozens of guards who surrounded the ship. Most of the soldiers in the group directly before the door were black, and they didn't look like Cubans. Around their necks hung necklaces made of colored beads and seeds called ox-eyes, and they had stuck little stalks of millet into their berets to distinguish themselves from the other guards.

As we descended from the plane, the soldiers began to shout fiercely and brandish their bayonets. But if the guards outside the plane were screaming and threatening us, the ones inside were even worse. "Get out! Now! Hurry up, quick! Jump!"

This time there were no boarding steps. The only way to get off the plane was to jump, and so prisoners were jumping out of the plane carrying the dead weight of the sacks. It was a mad marathon, a desperate jumble. Boitel dropped straight down and landed right in front of the door, and although he hardly scrambled two seconds to get to his feet again, one of the soldiers yanked him up by his arm, put his boot in his back, and shoved him away. Boitel fell on his face in the grass, handcuffed. He lost his glasses.

"Get on those trucks. Let's go! Hurry it up!" And they called us every name in the book. "You're on the Island, you sons of bitches! You bastards! We're going to see to it that you *like* it here! Let's go!" The noise, the confusion, the newness, the viciousness of our guards created a bedlam, ten endless minutes of pure panic. Prisoners ran like frightened animals, or at least I felt like one. I expected at any moment to be prodded with a bayonet or kicked headlong into the grass. Fear had overcome me. I felt a terrible tightness in my gut, like an iron claw squeezing and twisting my insides and slowly pulling them out of my belly. From that moment on, that sensation would remain with me for years, and I knew it was fear, panic, pure animal terror.

Hounded by the constant cries of the guards, we climbed up onto the trucks. There was one very fat, very slow-moving prisoner in the group, whom we called Tito. It was no easy task for him to get up onto a truck, and he stood there on the ground waiting for someone to give him a hand, but in those moments of fear and confusion, we had forgotten all about him. One of the guards raised his rifle and struck fat Tito with the flat of his bayonet, screaming, "Get up there! I told you to get on the truck!" And he hit him again. Several hands went out toward Tito and dragged him up onto the truck.

A rope bisected the truck bed. We prisoners were crammed into the front part next to the driver's cab; on the other side, as in the plane, were the soldiers. They were glaring at us fiercely, and when the truck began to move they raised their bayonets and held them up almost against our necks.

Carrión and I were among the prisoners closest to the dividing rope. The sharp points of the bayonets, just inches from us, swayed with each movement of the truck. A lurch of the truck, a quick stop, a pothole would have been enough to bury them in our throats. In the truck, too, we were forbidden to look out, even to turn our heads or speak. The bayonets kept swaying, moving forward and back to the swaying of the truck. Instinctively, your head drew back, and then the guard would push the rifle forward a little more.

"Are you scared, faggot?" And you had to swallow the insult. "You don't know what's in store for you. You're on Isla de Pinos now, and you're going to find out whether what they say about it is true," they said.

We had, in fact, heard a lot of talk about the prison we were being taken to, about the forced labor in the quarries, about the chilling searches in which some prisoners always wound up dead and hundreds wounded by bayonets. We had also heard about the sinister, dark punishment pavilions with their solitary-confinement cells. Prisoners, we had heard, were put in solitary confinement if they dared to complain about the injustices and abusive treatment committed against them on a daily basis; or they might be sent there simply because it pleased the jailers' taste for sadism to see the prisoners lying naked on the hard, cold floor with the cell door welded shut. They would spend months there, and every day the guards would throw pails of freezing water and excrement over them. Even if a prisoner managed to control his mind, to keep his mental faculties intact, he would still almost always come out tubercular, his lungs destroyed.

And that was where we were being taken. We rode in silence, breathing deeply, trying to fill ourselves with the free air we wouldn't breathe again for a very long time. And there were those bayonets too—swaying hypnotically, menacingly before our eyes like cobras in some nightmare, ready to sink their fangs into our throats.

But at that moment I seemed to wake up—the memory of my fallen comrades, executed by the firing squads of La Cabaña, came into my mind. I thought about Julio and his scorn for life as he defended his belief in freedom and patriotism; I thought about all of those men who marched to the firing squads with a smile on their lips; I thought about the integrity of those martyrs who had died shouting, "*Viva Cuba Libre!* Viva Christ the King! Down with Communism!" And I was ashamed to feel so frightened. I realized that the only way to honor the memory of those heroes was to behave with their firmness and integrity. My heart rose up to God, and I fervently prayed for Him to help me stand up to this brutality, and do what I had to do. I felt that God heard my prayer.

7 / A Model Prison

The prison on Isla de Pinos was at that time the largest in Cuba. It was the so-called Model Prison. The Cuban dictator Gerardo Machado had had it built in the 1930s. It had six enormous circular buildings, with a much larger capacity than was needed when it was first built. Someone asked Machado why he had had the prison built so big; they said it would never be filled. But Machado answered, "Don't you worry. Somebody will come along who'll manage to fill it up."

That somebody was Fidel Castro.

There were 312 of us in that particular group; we were the last contingent of the largest single transfer of prisoners that had ever been carried out in the Cuban prison system. Political prisoners were being concentrated in unimaginable numbers at Isla de Pinos.

The main gates of the first line of security opened to let the procession of trucks through. Handsome, well-cared-for gardens were the first thing the newly arrived prisoner saw. Common prisoners watered and weeded the rosebushes and hibiscus plants. The gardens were bounded at the rear by an arc made up of the Headquarters Building in the center and rows of houses for the officers on each side. Behind that arc rose the enormous masses of the "Circulars," which housed the inmates.

"Get out, you sons of bitches! Now you're *really* prisoners! You're on the Island!"

The insult slapped us in the face, but no one responded. We began to jump out of the truck. In front of me, two of my comrades were handcuffed together; one of them tried to find some support before he jumped, but a guard came up behind him and kicked him off the truck to the ground. As he fell, he pulled his handcuff-mate off with him, spraining his wrist with the metal bracelet. Up on the truck, the guard broke out into a mocking laugh picked up by the rest of the soldiers. One of them walked over to the two prisoners trying to stand up, battered and bruised by the fall, and said to them, "See how nice we are here? We even help you get off the truck."

And once again came the mocking laughter. The rest of us there were completely powerless. We didn't even dare protest, because we thought that if this was just the beginning, who dared find out too soon what the rest would be like.

Immediately a jeep pulled up; they asked about one of us, a man who had been involved in an incident in which a militiaman had been killed in an exchange of fire with anti-Castro rebels. Two men also engaged in the incident had been executed by firing squad; this man had been sentenced to thirty years.

"Where is that son of a bitch?" screamed a sergeant, getting out of the jeep in a fury.

"That's him," one of the soldiers who had escorted us from Havana answered. "Let's go, get a move on. Now you're going to see who it is you're dealing with."

They pushed the prisoner toward the jeep, and the sergeant and his troop rained blows on him as they shoved him in. One of the guards struck out with the butt of his rifle, and a low moan escaped the poor man's lips. He was hardly more than a boy yet.

"Take him to the punishment pavilion," yelled the tall fat sergeant, who seemed to be the one in charge of that group. "And the rest of you," he went on, speaking to those of us standing there waiting, "get into formation over there. On the double. Get a move on."

We lined up in ranks, and they began to check our names against the list the escorts had brought from Cuba.

"Now then, which ones were in the 'little strike'?" the sergeant sneered.

The guards called out Cheo Guerra, Guillermo, and others. Several militiamen broke off from the group, their rifles raised, their bayonets fixed, and pointed to the path the prisoners were to take, a road running into the rest of the prison installations.

"Run! On the double!" they shouted at the prisoners' backs. They prodded and jabbed at them with their bayonets. We saw them run off, and we were horrified to see, as blood tinged their thighs, the color of their pants grow darker and darker. One of them stumbled and fell, and on top of him landed the guards' boots; they kicked him until he lay there unconscious in a pool of blood. He was dragged away by his arms. This was one of the favorite diversions of the guards, as we later learned. But for us, at that moment, it was a spectacle out of Dante. How far we were from imagining that there would be many times when from our cells we would see that same ferocity, that same viciousness, unleashed against other prisoners who kept arriving, day after day, at the Island!

"Okay, let's go. Up these stairs!" said the leader of the escort, and we began to walk up the steps, which led to some minor offices and the General Headquarters of the prison; once there, we were led along a corridor. Not for a single moment had they left off insulting and harassing us.

We came to the end of the corridor and went down a stairway to the back part of the central building, a kind of basement where militiamen were already waiting for us before several piles of prison clothes. These were the uniforms of the old Army, but with one black *P* on the back and two others on the trouser legs.

"All right! Get those clothes off, all of you! Everybody! Strip!" Everything was a rush, everything had to be done in a hurry, under the constant menace of being beaten or run through with a bayonet. We began to take off our clothes—shirt, pants, undershirt and underwear, everything lay at last at our feet.

"Shoes, too, goddammit!" another guard yelled. And we took off our shoes and socks too.

It is impossible for me to describe what I felt at that moment. I suppose the other prisoners thought and felt the same thing I did, standing there like that, naked, facing the wall, with those militiamen and guards laughing and making fun of us, cracking jokes about our nakedness. There is nothing so depressing as being trapped in such a situation.

"Okay, turn around now and stand still until you're called," said one of the soldiers.

They began calling us one by one over to a bench which stood between us and the guards, where they would carry out the search of our property, if the little that we had brought with us—some cans of jam, medicine, toothpaste, soap, underwear—could be called property. But they looted it anyway. Anything that was of any value, or that they simply took a liking to, was "confiscated." My watch attracted Lieutenant Paneque's attention, and he almost broke my wrist when he ripped it off me. Now I definitely gave it up for lost. They were like Vikings or Huns, dividing up the booty right there in front of us. With what seemed unlimited brazenness they argued over the most trivial items—some socks, a razor, a pen or ballpoint.

I was wearing a crucifix that a young friend of mine, Neno Medina, had given me as a gift. Neno was hardly sixteen years old, but Castro hadn't managed to deceive him. His whole family had asked for political asylum in Venezuela during the dictatorship of Batista because his father was one of Castro's revolutionaries. Neno may not have "known," but he intuited that Communism was no good for Cuba. Neno called Fidel "Fidelovsky" as early as 1960. He was forced to enter the militia, though he knew the Revolution which his father had fought and died for had been betrayed. He was sent to the mountains of Escambray as a driver in a military operation intended to besiege and strangle the guerrilla strongholds from which the rebels launched their attacks against Castro. Neno could not stand that— after all, he was on the rebels' side—so he made a mortal decision: driving a truck full of troops, he floorboarded the accelerator and steered the truck over a precipice. Everyone died.

Lieutenant Paneque's hand stretched out toward the crucifix and grabbed it with fury. He brutally stomped and kicked the wooden cross until it was scattered in pieces across the floor.

Suddenly, at the opposite end of the room, there were bursts of laughter and outcries of indignation, and almost immediately a prisoner who was protesting lunged at one of the guards searching him. Several militiamen jumped on him. The prisoner fought, bit, scratched, until the guards beat him to the ground. His head was smashed and his face was covered with the blood gushing from his nose. He tried to stand up, but they booted him to the floor once more. The rest of the guards surrounding us stepped back immediately when the fight broke out and gripped their rifles and machine guns nervously, though nonetheless menacingly.

"Nobody move! Put your hands up and careful what you do or we shoot!"

They were afraid, they were nervous; they were actually fearful that unarmed, naked men might try something, and I felt that we somehow grew before that rabble who could hardly hold their weapons up for the trembling of their hands. Immediately they took out the man that had attacked the guard. We didn't know what had happened, what had provoked the incident, we only saw his wounds and the marks of the boots that had kicked him senseless. Two guards dragged him out of the room, leaving a trail of blood on the floor. Many of us thought he'd surely die from the beating and the wounds.

Later we found out that the guard who was searching him had come across a photograph among the articles he was rummaging through and had asked the prisoner what whorehouse the woman in the picture worked in. That was the last straw. It was a photograph of our companion's mother— a mother like mine, like everybody's, one of the many mothers who suffered the terrible pain of separation from her children, of knowing that they were confined in jails where outrage, physical and psychological mistreatment, and abuse were the order of the day. The man couldn't control himself when the guard sneeringly insulted his mother. Blinded by rage, tears of fury in his eyes, he attacked his offender. If only that poor mother could know that far from home, her son was being dragged out of the room almost dead from a beating the guards had given him for defending her!

Once the search and sacking were done, each inmate was given a change of clothing. Those who wore small or medium were given large-sized clothes, and the big or fat men were given smalls; we had to put the clothes on and leave the room dressed.

The thin ones had no problems—we simply wadded the pants around our waists and rolled up the cuffs and the shirtsleeves. For the fat prisoners, though, it was an ordeal. Tito struggled to try to pull on pants he couldn't possibly wear. At last he managed to get into them, but there was a gap of six inches at the waist; there was no way to button them. They were so short they came halfway up his calves. This was another of the garrison's diversions.

As we left, we passed a poster on the basement wall with a thought from Fidel Castro:

THE REVOLUTION IS GREENER THAN PALM TREES

We formed up in twos and began to walk. Guards prowled back and forth down both sides of the files. The entrance gate in the second security cordon opened; a guardhouse of concrete, with spotlights and a machine gun pointed toward the buildings, stood as though at attention at the gate. Now we were inside the prison.

From that point, the gardens were completely lost to sight. The gate behind us had opened onto a completely foreign world, which many of us now entering would never leave. We walked between Building 5 and Building 6—enormous rectangular buildings, five stories high—and before us rose the huge, seven-story iron-and-concrete piles which were the Circulars. Though built to house 930 inmates each, they would come to shelter 1,300. There were four of those buildings; at their center, as though the prison area were a great die with the number five up, stood the dining hall. It too was circular, though only two stories high. It could handle five thousand men at one sitting; the kitchen and storerooms were in that building too.

We kept walking, on between Circulars 1 and 2. From dozens of windows prisoners waved and shouted at us, but the guards told us not to shout or raise our hands to respond. Anyone who tried it was beaten. We marched along an asphalt walk around the side of the dining hall and stopped before the large iron gate of Circular 4, our destination. Above the door there was an ironic sign: WELCOME TO CIRCULAR 4.

The entrance had a large guardhouse made of unpainted concrete blocks and roofed with corrugated sheets of cast fiber-cement. Through the windows, the prisoners who had arrived the day before shouted at us, called by name to those of us that they had met at La Cabaña. But the guards were not speaking. It was as though when they arrived at that point, they didn't have to have any relationship with us whatsoever. We were utterly *other* to them now. And that lifted my spirits; I dared to raise my head and look up, up to the highest barred windows of the fifth and sixth floors, from which hands were waving in greeting. Then I slowly lowered my eyes down the side of the building to the windows of the first floor, which were very near me. The men behind those iron palisades looked like skeletons; their faces were white and waxen from lack of sun. One of them was so emaciated that he seemed unreal. He didn't speak, he didn't wave or gesture, he was simply there, staring—he looked to me like a figure in a wax museum. However, not one of the men there could have spent more than two years and a few days in that jail. Just thinking about it sent a shiver of terror up my spine. Two years! I would never be able to stand it. How could they still be alive? Why hadn't they died?

At last they opened the entrance gate, after having counted us several times. A throng of prisoners waited on the ground floor in a circular prison yard about eighty yards in circumference. In the center, a concrete tower rose to the height of the fourth floor. At the top a little balcony with a railing for the watch ran around it. A low metal door opened onto the balcony. The tower could be reached only by way of a tunnel which ran from the outside, so that soldiers could enter it without having to come inside the Circular itself.

Around the Circular, opening onto the inner well like an enormous beehive, were the cells. They were lined up one after another, ninety-three cells to a floor. In front of them, circling each floor, was a balcony with an iron railing, so that the balconies were hallways of a sort, along which one could safely walk. Communication from one floor to another was by way of a large marble stairway and four other, smaller stairways, which connected the ground floor to the first floor of cells. In the prison yard, there on the ground floor, there were no cells, only washbasins and showers. The cells themselves were small, with one large window barred with square iron rods. The sixth floor had no walls or divisions—it had been used before as a confinement and punishment area for common prisoners. Several cells had been there at one time, but they had been demolished. Now, because of the overpopulation, they were being used as well. This building, Circular 4, had bars on the cells of the first floor, unlike any of the other Circulars. These cells too had been used as punishment cages before the influx of political prisoners. The rest of the cells had no bars, and one might stroll along the corridors or go up and down the stairs from one floor to another.

The building was like a Roman circus. Everyone was talking and yelling at the same time. A few of us went up to the base of the tower and dropped our bundles so we could rest and take our bearings. High up on the other floors, leaning on their elbows on the railings, many inmates looked down at us curiously. Some of the newcomers were helped by acquaintances, already installed, to take their bags and bundles up and to find a place to sleep in the cells. Boitel, Carrión, and I watched all that as though dumbstruck—that absurd world where everything seemed to have some strange "otherness" about it. "How those cursed wretches shout!"—that was one of Carrión's favorite phrases; he had taken it from *Don Juan Tenorio* by Zorilla, and Alfredo would repeat it whenever it most seemed to fit, like now, when the yelling and screaming threatened to drive us all crazy.

"Gentlemen! Gentlemen! Silence, I implore you!" That was the voice of Lorenzo, the Major of the building, a six-foot-tall, two-hundred-pound mulatto who had been a motorcycle officer in the police force of the previous regime. By secret ballot the prisoners elected a kind of internal government they called the Mandancia, a half-joking argot word that might be translated "Board of Directors" or "Boss-ship." It was the responsibility of the Major to appoint those who would be in charge of the daily operation and maintenance of the building—cleaning, serving the mess, and other tasks. The Major was the man who dealt directly with the guards and who brought us any messages or orders they wanted sent to us. At the beginning of 1959 the ex-soldiers of Batista's army sent to that prison had to tolerate Mandancias made up of common prisoners and imposed on them by the garrison. Those Mandancias collaborated with the garrison, of course; suffice it to say that the common prisoners had portraits of Fidel Castro in their cells and enjoyed the protection of Prison Headquarters. Within a few months, thanks to the efforts of a man named Beruvides, one of the Air Force pilots who was imprisoned there, the military managed to oust common prisoners from leadership. The first groups of political prisoners had not yet arrived; the only prisoners kept there then were ex-officers and soldiers from Batista's army.

"Well, let's go up," said someone in the group, and we picked up our duffels and began to walk over toward the stairs.

We had to pick our way through long ranks of pails and every other imaginable kind of container, set out in the prison yard in meandering files like the course of some strange river. We soon found out why: Water was rationed in the prison. Each man was allowed five liters of water per week. That was the only water—for drinking, for washing your face, for bathing, for washing clothes. Naturally, it wasn't enough. The reason for this rationing was that the installations which supplied the prison with water were being repaired. The trucks they used now to deliver water belonged to another agency, and they couldn't be relied on. On this particular occasion, nine days had elapsed since the last delivery. We were informed of all this when we asked one of the "veteran" prisoners where we could get some water. One of the men, who had been a patient in the National Psychiatric Hospital, knew Boitel, and he had invited us into his cell to rest for a few minutes. He lived on the first floor. He told us he'd ask around to try to find us a little water, but that there would be very little of it. That same afternoon, the militia had said, the tank truck would be arriving, but hardly anyone believed it. The prisoners hoarded their water like the real treasure it was.

The man who finally shared some of his water with us was an old fellow who lived alone in one of the cells on the first floor. When Boitel's friend asked him to give us some, he peered at us keenly and took a pail covered with cardboard out from under his cot. We saw that there was a little water in the bottom.

"I don't drink much, very little, you know, and that's why I still have some left." He gave us each a sip. I became even thirstier—I realized I could have drunk down the whole pailful.

We made our way on up to the sixth floor. The men who had arrived the day before had managed to get empty cells, so they took many of us in. The traffic on the stairways never stopped—cots were moved from one floor to another, from one cell to another. The cells had two of these beds, which prison slang called "airplanes." I never managed to find out why, though probably they called them that because they folded up like wings. The frame was made of tubing to which a piece of canvas or burlap was sewn. They were held to the wall by two steel eyebolts sunk into the concrete, and hung by two chains attached higher up, so they were cantilevered. They could be taken up during the day, and were opened out only when they were going to be used. Having one of those canvas "airplanes" in good condition was the height of luxury for a prisoner.

Carrión, Piñango, Boitel, Jorge Víctor, and I, with a few more friends, had stayed together through all the bustle of the move. We were utterly exhausted when we finally managed to reach the sixth floor. In prison one has dozens, hundreds, of friends, but there is always a smaller group with whom you spend most of your time. Those are the ones with whom you share not only most of your hours but that necessity to communicate as well, which for some prisoners is more important than all the rest. Jorge Víctor was a quiet type; he hardly spoke, and he gave the impression of being solid and equable, as he in fact was. He had been studying to be a priest, and it always seemed as though he were wearing an invisible habit. He was an extraordinary companion, and Carrión joked with him all the time. He had been detained the same morning the rest of us had. Jorge Víctor immediately plunked down on the floor, impassive, and in a while the rest of us followed suit. We each found a spot in that square cell, took out our blankets, and settled down to sleep as best we could. The next day we'd try to find some mattresses, get our hands on some "airplanes," and stake out our own cells, but meantime, in spite of the discomfort of the tiny cell with its unfinished floor pocked with holes, we almost immediately sank into deep sleep. The last few days had exhausted us.

Carrión woke us up just a few minutes after we had fallen asleep. There was a rat running around all over us. Rats were another of those things that were to keep us company as long as we were in jail. It wouldn't be a prison without rats, but they were insignificant on Isla de Pinos, compared to what we would see in the future.

As a matter of fact, events of all sorts conspired to keep us from getting any sleep to speak of that night. In the early hours of the morning, a screaming and crying and infernal noise woke us up with a start. We got up and looked out over the railing. We could see the entrance bars from where we were standing; the spectacle appeared to be from some strange hallucination. They had finally brought the tank truck of water. But what they did was stick two four-inch hoses through the bars and open the valves—the precious liquid was being poured out onto the ground, and the first prisoners, half asleep, were running down the stairs screaming *"Water!"*

Prisoners rushed frantically down the stairs into the prison yard, carrying pails, cans, jars—anything that would hold water. Hundreds of men were filling their containers as their turn came in the snaking lines. They were running down the stairs like demons, yelling and screaming. Above that howl Major Lorenzo's thundering voice could be heard: "Stay calm, gentlemen, stay calm!"

But those men were no longer civilized beings; they acted like a herd of thirst-maddened animals that suddenly get wind of water nearby and break into stampede. They ran up and down the stairs; some of them, more agile than the rest, swung from the railings and jumped from floor to floor like monkeys, running the risk of falling headlong into space.

"Please, gentlemen, let's act like human beings!" Lorenzo kept crying, shirtless but still wearing his dark glasses. I don't think he ever took them off. He was up next to the bars beside the hoses. The volume of water the hoses spewed out was enough to fill the containers immediately, and as the hose went from one pail to another gallons and gallons of water were wasted. There was already a great pool in the prison yard. Someone was running and slipped and fell . . . but men kept on running down hallways and stairs.

I stood there looking at all that as though I were hypnotized, until a prisoner ran along behind us with a plastic pail.

"Hey, you guys, get a move on or you won't get any water!" And those words of his woke us up. It was true, and we were very thirsty. We picked up our pails and took off running; we hurtled down the stairs. I felt that I was going through my initiation, that I was becoming just another prisoner, just another one of those men.

8 / Animal Protein

At five o'clock in the morning a cornet's Reveille called us to the headcount, which officers took every morning at six. The cornet player was a common prisoner who stood near the dining hall in front of Circulars 3 and 4. He played very well. Later I would sit and watch him often in the afternoon. He would get drunk whenever he could on alcohol mixed with sugar, and those days he had to lean up against one of the columns of the building, because if he didn't he would've fallen over. Curiously enough, the more plastered he was, the better he played. It was this cornet player who played Taps when they carried out the corpses of men who had died in the prison. The Major would call us all to attention, we prisoners would stand straight and tall, and everything would stop for a few moments. The only sound was the notes of Taps echoing movingly through the presidio.

Carrión and I had managed to find a cell on the second floor, number 64. Boitel didn't want to move in with us; he liked to sleep late in the morning, so he had found a cot on the sixth floor, which was an ideal place for sleeping late. Jorge Víctor, Piñango, and the rest had already settled in with some other companions. But we would all get together to eat, and into our group came Manolito and Vladimir Ramírez.

Ramírez was a psychologist who had organized an action cell which was planning an attempt on Castro's life, using Ramírez' apartment as a base of operations. His apartment was located across the street from El Carmelo Restaurant, which the dictator frequented. They were discovered, though, and a shoot-out led to their arrest. Vladimir and Fernando López del Toro blockaded themselves inside the walls of a colonial mansion in El Vedado, and it took a huge police siege to make them surrender.

Mealtimes became a time for conversation, with talk about all sorts of things but especially about political events in the country. The track of the conversation always led to the fall of the regime, because every day more and more rumors were coming in about the rise of internal resistance, about

acts of sabotage, about the number of counterrevolutionaries in the countryside, and about the gigantic military operations which the government had
been forced to carry out against the new anti-Castro guerrillas.

The mess we ate at those times was cooked by common prisoners. The
food was so tasteless and unseasoned, so flat, so dull and unappetizing, that
we jokingly called it La Boba—"The Old Maid"; nobody really wanted to
try it a second time. When the prisoners pushed the cart loaded with the
vats of food up to the gate the Major or the gatekeeper—another member
of the Mandancia, whose job was to stay by the front gate for just this sort
of duty—would cry out, "Here comes La Boba! Get your tools ready!" This
announcement simply meant that all the prisoners were to line up floor by
floor; each man was to have his plate and a canteen cup or jar at the ready.

The menu was not very varied. For lunch, there was rice and split peas;
in the afternoon, there was boiled cornmeal and a greasy, watery soup.
Generally the split peas or some other kind of peas or beans had been sent
to the prison because they were spoiled, and often enough they were wormy
as well. When the food was prepared from such a shipment, a layer of tiny
animals floated on top of the vats. But in even the most unpleasant circumstances the Cuban will find a vein of humor; so when the beans full of worms
were coming, the gatekeeper would call out, "Split peas with protein!"

For many days at first I virtually lived on bread, for I had a certain
squeamishness about what I ate. But prison and hunger cured me of that
soon enough. Weeks later I would devour those peas, any food, as fast as
the next man. When someone would say that the food was spoiled or tasted
bad, Carrión always answered, "Who's ever heard of a prisoner eating
because he likes the food? Prisoners eat to survive."

And it was true. You had to eat whatever they gave you, in order to
survive, and I swore to myself to put aside all those scruples and swallow
whatever came along. We would sometimes have macabre contests with our
spoons, fishing out the little worms and pushing them to the side. They were
small, yellowish-white worms with a kind of caramel-colored spot on the
head. Little by little you lost your disgust for them, and rationalized the
situation: "The little worms are dead, they've been boiled in the steam vats,
so what harm can it do to eat them?"—"Absolutely none; the only thing is
that you're not accustomed to eating them. But just remember, in Asia they
eat insects." All these arguments prepare the mind, condition it, and that
is the real secret of survival—mental control. We wound up stirring the soup
up with the rice without wasting any more effort fishing out the worms.
After all, it was true—they *were* protein. I never got sick from eating them,
either.

Since it was the common prisoners, supervised by a militiaman, that cooked
the food for us; since we were counterrevolutionaries while they were revolutionaries—even if *criminal* revolutionaries; and since a revolutionary is

defined by, among other things, his hostility and aggressiveness toward counterrevolutionaries, some dreadful things happened to our food from time to time.

One morning the breakfast sugar water that was brought to us in a fifty-five-gallon drum—one of those used for holding fuel—began to taste funny as its level dropped. When there were only six or eight inches of the water left, it grew bubbly. The constant churning of the big serving ladle had whipped it into a froth. The inmates stopped serving it and ran a wooden paddle around in it; the paddle bumped something hard on the bottom. They decided to pour out what was left of the sugar water—and there were two bars of soap in the bottom of the drum.

On another occasion more than half the length of a thick cow intestine, rectum included, was floating on top of the soup; the intestine was still full of cowshit. We sent the soup back.

Complaints were made to the soldier who was head of the kitchen, but he always shrugged off any personal responsibility for things that happened. He would allege that whatever happened was the cooks' fault. We frequently found pieces of broken glass. One day the food they brought in had dead rats in it. But the worst consequences of eating spoiled food occurred when we were served poisoned split peas one day. Thousands of prisoners came down with uncontrollable diarrhea and quickly dehydrated. The authorities became frightened, since dozens and dozens of prisoners, almost unable to walk, or even speak, came down into the prison yard. Intravenous kits and saline solution were brought over, but there were not enough to go around, so they had to notify the civilian hospital in Nueva Gerona. They didn't have enough supplies to send, either. Therefore the Ministry of the Interior sent a plane from Cuba with a shipment of intravenous equipment and other medicines and supplies. The authorities admitted that the common prisoner who was head of the cooks had stirred some toxic substance into the food. They even knew what the substance was—they said it was a liquid sprayed on the split peas to protect them against insects. They assured us that punitive measures would be taken against him. But that inmate continued as head of the kitchen for a long time—until all common prisoners were removed from the prison, in fact, which was then staffed solely by political prisoners.

Until the spring of 1961, every forty-five days the prison sold certain articles to prisoners: spices, oil, salt, cigarettes, and cigars. With these items we could disguise La Boba, fix her up. We recooked the food and added salt, a little oil, and some spices. All that came to an end in April 1961. However, even though there were no visits, every so many days they did allow prisoners' families to send a little package containing powdered milk, sugar, and *gofio de trigo.* (*Gofio de trigo* became a staple food additive in the prisons. In the absence of really nutritive foods, this roasted wheat flour, something

like prepared wheat germ but gummier when wet, supplied what few vitamins, even calories, we subsisted on.) Prisoners also persuaded the authorities to let our families send mattresses in to us. Cuba was still in the dying
days of capitalism. Those packages would lead to another of our macabre
jokes, as I'll tell shortly.

Bathing during those first months was not possible. Water still had to
be brought to the prison in the tank truck, and the quota allowed us only
enough water for drinking.

At dawn and at evening, there was always the headcount. We had to
stand in the cell doors, but only two men per cell; all the rest of us lined
up in the prison yard. All the officers were very good at the counting, but
the most talented of them all was a sergeant who had served in the ranks
of Batista's army. He was very soldierly—he clicked his heels and everything. Prisoners called this sergeant by the nickname Pinguilla—"Little
Prick." With one quick glance, his eyes flew over the six floors, and if, by
the way the men were arrayed, his headcount did not balance out with the
list he had, he would discover it instantly.

If a prisoner so much as leaned against the cell door at the moment the
count was being taken, he would be carried off to the punishment cells. He
would be beaten by Sergeant Naranjito, who never failed to carry the cavalry
sword which he had inherited from the days he was in Batista's rural guard.
Naranjito was a true sadist; his favorite pastime and greatest pleasure consisted of running the prisoners to the punishment-cell pavilion, hacking at
them with the broad side of the saber all the way.

The punishment-cell pavilion was located beyond the Circulars and the
two rectangular one-story buildings, alongside the chapel, in some of whose
large rooms common prisoners were lodged. The other building in that area,
exactly in front of the punishment pavilion, was the hospital. Batista had left
it very well equipped—it had a modern X-ray laboratory, a medical laboratory, an operating room, a pharmacy, a dental office, and all the rest—but
its use for medical care of prisoners was kept to a minimum. All its rooms
opened onto an interior patio.

Fidel Castro had been held prisoner in one of the rooms of that hospital,
but he had been allowed visitors, national and international news, uncen-
sored books, sun, unlimited correspondence, a conjugal pavilion, and any
food he wanted. He had never been mistreated; they had never so much as
pushed him. Now the authorities had Húber Matos there, one of the men
who had fought beside Castro in the mountains. Húber Matos had come
down from the Sierra Maestra with Castro holding the rank of commander,
a title he had well earned in combat; but he diverged from the Marxist line
of the Revolution, so he wrote a letter to Castro resigning his commission
and his office as Military Chief of the Revolutionary Army in Camagüey
province. Castro accused him of being an ingrate and a traitor and sent him
to jail, sentencing him and several of his officers to twenty years in prison.

There was a special guard for Húber Matos. He was not guarded by the garrison of the presidio, but rather by a special group selected very carefully from among the Political Police. Castro feared the sympathies which the ex-commander could draw on among the ranks of the rebel army. Matos was held completely incommunicado from the rest of the prisoners. Even his food was brought in uncooked to his place of detention, so as to avoid any contact with other prisoners. It would be 1966 before Matos would finally leave his solitary confinement for the first time and enter into contact with the rest of the political prisoners.

One afternoon, from a window on the fifth floor, someone shouted that they were taking prisoners out of the punishment cells. The punishment-cell pavilion and the hospital could be seen perfectly clearly from Circulars 3 and 4. Every two or three months the authorities took out a number of prisoners, generally when the pavilion was overcrowded and they needed space to punish others. Among that group of released prisoners were Cheo Guerra and Guillermo Díaz Lanz, who had been sent there on our first day at Isla de Pinos. They had grown so gaunt that their bones were practically tearing through their skin. Their eyes were sunken, they were as pale as candlewax, and their faces were covered by a months-long growth of beard which made them almost unrecognizable.

They told us about the torments and miseries they had been through there. The common prisoners controlled everything. The punished prisoners were shut up in cells with the doors almost completely sealed with a sheet of iron. They had not had a bath in all that time, and they had known nothing of the outside world. Sometimes the common prisoners, by order of the posted militia, would throw pails of cold water on them, and sometimes dirty water as well, which had been used to rinse out the rags used for cleaning the floors.

News, rumors, and gossip were like a drug for a great number of prisoners. I had read about this phenomenon in books about concentration camps, but I had never thought it would be anything so complex, or that so many men would be sustained, in many cases, by simple information. Communists are perfectly aware of what information means to the prisoner, since by keeping him in touch with outside reality it allows him to put prison reality into perspective. Everything the Communists did, then, was directed expressly toward breaking that link, toward isolating the imprisoned man even more. During this period, they were still a little clumsy and green in their practices, but slowly, as the staff of the prisons and the Political Police were sent off and trained in East Germany and Czechoslovakia, their techniques grew more refined, more scientific, more inhumane, more psychologically destructive.

The mail was a constant frustration for us. When we first arrived we were allowed to send a brief telegram telling our families where we were. The prison rules permitted us to receive one telegram and one letter, written on one side only of the paper, from our families monthly. Those of us who were lucky enough to receive the letters sent to us, which not all of us were, sometimes could hardly read them. Slogans—"The Fatherland or death," "We will overcome," and the like—would be rubber-stamped one on top of another, so that the dark ink of the rubber stamp would obscure the text of the letters.

About that time, I received a letter from my mother. She told me that she and my father had come to the prison to try to persuade the authorities to let them see me. Obviously nothing had come of that.

Newspapers were never allowed into the prison, and if one of the guards discovered a prisoner with one, the prisoner was taken to the punishment cells under a hail of blows. But in Circular 3, Macurán, an ex-soldier of the defeated army, had managed to put together a rudimentary radio which drove all the soldiers of the garrison crazy. They had conducted one search after another trying to find it, but it had always eluded them. When news came in over Macurán's radio, six copies were made immediately, one for each floor, and the news would be read out to small groups of men. The guard on the tower had to be watched, but very few times during that period did the guards go up to the observation tower. Good news lifted the prisoners' spirits into the clouds, and when the group dissolved, many men would exhibit signs of almost manic optimism and elation. There were even those who would follow the one man who had read the news into the next circle, to hear him read it again. It was really like a drug, an addiction.

The prisoners had invented a sort of sign language using their hands and fingers. It was similar to the sign language used by deaf-mutes, but not nearly so sophisticated. For example, circling one of the railings with the whole hand, as though gripping a baseball bat, was the letter D. Putting two fingers across a bar corresponded to the letter N, and three fingers stood for M. This permitted the prisoners to communicate with amazing speed. It might easily have looked like something out of bedlam to a spectator who didn't know what was going on, seeing those men behind their bars moving their hands like men possessed, opening and closing their fists or touching the iron bars several times. The news from Macurán's radio—or gossip, for that matter—could be sent by this method over from Circular 3 and copied down by us in Circular 4. The two buildings were separated by only the thin strip of asphalt walkway.

But Circulars 1 and 2 were farther away, so hand language was impossible. We established communication with them, though, using Morse code. There were quite a few telegraph operators among us, and others of us learned it from them. A cardboard ruler or some other little piece of stiff white paper would be employed as a transmitter. One slap sideways with this little ruler was equivalent to *dot;* toward the front, *dash.* A while later communications were perfected when we put together a homemade blinker.

Whistles made out of empty toothpaste tubes were also used, and thus was sonic communication born.

Speaking or calling from one Circular to another was prohibited. If someone was caught at it, he was sent at once to the punishment cages. And it wasn't hard for the guards to catch prisoners. The guards walked beats around the Circulars. Outside each cell, under the window, the cell number was painted very prominently. The guard could easily see, then, which cell contained the rule-breaking prisoner. And of course there was no way to escape.

Keeping up communications was a first-priority task, and someone had managed to string a line for sending letters between the two Circulars. To shoot them over, all folded up, they used a sort of slingshot made of pieces of rubber tubing taken from the intravenous equipment. The projectile was a piece of lead to which a fine thread was attached. This thread was obtained by unraveling a nylon sock with much patient labor—the same work the textile factory did, but in reverse. T-shirts, sheets, or any other woven fabric might also be used.

The first times they tried to shoot a thread across with a letter, a problem became evident: the shot was so fast that however much trouble they took in winding the thread at the shooter's feet, it always got tangled. Someone thought of the bobbins on looms, and the problem was solved. Thread was coiled around an aluminum cone, exactly as it comes from the factory on bobbins, one wind on top of another. When they made the shot with this new apparatus, another prisoner stood next to the shooter, with his hand stuck into the cone to steady and hold it. The lead piece shot off, and behind, with dizzying speed, the thread unwound cleanly.

On the other side, they stuck two broomsticks with a thread strung between them out the window of one of the cells closest to our Circular. They caught the piece of lead on the fly.

Prisoners kept adding refinements to the system—the latest advance consisted of using nylon fishing line that somebody had gotten from somewhere. This had the advantage of being almost invisible, so that it could be left in place. And since all this "archery" took place on the fifth floor, the guards couldn't see anything from the ground. This system lasted until one fine afternoon when Lieutenant Paneque, walking unconcernedly along between the Circulars, looked upward, did a double-take, and stood petrified with his eyes glued on the heavens. There before his eyes was a little bird sitting in midair, unmoving. That is how they discovered us—a beautiful, free little bird ruined our line of communications by perching on it.

"Search!" was the alarm cry among us. The garrison barracks was situated at the back part of the prison, very clearly visible from Circular 4. When there was going to be a search, platoons of soldiers would run out of the building. If they got onto trucks or came toward our Circulars, the alarm

"Search!" was cried throughout the building. We could never know which Circular they were headed for, but the alarm was given in all four. They could never surprise us, since we had organized a twenty-four-hour vigilance committee. There was one man per floor, relieved every two hours, around the clock. Although the notification gave us only about a two-minute head-start on their arrival, this was enough to allow us to destroy any compromising papers and hide the radio or any other proscribed items. When the platoons of guards formed up in front of the entrance to the buildings, the prisoners were already on top of the situation, following every movement with full attention.

The guards, armed with machetes, truncheons, rubber-clad chains, and bayonets, would fill the prison yard in seconds. Several of them carrying rifles would appear on the central tower to keep watch on the high floors and on the movements of the prisoners. If they saw some suspicious operation, they would fire off a warning shot and point at the cell involved, screaming at the prisoner to raise his hands and not to move until the other guards below came to his cell.

Within the presidio there were two enclosures or corrals about ninety yards square, formed by nine-foot chain-link fences crowned with barbed wire strung in a V. Two files of guards lined up from the entrance to the Circulars out to those corrals. They would be armed with fixed bayonets, and prisoners had to pass naked down that gauntlet at a dead run. The guards gathered at the main gate and flailed at the prisoners as they ran out. Then the guards in the two files prodded us in our backsides and thighs with their bayonets—always from behind. Every search left a toll of more than a hundred wounded by bayonet stabs, over and above the number of men beaten. And we returned to the Circular in the same way.

On our return we would find the Circular looking as if a hurricane had blown through it. Clothes, shoes, toilet articles would be jumbled and strewn through the prison yard as they had been thrown down from the floors onto the ground floor. That is why we had put our prisoner number on everything, from our underwear and socks to our toothbrushes. After every search many men would find their canvas or burlap cot covering slashed by a bayonet, or the sugar or powdered milk their families had sent them, and that they carefully rationed so that it would last forty-five days, poured out over the bed. Sometimes the powdered milk would be dumped into our pails of water. Cigarette packages would be cut in half, as would bars of soap.

The most important task after a search was to try to help the wounded. If a case seemed especially serious, because of a deep bayonet wound, for example, the guards on post would be notified so that they in their turn would inform their superior officer. The object of this long process was simply to get the wounded man taken to the little hospital where the authorities held the prisoners who were doctors. In subsequent weeks more doctors came into the prison, and they usually came to the Circulars.

Among the common prisoners in that prison could be found the most dangerous kinds of criminals. Early in 1961 the authorities began several programs of indoctrination talks for those prisoners. They told them that the Revolution would give them the opportunity to become heroes, liberators of other countries laboring under the weight of dictators. They explained to them that the unjust society they had lived in before had forced them to become criminals, but, they told them, the future could be different. Then these prisoners were put through military training and sent off on an invasion of the Dominican Republic to topple Trujillo. But the Dominican dictator had his air force waiting for them. Not a single soldier managed to land; their ships were sunk many miles from the coast, and no one survived. Castro had notified Trujillo's Intelligence Corps, giving them all the information they needed to intercept the military contingent.

Among the mass of common prisoners on Isla de Pinos at that time, however, there were also many men who sympathized with the political prisoners; they too loathed the system. These men helped us in many valuable ways and risked the danger of reprisals by doing so. Communication with them was not easy, since they were under absolute prohibition to speak to us. If he were caught at it, a common prisoner would be identified with us, with what we represented, and he would rot in the punishment cells.

Through the window of one of the cells on the first floor, right above the little road, Boitel and I managed to establish contact with one of those common prisoners. It was a labor of many days' duration. The prisoner worked in the bakery, and at evening as he returned to Building 5, where the common prisoners then lived, he would pass three or four yards from the cell window, but he couldn't stop. We would sit there next to the window and every day we would softly call one or two phrases to him. We had written them down and we would repeat them day after day. We asked him to find a newspaper for us; we asked him about the possibility, a little farther on, of smuggling some correspondence in and out for us, a relatively easy thing for prisoners held for ordinary crimes to do, at least at that time. Finally we managed to win him over. He agreed to collaborate with us in spite of the fact that we had warned him about the risks he was exposing himself to. And he didn't do it for money—it was his way of undermining the regime.

We figured out a way to get the newspaper through. It had to be smuggled in not directly in front of the cell but several yards away from the Circular, so that anyone who saw him from a distance couldn't possibly suspect anything. You had to take care not only against the militia, but also against the other common prisoners, among whom there were informers, collaborators with the garrison; they might easily denounce him.

That afternoon Boitel and I were posted at the window and Carrión was standing watch at the door when our man appeared at the end of the walkway coming toward us. We got our equipment ready.

We were going to snare the newspaper using a piece of green-dyed cord with a lead weight tied to the end of it. We would shoot the string through the bars of the window with a slingshot. I shot, and the string looped out to the edge of the little road. Then we let out enough slack so that it hung down right against the green wall; that way no observer could make it out.

Our friend was coming closer, looking surreptitiously at the edge of the road. Boitel gave a little tug on the string, which ruffled the grass. That was enough for the man to see the thread. He squatted down as though he were tying his shoelace and quickly took a small flat package out of his sock, made a lightning-quick gesture, and continued his walk. It took only a few seconds. We waited five very long minutes to give our friend time to get to his building, then Boitel very slowly pulled in the cord. Suddenly a guard jeep appeared, turning in from behind the pavilion. Hurriedly, we played out a little string to keep it from being seen and jumped away from the window. It was getting dark now and that helped us. The jeep passed, and we breathed a little easier. We hauled up the package. What came into our hands was a copy of the newspaper *Revolución,* wrapped into a tight little bundle with a piece of thread.

From that day on, we had newspapers with some frequency. But we couldn't talk about it—we knew that there were informers also planted among the thousands of men in our Circular. Boitel, Carrión, Ulises, and I decided to edit a bulletin with the most important news of the day and to distribute it, as we did with the news that Macurán gave us as well. We called our new little newspaper the *Free Press.*

Books were prohibited. There were only two which had been saved—no one knew how—when, months before, at the end of 1960, before our group arrived, the garrison took everything away. The two books which remained were a biography of Marie Antoinette by Stefan Zweig and *El Hombre mediocre (Mediocre Man)* by José Ingenieros. Several hundred men were signed up for their turn to read them.

9 / Searches and Mass Relocations

There was search after search in Circular 3. The authorities constantly, if vainly, kept trying to find the clandestine radio. Guards would mass at the exit of the Circular and wield their chains and bayonets with complete impunity. Their victims would dodge through the hail of blows, ducking and trying to cover unprotected, vulnerable heads with arms already aching and bruised.

In one of these searches a prisoner stumbled and fell headlong from the beating the guards were giving him, and he lay there inert. Other prisoners ran around him or jumped over his prostrate body. Each man's private terror was all that existed at those moments; stopping to aid a fallen companion would have meant getting more kicks and blows for your trouble. Under those circumstances the instinct of self-preservation won out over pity—the prisoners kept on running, dodging, running.

And the guards were screaming, yelling; they always did that. It was a mechanism for firing themselves up, getting themselves agitated. Probably striking other men for no cause, no motive, was not easy, even for the most heartless of our guards. They were men with wives and children. Some of them lived in the little houses at the exit of the prison. They would have just come in, still wrapped in the warmth of their homes, still not fully free of sleep, and they would immediately be given a bayonet, a chain, or a truncheon to attack men whom they had never even crossed words with, had never taken even verbal, let alone physical, offense from. What must those guards have felt when the first prisoners looked fearfully out the bars and they had to raise their bayonets and strike them?

After passing through the main gate, the prisoners kept running, into the corral, trying to dodge through the gauntlet of guards. Suddenly, a tall black prisoner appeared, dressed in full uniform. He was wearing little round, gold-rimmed old-fashioned glasses; on his left forearm he was carrying a small wooden bench; in his right hand there was a fan, which he was calmly fanning himself with. This was Dr. Velázco, one of our best doctors. He spoke the same way he walked—deliberately and unhurriedly, pronouncing every letter, every syllable. He was utterly imperturbable. Other prisoners were still running past, but Dr. Velázco maintained that same rhythmic pace, giving the impression that he was strolling through his garden at home on a gentle afternoon.

There was another search a while later, in Circular 2, when I saw Dr. Velázco act the same way. The guards were standing on the stairways savagely beating the men coming down the stairs. Already almost all of us were downstairs in the prison yard; there were only a few stragglers, among them Dr. Velázco. As always, he walked slowly, unhurriedly, deliberately. From the yard his friends called out to him, begging him to hurry so the guards wouldn't beat him. When he came to the last flight of stairs, though, the guards in fury unleashed a rain of blows on his back. Dr. Velázco didn't move a muscle, as though it weren't his back taking the beating. A howl of indignation arose: "That's the doctor! Stop hitting him!" we called. But what did the guards care if he was a doctor?

Dr. Velázco came down the last steps, and even though the blows did not cease, he did not flinch, he did not move one whit faster. One of the guards, who was just about to reach the second floor, came back down a few steps and leaned out over the railing, holding himself with one arm. With the other arm, the arm wielding a machete, he let fall the last blow. Those of us awaiting Dr. Velázco below surrounded him; we were very concerned. Still speaking deliberately, he told us that it was nothing . . . and he found a place next to the tower, set his little wooden bench down, and sat down to fan himself. I knew how much his back must have burned and throbbed; I don't think I could have kept my composure in such pain. But he was unmoved and apparently undaunted.

One afternoon during this time they called Boitel out. They were transferring him to La Cabaña, where they were going to put him through another trial; he was to get twenty-five years for the *cause célèbre,* Capri No. 600.

Prisoners were frequently sent to Isla de Pinos from various jails across the island. About that time, the Ministry of the Interior had begun the practice of sending the prisoner as far away from his family as possible, so as to make contact among family members more difficult and keep the doors to the jails from always being thronged with mothers and wives. This meant that prisoners whose homes were at the extreme western end of Cuba were sent to jail in the province of Oriente, five or six hundred miles away, where it would be virtually impossible for their families to travel with any frequency to visit them.

The government followed this strategy not only with prisoners or captured guerrillas, but also even with private citizens, especially campesinos. Long before the "strategic hamlets" had been employed in Vietnam, Castro had already put them into practice in Cuba. The first of these hamlets was called Ciudad Sandino, Sandino City.

Early in 1961, prisoners who had belonged to the rebel bands began to flow into the Model Prison on Isla de Pinos; these were those rebels who had been operating in Escambray out of numerous pockets of guerrilla concentration. Through them we learned details of the gigantic operation that the government had set in motion—more than sixty thousand troops, most of them militia, were participating in what was called the "Cleanup" of Escambray. This led directly to the relocation projects and the "strategic hamlets."

Suppression of the guerrillas was expensive for Castro. In the newspaper *Granma,* the official organ of the Party, in May 1970, Raúl Castro retrospectively added up the toll of those years of struggle against the rebel forces that had been fighting throughout the country, and he admitted that more than five hundred soldiers had died and that the struggle had cost some 800 million pesos. There had been 179 guerrilla bands made up of 3,591 men, Fidel's brother reported.

To hide the fact that there was such fierce resistance to the Communist government on the part of the people living in the countryside, the government called them "bandits," and a special force was created to deal with the insurgents. This force was called the Batallones de Lucha Contra Bandidos, the Bandit Control Battalions, better known by the Spanish initials, LCB.

In the government's attempt to wipe out these forces, not only guerrillas themselves but also those campesinos who acted as guides, messengers, and contacts were executed. In the area of Escambray, campesinos in great numbers were opposed to the Castro regime, and those who did not actually join up with the guerrillas cooperated with them in many ways. The land was very fertile and under the campesinos' hands yielded plantains, various kinds of tubers, and all sorts of other foodstuffs. The people also raised pigs and poultry on their little parcels of land. The government believed, not unnaturally, that the rebels were being supplied from these sources, so the leaders developed a reconcentration plan to keep supplies from the rebels. All the families with land in Escambray and its foothills would be cleared out.

The day the evictions began, trucks from the INRA (National Institute of Agrarian Reform) and Soviet-made ZIL campaign trucks full of troops stopped in front of the humble houses, some with dirt floors and roofs thatched with palm leaves. The countryfolk were permitted to take only a few clothes and personal articles with them. Their fruits and vegetables, poultry, pigs, and the occasional cow were confiscated by the INRA. The troops destroyed their garden plots, set fire to their houses, and poisoned their wells. This scorched-earth policy, eliminating the sources of supply to the guerrillas, was carried out most thoroughly and methodically.

The women and children of the campesino families were separated from the men and transferred to Havana. They were sent off to residences in the luxurious Miramar section of the city, but they were shut up there as though they were in jails. Several families would be packed into those houses. Still not satisfied with this, the authorities informed the women that they had to go into the country to do farm labor. The old women among them would stay behind to take care of the children.

The situation lasted for years, and in all that time they never saw their husbands or brothers. The children of school age were separated from their mothers and sent off on "scholarships" to government schools for indoctrination in Marxist thought, to wipe out the "harmful" effects and influences of the adults.

The men were taken to the Guanajacabibes peninsula, the most westerly part of Cuba, and one of the most inhospitable, hundreds of miles from the theater of war, and even farther from their families in Havana. These campesinos were never brought before a tribunal, but they were prisoners all the same. They were threatened with execution if they tried to escape, and they were told that reprisals would be taken against their relatives. Those poor wretches did not even know where they were. They were put to hard farm labor and the construction of Sandino Concentration Camps 1, 2, and 3, which still exist.

When these three concentration camps were finished, the government told the campesinos that they were going to build a little town. When they were finished with it, they were told, they could go and live in it with their families. Before they began the construction they would be allowed to go and visit their families in Havana. And after that meeting, the campesinos would be allowed to send and receive one letter a month.

So with the dream of building a town for themselves and their families, the men worked day and night and raised the blocks of buildings. When they had finished, the women and children were brought there. And they did live there together, but they were forbidden to travel outside the borders of the province. That way, the authorities kept them from trying to return to the mountains. This strategic hamlet, Ciudad Sandino, still exists.

Very little is known abroad about these hamlets and the terrible tragedy of those families. The men were prisoners, separated from their wives and families, forced to do hard labor. Nonetheless, there is not a piece of paper, not a document—nothing, even for form's sake—which speaks of that spoliation and exile and what happened in the years afterward.

10 / On Top of a Powder Keg

T he presidio was located so near the north coast of Isla de Pinos that
you could see the waters of the Caribbean from it. There was a cay
offshore called Monkey Key (Cayo de Monos); it had gotten its name, so
the story goes, because years before, monkeys used in research and laboratory experiments had been kept there. Some natives of Isla de Pinos swore
that monkeys still lived out on the cay. To the west of the prison complex
were the Sierra Caballo mountains; to the south there were extensive fields
used for Army and militia exercises, tank practice, and a firing range; to the
east were green pine groves, from which the island had no doubt gotten its
name, and some low hills. Besides the garrison for the prison there were
several military encampments, especially militia posts, scattered all around
the area.

From the fifth floor of the Circular you had an uninterrupted view for
several miles around. Firing practices were held regularly, and whenever
there were night exercises the artillery officers in the Circulars would stay
up and watch. They could classify the guns and other weapons used and
locate the nearby emplacements with considerable exactness. You could
easily see the flares of the cannon blasts on the peaks of the nearby mountain
range.

At night from my cell, overlooking those mountains, I could sometimes
make out the yellowish flicker and glow of matches the soldiers struck for
their cigarettes. Toward the south, tanks shot their guns and machine guns
stuttered. The orange trail of tracer shells would often sear through the dark
night.

For some men the firing was exciting—they'd hurrah and shout, even
though they knew it was the enemy out there practicing. Those were always
the men of action, men who had fought with the guerrillas, men for whom
the memory of the roar of combat against the Communist militia was still
fresh. They still seemed to yearn for those difficult and trying times, the
privations, the thrills and the anguish—they had been free, then, at least,

and brave, and they had been fighting for others' freedom as well. But there were other men who grew nervous, some almost hysterical. You could see that the very sound of the firing affected them.

Ernesto Piñango and Armando Rodríguez, with the help of some technicians jailed with us, managed to put a radio together. Later Rafael del Pino joined them in taking charge of the radio operation. Del Pino had been an early supporter of Castro, but had abandoned the cause and now was in prison for it.

The radio they made was very crude but it could pick up international news reports. The sixth floor was the ideal place for picking up those broadcasts, which sometimes mentioned the situation on the island. Piñango and Viscaya, as everybody called Armando, even put up an antenna at night, when the darkness and height made it safe. They would unscrew one of the roof tiles, slide it to one side, and stick the antenna up through the opening.

Batteries for the radio were made right there in the Circular. I don't know all the details of the process, but I do know that once in a while somebody had to urinate into some jars because the technicians needed the urine. They used pencil lead, too; it seems several sticks of graphite bundled together could replace that core batteries have running down the middle. And through a contact in the hospital they got copper sulfate, another of the substances necessary to the recipe.

We heard the news over earphones made out of intravenous tubes. There were three sets of earphones. Men would copy out the news in shorthand, then write it out in longhand afterward. We made several copies, and then next morning each floor would get its morning newspaper.

The radio lasted for several years, partly because Piñango and Viscaya developed a hiding place that was practically discovery-proof. Actually, I should say hiding *places,* because they'd take the radio completely apart and hide it all over the Circular. The guards might have a piece of it in their hands and not know it had anything in the world to do with a radio. The two men would have to take special care in hiding the pieces, though, in case some spy was watching. Sometimes Piñango would leave the cell with a little package, apparently casually and equally apparently sneakily, and stuff the package into a hiding place. But that wasn't the radio, or even a piece of it. That was a red herring he was dragging through the Circular. Meanwhile, somebody else would scurry off and hide the parts.

Carrión slept on the upper bunk. He slept so heavily you had to shake him if you wanted to wake him up. One morning just at dawn I heard machine-gun rattle and the boom of cannons. I jumped to the window. On the peak of the hills the red-orange blaze of the batteries installed there lit up the early morning. Tracer shells scored the dark-blue sky; I couldn't see or imagine their target. It didn't seem like the usual firing practice, though.

I shook Carrión by one foot and rushed upstairs to the sixth floor to see if I could tell any better what it was all about.

In the Circular there was already a general alarm, and the confusion was incredible.

"They're attacking *us!*" people were shouting. "They're aiming right at us!"

But the Circular couldn't have been the target of those projectiles; we'd have been blown to bits immediately if it had been. I came to the sixth floor. Men were standing on cans, on cots, or just on tiptoe, looking frantically, worriedly, out the windows. Some men had pulled themselves up to the window bars by the strength of their arms.

Just to the east of the presidio, almost directly above us, anti-aircraft shells were blooming into black popcorn clouds, and through them floated a B-26 bomber, its silver fuselage gleaming in the morning sun as the explosions peppered and sputtered all along its path.

I watched it fly into the distance, toward the mouth of the Las Casas River. From there a Cuban Marine emplacement began to shoot at it. The frigate *Baire* began to fire on it now.

The pilot of the B-26 suddenly saw the *Baire* and dived at it, machine guns blazing. It was like watching a war movie from the windows.

The frigate began to move, to take evasive action; the plane released its first rocket, and a huge spout of water rose before the frigate's bow. The boat began to speed away.

Then the B-26 banked to the left. The guns began to fire at it from the hills again, and again it sailed peacefully, as though with Olympian detachment, through the artillery shells furiously hurled at it. That pilot must have had icewater in his veins. The plane's blithe flight seemed to mock that curtain of fire aimed at bringing it down. The pilot headed the plane once more toward the ship, which was now firing on him again, and this time his aim was sure. The explosion of his rocket made the ship's stern leap out of the water and wrapped it in a whirlwind of black smoke. The plane then flew off toward the northwest.

The Bay of Pigs invasion had begun. It was April 17, 1961.

The scene we had witnessed produced incredible excitement among the prisoners. We immediately took the little radio out of hiding and set it up. Every imaginable theory of what was happening was vehemently expounded by one or another prisoner. Suddenly military trucks lined up at battle stations around the Circulars, and the troops they were transporting, largely militia, jumped out, firing up at the windows.

A group of them ran to the main gate. There was no one in the prison yard or on the lower floor. They stuck the barrels of their machine guns through the bars and fired off several bursts, which whined off the tower and went on ricocheting off bars and railings. I threw myself headfirst onto the floor, and though I didn't have time to look to see, I imagine everyone else did the same.

They completely surrounded the Circular. They then called Major Lorenzo to the main gate. Even up to the sixth floor we could hear the officers shouting at the top of their lungs; we heard every word of the orders our comrade was to pass along to us. "Listen, tell the men that we have orders from General Headquarters to fire on anyone who comes to the windows. If anyone has clothing hung outside, it's to be brought in immediately. We'll give you three minutes to do so. After three minutes, nobody comes to the windows for any reason. Anyone that does will be shot immediately."

Lorenzo was on his way up, but we intercepted him on the third floor. We surrounded him and shouted questions at him. Had they said anything else? Did we miss anything? A prisoner always does that—he pesters you to find out whether there wasn't something left out, whether there wasn't some meaningful gesture that might have been overlooked. But this time there was absolutely nothing left out. The officers' shouts had been heard throughout the Circular and there was really no need at all for Lorenzo to repeat what they had said.

What followed was a very tense situation. If anybody overly curious, and there are always some, got too close to the window, the soldiers fired off a burst of machine-gun fire. Out there, gazing up vigilantly, the guards looked like hunting dogs with treed quarry, and as though to make this image even more convincing, some of them were wearing those caps with earflaps that hang down like hounds' ears. In cells 46 and 47, which were the bathrooms, things were even more difficult. It was hard to use the bathrooms because you had to be close to the window to get to the toilet. Those who tried to go to the bathroom at first got scares they never forgot. The guards shot without the least hesitation.

That afternoon after lunch a tarpaulin-covered truck with several armed soldiers aboard, escorted by two vehicles, screeched to a stop in front of the main gate. Now during this period the prison authorities often delivered packs of cigarettes, cans of milk and sugar, and cookies or crackers acquired by prisoners' family members in the prison canteen. The family member purchased the items, which he could not even touch, paying exorbitant prices, and then the purchase was sent in to the prisoner. A garrison truck was used for the deliveries. We had a friend, Sánchez, who was in charge of receiving the packages, putting them out in order in the prison yard, and then calling the men they were sent to to pick them up. So when we saw the military truck pull up, someone as a joke called out, "Sánchez, the packages!" But it wasn't the packages, at least not for our consumption—although they were in fact in a way destined for us.

They were boxes of Canadian-made dynamite.

The soldiers, led by Commander William Gálvez, began to unload the frightening cargo. An officer called Major Lorenzo out to tell him that the whole front part of the Circular had to be cleared, that the prisoners were to move to the back until the truck had been completely unloaded. The dynamite was to be deposited underneath the Circular, in the tunnel to the central tower and along the foundations.

That event completely changed the psychological climate of the Circular. Men speculated endlessly about the reason for the explosives. Some thought they had been deposited there to have them in a safe place, protected from attacks like that morning's—planes would never bomb the Circulars, since it was known there were prisoners inside.

About nightfall we got the first hard information through the clandestine radio. There had been fighting in the swamps of Zapata, at the Bay of Pigs, since very early that morning. The communiqués were very encouraging, and the prisoners' euphoria knew no bounds. There were those who shouted at the top of their lungs, jumped around, and embraced their friends, possessed by a joy the reader can easily imagine—our situation had finally begun to look hopeful. And those bulletins continued.

Very early the next day, soldiers supplied with jackhammers went to work inside the tunnel leading to the central tower. They were opening niches to store the dynamite in, drilling through the thick foundations of the enormous structure. This operation now took on a macabre significance for us—the explosives could blow us sky-high.

Demolition experts arrived with the soldiers who were drilling, and we watched them unload boxes of detonators, rolls of fuse, and other equipment used for setting off explosions.

Meanwhile the communiqués from the international press kept coming in. The inmates who handled the radio never stopped to rest. They hardly slept for two days. Very early the next morning, Radio Swan, the station that transmitted to Cuba, issued a call for help from the internal resistance underground in support of the invasion:

People of Havana! Attention! People of Havana! The brave patriots of the Army of Liberation need your cooperation. Electric plants must be kept from furnishing electricity to the few industrial facilities the regime is attempting to keep in operation. This morning at seven forty-five a.m., when this station gives the signal, we ask that you turn on all the lights in your homes and connect all electrical appliances. This concerted action will increase the load on the generators in the electric plants and overload the system.

Other cables reported that the invading forces, sweeping down every-thing in their path, were triumphantly approaching Havana. This was false, of course; the invasion had failed.

Castro, the very man who had declared a thousand times that he was not a Communist and that "the Revolution is greener than palm trees," had stripped off the disguise that had fooled so many people and now had proclaimed the true nature of the Revolution, the nature it had had from the beginning: "This is a socialist revolution," he said. "And we will defend it with these rifles!" And he ended his proclamation with an unmistakably Communist finale: "Long live the working class! Long live the farmers! Long live the humble! Long live the Socialist Revolution! *Patria o muerte!* We shall overcome!"—the demagogic phrases of a system which promises the worker, the poor, the humble his freedom, and then enchains him.

From the moment of the first attack, on the 15th, when the B-26s began bombing airports and various other places throughout the Island, the gov-ernment unleashed fierce repression against everyone considered unsympa-thetic to the regime. Roughly half a million people were arrested throughout the country. Priests, workers, the elderly, women, soldiers, students, people from all walks of life were confined in public buildings of every sort imagin-able—theaters, stadiums, government buildings, police stations, schools, and other locations—and the jails were packed to the rafters. The wholesale roundup brought into the jails hundreds of Cubans who were working in the underground, infiltrators who, once identified, were shot immediately with-out any trial whatsoever. Ironically, it also brought in government function-aries such as several members of the board of governors of the Banco Nacional, a Marxist elite who had been detained as they were having dinner in a restaurant and spent two days locked up.

As the jails filled, hundreds of people, including some women with children, were crammed into the prison yard of La Cabaña in the open air. There were prisoners in the moats as well, surrounded by machine guns. The only moat left free of people was the one in which the firing squads operated. In the moats of Castillo del Morro, too, a fortress in Havana, thousands of people were held for two days without food or water. At the end of the two days, the authorities turned a hose on them so they could quench their thirst.

Dozens of people died in those overcrowded conditions. Some pregnant women miscarried, and others gave birth right there on the ground, assisted by the other women. The guards threatened all and sundry with machine-gunning if the invasion triumphed.

The Blanquita Theater, the largest theater in Cuba, was converted into a gigantic prison which lodged more than eight thousand people. In five days the people jammed into the theater received food on only four occasions. The Sports Palace sheltered thousands more. One night, just for kicks apparently, the militiamen guarding them began screaming for everyone to get down on the ground. They fired their machine guns over them; several people were wounded.

The persecution and repression became almost annihilation—every citizen was a potential enemy. If you weren't in the armed forces or the militia or couldn't prove your revolutionary militancy, you would be detained—or worse.

There are no data on the number of people shot throughout the Island during those several days, but execution squads were functioning in the regiment at Pinar del Río, on the military base at San Antonio de los Baños, in El Morro, in La Cabaña, in El Castillo de San Severino in Matanzas province, in La Campana, and in Camagüey and Oriente provinces. Often they didn't even put the bodies into coffins—they merely stripped them and put them into plastic bags and buried them.

It was April 16, 1961, in the Colón Cemetery in Havana, and as Castro was shaking the hands of the mourners for the men killed in the bombardments of the 15th, six anonymous corpses were brought in through the back gate, in silence, with no flowers, no wreaths, no family members or friends to say a few words of farewell. An officer from the Political Police and two soldiers in a white Volkswagen van picked up the corpses and carried them to an area under military control, where they were thrown into a common grave. Juan Hernández, one of the soldiers in that detail, was later sentenced to prison for conspiracy. He told us about the operation in detail. The bodies were those of men executed peremptorily as soon as the invasion began.

Emboldened by the government's turning back the Bay of Pigs invaders, the prison authorities felt they could exercise ruthless control over us. Repression became more violent and systematic, less "occasional"—we were informed officially that the dynamite would remain in the foundations, to blow us up if there was another invasion attempt. Many prisoners simply refused to accept the fact that the dynamite was planted down there, and there were even those who said that the boxes had never contained explosives, that it was all a great charade to intimidate us and keep us in line. Others did face up to the reality of the dynamite, but they couldn't bring themselves to believe that the dynamite would be used—rather they believed it was an instrument of political blackmail. The psychological defense mechanisms at work in their minds were very complex—there was a flat rejection of an infinitely threatening reality. It was, indeed, very difficult to accept the fact that we were living on top of a powder keg.

Some men dreamed up elaborate "security" measures to be taken in case worst came to worst—poor wretches grasping at anything anybody said. One guy said you had to bite down on a piece of wood so you wouldn't burst when the dynamite exploded. So people hung pieces of wood about the thickness of a cigar around their necks; they planned to bite down on them as they flew through the air. There was an exodus to the sixth floor—many prisoners thought the farther they got from the basement, the better chance there was of escaping unharmed. Other, more realistic prisoners scratched their names and prisoner numbers on little homemade metal tags and hung them around their necks so they could at least be identified afterward.

One man, Luis Lemus, known as Americanito, decided he'd go have a look for himself. He wanted to test some of the theories, I suppose. He managed to get down into the basement by a complicated operation which involved sliding down through one of the vertical tunnels for the plumbing pipes. Someone else went to where three American CIA officers were being held, to find out what they thought about the matter; they might have a more professional opinion. These men were trained in explosives and demolition; one of them, Daniel Caswell, was really an expert. He was given all the information we had, including samples of the explosives, detonators, and so forth which Americanito had brought up from below. They came to the conclusion that everything was set to blow us up. There was a double, "fail-safe" detonation system—electrical and mechanical. There were enough explosives to reduce our building to rubble, and the same was true for the other Circulars, which had been mined with dynamite the same day ours had.

At the back of the punishment-cell pavilion some two hundred fifty to three hundred yards from the Circular, behind a little earthen bulwark, was the control hut from which the charges would be detonated. All the connections and underground plastic tubes led to that site. The explosion would be so shattering that even those who depressed the detonator handles would die, and the entire presidio would be converted into a blackened crater.

Commander García Olivera, chief of the Army Engineer Corps, and the captain from the Political Police known as Mario were the leaders of the mining operation. A group of technicians led by another soldier, a thin, gawky man called Chanito—sarcastically, "Lightning"—was in charge of checking, every day, all the machinery of death that had been installed.

This group of technicians would often walk smugly between the Circulars and make motions with their hands as though pressing the detonator, and then they would make a gesture simulating the explosion.

Those soldiers' mission was to murder six thousand prisoners. What must they have felt? Their sadism marked them as truly mentally ill. Years later we learned that two of them wound up in an insane asylum which the Ministry of the Interior maintains for its employees. There the authorities house the military, so that no one can find out about the horrors that drove them mad.

One morning the technicians and some soldiers arrived in several trucks and began unloading boxes and taking other boxes out of the basement. They were replacing the dynamite with a surer and more powerful explosive, one which wouldn't go off "sympathetically," but only from an initial blast from another explosive. They filled in the tower in the prison yard with a ton of TNT, thereby converting it into a four-story fragmentation grenade of thick concrete, whose explosion would generate tremendous heat and tons of shrapnel, and produce a shock wave more than sufficient to kill us all.

A group of our men, expert in explosives themselves, set about organizing teams to try to do something to neutralize the authorities' plans. All their energy was concentrated on deactivating the explosives. But the operation had to be discreet; not everyone could know about it, and the team members never went into much detail about what they were doing. They tried to work in secret as much as they could. But even the informers cooperated. After all, they were sure they would be blown up like everybody else; the Communists weren't likely to come take them out of the Circulars when they decided to kill the rest of us. In order to stop leaks to the outside, a group of inmates was assigned to read all the letters which once a month or every forty-five days we were allowed to send. This was to keep anyone working on the project from inadvertently writing something that would give away the plan.

Americanito went on exploring the basement. He brought up samples of the fuses that had been left behind down there, and he drew up plans with the placement of the charges.

The mechanical system, using a fuse called Primacord, was the first system deactivated. The men in charge of that task did impeccable work. We knew that government technicians tested to make sure the fuse had not been cut; they picked it up at its two ends and yanked on it. If it grew taut, they assumed it was still intact, that it hadn't been cut or tampered with. The fuse was somewhat like a garden hose—a hollow tube of insulating material filled with powdered TNT. Our deactivation team made a cut on the bottom and took out about two inches of the powder. They cleaned out this space well and put a cylindrical tube into it the same diameter as the fuse. Then they carefully sewed up the cut. The fuse lay on the ground, so when they applied a little dirt to the seam, the alteration was perfectly camouflaged. If the authorities tried to use this fuse, it would be interrupted and the detonators would not go off.

The electrical detonation system was much more complicated. Basically, it was neutralized by an electrical bridge which detoured the current, a sort of short circuit.

Nonetheless, all these measures, assuming they worked according to our plans, would give us only a few minutes, because when the authorities saw that the TNT didn't explode, that we weren't flying into the air in pieces, they would try some other way to do away with us. All they would have to do was fire cannons at any of the Circulars, since every one of them was still a powder keg. And so for those few moments left us, our action groups had organized a second-stage plan. They partially cut through some windows so that just a few quick strokes would sever them completely. They also took off the grating, almost a yard square, from one of the entrances to the drains and excavated a tunnel that ran underneath the foundations and came out several yards away from the Circulars, but they didn't remove the last few inches of dirt at the exit. Many of the TNT sticks were half emptied, and homemade grenades were fabricated with fuses made out of match heads.

Although all the work in our Circular was well conceived, well planned, and well executed, if the men in the Circular next to us didn't do the same things, nothing would come of it. If one of the huge powder kegs exploded, it would be enough to set off the adjoining ones.

No one could tell whether the work that had been carried out would produce the results we hoped for. There was, however, absolutely no doubt about the authorities' criminal intentions. After a great deal of effort, we managed to leak the news about what they had planned to the outside world. In Miami, articles were published about the government's monstrous plans. But all our pleas and the pleas of our families to international organizations, especially the United Nations Commission on Human Rights, were futile. Nobody paid the least attention to the act of barbarism which the Cuban government had laid plans for. There was not a single voice raised in protest.

II / Operation Reprisal

Knowing that we were, so to speak, sleeping on a mattress full of explosives destroyed many prisoners' nerves; some went completely mad. They felt they were trapped, and they gave way to sheer animal panic. On two nights we were awakened by the blood-curdling shrieks of prisoners who threw themselves over the sixth-floor railing onto the prison yard below. One of them had been in the jail for two years. The other had arrived with the last consignments of prisoners from Oriente province. I remember that this latter prisoner's name was Arturo; I had spoken with him several times.

Every time the group of technicians under Lightning's command went down into the basement, several prisoners would be seized with hysteria.

"They're down there! They're sure as hell gonna blow us to smithereens! I hope they don't connect us up by mistake!"

Dozens of men lived in that state of anxiety. They kept watch on their own (they would hardly sleep), and they practically leaped out of their skin if it grew too quiet outside. They had evolved a grisly interpretation of a too-silent night—the guards on post had received orders to evacuate because they were going to set off the TNT.

And in the aftermath of the Bay of Pigs failure, not only our psychological state, but living conditions generally in the prison became much more severe. Even food was much scarcer. At that time, they would bring in vats full of greasy water with some vegetables floating in it—potatoes, pumpkins, yams—frequently dirty and rotten, at that. We found out from men working in the kitchen, who belonged to Circular 4, that one hundred pounds of foodstuffs per day were allocated for the six thousand prisoners on Isla de Pinos—that worked out to less than a pound for every fifty prisoners. And that was the extent of our food. The bread had not a drop of fat or lard in it, just salt, and not always that. Its texture was so rubbery that you could stretch it out to more than a third longer without breaking it.

Filth, cockroaches, and rats continually appeared in the food.

The hot sugar water they served as breakfast was prepared with sugar dyed green. The sacks the sugar came in had a notice printed on them: NOT FOR HUMAN CONSUMPTION. It was waste sugar, swept up off the factory floors or picked up with shovels, and it was full of trash and impurities. It was meant to be used as cattle feed.

It was during those months that guanina came to Isla de Pinos. The guanina bush, related to the tree called fustic which produces a strong yellow dye and is sometimes slightly toxic, yields a small bean somewhat like a lentil, and about the same color, but it tastes terrible. It has a strong, bitter taste of bile—another of its relatives is called, for good reason, the kidney tree. Campesinos sometimes used it as a substitute for coffee. It, like the green sugar, was ordinarily used for cattle feed, but only when mixed with other grains, since it has hardly any nutritional value of its own. It is not used for human consumption. But that didn't matter much to the prison authorities.

There was a man named Vivas Bartelemí in our Circular. He had been a medical student who had gone as a member of a diplomatic mission to Communist China, and he had appeared in the newspapers in a photograph shaking hands with Mao Zedong. Somebody started a rumor that he had bought the guanina during his trip to China. Vivas thought that was funny. Knowing his sense of humor, I suspect he himself had something to do with the spread of the rumor. Irony seemed to crop up all around Vivas. He had been fighting against Batista and was taken prisoner during the Revolution. When Castro came to power, Vivas was arrested again and confined to the same Circular he had been in before.

One of the dishes they served us was guanina with cornmeal ground very fine, but still full of worms, and very bitter-tasting. The rice also had worms, and a very unpleasant taste—they didn't wash it before cooking it. It seemed that any foodstuff that had spoiled was sent to Isla de Pinos, for us to eat. It was about that time that macaroni and spaghetti began appearing constantly; this food became the staple of the Cuban people, as it also did, of course, for the prisoners, for the next twenty years. But you should not imagine a tasty dish of macaroni Italian-style. What they served in the jail was boiled with a little bit of salt until it all stuck together in a gummy paste; that was all. You had to cut it into pieces to serve it, and even to be able to swallow it, you had to add sugar. The sale of cooking oil, spices, and salt that we had taken advantage of before was now suspended. There was no protein whatsoever in our diet. So not only was our food unbearably monotonous and unspeakably foul-tasting, it lacked all vitamins and other elements necessary to the organism as well, and that would have further consequences later on, when the effects of vitamin and protein deficiency were felt by all of us.

.   .   .

One day they called us out in groups of twenty-five to take us to the records office, which had been set up in the back part of Building 5. We went up some steps leading to a large room. They shaved my head, took clippings of hair around my temples, and fingerprinted me several times. They went all over my naked body, looking for tattoos, marks, or scars which might be used to identify me. Then they photographed me and gave me my prisoner number—26830. From then on, my name would not mean anything to the garrison, and I would be just a number.

We were made to sign a card authorizing the prison to open and read our correspondence. One man refused to sign, so the guards were sent for. They beat him until he signed. There was another prisoner, named Mitre, who couldn't be forced to sign. He was a calm, quiet man, but he had an indestructible will.

Given all these conditions, who could have been surprised when one rainy, stormy night in July, Cheo Guerra, Pedro Carlo Osorio, "El Mexicano," Edmundo Amado, and two other men decided to escape. They cut through a window on the hospital side of the Circular. The rain was coming down in sheets; the sound of it was deafening and the spotlights were useless, since the curtains of water cut off their light. The men managed to climb down without any trouble, but they got no more than a few yards away. Someone had seen them. An intense burst of fire, muted somewhat by the sound of the rain, sounded the alarm. They were captured, and on the spot, dripping wet in the driving rain, they were given a brutal beating. The soldiers, blind with rage, couldn't even wait to get them to the punishment cages, where they were to spend many months. That was Cheo's second visit to the dungeonlike cells, and it would not be his last.

The next morning, Lieutenant Julio Tarrau, the prison director, came in at the head of the garrison. Wielding his Russian Makarov pistol, which no one had ever seen him shoot but which he thought gave him more authority, and which certainly gave him more courage, he screamed at us, "I'll kill any son of a bitch that moves. Stand in front of your cells, at attention!"

The garrison, which amounted to some two hundred soldiers for that search, filled the prison yard. The first wave entered without firearms, carrying only bayonets and truncheons. Behind them came the guards armed with rifles and fixed bayonets.

"Okay!" Tarrau began speaking again. "Everybody strip! Everybody take off your clothes and stand there in front of your cells!"

Carrión and I stripped. In the next cell, ex-Captain Tápanes-Tápanes, from the city of Cárdenas, and his cellmate Chávez followed suit.

There was someone on the fourth floor who did not take off his underwear. Lieutenant Tarrau screamed at him to come downstairs. The atmosphere grew even more tense, more frightened and expectant. Thousands of eyes were fixed on that man slowly walking down the stairs. In everyone's mind was the same question—and it was almost like a plea there was no longer enough time for: Why didn't you take off your underwear like everybody else?

When the man came to the prison yard, Tarrau himself shoved him, and a group of guards fell on him. The prisoner struggled, but only for a few seconds. The hail of blows flattened him, and staggering, almost unable to walk, he was dragged and shoved out toward the punishment cells, while they ripped his underwear from him in shreds. He had not even reached the main gate before he was naked.

A murmur of protest and indignation arose throughout the Circular. Tarrau shot his pistol into the air, and the guards cocked their rifles. You could hear the bolts of the machine guns click too, as the guards in the tower cocked them and took aim at the prisoners before the cells. The rifles' power of persuasion silenced us. We learned later that the prisoner hadn't wanted to take off his underwear because when he was fighting in the mountains with Castro's troops an enemy mine had torn off his member and destroyed one testicle.

The spectacle in the Circular beggared description. All you could do at the moment was stare—there were hundreds of completely naked men formed into a surrealistic legion, standing at attention in perfect formation.

"First floor, down here!" Tarrau was the only one giving orders. He was livid with rage. *He* was the director, and these prisoners had tried to escape on him.

We began to descend, and he ordered us to stand in front of the wall next to the washbasins. Some of us were randomly clubbed and pushed. When we were all downstairs, the garrison went up into the cells. Five or six hours later we were still standing there; several older men's ankles and legs were swollen and inflamed. No one was allowed to raise his head, under threat of being beaten and dragged off to the punishment cages. Some of those who couldn't resist the temptation to look up to watch the destruction of our possessions were caught at it and brutally beaten and then spent months naked in the punishment pavilion.

When the soldiers were finally finished with their work and the bars of the main gate closed behind the last guard, we were released from our formation. In the prison yard, in front of the showers and washbasins, there were piles of clothing from all the cells on all the floors. Several inmates later took charge of sorting the clothing and calling out the owners' numbers. We headed back to our cells. More than a thousand naked prisoners filled the stairways. We were all eager to be the first to arrive, less to see what the guards had done than to cover ourselves. . . .

There is nothing more humiliating or more degrading than forced nakedness before your oppressors—you feel especially vulnerable. The authorities knew that, and they used our nakedness against us, another in their arsenal of psychological weapons. The interrogators from the Political Police never failed to keep prisoners, both men and women, naked. They took the women in naked for interrogations by groups of officers. If for a man it's embarrassing to be forced to stand there completely stripped before a phalanx of interrogators, for a woman it is much more terrible, and many of the suicides and attempted suicides among the women were triggered precisely by that humiliation. Even today the government still employs this practice with women political prisoners. When they are confined to solitary, they are completely undressed and then officers from the jail, Prison Headquarters, and the Political Police stop by to see them.

We arrived at our cells. On the floor, all jumbled together and scattered, were the few things we owned—underwear, socks, uniforms, and our pillows. Over the heap they had poured the little *gofio de trigo* and sugar we had left, our only reserve of real nutrition, which we very carefully doled out so as to keep down our hunger a little. Then, on top of all that, they had poured out the water from the pails.

Dozens of cots had been slashed by bayonets, and in some cells they had mixed salt and washing detergent into the food.

This had been the reprisal operation which never failed to follow an escape or escape attempt. "Those who remain will pay for the desires for freedom of those who try to get away"—that was the unmistakable message the authorities were sending us, and the Communists made sure the message sank in: The prisoner who tries to escape has no sense of *esprit de corps* or comradeship; he is an egotist who thinks only about making his own lot better, a man who cares nothing about those he leaves behind; he simply abandons them to their fate. Sadly, there was always someone who at least half believed those sophistries.

It was after Cheo and El Mexicano's escape attempt that the authorities began assigning soldiers with dogs to walk guard all around the Circulars. Our guard came on duty at six o'clock in the afternoon, his rifle on his shoulder, and he walked by looking at all the windows. Whenever he and the guard who was on patrol at Circular 3 crossed paths they stopped, chatted for a few minutes, and took up their rounds again. They must have been bored senseless by their rounds, but that habit of talking to each other when they met would be quite helpful to us in the future.

Our cell on the second floor was the place a group of friends, almost all students, would get together. We would have interesting conversations there, which would take our minds off the reality of bolts and bars for a time. Often someone would recite poetry, Villanueva would sing his latest songs to us, or we would laugh at one of Díaz Lanz' imitations.

Transports of prisoners from various prisons in Cuba would frequently arrive. In one of the transports Benito López came in from La Cabaña. He was a businessman arrested only because he had spoken out against Communism. His refusal to join the mass demonstrations and his open expression of disappointment with the Revolution's course were enough for the chairman of the CDR to denounce him to the Political Police. One of the "terrible" accusations they brought against him was that he had sent his son, Rubén, to the United States.

Benito came to our floor. He seemed completely disoriented, lost, and miserable. His sadness struck me, and I tried to cheer him up. He had been assigned to Celestino Méndez' cell, near mine, but there were no beds left in the cell, so he had to sleep on the floor. Besides the discomfort, he had to get up very early to get out of the other men's way. So I told him he could come into my cell during the day and rest and sleep on my cot. Our friendship began just that casually; neither of us could imagine that one day we would be relatives. I don't know how he had managed to keep some tiny photos of his children. His youngest daughter, Martha, was a girl with little round glasses, and even when I first saw her face to face, I saw nothing special about her.

Benito's family was almost an obsession with him, and he never stopped talking about them. To raise his spirits a little, there was a phrase I often repeated—"We're out on the streets!"—and the two of us would joke about that pet phrase of ours, which became a sort of sign of our optimism, our common dream.

12 / Preparations for an Escape

After the failure of the Bay of Pigs, Boitel, Ulises, and I sat down to analyze our situation, and we came to the conclusion that the Revolution would remain in power for many long years yet. That view of the matter left us with only one thing to do—try to escape. That idea, that dream, lies in the heart of every prisoner. It's an idea not all prisoners rise to, not for lack of decision or courage alone, but rather because very specific factors hold them back—their families, the scant possibility of success, and the great possibility of dying. And there are, of course, those prisoners who simply resign themselves to their fate and sit down to await the outcome; those are the majority in every jail in the world.

From the moment we conceived the idea of escaping, our minds were constantly at work on a way to realize the faint dream. Each of us thought about how it ought to come off. There were days of intense consultations; one of us would propose a plan and the others would pick it to pieces. We discarded cutting through the barbed wire in the classical manner, using a pair of strong pliers to cut through the steel chain-link fence and escaping through the breach. The escape could not involve violence, either, since then the chance of success was substantially reduced. It had to be as simple and easy as possible, so as not to arouse suspicion.

During the planning stage, I was in charge of mapping the surrounding area. I was to locate on a map, as precisely as I could, the roads, elevations, guardposts, and whatever other details might come into play at the time of the escape. Even though from the fifth floor you could see for many miles all around, we managed to find a prisoner who had accompanied Batista's children when they traveled abroad, a man named Tasi, who we understood had a telescope made right there in the prison from lenses that someone had smuggled in. With the aid of the little telescope, I spent hours both during the day and at night closely observing our surroundings. Little by little, I added new details to the map—the little militia encampments to the northwest and the Cossack guardpost on the other side of the military cordon, among the pines, which could be made out only because of the glow of the cigarettes they lighted at night.

Over and above the physical details, I familiarized myself with the routine and movements of the garrison. The prisoner-gatekeeper was authorized to wear a watch, and we persuaded him to lend it to us. It was a tremendous help; with it I could measure how long it would take a soldier to go from the little guardhouse to the last guard hut which could be seen, or to a house just beyond the fence to the east, beyond the little stand of pines, where another guard hut was tucked away. It was at this house that the guards' uniforms were washed and ironed. You could almost always see long clotheslines with olive-green uniforms flapping in the wind. The house became very important, since it gave us a plausible way to escape from the prison.

The preparations for an escape generate a tremendous amount of activity. A thousand details have to be taken care of, each one of vital importance in its own right. Another of the common prisoners who sometimes collaborated with us gave us invaluable help. We got in touch with him because we needed contacts on the outside, friends and relatives of Boitel and Ulises who could furnish certain articles we needed. You needed some luck, too, and some came our way. While our planning was going on, the Director-General of Jails and Prisons, in an act of "generosity," decided to permit us two visits a year, one in June and one in September. That was a real piece of news for the presidio, but for us, and our escape plans, it was a blessing.

Pieces of information we would need were fed to us by some of the common prisoners. Boitel was the one who took charge of those contacts. I was in charge of vigilance and other details, as I've mentioned. I'll speak about Ulises' responsibilities in a moment. There was a fourth man, Benjamín Brito, who would go with us as our guide and navigator. Brito was a sailor, an expert in everything connected with the sea, and he was doubly valuable because he knew the swamps of the Island. He had been a caiman hunter in that area for years. Besides Brito's knowledge of the Island, we were fortunate to have, from the common prisoners, a detailed map of Isla de Pinos with topographical and elevation isobars, rivers, and creeks marked on it, and also indicating the swampy regions.

Measuring time with the watch and counting the guards' steps, I put together a table of distances and times between one point and another—as for example from one guardpost to the main guardhouse, from the guardhouse to our Circular, and so on. The hours of the changing of the guards were also very important, since if an escape was to be attempted a short while after the guard had come on duty, it ran the risk of being stymied because the relief would be wide awake and watchful. Quite the contrary if the escape took place toward the end of a shift when the guard was tired and ready to go in—his watchfulness then would not be so sharp, he would pay less attention. The only thing he would be thinking about would be his replacement.

I knew that between the little guard huts there was a distance of about fifty yards, so guiding myself by this fact, I observed several soldiers to get an average time for a fifty-yard walk. Then, once that number was known, I could estimate other times for known distances, and other distances from known times. I rechecked my calculations—for time and distance from the main guardhouse to the house where the clothes were washed, for example —both by the time a guard actually took and by the fact that I knew the distance between one point and the other was approximately four hundred yards.

The barbed-wire fences had a watch it would be fatal to take lightly. Every fifty yards there was a guard hut, equipped with spotlights, with an armed sentinel stationed inside. The two endmost guard huts, at the front and the back of the prison, were taller and armed with machine guns. The chain-link fences had been restored in 1960. They were erected on deep concrete foundations, which had trenches dug in front of them; the fences were topped with metal V's which carried ten or twelve barbed-wire strands. After six o'clock in the evening a guard jeep made uninterrupted patrols outside the presidio, traveling always parallel to the barbed wire, as another one did the same inside.

We decided to escape dressed as militiamen. The decision was virtually inevitable for several reasons: They were the ones constantly going in and out of the presidio; there were several militia encampments in the surrounding area; and it would be much easier to get lost among them than among the soldiers from the regular garrison. The militia uniform we would need consisted of a pair of olive-green pants, a blue shirt, a black beret, a military web belt, also olive-green, and black boots. Ulises was put in charge of the uniforms.

We needed militia shirts and berets above all. The khaki-colored pants from the old army were the uniforms we always wore, and it was easy enough to dye them olive-green. Many of those pants, from having been constantly worn and washed, had lost the letter *P* that had been stenciled on them. The military belts were part of the prisoners' uniforms anyway, and we already had the boots. We also needed hacksaw blades to cut through the bars, Cuban and American money, a first-aid kit, knives, water-purifying tablets, and a whole list of other little things.

While I was gathering my information, we got two lenses for a more powerful telescope. We made the tube out of cardboard pasted together with glue made from macaroni. We dyed the tube inside with soot and smoke given off by burning kerosene we got sometimes to kill bedbugs with. The telescope was made so you could take it apart, and I always took the precaution of not leaving it assembled if I wasn't using it. Hiding the lenses was very easy—when we were finished using them, we simply dropped them into a pail of water. Even if there was a search, however much they looked the guards couldn't find them.

At last the day of the visit was upon us. Twelve hundred prisoners were to receive family members at the same time and in the same place, in the corral a hundred yards square with its high barbed-wire fence. In 1960, General Headquarters had permitted one visit, but this new visit really was unprecedented because of the number of inmates and family members who would come together.

The eve of the visit made me aware of some startling ways veteran prisoners prepared to meet their families. I heard one of our neighbors in an adjoining cell say he had to iron his uniform for the visit. I did a double-take—there were no irons there, or even electricity, nothing of the kind. I asked him how he proposed to iron his clothes under those conditions, and he smiled at me and said he'd show me—a friend of his was already doing the ironing up on the fourth floor.

When we arrived, I saw how they went about it. The iron was an aluminum canteen cup to which they'd nailed a heavy wooden handle. They put plastic bags inside, all rolled up and knotted, and set them afire. This produced high temperatures in the canteen cup, which they ran over the clothing to iron it. Through a long, laborious process, they also extracted starch from macaroni. Some men ironed with bottles full of hot water. The efforts of these men was admirable, but I told myself that if that was the way to go elegantly dressed to the visit, I without a doubt would never be able to manage it. I contented myself with putting my pants carefully on top of the canvas of the cot and then some blankets on top of that, and sleeping on the pile. This method of "ironing" was the most popular among the prisoners.

Many people's nerves had a profound effect on their digestive system, so it seemed there were never enough bathrooms just before a visit. There were many people who did not ordinarily have stomach or digestive problems but had them unfailingly the day before a visit.

Boitel, Ulises, and I had made up three minuscule notes, all three identical, to try to get at least one of them through the search. In the note we asked Boitel's outside contacts to send us the things we needed for the escape and explained how to get them to us. We also asked them to make arrangements for a boat to pick us up on the coast at a certain place, day, and hour. We could confirm this last on the next visit. And we asked for an answer. The notes were in code; we were to furnish the key aloud to the person we gave the notes to. The key was a single word of five letters—it was unforgettable, since it was the last name of the Maestro, the Apostle of Cuban Independence: Martí.*

The main city of Isla de Pinos, Nueva Gerona, is located several miles from the prison. A road running from the town crosses the Las Casas River and comes right to the door of the prison. The hotel capacity of Nueva Gerona and its environs was very limited; there were two little hotels and several small guest houses. But some four thousand visitors had arrived for that visit in June. They slept in parks, in doorways, right in the middle of the street. Beginning the afternoon of the day before the visit, they came to the gates of the prison and formed enormously long lines, carrying the little packages of food they had been authorized to bring. They waited there through the night.

Starting early in the morning, we were up out of bed, standing in lines for the latrines, shaving, getting everything ready. We went over our clothes carefully, looking for bedbugs and lice so we could get them out of the clothes. These disgusting creatures were an ineradicable plague. There were millions of them. That entire gigantic building, all six floors of it, was full of bedbugs. We struggled against them constantly but they hid in the most unexpected places—the soles of shoes, belt buckles, the seams of clothing. The walls of many cells had lost their cement outer layer, and the bricks underneath had holes full of these tiny little bugs. But in truth not everyone tried to exterminate them. It didn't matter very much to some men. They would fall exhausted onto their cots, and although throngs of those insects began to suck their blood, the men didn't even wake up. When the bedbugs were full, they moved very sluggishly, so the prisoner, dead asleep, would turn over in bed, squash them, and the next day the canvas covering of the cot would be covered with bloodstains. The blood sucked out by bedbugs gives off a characteristic piercing, sickening odor. On some walls, you could see a dark stain about the size of an egg. If you touched it, it would disperse in all directions. It would be a colony of thousands of bedbugs.

To combat them, there were two preferred methods—there was kerosene, which was especially difficult to get hold of, or there was washing the cot with a brush, scrubbing the seams of the covering. The cots with burlap were a trial for the prisoners and a real paradise for the bedbugs, which were camouflaged by the dark fabric; since they were so tiny it was almost impossible to make them out. When a solution of water and detergent was applied to them, they died immediately in that characteristic way of theirs

*José Martí (1853–1895). Martí was an essayist, poet, and liberator of Cuba from the Spanish · Colonial regime. Jailed in his adolescence for his opposition to the Spaniards, he went on to campaign vigorously for Cuba's independence and died in the struggle. Even during his war campaigns, he wrote diaries and poetry, which contain some of the most moving and beautiful writing in the Spanish language. He is modern Cuba's greatest hero, seen almost as a saint. —Trans.

—they stiffen, then arch their bodies, and then they quiver and die. But getting detergent was not easy either. Instead, after washing the cot, you could rub a piece of soap back and forth over the seams, coating them with a paste of the soap. The bedbugs hated the smell of the soap we used. Therefore some prisoners, when the guards were about to make a sweep of the cells, would lay down a barrier of soap around their cells by rubbing the bar across the floor. That way bedbugs from adjoining cells would not cross the "magic circle" and invade their own. Old campesinos used still another method—they put stems or veins of tobacco leaves down, since the odor of tobacco also drove the bedbugs off. There were men who kept some sense of black humor, and they would say it made them sad to kill the bedbugs because they were blood of their blood.

Appeals to the prison authorities to fumigate the cells bore no fruit for the almost ten years I was there, so that on top of all the other sufferings we had to go through was that plague. The bedbug bites were terrible for me, since I was allergic to their bites; they formed large welts which lasted for days.

At seven o'clock in the morning, the platoon of guards that would search us before we went out to the visit finally arrived at the front gate. The gatekeeper told all the inmates to start getting ready because in a few minutes the guards would start calling off men from the lists.

The first prisoners were going out. They had to strip completely. The guards then carefully went over the men's clothing seam by seam, the cuffs of their pants, the double seams of their flies. They stuck their hands into their shoes, looking for notes. They did the same with their socks. They ordered the men to raise their arms and checked their armpits. When the search was over, the prisoners dressed again and went out toward the corral. Six or eight guards were posted all along the walk, but this time the prisoners didn't run in terror.

Ulises, Boitel, and I crowded together next to the bars at the exit to see how the others were searched. If they did a search on me like the ones I was watching, I would have no problem. When my turn came, I was nervous, but the hidden note was very difficult to find. I had packed it flat, so there was hardly any bulge, into a heat-sealed plastic protector. Ulises was searched at the same time I was. Since we were being called out in alphabetical order, not by prisoner number, Boitel had been one of the first ones through, and he hadn't had any problem. When the guard turned my clothes over to me, I breathed a deep sigh of relief. The search had been thorough, but not sufficient. The notes had gotten through, taped under our testicles.

13 / The Visit, Its Aftermath, and Continuing Plans

When all of us were in the corral, guards armed with rifles were stationed at all four corners outside. We all looked toward the walk down which our relatives would come; since the night before they had been waiting in the open in front of the prison, lying on the shoulders of the road, under trees, and forced to perform their bodily functions among the shrubs which grew alongside the road. At last the throng of family members came into view. A soldier was leading the march; he was walking a few yards ahead to keep anyone from rushing forward. The visitors were anxious to arrive, almost desperate, but he didn't allow anyone to get too close to him; they had to stay far back. Five or six times he stopped dead and turned and gestured and shouted at them, and the human mass behind him also had to stop. We couldn't hear what he was saying to them, since they were still too far away.

As they neared, the guards opened the gate and we bunched together, waiting for our families. Men who had already made out relatives in the crowd shouted and waved their arms. When they came in at last, there were moving, pathetic, dramatic scenes as women and children cried and hugged prisoners they had come perhaps hundreds of miles to see. My mother and sister arrived among the first groups, but my father waited outside. Men were forbidden to come into the corral; they had to stay outside the fence.

The visit took place under the most uncomfortable circumstances. We had to stand or squat on the ground, under an implacable sun—which in the month of June, in the tropics, is truly exhausting. There was no water. Children were complaining of thirst. Adults stoically tried to bear up under that long exposure to the scorching sun, but some visitors fainted.

The visit ended at three o'clock in the afternoon, and by then elderly ladies, especially, were ready to drop from so many hours in the sun, but the families could not leave immediately. They had to stay inside the prison until we had been counted and the guards had verified that no one had escaped. Children shouted to their fathers—"*Adios, papá!*"

One of them, clinging to his father's neck, crying inconsolably, was begging him not to stay there, to go back home with him. The pathetic scene was interrupted by the guards who invaded the corral to hurry the straggling family members along. They goaded them with cries of "Move along. Outside. It's over. Out. Outside, now."

When they had all left the corral, the guards counted us, and at our return to the Circular they stripped us again. At first most of the prisoners seemed sad and nostalgic; we were downcast. However, once inside, we joined our friends to talk over the visit, family gossip, politics, rumors.

We four would-be escapees were elated at our success in smuggling out the notes during the visit, but for some prisoners the visit had only brought on terrible, anguished depression. Cuco Muñiz and I, each with a foot propped up and leaning on the first-floor railing in front of cell 35, were chatting about the latest news we had learned during the visit and about the situation in the prisons on the Island. Suddenly from above something bulky dropped in front of us—very close, because we were leaning out a little. It landed on the ground in the prison yard with a heavy sodden crunching sound. I will never forget the sound made by the man's head as it burst against the ground. The man fell face down almost directly in front of the washbasins with his face turned aside and one leg drawn up. The mass of his brains was seeping out through his nose. Jesús López Cuevas had committed suicide by jumping off the fourth floor. I stood with my eyes fixed on that poor man's body lying before me, nine feet below.

Some rebels captured in the mountains of Escambray lived in Circular 4. One afternoon shortly after the visit they were called to trial. The tribunal was assembled from militiamen and soldiers of the presidio; it sat in a little garrison theater. All four of the rebel campesinos were sentenced to death. They were transported in a dump truck with their hands handcuffed behind them, under heavy guard, to the foothills of Escambray, the rebel zone, in the province of Las Villas. Another prisoner was being carried in a military jeep separate from the others. He was also handcuffed.

Two of the prisoners in the dump truck, Aquilino Cerquera and Macario Quintana, were taken out of it and executed in the town square of their hometown, the city of Trinidad, so as to inspire terror in the other inhabitants of the region. The truck then went on toward La Campana, and the trip continued over highways curving up into the mountains. The truck stopped, the guards got out and surrounded it, and they began to fire their machine guns and rifles into the two handcuffed men. It was simple butchery. That spectacle unfolded before the horrified eyes of the prisoner traveling in the jeep, Cristóbal Airado. He was the only survivor. After the machine-gunning, the soldiers engaged the dump-truck mechanism and the bodies rolled out of the back of it to the ground. One of the officers said to

Cristóbal, "This is so you'll know what we do with people who oppose the Revolution."

They had taken Cristóbal along so he could tell others what had happened. The Communists knew that soon the event would be common knowledge throughout Cuba, and the people themselves would spread the message of terror.

We, of course, soon found out about this latest act of barbarism. The growing intimidation and repression, not only in the prison but throughout the Island as well, led us to think that if we failed in our attempt to escape the consequence would be death, but we went on with our preparations. We had given our relatives instructions to send certain sums of money to an address which our contact, the common prisoner that was helping us, had given us. We had also asked them to send ID photographs. Two weeks after the visit, our friend delivered to us, using the string-through-the-window method we had perfected, four gorgeous militia ID cards with our photos. It was professional work. According to those documents, each of us belonged to one of the militia companies camped near the presidio. And the names on the ID cards were not invented, they actually existed. I was called Braulio Barceló and I belonged to the 830th Battalion, quartered at Los Mangos, a nearby camp. I could have been arrested somewhere on the island, but if they called up my battalion and asked about the man whose name appeared on the ID card, they would be told that indeed that militiaman belonged to that military unit.

A friend very skilled at making knives cut up the blade of a machete to make us four excellent ones with wooden handles. Step by step we were getting together the necessary provisions and equipment. For example, in a little plastic pouch sewn inside a larger plastic bag filled with *gofio de trigo,* we hid Halazone tablets for purifying water.

I was still making observations of the area with the telescope. I finally even came to recognize the faces of the soldiers in the little guard huts and the ones posted in front of the main guardhouse; I could see their faces as clearly as though they were only an arm's length away.

Around the middle of August a thick mattress arrived for Boitel. In Cuba, mattresses are filled with raw cotton stuffing and sewn with a piping about an inch in diameter all around the top and bottom. The guards had slashed this one, as they always did, from head to foot to poke around in the raw cotton padding in search of objects or letters hidden inside and smuggled in. Then they had folded up the mattress with the cut inside so the filling wouldn't come out, and tied it up with a piece of twine. It was a harmless-looking mattress, apparently thoroughly searched. But inside its piping were packed four militia shirts. They had been stretched out, twisted into tight spirals, and wrapped and braided with strong thread. They had then been padded with a thin layer of cotton inside the piping, two shirts on top and two underneath. Carmen Jiménez, Boitel's girlfriend, had come to Isla de Pinos for the express purpose of observing the searches performed on mattresses. Since the inspection of the articles was carried out in the presence of the family members, so they could be held responsible immediately if they tried to smuggle in some forbidden item, three or four inspections were conducted before her eyes. What she saw was that there was only one place they didn't search—that thick piping around the mattress. With this information, she left for Havana, and some friends made up the mattress at home. She brought it to the prison herself. If they had caught her, Carmen would have wound up in jail.

The berets had come in the same way the shirts had. The hacksaw blades had also, though we didn't find them immediately. We were lucky, because that was the last time they allowed mattresses to be brought in. Now all we needed to do was dye the pants and the web belts.

We began workouts to get into shape; we walked to build up our stamina. Every day we walked the circumference of the Circular dozens of times, and also up and down—from the fifth floor to the first floor and from the first floor back up again. And every day we added two or three laps and built up speed. There were many prisoners who did this for exercise, so we didn't arouse any suspicions. We calculated that finally we were walking fifteen miles a day. We took turns on lookout—when I walked, Ulises watched, and vice versa.

One detail which might have aroused attention once we were outside was how pale we were; we hadn't had any sun during all the months of our incarceration. We needed to get a little better color, such as the militiamen had. That was indeed a complicated undertaking. We had to follow the sun from one cell window to another to expose our faces to the shifting sun as it came in between the bars. We were managing to get a little tan.

All this took time, but a prisoner learns patience—and things were coming together well.

14 / "Squares": The Political Rehabilitation Program

The morning the Major told us that the penal authorities were going to authorize books and newspapers to be brought in, a general murmur and exclamations of surprise stopped him. He called for silence and went on. Every inmate would be allowed three books per month, but they had to come from the National Press of Cuba. Foreign books would not be allowed, nor would Cuban books from other publishers. Magazines and books printed in socialist countries and their national newspapers would be allowed, but nothing from the free presses of the world.

Two weeks later, a truck full of books and magazines pulled up in front of the Circular. They had all been printed by the National Press. Among them there were some classics like *Don Quixote,* which had been published at the beginning of the Revolution when Castro and his henchmen kept denying they were Communists, but most of the texts either were explicitly Marxist or while not openly Marxist implicitly carried severe criticism of free societies and democratic countries. I recall, for example, *Elementary Principles of Marxist Philosophy* by George Pulitzer, translated into Spanish; Soviet economics textbooks; and Russian novels from the Communist period. There were also propaganda magazines published for foreigners by the Eastern Bloc countries of Poland, Hungary, Rumania, Bulgaria, and others.

The objective of the easing of the rules against reading matter was to flood us with propaganda and indoctrinate us. The authorities knew that the majority of the prisoners were campesinos, workers, and soldiers, and that well-educated and politically aware prisoners were in the minority. Reading the material the propagandists sent in to us would confuse more than one of the prisoners, and we would have a continuous struggle against the massive indoctrination which they were trying to pull off with those books.

On one occasion Boitel suggested a drastic solution—burning all the Marxist books. But we immediately rejected the idea. We were prisoners precisely because we had defended a model of society in which no one would ever burn his adversary's books.

That was the beginning of a new phase. I little knew that in resisting the authorities' measures I would go almost literally through hell for the rest of my prison life. The government had decided, taking its cue from what the other Communist countries had done, to set up Political Rehabilitation Programs for the prisoners.

At first, the objective of Political Rehabilitation was to reduce the number of men within the prisons who continued to repudiate the government. Therefore the authorities promised better treatment, frequent family visits, correspondence, segregation from the "rebel" prisoners, prompt return to freedom, and reintegration into the new society. In exchange for this, the authorities demanded at least neutrality on the part of the prisoner or, better yet, the renunciation of the attitude which he had theretofore maintained. But in order for your file to be closed once and for all, you had to collaborate with the Political Police—you had to turn in reports and make a self-criticism, write an apology for your previous counterrevolutionary activity, and confess everything you had hidden during the interrogations. Initially, prisoners had to sign declarations in support of the government and against the Vietnam War and the United States.

It was not easy to make the men in charge of the prisons and their repressive forces understand the purposes of Political Rehabilitation. Theoretically, the inmate who agreed to join the Rehabilitation Program would be immediately treated differently, better. But how to take away from the hordes of bullying guards in the jails and prisons and from the rank and file in the Political Police the pleasure they derived from torturing, abusing, and mistreating their prisoner-victims? Only by strong pressure from the high leadership of the Party were they forced to obey the order not to beat up the men who came into the Rehabilitation Program. They were made to understand that the Soviet Union demanded the establishment of Political Rehabilitation, and they were finally convinced that beatings were not the only means of revenge against the antagonists of the regime, that there existed other methods by which they could vent their hatred and sadism. They were made to see that the ultimate aim of Political Rehabilitation was the internal annihilation of the prisoner, the destruction of all his principles. Turning a man into a moral zero would be the supreme vengeance.

The Rehabilitation Program was implemented by steps, using various techniques. One of the best-known preliminary techniques was that employed in the prison of La Cabaña. The prison authorities created an *escuelita*, a "little school." (The diminutive form seemed, or so the authorities must have thought, to make it a thing of little importance.) Those who attended took classes given by other inmates. But this little school did not have the laudable aim of raising the educational level of its students; instead it aimed to create a political about-face. Marxist theory was explained there, there were talks about defending Communism, and the students had to participate in activities in support of the Revolution. Meanwhile, every night patriots were falling before the firing squads.

The directors of the prison offered certain privileges to those who attended the little school. The remaining inmates' discontent with and rejection of this group, who were fraternizing with the enemy, began to create an atmosphere of open hostility, which came to a boil when Headquarters announced that the Rehabilitation Program was being put into effect.

I was told that about that time two hundred minors were jailed in *galera* 13 in La Cabaña. They had been accused of political crimes; some of them were sons of the many patriots who had taken up arms to fight against Castro and were even now fighting with the counterrevolutionary rebels in the mountains. As a reprisal, because the government had not been able to capture the fathers, it jailed their sons. There were boys fourteen and fifteen years old there. This group of boys presented a completely unified front to their jailers. There had never been a more feisty, stubborn, combative group, a group readier to stand up to the garrison physically, even though the guards attacked them with bayonets, iron bars, and chains. The minors' gallery wrote memorable pages in the history of La Cabaña prison.

It was those prisoners who awaited the "rehabilitated" prisoners when they came back from the little school; they greeted them with a hail of orange peels and other rubbish picked out of the garbage cans in the kitchen. That was a juvenile sort of way of showing them the contempt they had for the Rehabilitation Program. And it also showed that they wanted those who agreed to join the program to be housed separately; the two "classes" of prisoners could no longer live together.

Throwing the orange peels and other trash started a fight between the two groups, a general brawl, which turned the prison yard into a coliseum. The guard posted on the roof shot into the air and sounded the alarm, and the garrison in combat formation broke into the prison yard and dealt the prisoners one of the most savage beatings that had ever been given.

When this first attack was over, the chief of the Political Police in the prison, in company with the director, the head of the garrison, and other officers, and followed by the inmates who were attending the orientation classes, went *galera* by *galera* and made the men from the little school point out the ones that had assaulted them. The rehabilitated prisoners tried not to identify anyone, but at a signal from the Political Police chief, the guards took them by the scruff of the neck and shook them and forced them to inform on their comrades. Those men, terrified, pointed indiscriminately into each gallery, mixing those who really had participated with others who were completely innocent. Those who had been pointed out, most of them boys from the minors' *galera,* were taken out and given another beating— kicks and blows with rifle butts, which left even more of them hurt, some with fractured arms and ribs.

The first time the Political Commissioners themselves came to the prison on Isla de Pinos, they headed for Circular 4. Their leader was a venerable-looking soldier with white hair and a kindly, avuncular air. His last name was Méndez. There were quite a few men in the prison yard talking at the time, and he called us over to the gate. He did this very respectfully, and it puzzled us—that was hardly the way we were used to being treated. Soon there was a little group of prisoners standing there listening to him, among them Alberto Vivas.

Anyone who heard Méndez talk and who didn't know what he was *not* saying, who didn't know the nature of Communism, might have thought that Marxism was the solution to all humanity's problems, its only escape. He told us he was there to help us, to solve our problems, and our families' problems as well. He asked us not to think of him as a soldier; for him, we were more like his grandsons. From that moment on, he was always called Grandpa Méndez—in fact, that's the reason all the Political Commissioners in Cuba came to be ironically called grandpas.

Vivas would spend long hours chatting with Grandpa Méndez, who didn't realize that Vivas was having fun at his expense. One afternoon, Vivas showed him the magazine *Popular China* in which the famous photo of him shaking hands with Mao Zedong appeared. At that time Cuba and China were having a sort of political honeymoon, so when Grandpa Méndez saw the photograph his eyes widened in surprise.

"But Vivas, what're you doing in jail? . . ."

Vivas hung his head abashedly (he was an artist!) and answered that he had been wrong about everything, that he only wanted the Revolution to give him another chance, to let him out of that terrible prison, that this time around all he wanted to do was devote himself to a little piece of land he had. The Commissioner immediately noted down in his ever-present note-book what Vivas had told him. For the next few days Vivas kept asking him to do what he could to get his request approved—he was dying just to go off and work his little piece of land.

Meantime it had quickly become almost a ritual for a group of jokers to run up to Grandpa Méndez at the gate and make fun of him. A guy called Caribe had asked him to bring him a kite and a ball of string so he could "fly" from his cell on the fifth floor.

"Didn't you say we were your grandsons?"

And then every time the Political Commissioner passed anywhere close to the Circular, from the fifth floor Caribe's voice would ring out, "Grandpa, what about my kite?"

One afternoon the Commissioner called to Vivas. There was a pretty large group standing around.

"I've brought up your request, my son. But I need a little more information. You told me you had a little piece of land you wanted to work on, but you didn't tell me where it was. Is it here in Havana province?"

"No, Grandpa, it's in California."

The Political Commissioner looked as if he'd been slapped. He was speechless; he turned as red as a tomato and his chin trembled. I thought he was going to have a stroke or an attack of apoplexy. The whole group erupted into howls of laughter. That night, and for many more nights, Vivas slept in the punishment cells with his back stinging from blows dealt him with the flats of machetes, and Grandpa Méndez never stopped again at the gate to chat with us.

Toward the middle of that year, they took out two small groups of volunteers who had been sentenced to short terms. One of them was to work in the kitchen and the other was to do some work inside the security cordon. One day they gave this latter group an authorization card so they could go in and out of the prison during working hours, accompanied by guards, since they were to build some chicken coops right at the exit of the prison.

The construction began. The prisoners went out in the morning and came back at dusk. The authorities never made any undue demands on them until the day the guards took them not to the chicken coops but over to one side of the Circular, where everyone could see them, and ordered them to perform the most humiliating, most degrading of tasks. They were to dig trenches for the Communist soldiers to take shelter in if the rebels attacked Isla de Pinos. At first the prisoners refused. Then a platoon set a machine gun down in front of them and threatened to shoot them all if they didn't dig the trenches. In that group there were men with high academic and political credentials—university teachers and students. But the first of them to speak was a relatively uneducated black man whom everyone knew by the nickname Chameleon. He turned to the platoon and told them that even if he was almost illiterate, he still knew that you didn't dig trenches for your enemies. They could go ahead and shoot. Other men then joined him in the protest. Those men were returned to the Circular, while the rest of the group stayed and dug trenches.

From the windows of the cells that looked toward the east, hundreds of their comrades watched them in silence.

The prisoners watching came to the decision to ostracize those who had given in and dug trenches, but the authorities preempted us—they already had everything arranged. They took the prisoners to a room they had previously prepared for them in the punishment-cell block. A few days later they transferred them to Building 6, one of the two rectangular buildings. It was because of this that the rehabilitated prisoners were given the name Squares, to distinguish them from the prisoners in the round buildings, the Circulars.

The Political Commissioners then began interviewing campesinos, workers, and ex-soldiers who did not have long sentences to serve. It was the ideal psychological moment. The Bay of Pigs had failed, so the Commissioners' talk was based on arguments they would go on using for the next twenty years—the Americans had forgotten about us, they had betrayed us, the United States had been defeated in the invasion, the Revolution had been consolidated and was now indestructible. The Commissioners argued that the men's families were going through hard times, that their children sometimes didn't have enough to eat. But the Revolution was generous with its enemies; it would give them the chance to rectify their conduct. With simple, sincere repentance they could win their freedom and return to their homes.

And to mark an even greater difference between the two kinds of prisoners, as well as to force those still wavering to join the Rehabilitation Program, repression within the Circulars grew more pointed day by day. The hostility and savage fury kept growing, the physical mistreatment and harassment made our lives more surreal than ever.

15 / Martha in the Rain

Boitel, Ulises, Brito, and I were impatient and anxious for the day of our escape to arrive. Once this idea lodges in the mind of a prisoner, it becomes an obsession. I could hardly wait for the day when we would try to shatter the myth that the guards in that prison had sown—that it was impossible to escape from Isla de Pinos. We had political reasons, too, for attempting the escape. In October an important meeting was to be held in Punta del Este, Uruguay, convened by the Organization of American States (OAS), and we were going to try to attend so we could denounce the situation in Cuba and the human-rights violations in the prisons.

I made maps of all the prison surroundings, but I paid special attention to the southeastern zone, through which we had decided to make our escape. There were fewer populated areas and highways in that direction. We were only waiting for the next visit to confirm that our outside contacts could send a boat to pick us up at a certain point on the coast. The date would be decided at the September visit.

We still didn't realize that the hacksaw blades to cut through the bars had arrived inside the mattress with the uniforms. Everything else had been taken care of. One of our greatest worries was that in some search or other they might discover the paraphernalia we had hidden away. That would have been catastrophic.

There had been one failed escape attempt which frightened us all. A great number of the officers who had fought in Castro's army against Batista did not want to become proponents of Communism, so they stood up to the new Marxist tyranny. Therefore, they were there in Circular 4 of the prison on Isla de Pinos. Among them was Captain Regino Machado and quite a few officers who had fought under his command in Escambray. Machado was highly respected by all the combatants who had known him, some of whom were members of the military forces at the presidio. One of them arrived one morning as a guard at the main gate. They recognized each other and established contact. This guard carried a message to one of the officers who had fought in Machado's unit, so that at that moment began a conspiracy in which almost twenty soldiers assigned to the garrison would be implicated.

The little pine woods located to the east of the barbed wire, where we had discovered a small cabin in which a few soldiers stayed, was used by the conspirators to communicate with Machado and his group inside the Circular. The communication was carried out in Morse code. A blinker was made from a can with a little kerosene lantern inside and a flap which could be rhythmically opened and closed.

The Political Police discovered the conspiracy, and no less than seventeen of those soldiers were arrested. Several of them were executed on the firing range at the rear of the jail, beyond the barbed wire and a plantain field—nobody ever found out exactly how many or who they were. It was the first time there had been executions in the Model Prison. A little while later in the same place, political prisoners would be shot as well.

Boitel slept until almost noon and went to bed very late. We would talk until they gave the order for silence. At any rate, we could have gone on talking only a few minutes more because the whispering would have disturbed the prisoners in the neighboring cells. Every night for those few minutes before sleep came, I thought about my family and I prayed to God to strengthen my faith and allow me to keep firmly in mind the resolve which I had taken, not to allow myself to be spiritually destroyed. I prayed that my soul would not be hardened and degraded by rancor or hatred. My greatest concern at every moment was not to grow discouraged or desperate; I saw the ravages of depression and desperation on many of those in jail with me. In my conversations with God in the solitude of those few minutes I penetrated to the foundations of that faith which would be so severely tried in the course of years, but which would finally be victorious.

Still, because of my anxiety, the days passed slowly. The searches were frequent, and the repressive measures were harrowing. All an inmate had to do at headcount time was rest a shoulder on the cell wall, put his hands on his hips, cross his arms or raise them, and he was dragged down and beaten all the way to the punishment cells, where he was confined for months. Lieutenant Julio Tarrau, the prison director, had established a reign of terror. This man, a mestizo who had been a militant in the Communist Party ranks since the 1940s, never let an opportunity slip by for expressing his hatred of the political prisoners. Tarrau named Lieutenant Bernardo Díaz, an old Party comrade of his, to be chief of Internal Order.

Finally, September 5 dawned—a gray, rainy morning. One of the seasonal Caribbean hurricane fronts was approaching Cuba, and in the days before its arrival there had been frequent heavy rainstorms and a great deal of wind. The visit that day would be of the utmost importance to us four planning the escape; for me it would be even more important, even though

I had no inkling of it, for I would meet my future wife at that visit. And it was precisely that contact, even more than the one we were eagerly waiting for, which would finally get me out of jail twenty-two years later. . . .

There was at first a gusty rain, then the rain stopped and the low clouds scudded before an easterly wind. We all prayed that the weather would improve a little, and we worried about our relatives, who we knew were out there waiting, since the night before, with no place to take shelter.

Along the horizon the sky opened up a bit, and a pale sun came up. That promise that the day might at last dawn filled us with joy and expectancy.

We left the Circular as we always did for the visits—they called us out by number, they stripped us, they inspected all our clothing, and they herded us into the corral. The ground had become a mudhole. Our shoes picked up globs of mud as we walked. At the center the water had formed a pool four or five yards wide.

Around nine o'clock we made out the first groups of visitors. I kept looking up at the sky; the clouds were still running fast before the wind, so it began to look as if it wasn't going to rain that morning after all. Two hours later, most of the family members were inside the corral, but mine and some others' hadn't appeared. We learned from some visitors that two days before when they were on board the ferry that carried them from the port of Batabanó on the south coast of Cuba across to the Island, they were forced to get off the boat so a contingent of militiamen and arms could be transported.

The transits to Isla de Pinos were made on two boats inherited from the previous government: *El Pinero,* with a capacity of more than three hundred people; and the ferry *Isla de Tesoro* (*Treasure Island*), whose engines had stopped running sometime in 1960 from lack of maintenance and repair—it had to be pulled over by a tug. Its capacity was five hundred seated passengers, but up to fourteen hundred people crowded into it. A trip which a slow boat would normally make in three to three and a half hours sometimes took fourteen and sixteen on the towed ferry, depending on the strength and direction of the wind.

Our families even tried to find space in the holds among the cargo. As soon as they had squeezed in a little, still others tried to enter. Many had made the voyage to Batabanó on foot and arrived with swollen legs and ankles. Some were carrying pallet quilts to spread on the deck. To walk they had to step over the others. There was only one bathroom for women and another for men, and rowdy lines grew at their doors. Even the deck was full, and when it rained all of them simply didn't fit under cover, so they had to stay out in the rain and wind.

I was struck by the foreboding that I was not going to have any visitors. I was wandering concerned and dejected through the corral when Benito called me over to introduce me to his family. "This is Armando. He's been like a son to me." They thanked me emotionally. His wife and young daughter had come to see him; she was the same little girl I had seen in the photograph that Benito had showed me weeks before, but that picture must have dated from some time ago, since here before my startled eyes was standing not the insignificant little girl in glasses, but a pretty teenage woman, tall, elegant, and well mannered, with a sweet baby face. In her eyes shone a firm will, a mixture of tenderness and courage. I think that was what most impressed me about her.

I asked them whether they knew anything about the people who had had to get off the boat two days before. They said they had been told they would be brought over somehow, and they asked me to stay there with them until my relatives arrived.

Martha and her mother had come on the first, smaller, boat, and had been in line in front of the presidio since the day before. They told us there was a throng of thousands of people—old ladies, children, pregnant women —along the highway. There were some cars pulled off onto the side of the road which had served as shelter for the people who had had the incredible luck to be able to rent them. There were only a few taxis in Nueva Gerona, not nearly enough for the five thousand people who had come to the visit. This visit was the largest in the history of the prison, and by far the most uncomfortable, since it took place under alternating rain squalls and insufferable attacks of swarming mosquitoes. So the night had passed for them. When a woman needed to relieve herself the others formed a circle around her to shelter her.

At six o'clock in the morning, the order had been given to enter the prison, and the lines had formed up again, but now within the prison fences. There was one file to inspect the little food packages that they brought to their prisoner, then another where people were physically searched, men to one side, women to another. They were completely stripped. The strip-searches of the women were conducted by women soldiers, and they were so repugnant that some altercations arose, especially with one of the soldiers named Zenaida. They didn't even have any respect for the old ladies. Iglesias de la Torre's mother, who was sick and almost blind, had to strip in spite of being seventy years old.

Knowing that our mothers, daughters, wives, girlfriends, and sisters had to undergo every imaginable humiliation was infuriating—even more so when there was no need to search them, because we ourselves were stripped and thoroughly searched both in coming out and returning to the Circulars after the visit. They did not do it for reasons of security, but simply to humiliate, torment, and vex our relatives—out of spite, cruelty, and hatred. Women who were having their periods were forced to take off their sanitary napkins, open them, and allow them to be inspected, since the guards alleged that inside them they might have a note or money hidden.

Martha visibly reddened when I started besieging her with my questions, asking for details. The visitors tried to avoid telling us about those indignities and harassments so we wouldn't get so upset that we'd ask them not to visit again.

In that huge corral now become a quagmire, there was not so much as a bench or any sanitary facilities. There was no place to get water.

The sky grew dark in the east, and thick heavy clouds appeared. With a great rush, it began to rain. Something like six thousand people were standing there in the rain. I stood in front of Martha with my back to the wind, trying to keep the gusts of water from flailing her directly. It was all I could do. In only a few minutes we were all soaked to the skin. I unbuttoned my shirt and opened it around her for a little more protection. The depressing spectacle of those women and children shivering with cold, the futile attempt by the prisoners to protect them from the rain, is something I have never forgotten. After dozens of pleas, we finally were allowed to cross the street into the dining hall; we would all fit easily, since it was built to hold five thousand people at a time. They opened the corral and the visitors began to move out. The rain never let up. The caravan of visitors, huddled over attempting to keep the little packages dry, entered the dining room one by one. Seeing the old women with their soaking dresses, their white hair dripping streams of water and the guards giving unnecessary orders, all inspired pity and fury.

Male visitors were not allowed to go into the dining hall, either. They had to stay on the other side of the fence, and even when we prisoners entered they had to stand in the torrential rain. They couldn't leave the prison until the visit was over, the prisoners had all been counted, and the guards had made sure that no one had escaped.

We formed up in the rain, they counted us, and only then could we go into the dining hall. Our relatives broke into applause as we came in. It was a very emotional moment. Water was streaming from our soaked clothing. The guards standing on the tables banged on them with their rifle butts and ordered the applause to stop. They jumped from one table to another, frightening women and children with their blows and cries.

I stayed with Benito and his family. Martha and I sat down across from each other at a narrow table. I took off my boots, turned them upside down, and poured out the water as though they'd been pitchers. Her hair was dripping wet; the simple light-colored dress she was wearing clung to her body. I found her radiantly beautiful. She did not wear any makeup; in fact, this was the first time her mother had let her do her eyebrows. They invited me to eat a few bites with them. When we bit into the food, water ran down our chins—it was practically mush.

My conversation with Martha that day of our first meeting was trivial yet unforgettable for both of us. In just a few hours a mutual sympathy made us feel as though we had been friends all our lives. She was fourteen years old and I was twenty-four, and it was precisely her almost childlike youth that attracted me. We started a conversation about nothing in particular; I asked about what she did, what she liked. I remember that she crossed her arms on the table and rested her head on them. She was more comfortable that way, and the exhaustion from the trip and the forty-eight hours without sleep did the rest. She lay there asleep while her admirer and future husband talked. I stood up carefully and went over to one of the barred windows through which the wind was blowing, to try to dry my clothes off a little, but I wound up shivering with cold. My pretty friend was still sleeping, and I stood there contemplating her. I felt a great tenderness at that, a tenderness I had never before experienced.

When Martha woke up, she apologized, embarrassed, for going to sleep. We laughed, and our new friendship seemed to glow as well.

A half-hour before the visit was to end, my mother and sister, along with some other relatives, came into the dining room. The guards didn't allow them to give me the package they had brought me. They had been made to get off the boat, they had been kept from arriving on time for the visit, and now they were being told that they had come for nothing. We barely had any time for conversation. They had had a terrible trip, on the deck the whole time, under the never-ending lashing of the wind and rain.

When a soldier got up on one of the tables and began to shout for all of us to be silent, I knew what it meant.

"The visit's over! Everybody out!"

And dozens of guards began repeating his cries, banging on the tabletops, separating the prisoners from their relatives. Nonetheless several went on talking and embracing, even through the soldiers' hullabaloo. The visitors were crowded into one side of the hall and a cordon of guards, brandishing their rifles, kept them from approaching us again. I saw a little three-year-old boy who could barely walk run over to hug his father one last time. A guard stopped him by throwing the butt of his rifle in front of the child. The little boy grabbed it, and the guard pushed him backward. He broke out crying. They also pushed old ladies back with their rifles. Seeing that, a roar of indignation arose from us, but there was a picket of bayonets pointed at us. That incident left us all with a bitter taste, but then they were constantly trying to find some provocation to beat us and send us to the solitary-confinement cells.

Martha had told me that when they were going to get on the boat there in Batabanó, one of the soldiers had made a pass at a prisoner's wife. She didn't let him get away with it, and the guard told her she had to apologize to him for having sassed him. The soldier wanted to humiliate her before the rest of the people, but the woman stood her ground. Then he told her that if she didn't apologize, he wouldn't let her go to the visit. She refused again, so the soldier made her get off the boat and miss the visit, and then spitefully refused to let any of the other women take the package she had brought for her husband.

These incidents with the prettier wives of the prisoners occurred with some regularity. The guards insulted and blackmailed them, as though the wives of defeated men should be part of the victorious forces' booty—if they didn't get what they wanted, they threatened to keep the wives from visiting, thinking that way the women, out of love for their husbands who were being kept prisoner, would give in.

16 / A Harrowing Obstacle Course

As soon as we returned from the visit, Ulises, Boitel, Brito, and I got together in my cell. Everything seemed to be going well. The people who were handling the arrangements for the boat had sent a man to the visit. Boitel spoke with him a few minutes through the fence. The man wanted to know how we planned to get out of there, because the contacts on the outside thought an escape was impossible. Boitel told him we had a plan— we couldn't talk about the details of it, but we were almost certain it was going to work.

It was agreed that a boat and crew would pick us up at the mouth of the Júcaro River, several miles southeast of the presidio, on the night of October 21, or one o'clock in the morning, that is, of October 22. We would wait for them there for two days. The signals for identifying the ship were agreed upon. We asked about the hacksaw blades, which we had not yet discovered, and were told they'd been in our hands all along. We were sheepish but delighted.

Knowing that our escape plans were moving ahead elated us. The dozens of news reports and rumors which the visit had brought us really held little interest for us now; in less than two months we would be trying to gain our liberty on our own, more or less independent of outside events. This thought made me feel that I was already outside the bars. As long as you can plan for your freedom and strive to attain it, even if you're chained hand and foot, you don't feel like a slave.

With a small bottle of kerosene and black pepper to stop the dogs they were sure to put on our trail, and with tablets to dye the pants olive-green, we now had everything we needed. All the other equipment and supplies were hidden where we could get at them within moments.

Our families didn't know anything about what we were planning to do. We had decided not to tell them—what we were about to do was so dangerous, and the potential repercussions so serious, that we had wanted to spare them the worry and anguish they would suffer for us. Carmen, Boitel's girlfriend, was the only person who was kept abreast of everything, because she was the coordinator of all the activity going on outside. Her participation was crucial. Without her we wouldn't have been able to consider such an undertaking and thus shatter the myth that the man wasn't born who could escape from the prison on Isla de Pinos.

We never left off our observation of our surroundings. All four of us now were on watch; we all had to familiarize ourselves with the ground we were going to have to cross. We had to know the smallest details of the movement of the troops from the guard station, all about the posted guards and the guards who walked the rounds. It was boring, but thanks to our continual observation, even weeks later we would have been able to walk every step of that area with our eyes closed.

The lancewood-bordered path which led to the house where the soldiers' uniforms were laundered would be the first leg of our escape. Anyone who was watching us would see us headed toward that house, but we wouldn't arouse suspicions because everybody went there from time to time. To one side of the guardhouse, where the red-earth path ended, there was a little gate. The guard posted at the entrance to the guardhouse beside that walk always stayed about ten yards away from the gate. Vehicles never passed through it; it was only for soldiers and militiamen on foot. If they hadn't been able to use this route they'd have had to walk a half mile at least, all the way around the presidio, to get to the wash house. That exit was quite useful, to say the least.

One day Ulises noticed that there was not a single militiaman inside the prison. And in fact, we didn't see one the whole day. Nor the next. We thought they must have been confined to quarters. However, the movement of troops confined to barracks as they settled in would have been detected by us immediately. Apparently, then, that wasn't the reason for their absence. The routine of the guardpost went on as usual. It didn't take us long at all to discover the real reason. They had been prohibited from entering the prison grounds.

The order had been issued for security considerations. The Political Police knew perfectly well that not all militiamen sympathized with the regime, and besides those who were not exactly supporters, there were even counterrevolutionaries within the ranks. The massive coming and going of militiamen at the prison might be used to establish contact with prisoners, to get information in to them, and even to make escapes possible. Unknowingly, the Political Police had put a snag into a very real escape attempt by four of their prisoners.

This news was shattering for us at first. Getting the four shirts and the berets into the prison to disguise ourselves as militiamen had been a tremendous job. What were we to do now?

There was only one solution left us. We had to dye the shirts olive-green too and try to pass ourselves off as soldiers. In order to do that, we had to manufacture four new pieces of headgear, and as soon as possible. This, actually, was not so difficult, since the Army used fatigue caps. There were tailors, harness makers, and all sorts of other craftsmen there with us. The caps, which had become essential, wouldn't really be an insurmountable problem. And there turned out to be enough dye for the shirts as well.

Besides the fixed floodlights and the movable spotlights installed on the guard huts, which swept all across the prison with their beams of whitish light, a few yards away from the building the authorities had stretched an electric cord strung with 500-watt light bulbs. Those lights were never turned off; they remained lit night and day. It didn't matter if the sky was blue and a glaring sun illuminated everything—they were still lit. At dusk they turned on the other spotlights and began to sweep the whole prison— buildings, windows, green areas. The hour decided upon by us for our escape was minutes before nightfall, so as to avoid the danger of being caught in the spotlights. However, one of those 500-watt bulbs was directly in front of the cell, so we decided to put it out just at the moment of our escape. For that we would use a slingshot; from the second floor the light bulb would be an easy target.

I was on watch when they began some work outside, and what I saw made my heart sink. The little gate through which we had planned to make our escape was being closed up. They dug some post holes, put metal posts in them, and between the poles stretched an unbroken web of steel chain-link, like that the security cordon was made of. The gate simply disappeared, just like that, and with it the possibility of our escape.

I called the rest to tell them the terrible news. I don't think they had received such bad news in all the months past. Now our plan would be worse than difficult. But we decided to keep watching; something might come up. We might still find an alternative way.

Around the main guardhouse there was a fence about five feet high strung with several strands of barbed wire. The soldiers hung socks and underwear on those lines to dry. They went on carrying their uniforms to be washed over to the house, and it didn't matter to them that the gate had been sealed up. They simply made a new path—they pulled the wires on the fence apart and crawled through to the other side. So the new route we had been looking for was established by the soldiers themselves. We knew that if we proposed to escape, we'd have to do what they did. But the enterprise was much riskier now; we would have to actually enter the guardhouse, and this raised the odds against us tremendously.

After you've spent months preparing for an operation of this kind, it's really impossible to stop, so as obstacles arise you skirt them or eliminate them with new variants on the plan. We decided to take that route, the only one that existed for us, even if we did have to pass through the guardhouse. Our attention was focused now on the guardhouse activity. We observed how the soldiers came and went. Closing up the gate allowed the guard posted in the little yard more freedom of movement, since he didn't have to stay right next to the gate. This was a help to our plan, actually, since, of the two entrances to the guardhouse, we could use the one farther from the guard on duty at the moment we came to the house.

I can't imagine there was ever an escape plan with more difficulties to be overcome, more obstacles to get around, more interruptions, than ours. And still soldiers continued reinforcing the defense systems. They cleared the land at the back of the guardhouse, tearing down trees and shrubs with bulldozers and leaving more than a hundred yards as smooth and level as an airport runway. At the same time, they set up a barbed-wire fence more than nine feet high to replace the previous flimsy one. On this new fence they used special barbed wire with the barbs set every three inches. If the guardhouse was attacked from the outside, the assault would be much more difficult. It looked as though that barbed-wire fence closed up our hopes for escape once and for all. We really were in despair now. We anxiously scanned everything within sight, trying to find some place, some corner, some possibility for flight, and it would have to be before the date we had fixed for our being picked up on the coast.

I had taken up the watch the morning that several guards, equipped with picks and shovels, began to make an excavation at the foot of the barbed-wire fence. What in the world were they doing? I didn't for even one second take my eye from the telescope, the telescope from them. They had already made a hole about knee-deep, but they kept digging. The earth piled up next to it made a slowly growing mound. It turned out to be a ditch underneath the fence! When all the digging was done, they brought in a machine gun and emplaced it next to the ditch, and on the guardhouse roof they set up a powerful floodlight with its switch operated from below. Its fixed beam illuminated the area of the ditch and the cleared area at the back. The guard in charge of the machine gun sat on a stool leaning against the wall behind the guardhouse, about five yards away from the machine gun.

Once again, that campesino house where the guards' uniforms were washed had come to our aid. The ditch was used exactly as though it had been a gate. We practically jumped for joy when we saw the guards going in and out through the ditch when they took or picked up their laundry.

There were very few days left now, so we hastened our preparations. Boitel took out the hacksaw blades to cut through the bars. That was when we discovered that the blades didn't have pegs on the ends to attach them to the slot on the metal handle they were supposed to be used with. So with the handle from a pail I made a saw frame narrow enough to fit between the two bars. I made slots in it with one of the hacksaw blades itself, but there was no way to attach the blades to the frame. Boitel came up with the solution. They could be bent into a U or L at each end, but they broke if you did it while they were cold. So we took a kerosene lamp, the plastic tube off an intravenous kit, and an empty ballpoint-pen refill, and improvised a blowtorch. I blew the flame across one end of the hacksaw's steel blade as Boitel held it, and we heated the blade red-hot. With a pair of pliers we bent them, without breaking them, around some nails and punches. Once they were bent double we fired them again, and submerged them red-hot into a little pan of oil to retemper them. We made up half a dozen of them that way.

Ulises' job was dyeing the caps—which, by the way, had turned out better than the ones the guards themselves wore.

We worked out the ideal location for the cell we should escape from, and it turned out that cell 64 offered us the greatest security against being seen. That was in fact our own cell—but ours was on the second floor, and we needed the one on the first floor. It could hardly be any other, since using 63 or 65 would expose us to being seen from the guard hut in back, to the west, or by the guard posted in front of the main guardhouse. The prisoner who lived underneath us, in cell 64 of the first floor, had been a combatant in the struggle against Batista. Boitel and I went to speak with him and told him very frankly that we needed his help for our escape. The only thing he had to do was change cells with us; there would be no risk involved for him. We explained that if we had to jump from the second floor, which in reality was the third floor, since the ground floor had no cells, the fall could be very dangerous. But the first-floor cell was ideal for our purposes. But there was no way to convince him. He just refused—the excuses he trotted out were farfetched and unconvincing, but we could tell he was unshakable. Then we spoke with Gomila, a very good friend of his, and asked Gomila to try to persuade him. Gomila had no better luck than we did. The man was afraid; his fear of reprisal was overwhelming, paralyzing. It is interesting to note how some men's courage is undaunted by certain circumstances but quails before others.

We couldn't use any other cell—only number 64 would do. So we decided to jump from the second floor. Of course that increased the risks, but we had to act without any waste of time or we would literally miss the boat which was to pick us up on the coast. So we set to work.

Since Carrión wasn't going with us, he changed places with Brito; if Carrión stayed in the cell the escape was launched from, the reprisals that would fall on him would be mortal, more than likely.

To cut through the iron bars of the window, Boitel and I had to take all sorts of precautions. They were then letting us hang clothing outside the bars until five o'clock in the afternoon. We thought that hanging a towel out to dry would keep us from being spotted from the outside. One person would cut the bars while another stood watch, since even with the towel the movement might attract some soldier's notice. When someone approached, we stopped sawing. To protect ourselves against the improbable event of a guard coming up into the central tower, we took down the cot at the front of the cell and hung another towel up horizontally across the bars while

Carrión stood watch in the narrow hallway and obstructed the vision not only of the possible guard, but also of any indiscreet prisoners within the Circular itself. We knew there were informers who if they saw something would announce it to the whole garrison.

There were three bars we needed to cut through. Although Brito, Boitel, and I could squeeze through the space left when two bars were taken out, Ulises, the *gordo* in our group, wouldn't fit. We didn't cut all the way through them; we left two points of union which later, in just a few moments, we could saw through completely. We did it that way for security. Into the slots left by the cut we forced razor blades, because when the guards performed their inspections they ran an iron rod across the bars and the windows then were like a rigid harp that produced a single note. If one of the bars had been cut all the way through, it would ring false and the plot would be discovered. By not cutting totally through the bars and by filling the slots with razor blades, we would keep the iron music harmonious, as it were. Or if not harmonious, at least it would sound like any other window. Once the razor blades were in place, we camouflaged the cuts with a very thick mixture made of toothpaste and powdered milk, and the sole of a shoe run over them to "age" and dirty the bars a bit completed the work. Once all that was done, the cuts were perfectly undetectable.

From aluminum we made six little rings which were to be used after our escape to put the bars back into place and hold them there. They would be attached with wire, and since the rings had been painted the same color as the bars, the guard walking his post below would not be able to distinguish anything out of the ordinary. We couldn't leave a hole in the window, because the guard would see it immediately as the spotlight swept across the Circular, he'd give the alarm, and we wouldn't even get to the main guardhouse. Our rearguard would win the time necessary to put the bars back in place by keeping the guard who was walking the rounds busy. They would employ the simple stratagem of putting a towel out to dry—an action forbidden at that hour. The prisoner would ask the guard's permission. The guard would tell the prisoner it wasn't authorized. The prisoner would ask him, please, to give him just one hour, there was no other towel he could use—and those seconds of conversation would give Carrión, Vidal, and Chaguito time to put the bars back into place.

In our equipment packs, we included olive-green mosquito netting to cover our heads (since the mosquitoes of the swamps were enough to drive anyone mad) and black gloves, and under our shirts, T-shirts with several rows of pockets sewn in, to carry water-purification tablets, bars of chocolate, emergency medicines, razor blades, matches in jars sealed watertight, a little mirror for signaling, and other small items. We would have no difficulty with orientation, since we had studied the maps and even at night we were sure that we wouldn't get lost, but just to be sure we carried a little compass with us—the kind used for keychains, more decorative than useful in ordinary circumstances. I knew the most important constellations, as, of course, Brito did; he was the one among us with the strongest sense of direction. He had, after all, spent his whole life sailing.

Boitel was still obsessed with the idea of getting to the conference at Punta del Este.

17 / The Escape:
Destroying a Myth

We had a courageous group of friends in the prison whose coopera-tion helped make it all possible. Without their collaboration and assistance we would never have been able to escape. We spoke with each of them separately to thank them and to put the finishing touches on the plan. Lookouts had to be posted at the moment of our escape, to be sure that there was no vehicle approaching the Circular. Therefore three of our cellmates would spread out through the floors and make sure "the coast was clear"; they were to give the okay to Chaguito, who was to be at the entrance to our cell.

Ulises had had a rope made which we would slide down. The rope was made by unraveling the threads of a piece of the burlap covering of a cot —ten or twelve of these threads would be skeined together to make a thick strand. Then the rope itself would be braided from four or five of these strands. If it was well braided such a rope was strong enough to support the weight of one man.

Now the uniforms were dyed and ironed and the caps were impeccably tailored. Our day dawned—October 21, 1961. They were having a visit at Circular 3.

We had to talk to Perdomo, since we knew that he and León, in cell 13 on the first floor, were sawing through the iron bars with an eye to escaping next. We told them that afternoon for the first time about our escape planned for that night, so they could take precautions and hide their equipment, their hacksaw blades, camouflage the bars, and so on, for the guards would swarm over the Circular when our escape was discovered.

If everything went well, according to plan, we would have until the next day's headcount at dawn to get to our pickup position. At dawn the escape would be discovered.

The last of our preparations got under way immediately after the after-noon headcount. With the slingshot we burst the light outside the cell window. From that moment on, everything had to go with clockwork precision. But suddenly we realized that the rope was missing. Carrión ran to get it. Then we got dressed. We put on the T-shirts, the rubber-band "garters" holding knives to our legs, loaded up with the cigarettes and matches, Cuban pesos and American dollars which I was carrying in an old wallet, the ID cards, and all the rest. It began to grow dusky. The guard who walked the rounds of the Circular had already arrived and made one desultory circuit. He was smoking as he and his dog walked their post.

We rubbed our underarms and genitals with a piece of cloth moistened with kerosene so the dogs couldn't pick up our scent. Brito would be the first to jump. Then Ulises. Chaguito at the entrance would give the all-clear signal when the lookouts we had stationed around the building said it was safe. Obregón would cover the stairways.

The guard stopped and chatted with his comrade making the same round at Circular 3; then the two of them continued on.

We sawed the rest of the way through and took out the bars. We tied the rope. Chaguito gave the thumbs-up, and Brito went out the window and slithered quickly down. Behind him went Ulises, followed by Boitel. But just at that moment, all the lights went out. There was a general power outage. I didn't know it, but the rope had meanwhile come unraveled on Boitel, which forced him to drop to the ground. He fell heavily, and two fracture lines were produced in his heel. When I jumped, the raveled rope was not nearly thick enough to hold me. I was just about to do a quick arm-over-arm down the rope, and I was left holding a few shreds of old burlap. I plummeted and landed on a pile of cement rubble. I felt a terrible pain in my right foot, but I stood up instantly. In moments of danger a man is capable of incredible acts, of overcoming terrible pain and physical limitations. It is as though your mind, bent on one single objective, blocks out all other sensations.

Later on I would learn that in the fall I had fractured three bones in my foot, and that another bone, caught between the fractured ones, had been dislocated. Nonetheless I walked normally, without limping, and joined Boitel, who was lighting a cigarette as he waited for me beside the walkway. We started walking away.

We hadn't had time to exchange a single word when Little Prick came out of the hospital; he was the one who did the headcounts. He had a Czech submachine gun slung on his shoulder. Brito and Ulises, who were walking about thirty-five yards ahead of us, were going to walk within inches of him. Ulises had a round, quite memorable face, and in fact when they crossed paths, the sergeant stopped and did a double-take at that face he couldn't quite place. There was a moment of indescribable tension.Ulises had become suspect. Boitel and I were approaching the sergeant, and we began to talk rather loudly:

"Fatso's in such a hurry—he can't even wait for us! He's desperate to get back to Havana. If Captain Quindelán were here now, we could leave first thing tomorrow."

The sergeant could hear my words perfectly clearly; they answered his doubts, his questions. He didn't know the two "soldiers" because they were from Havana; they were there to see Captain Quindelán, the head of the garrison. Undoubtedly his simple mind was satisfied by my quick comment. When we passed along beside him, Boitel and I were talking naturally. As we passed, I greeted him—"How are you, Sergeant." "Just fine, son."

I think that for the first time in the last two minutes, we breathed. If that sergeant had come out of the hospital thirty seconds earlier, he'd have surprised us coming down the rope. That was one of the unforeseeable risks we ran. A few seconds had meant the difference between staying alive and dying—but thank God nothing had happened.

Night fell suddenly, with no other warning than that dusky shadowiness which in the tropics gives way to total darkness within seconds. As we were walking toward the guardhouse, they turned on the searchlights. Our plan was to walk around the side of the military building, through the side yard, like guards going to get our socks and underwear off the fences. Or like guards headed for the house that had been converted into a laundry. We were to leave by the ditch beside the machine gun and move off toward the right, toward the undergrowth at the edge of the cleared area. Those minutes would be decisive, since all the guard at the machine gun had to do to discover our escape was to turn on the fixed floodlight on the roof. But our observations had led us to expect them to do that only later, when it got really dark.

We saw Ulises and Brito enter the guardhouse yard, as though they were strolling up to their own house. The guard was to their left. They bent off to the right, and we lost sight of them.

It was already dark and murky. My leg hurt terribly, but I knew it would be fatal to allow myself to limp even for one step. Standing straight, as though the leg that was killing me didn't belong to me, I put myself in God's hands and with His aid made it the whole distance.

Now Boitel and I were almost to the little yard, still talking in a normal tone, trying to make our presence as natural as we could. The guard, whom we passed about fifteen yards away, didn't notice anything strange—we were just two more guards of the many who came and went.

We too turned off to the right. A broad, open doorway was the entrance to the showers. A guard called Chinaman by his buddies was taking a shower. He was often on duty in our Circular. Boitel called out to him, "Hey, Chinaman, don't forget to wash your back!" That shout eased a little of the tension we were feeling.

We came to the rear yard. A tall blond guard leaning on his stool against the wall was singing *decimas,* typical songs of the Cuban countryside.

They're ten-line verses with sometimes complicated rhymes, very fixed forms; you've got to keep your mind on what you're doing if you sing *decimas*. The grass in the yard grew almost knee-high. We didn't see a sign of Brito and Ulises, who had already gone through. Boitel and I looked for the ditch, but we couldn't find it in the darkness and the weed-overgrown yard. We had a few desperate moments. I told Boitel to wait for me a second, I was going to take a leak at the foot of the fence. I turned my back to the guard, who was still deep in his singing, and pretended to urinate. This gave Boitel time, slipping along the fence, to locate the ditch. As soon as I saw him squat down in the shadows, I followed him. I stumbled against something hard, and made out some toothed iron wheels in the weeds. They were jumbled one on top of another, and I almost fell over them a second time. The process of getting through the ditch made my foot hurt so much I almost screamed. I was in a cold hard sweat. Boitel was waiting for me on the other side. We turned off to the right, crossing close to Lieutenant Antonio's house; he was called The Shadow because of his cruel, sinister personality. Ulises and Brito were waiting for us there. Lieutenant Antonio's dogs were barking, but those weren't the ones that worried us—we were worried about the Ministry of the Interior's bloodhounds.

We moved along behind a border of shrubs which the bulldozers had left when they cleared off the area. Now even if they turned on the guardhouse floodlight, the guard wouldn't see us and sound the alarm. We walked more than a hundred yards parallel to the cleared land. At the far end, we turned to look back at the brooding piles of the Circulars. Ours, the closest one, was truly imposing—its windows were illuminated by the ghastly light from the central tower's spotlights. No prisoner had ever been able to look upon the Circulars from that perspective. We had just put the myth of the impossible escape to rest; we had demonstrated that the fortress was, indeed, vulnerable.

We moved farther into the woods, then we made a little halt to leave traces for the dogs—three swatches of cloth that we carefully sprinkled with pepper. When the bloodhounds came up and sniffed at them in that characteristic way of theirs, deeply snuffling and inhaling, the peppery powder would fill their noses, they'd start sneezing, and their sense of smell would be out of commission for a good while. We placed the pieces of cloth a few feet apart.

As soon as we'd cleared the window, our rearguard in the Circular went to work. The bars were put back into place in the way we'd planned, and the materials left over, such as hacksaw blades, dye tablets, and so forth, were turned over to friends for future escape attempts.

The most important thing was to take security precautions, to keep one of the internal informers from tipping off the garrison. Vladimir Ramírez and another man planted themselves in front of one of the cells on the first floor, occupied by a prisoner about whom there were certain strong suspicions—people said he was a stool pigeon. And sure enough, the prisoner saw us slide down the rope and tried to run out of his cell—but Vladimir stopped him. He held a knife to his throat and pushed him into the back of the cell. The same thing happened with some other suspicious types. The escape was now general knowledge, and to silence murmurs or even shouts that might alert the guards that something out of the ordinary was afoot, our friends banged out a rumba with cans, pails, and spoons. It was typically Cuban— the beat of that rumba shook the Circular. At that time, a dozen prisoners from the Circular were working in the kitchen on the first shift, which began at midnight. They had already been called together and told that they would be held responsible for whatever happened to us if one of them committed an "indiscretion." It was generally thought that an infiltrator had penetrated that group.

When there was an escape, the garrison took reprisals against the head of the Circular, because they considered him an accomplice. Prison Headquarters tried in that way to make some prisoners stool pigeons against others. The director, Lieutenant Tarrau, had threatened the Major of the Circular and the men in charge of the various floors that if an escape was tried and they didn't notify him immediately, they would be assumed to be collaborators in the escapees' plan. That was the Fascist way of doing things —taking vengeance on innocent men to intimidate them into collaborating with the authorities. So when the prisoner in charge of the second floor found out that we had escaped, he trembled in horror. He could foresee the reprisals that would come down on him, and he went through a crisis of conscience, struggling between his instinct for self-preservation and his sense of solidarity with us. It was then that one of our comrades told him that he, our comrade, would take the responsibility of his position. When the garrison came, our friend would stand before them as head of the floor.

We heard dogs barking far off in the distance, and thought that the chase might already have begun. We had never believed the escape could really be kept secret until the following morning. We had hoped it could be, but it seemed only a remote possibility—after all, we knew about the collaborators, infiltrators, and stool pigeons among us.

We came to a stretch of uneven, bumpy land which would present very treacherous footing to us, walking as we were in total darkness. I was in great pain from my ankle, and the pressure produced by the swelling made walking even more painful still. We stopped a second, just long enough for me to take out a knife and cut my boot from the top almost down to the toe. That relieved the pain and pressure a little, and we continued our march until we came to some flatter land. The moon shed its white light over the yellow-brown landscape. We were at an open space, and even though there were no houses nearby, without the protection of undergrowth we felt quite exposed. Any campesino or militiaman passing by might see us.

We lay on the ground on our stomachs and looked all around. Brito said we'd have to run across that stretch of open territory. Since I couldn't run, Brito carried me fireman-style, with incredible agility and strength that came from some reservoir unimaginable to me. He ran for almost two hundred yards with me on his back. When we came to wooded ground again, Brito was as fresh as though he'd not been carrying a thing.

Soon we came to the first road. It was wide, and on each side was a barbed-wire fence for cattle and a ditch razed of vegetation which was the only shoulder of the road. We had to cross with all possible care that a vehicle coming along wouldn't catch us unawares in the open. We heard an engine far off, and we flattened ourselves against the ground as much as we could, hiding among the weeds. The vehicle approached. It was a Soviet-made ZIL truck. It sped by, raising a huge cloud of yellowish dust.

"Let's go! Now!"

And in the same breath, Boitel slid on his back under the lowest strand of barbed wire. Then I went, and Ulises and Brito brought up the rear. We rolled across the highway, since crossing on foot would have given us too high a profile. Before we went into the little pine grove on the other side, we put out some more pieces of cloth sprinkled with pepper for the blood-hounds. There was no more barking to be heard. The night was calm and quiet.

I found a straight stick to use as a cane. Twice more we had to cross open ground, and each time Brito carried me on his back, in spite of my protests; I didn't want to wear him down. But Brito had a truly admirable sense of comradeship and an optimism which breathed new life into the group.

I recall that Ulises, to cheer me up, told me that all I had was a simple dislocation in my ankle and that with much worse than that he had once finished out a soccer match. In spite of the desperate enterprise we had entered into, our morale was high, and we were delighted to be doing what we were doing. The one that felt worst physically was me. Boitel's stress fractures hurt him, but he walked without aid and was only shaky if he hit a hole or depression in the ground.

We came up on the second road. We were on course, and our map showed all the details we needed to orient ourselves exactly. We left a crude palm-thatched hut behind on the right. The house dogs smelled us and barked.

The vegetation began to change, and mosquitoes began to swarm around us in clouds and pepper us with bites. We were approaching the swamps of Júcaro, at the mouth of the Júcaro River. That was our destination—the boat should be there waiting for us at one o'clock in the morning.

Brito was in the lead, our scout. The river was only a few yards ahead.

To our right there was a dirt road which ran to the little wooden bridge indicated on our map. Here we had to veer to the left, toward the east.

Little by little the landscape had changed. Now we were in a thick undergrowth of high weeds and palm trees bristling with thorns on their trunks and the undersides of their fronds. We were advancing parallel to the river. A housing project appeared off to the left, and to skirt it we walked down closer to the river. We crossed another dirt road, and Brito went ahead to reconnoiter.

As we waited for him to come back and report, everything seemed quiet. The sounds of the night, the buzzing and chirping of insects, and the occasional frog were all we heard. The water in the marshes came up to our ankles. It was cold, and a light north wind began to blow a little stronger. That was a blessing for us, because it swept away the clouds of mosquitoes. I had lost one of my gloves, the left one, I didn't know where. I had realized it before we left the second false scent for the dogs. I couldn't take my hand out of my pocket, the mosquitoes had bitten it so much.

Ten minutes, and Brito hadn't returned. We began to get a little impatient. Why was he taking so long? Ulises offered to go looking for him, but Boitel said we should give him five more minutes. Finally Brito appeared. He had been watching a boat, but it had gone up the river. We were exactly on line with the agreed-on point. Boitel looked at the watch the gatekeeper had let us take. We had arrived thirty minutes early. In another half hour, we thought, our ship would be there, and by dawn we would be miles and miles away on the open sea, headed for Grand Cayman. We figured that was the route, south-southeast, that our enemies would least expect. They would figure we'd head north, for Cuba, or due west, to Mexico's Yucatán Peninsula.

We moved up as close as we dared to the shoreline. The swamp was almost impassable from time to time; the vegetation grew thicker and thicker. But we came to the shore at last. Boitel sent Brito ahead to survey the area and make sure we were in the right place; he was to keep looking out to sea, and if he saw our boat appear, he was to return immediately. We could see the ocean perfectly.

Ten minutes of one. A light gusty wind kept blowing, but there was not a single boat in all the area our eyes took in.

Brito came back with the results of his observations. On the other side of the mouth of the river was the militia camp that the map indicated, and to our left, as far as we had come, nothing but swamp and mangroves. But we knew that a little farther on there were some other smaller militia camps. We were exactly at the point we had agreed on.

Boitel looked at the watch impatiently, and when we gestured to him to tell us what time it was, he pulled down his glove and stretched out his wrist. We weren't speaking, because in the silence of the night our voices might carry and we might be discovered.

From the river, a few fishing boats went out to sea. They passed before us with their lanterns bobbing and swaying, but our ship did not arrive. One o'clock. One-thirty. Two. At three o'clock in the morning, we began to be really discouraged. What could have happened? We were in the exact place at the time and day that we had all agreed on. We couldn't understand. The people that were coming to pick us up knew that we were exposing ourselves to virtually certain death if we were captured.

At six o'clock in the morning, when the first light of dawn began to climb over the horizon and the sound of the militiamen on the other side of the river came to us like a distant murmur, we pulled back from the coast. The people in our boat had agreed to come to the pickup point two days in a row. That night we would be there again, in the same place, in eighteen hours. God would help us, and I entrusted myself once more to His care as the sun dyed the high clouds scarlet and seagulls began to soar and dive through the sky.

18 / The Pursuit

I t was Little Prick, whom we had almost literally run into the night before, who handled the headcount at the Circulars and who therefore sounded the alarm.

Carrión and the others had taken off the aluminum rings holding up the cut bars and thrown them on the cell floor. When Little Prick raised his head and saw the hole in the window, he stopped dead. More than a thousand pairs of eyes were watching him. He ran off shouting, "Escape! Escape!"

Within ten minutes Lieutenant Pomponio, debuting in his very first olive-green uniform, arrived at the Circular. He called Lorenzo to the main gate and ordered all the prisoners to form up for a physical count, a count which would be performed not by the numbers but by names and a comparison with an ID card with our photographs.

They discovered that the four cards left over at the end of the count were ours.

At the end of the count, they went out and tried to find traces we might have left under the window. Pomponio squatted down laboriously (he had an enormous belly) and raised now a stone, now a little blade of grass. From the Circular, inmates began to yell at him:

"Cold! Colder! Warmer! Warmer! *Hot!*"

The prisoners could make fun of the guards like that because even though they knew what was coming for them in the reprisal inspection, they felt that they had a stake in our escape. It was a triumph over the common enemy. We had put to rest forever the myth that no one could ever escape from the prison, and those of us who had pulled it off stood as symbols of the political prisoners' spirit of combativeness and rebellion. After our departure our friends could tell the authorities that our plans were to go to the conference in Punta del Este to denounce the human-rights abuses and violations and the tortures that political prisoners underwent in Cuba. They thought we were already off the Island, since Carrión knew we were going to be picked up at a point on the coast.

Political Police officers with dogs began to go along the fences trying to find the place we had gotten out by, but it was futile. All the fences were intact. The security cordon had not been violated. The guards posted in the guard huts had not noticed anything out of the ordinary. The guards making rounds around the Circulars had not noticed anything either.

"How did they get out?" Lieutenant Tarrau asked Lorenzo. Lorenzo told him he didn't know. Then Tarrau called out the prisoner who was head of the floor, the man who had assumed that responsibility the night before. He stepped forward. He wore a fearful look on his face—which he was very far from feeling, since he thought we were already far away. The prisoner told Tarrau that he had seen us climb down out of the window dressed as soldiers and that Lieutenant Paneque and another officer had been waiting for us in the street outside in a jeep. We had gotten into the jeep and the vehicle had driven off toward the Headquarters Building.

"I didn't say anything because that's a problem between soldiers," Rolando finished.

That "declaration" was a bomb. The director ran off to report what he had just heard.

Believing that story was the only alternative the authorities had. If the security cordon had not been broken through, then the escape could have been carried out only with internal assistance from guards or soldiers. That was simple logic. When coupled with the universal suspicion so characteristic of the Communist system, it led the Political Police to order all officers and soldiers who had been on duty since the night before confined to barracks, detained, and forbidden to leave the prison area. The suspiciousness of the system had once again fed mistrust between even closest comrades, had inclined the authorities to see everyone, even men they had worked with for years, as enemies or potential enemies, who had no doubt "sold out" to capitalist interests.

Major Lorenzo, several gatekeepers, and Rolando, the man who had stood up for us and then invented that story about the jeep, were all transferred to the punishment-cell building. There was a reception committee waiting for them there. They were ordered to take off their clothes and stand completely naked before Lieutenant Pomponio and his platoon. Pomponio was wielding a twisted electrical cord. His eight-year-old son, whom Pomponio often took with him to show him how to treat the enemies of the Revolution, accompanied him. The boy grew up in that climate of cruelty and barbarity and violence. By the time he was twelve years old, he too always walked around with an electrical cord to beat the prisoners with.

The prisoners refused to strip. Sergeant Naranjito raised the saber he always had hanging at his belt and dealt the first blow. The guards beat them until their clothes hung in tatters. Then they dragged them into the cells, helpless and dazed.

. . .

We camped at the very entrance of the most inhospitable part of the swamp. Before us was a flat area about a hundred yards wide on which grew a waist-high weed called *caguaso,* a grass with hollow tubular leaves about the thickness of a cigarette. The whole area was low and marshy. So was the place we were hiding in, though there were a few trees with tall, thin trunks and tan leaves. Some palm trees grew only about nine feet high, their trunks and leaves covered with long spiky thorns. They were very dangerous, since the least carelessness on our part could plunge one of those thorns into our face or eyes.

Scattered here and there were some small rises of dark, moist virgin earth. The area was a haven for birds and mosquitoes. The dangerous pools of quicksand, which could swallow up a cow, began a little farther south. Brito was the only one of the group with any experience of that kind of terrain; he had acquired his experience in his years of caiman hunting, a risky business he had gone into when he was just a teenager.

We maintained strict silence the whole time, anxiously awaiting the night, which would offer us a little more protection and moreover bring our boat. We ate a little bar of chocolate and another of sugar. We scooped water up into some small plastic bags and added Halazone tablets to purify it. We drank it an hour later. The mosquitoes were attacking us furiously. My unprotected left hand had been bitten pitilessly by then, and it was very red and itchy.

Brito went off a little way and climbed up into the top of a tree to survey our surroundings. Everything seemed calm. At about midday we heard the distant sound of an engine. It was coming closer. It was a small, low-flying plane, which passed just to the north of our position. The search had begun.

In the afternoon we had to hide even more carefully when we heard the unmistakable sound of a helicopter. This helicopter passed directly above our heads, almost brushing the tops of the trees, but there was no way we could be discovered in our olive-green uniforms and hidden in among the trees as we were. From time to time we could hear the sound of machine-gun fire, muted almost completely by the distance, but we didn't make any connection between that firing and the search for us. Instead we figured it was one of the military maneuvers the authorities frequently held in the area. But that was not what it was at all. The search, on an unprecedented scale, had been mounted that very morning. We later learned in detail what had taken place.

Since on the previous day, the day of our escape, the prisoners in Circular 3 had had a visit, thousands of family members were on Isla de Pinos, so the first thing the authorities did was prohibit their return to Cuba. They surrounded the villages of Nueva Gerona, Santa Fe, and Santa Barbara and performed house-by-house searches. The highways that ran toward the south were closed and only military vehicles and controlled traffic were allowed to travel. Family members in any way suspect, according to the criteria of the military, were detained. Soon the Nueva Gerona jail was bursting at the seams, so the military jammed the overflow detainees into the little park in the village and surrounded them with a cordon of armed guards.

We learned later from "the horse's mouth"—William Gálvez, the commander of the search operation—that when Castro found out that Boitel had escaped, he personally called Lieutenant Tarrau and told him that if Boitel got off Isla de Pinos he, Tarrau, would serve out Boitel's thirty-five-year sentence.

Naturally, then, a state of alert was declared across the Island. Thousands of militiamen and regular troops were called out to hunt us down. Patrols in vehicles covered all the roads and highways and set up roadblocks. The boats that had gone out to fish the night before from ports on the north coast were called back by radio, and patrol cutters ran up and down the coasts. The strategy for the land search was to throw out a dragnet of foot soldiers over the whole southern part of the Island. They were told that we were armed, so whenever a platoon came to a little stand of trees or some other overgrown area that they thought might offer shelter to us escapees, the troops fell full length on the ground, set up their Czech B-Z machine guns, and opened fire. Then they went into the woods to search. That, then, had been the cause of the bursts of fire we had been hearing off and on.

The hotels and guest houses nearby were assaulted by the Political Police. In one of them they arrested Carmen, Boitel's girlfriend. Lieutenant Gálvez interrogated her personally and threatened her with jail if her boyfriend escaped abroad.

In the late afternoon, Brito glimpsed soldiers aproaching the area where we were hiding. Before us lay the broad expanse covered with waist-high *caguaso,* and behind us was the little woods at the edge of which we were camped. When the guards began to fire into the woods, a rain of leaves and twigs cut down by the bullets fell on us. The bursts of fire were passing over our heads, but we hunched down to try to protect ourselves. We brushed out the marks our bodies had left in the place and crept off little by little toward the right of the circle of troops. The firm surface of the swamp where the vegetation began spread in a semicircle. The soldiers, as they continued their march, would have to come out onto the treeless area where only the *caguaso* grew.

When the first soldiers appeared, we were already moving along the edge of the rough. They were walking in a fan shape. They knew that the Júcaro military camp was just beyond the swampy fringe, and they didn't fire because of that. Probably the nearness of the military encampment led them to think that it was impossible that we would hide there, and that conclusion in turn no doubt caused them to be less than careful about combing the area.

Between the last soldier and the area of vegetation, to our right, there were about thirty yards without guards to close up the fan. We slunk along that flank, protected by the foliage. We crawled over some stretches. We had the advantage of being able to see without being seen. The real danger lay in their deciding suddenly to fan out, as they were supposed to, with soldiers inside the swamp. But they didn't do that.

However, the last guard detoured a little, toward our position; we heard the noise of his boots crushing the *caguaso* and squishing through the watery marsh. But he corrected his path and went once again straight ahead, passing bare yards from us. The guards didn't even enter the area that we had just abandoned. We were safe now; at least this time we had escaped the net. They moved off toward the south, looking for the dirt road and the little bridge that crossed the river, while we remained in the same place for about thirty minutes. Then we went back to our original camp. They wouldn't look there anymore. They had searched badly, but they would say, and even think, they had done it well, and their superiors would assume the zone had been scoured.

We didn't know it at the time, but in the port of Gerona a Canadian ship was loading grapefruit. It occurred to the Cuban authorities that we might have boarded the cargo ship, and they tried to search it. The captain of the boat flatly refused. During that time Canada maintained excellent trade relations with Cuba, and it was very important to the Cuban government to keep those relations in good repair. The Canadian captain's refusal to allow them to search the ship was interpreted by the Political Police as proof that we were aboard, but there was nothing they could do.

At eleven-thirty that night we were once again at the agreed-upon point, waiting to be picked up. The sky was clear and the stars were twinkling brightly. As on the night before, a few fishing boats were anchored to the east of our position. My leg hurt terribly. It was badly inflamed and swollen, and the efforts that I had asked of it during the day had worsened it. Around my ankle where the shock of the fall had been worst, the skin was purple. I had been taking aspirin all day long, but it didn't seem to help the pain. The fracture lines in his heel were bothering Boitel a little too. But all in all we couldn't complain; God had helped us and given us the self-confidence, security, and peace needed to carry out an escape like the one we had planned, which would now be engraved forever in the annals of the political prison. We had every reason to be thankful, because everything had gone smoothly for us so far—we were alive and full of hope.

One o'clock came. One-thirty. Two. Three o'clock in the morning, and the boat did not appear. We scanned the horizon anxiously, keenly, but there was nothing. They had not come to pick us up.

At dawn, as we were about to go back to our hiding place, we heard distant shouts, then some shots, and immediately heavy machine-gun fire coming from the mouth of the river. Then silence. A few minutes later, there were other voices, but we couldn't make out what they were saying. So we stayed there until the sky began to lighten.

We had slept from time to time, but we were exhausted from a general lack of sleep, and now the tension mounted even higher. The fact that the boat had not arrived the second night either discouraged us. Boitel proposed we steal a boat. Brito was a specialist in that sort of thing; he had seized several boats from the State Fishing Cooperatives to carry people escaping abroad.

The place we had settled in after the soldiers' first search operation was safe enough. Although our chocolate and sugar bars were our only nourishment, up to now they had been enough, at least in terms of calories.

At one o'clock that second day the Canadian cargo ship full of grapefruit weighed anchor and sailed down the channel toward the open sea. The Political Police believed we were hidden in its holds. An hour later, they called off the search in all areas of the Island, and they broadcast this decision to all commands, so their troops could return to their stations and camps.

The sun was beginning its descent when Brito alerted us to a large troop that was coming toward us. And in fact out of the little woods, just as before, the soldiers were advancing; this time they were practically on top of us. There were dozens of them, and before them, about ten or twelve yards ahead, a gray-haired man with an R-2 rifle was leading the march. The fan-shaped comb came right up to the edge of the swamp. We retreated as hurriedly as we could. Trying to repeat our maneuver of yesterday—that is, get a little more inside the woods and dig in a bit more—was impossible because there was so little distance between us and the soldiers.

We huddled down behind the thick trunks of the thorny palm trees. Ulises was nearest the platoon. To my right was Brito, and a little behind him was Boitel.

"Let's bear right and try to find the bridge," one of the guards shouted.

And I prayed they would do just that, since if they advanced straight ahead, we would inevitably be discovered. I frantically scrabbled in the swampy earth to bury the ID card and the maps I had. The others were no doubt doing the same thing, as we had agreed to do in case of a situation like this one.

"No, we'll have to detour if we do that. We won't go to the bridge. We'll go on ahead."

And they waded into the weeds toward our position. Just a few yards more and they would be upon us. I thought those were the last minutes of our lives. I commended myself to God and thought about my family; a flock of images rushed through my mind. I thought I was going to die there, in that horrible, smelly swamp, and I felt that invisible claw that always seizes my gut and squeezes, knotting my insides now.

"Don't shoot! We're unarmed!"

Ulises with his cry set off a chain of events. We heard the metal click of the rifle bolts, then the guards shouting at the man leading the march to get down so they could shoot.

"Don't shoot! We're unarmed!" Ulises shouted again.

The gray-haired guard who was leading the march turned to the platoon he commanded and shouted at them not to fire.

"No one shoots! That's an order!" he cried firmly.

Those were seconds of indescribable, almost unbearable tension. I believed we were going to be killed at any instant.

The gray-haired man kept shouting his order at the rest of the platoon —"Don't fire! Don't fire!" And then he turned toward us and yelled at us not to come out from behind the tree trunks, not to move until he gave the word. He wanted to keep us from being shot.*

Though only a few seconds had passed, the guards, knowing we were there and were not going to fire on them, had calmed down somewhat. They had stopped shouting hysterically at the commander to get out of the way so they would have a clear line of fire, at least. That man, to whose equanimity we owe our lives, immediately controlled the situation, controlled his men. He repeated once more for us to stay where we were. A few seconds, made hours by our anguish, passed.

"Okay. Come out now, one by one, with your hands behind your heads." Ulises came out first.

"Next." Boitel followed him, and then Brito.

"There's one of us with a bad leg," Boitel said. I limped out. There stood the four of us, our hands behind our heads, discouraged and utterly exhausted. A troop of about a hundred men surrounded us. They looked at us with fury and hatred. "We should kill them right here," one of them said, and pointed his rifle at us menacingly.

But everything had changed in a few fleeting minutes. I had never imagined that we would be captured alive. None of us, I think, even in the tiniest corner of our minds, had had that illusion. We knew our enemy only too well. And it was only the intervention of that gray-haired man, commanding the troops, that had spared us from death. And he knew that too—when he was standing near us so only we could hear him, he whispered to us that we were lucky he had been there, because if not . . . And he left the sentence hanging. We knew perfectly well what he meant.

Murmured orders and replies passed between the leader and some of his

---

*At about this point, if not before, one always asks why the boat never came. I asked Valladares and Martha this myself, and their answer was simply that the people who had said they would bring the boat never believed the four men could get out of the prison on Isla de Pinos. They had thought they were involving themselves in mere "prisoner fantasies."—Trans.

soldiers. Two of the soldiers went off to notify the nearby camp. The wind was gusting strongly. Accompanied by the leader and a small escort surrounding us, we began the march toward the dirt road to the west of our position.

I was dragging my leg, which had grown even more swollen and inflamed and was beginning to turn black around the ankle. The march over the swampy ground was extremely painful to me, since my feet kept sinking into the mud. I turned and leaned on Brito's shoulder until we came out onto the firmer ground of yellowish clay. When we came to the first fence, I went to crawl on my back under the bottom strand of barbed wire. That's the first time I remembered that I still had the old wallet with the wad of dollar bills and Cuban pesos in my back pocket. We had not been searched—we still even had the knives held to our legs with rubber bands. How was I going to get rid of that money? I decided to leave the wallet under the next fence, where there was a thick fringe of weeds and grass. Behind us came the troops. One of them kicked the wallet with the toe of his boot, and the dollar bills blew all over the field. The strong wind raised a whirl of green bills through the air.

"Dollars! Dollars!" he shouted, and rushed after the money the wind was carrying away. A mad scramble after the dollar bills ensued. The leader's order wasn't worth a centavo—his men ran wildly after what was to them the small fortune. And I never heard a word about that money again.

When we got to the dirt road, some other soldiers were already waiting for us. They fired several times into the air, as a signal to still others. We sat down on a stack of fence posts, and soon we heard the whir of a helicopter rotor. The helicopter came into view. It landed on the other side of the fence, and several officers got out. They didn't even salute. They were brusque and imposing as they approached Ulises, who was the closest one of us to them. They lifted his shirt collar at the back and turned it inside out. There they saw the labels with the factory name, which we had forgotten to cut out.

"Look, this is the work of those traitors we've got among us," one officer said to another, and he turned the collar loose with a vulgar gesture. "They gave them those uniforms."

Then he spoke to Boitel, whom he obviously knew. "Who smuggled these clothes in to you?"

Boitel just looked at him. The lieutenant repeated his question.

"There was a fat prisoner, a common prisoner, the one they call Chito," Boitel answered him at last. And from that moment on, that nonexistent common prisoner, so fat there could be no mistake, would be the one we constantly said was the person who had smuggled the uniforms and equipment in to us—uniforms and equipment the officers were incapable of suspecting had come in to us hidden in the piping of a mattress.

The officers from the helicopter walked away, and almost immediately a Soviet-made military jeep came to pick us up. We sat in back. A captain was driving. Another one was sitting beside him, turned toward us with a machine gun cocked and ready. Other officers were sitting on the jeep's fenders, and one of them, a lieutenant, took out his pistol, cocked it, and pressed it against Boitel's forehead. I knew him—he was a gangster type, one of those men the Communist Party had enrolled in the University for years and years and who never graduated, because their job was to stir up trouble, not to study. Years before, Boitel had unmasked that same agitator, who, by the grace of the Revolution, was now an officer in the Political Police. He was only too happy to be able to harass Boitel when he found him powerless, a prisoner.

I spoke to the lieutenant, because I knew Boitel would never speak a word to his tormentor. I asked him to take the pistol away from Boitel's head, since he was sitting perched on the side of the jeep, with his finger on the trigger, and all it would take was a bump in the road to fire the gun and blow Boitel's brains out.

"Tell *him* to ask me. Tell *him* to say please, very politely, to take the gun away, if he's scared."

Boitel was insulted, almost rabid. "I'm a thousand times more a man than you are under any circumstances, even with your pistol and your uniform. You're nothing but a punk, a loser."

The officer from the Political Police shoved Boitel's head back with the pistol. Ulises, Brito, and I began to protest, and the captain finally ordered the lieutenant to put the weapon away.

Soon we turned off the dusty, bumpy road onto the highway. On both sides there were mobilized soldiers making a living fence along the routes of travel. The helicopter was flying above the jeep.

We entered the prison through the main guardpost. We were going back into that hell, who knew now for how many years more. But we were ready for the revenge they would take against us. Leaning on Ulises and Brito, I began to go up the stairs toward the Headquarters offices, and I saw a big party of soldiers waiting to receive us up there. My leg still hurt terribly, but I was luckier than Sergio Bravo had been, a few hours before.

Perhaps at the very moment the guards were approaching our camp out there in the swamp, the reprisal inspection in the Circulars was being carried out. Incensed by our escape, the soldiers took it out on the prisoners. They set up sandbags with machine guns aimed at the doors of the Circulars and entered carrying their rifles with fixed bayonets. They wounded dozens of men.

Sergio Bravo was barely thirty years old. He lived on the fifth floor of Circular 3. He had an athletic build, and he was very agile, full of energy and enthusiasm. But he was dedicated to preaching the word of God even more than to athletics. His constant religious work was a great help in the prison in the struggle of love against hate, of Christ against evil passions.

Some time before, inspired to the most unimaginable tricks and dodges, he managed to smuggle in, page by page, and lovingly put together a tiny Bible —one of those no larger than a pack of cigarettes. He had managed so far to save the book from the searches; he had it carefully camouflaged in a niche in the cell wall.

When the screaming of the guards began and then the beatings down below, Sergio, who was lying on his cot, jumped to his feet and ran and looked down toward the open front gate, and the spectacle horrified him. They were committing butchery down there. He rushed down the stairs, three steps at a time, but when he got to the fourth floor, he suddenly remembered the Bible, which he had left under his pillow, outside the hiding place. There was no question that the guards would confiscate it. He knew the blows they'd give him for going back up would be dreadful, but that didn't matter—he went back up to hide the Bible. His powerful legs carried him back up the stairs. He rushed into his cell with his heart in his throat, but he managed to hide the book. It was only then that his situation came back to him in all its horror. He went out into the hallway again, running at full speed, the last race of his life.

The guards had already begun to fire. A rifle bullet shattered the bones of his leg just below his knee. The impact was like a blow from a hatchet.

While I was marching leaning on Ulises' and Brito's shoulders, Sergio Bravo's leg was being amputated. He would never run again. We learned later that the amputation wasn't really necessary, but the surgery to reconstruct his leg was too difficult for the military doctors, so they simply decided to cut it off.

19 / Punishment Pavilion

he escort pushed us into Lieutenant Tarrau's office. He was not there at the moment because he had gone out with Lieutenant Cruz, an old drunk I had known since I was a boy in the port city of Coloma. He was a Communist Party militant, even at that time, and the Revolution made him chief of the Political Police on Isla de Pinos.

On the director's desk we saw stacks of photographs of the four of us, the leftovers of the photographs that had been distributed all across the Island to identify us. They pointed us to a couch, and we sat down. Immediately Lieutenant Paneque arrived, the man our comrade had accused of having picked us up in the jeep, but none of us knew anything about that then. Still, his politeness did strike us as very strange and puzzle us a bit. He was always repressive, bullying, and despotic—but no doubt he thought we planned to implicate him in our escape, so he was treating us affably in hopes we would not. He knew that if we declared he had helped us, he'd instantly go to jail. Had we been in any other than that peculiar circumstance, you can be sure we would have seen very different conduct from him.

Suddenly a storm of soldiers broke into the office. At their forefront was Commander William Gálvez, territorial chief of Isla de Pinos, who like some of the others knew Boitel. Gálvez was famous for his eccentricities, such as roller-skating in full uniform through the streets of the city of Matanzas and right into the revolutionary tribunals, for which he was a prosecutor. He'd coast into the courtroom, still on his skates.

Gálvez was very interested in the details of the escape. He was by nature something of an adventurer, and he couldn't hide his admiration. At one point he said they knew a submarine from the Central Intelligence Agency was going to pick us up! Boitel denied it, of course, but Gálvez didn't believe him, and an argument erupted. Boitel kept denying that any submarine whatsoever had been going to pick us up.

"How were you going to get off the Island, then?"

"We thought we'd steal a boat."

"But who do you think you are?" this peculiar commander almost screamed, not imagining it was possible for us to have done that.

"Just think a minute, Commander—would it be any harder for us to steal a boat than to do what we'd already done?"

Gálvez was silent. He stood there looking fixedly at Boitel. He turned around and murmured softly, "Yes, that's true."

Nonetheless, the Political Police made sure the story of the CIA submarine was spread around, and they gave that version to Martha González, a Cuban exile who came back from the United States expressly to write a book full of that kind of falsehoods and lies. It was titled *Under Oath* and it was taken from materials she was given by the Political Police agency itself.

When Director Tarrau came into his office, total silence fell. He looked at us with rage and hatred almost boiling out of his eyes. He was snorting. The wings of his nose were livid, and it was obvious that he was making a tremendous effort to contain himself.

"You men are going to find out now . . ." He was so enraged he choked on the rest of the sentence. Director Tarrau did not make idle threats. In his hands he had all the power necessary to keep his word.

My spine froze. All this was like a dream to me, these experiences were alien to my entire previous life. I went over the last few days, and I could hardly believe that I was really one of the actors in such events. My life until the day of my detention had passed in a perfectly conventional way, like the life of any young man my age, unremarkable for any adventures or unusual circumstances, lacking anything worth other people's attention, much less worth being the talk of the whole Island. And suddenly, there I was, almost stunned by everything that had occurred.

Tarrau began the interrogation. The only one of the group that he knew was Boitel, and so all the accusations were directed toward him. He was called to account for everything. And for him there was the special hatred which had been personally expressed by Castro on many occasions. The rancor for Boitel showed in Tarrau's eyes. He couldn't forget Castro's threat to jail him if Boitel escaped.

It seemed to me that the responsibility for our escape should be shared, just as we had shared the hope of success, so I spoke up. I told Tarrau and Gálvez that Boitel wasn't the only one of us responsible—the escape had been started from my cell, I had cut through the bars of the window. Brito and Ulises took responsibility for their parts in the attempt, too.

Boitel smiled with satisfaction. He had known that his comrades would never let him down.

"Oh, don't worry—all of you are going to pay. You'll all be held responsible. The four of you will rot in the punishment cells. You'll never come out. And you're going to be sorry for what you've done to *me.*"

Tarrau took our desperation to escape, which was perfectly natural and legitimate in any prisoner, as a personal offense, and so he threatened us for what we had done to *him*.

Lieutenant Paneque, more solicitous by the minute, brought us pitchers of cold water; then he ordered food for us. The man's kind attentions made me fear a proportionately brutal reprisal when he got us into the cells. I took his concern as a perverted kind of sadism: He planned to make us believe nothing would happen to us, and then he'd turn on us with vicious fury.

They ordered us out of the office. We went downstairs to the entrance of the main security fence. Commander William Gálvez and Tarrau headed up the procession. Lieutenant Paneque took me by the arm to help me down the stairs.

"Thanks, Lieutenant, I can lean on my friends."

"No. They're exhausted," he insisted.

"Really, Lieutenant, I've got mud all over me, and you're going to get your uniform dirty," I told him, trying to find an excuse. But Paneque had made up his mind once and for all to help me.

"That's okay, it's nothing," he said. And he helped me whether I wanted him to or not.

What must that man have felt, seeing himself, in a manner of speaking, at our mercy? He was feared for his cruelty and his abuse of his position, and now he was afraid that one of us men, whom he might in other circumstances have beaten into senselessness, was going to implicate him in our escape. So he was making desperate efforts to keep us from dragging him into the punishment cells with us.

More than two hundred yards separated us from the punishment-cell block. They put me into a jeep, but they walked the others down the road, to exhibit them so the whole presidio could see that we had been captured. They wanted to parade their triumph.

When the jeep stopped in front of the punishment-cell pavilion, Boitel, Ulises, and Brito with their escort were just walking between the Circulars. As the prisoners saw them, they began to call and wave to the three men. The soldiers were enraged by the show of comradeship and friendship, and they shoved Boitel on. He stumbled several steps and almost fell.

That abuse provoked a violent reaction from the prisoners. Dejected and frustrated at seeing our capture, they vented all the hostility and disgust they were suffering in their shouting at the guards.

Commander Gálvez put his hand to his crotch, cupped his testicles, and gestured vulgarly at the prisoners. A voice cried out above the rest then, the voice of Ubaldo ("Manino") Alvarez, one of the bravest and youngest men of the presidio, a man who had been a comrade of Gálvez' in the struggle against Batista.

"William, this is Manino talking. You're a coward. Come in here and push *me.*"

Manino was a brave man, indeed, to have identified himself like that and yelled "Coward!"—daring one of those who could dispose of any prisoner's very life without having to answer for it. And Commander Gálvez, stung by the cries and shouts of the prisoners, practically went berserk. He bent down by the edge of the walkway, picked up some stones, and began throwing them at the cell windows. As the troop of soldiers finally came up to where I was waiting, the cries of the prisoners were still following them.

"I need to see a doctor," I told them. Commander Gálvez looked at me furiously.

"Do you mean to tell me that you're cynical enough to ask for medical help?"

When we were all together, they took us into the first large room, where the punishment cells were located. The area had been evacuated for our arrival. Eleven cells were built into a large space which had not originally been designed for that purpose. The old-fashioned, high-ceilinged construction of the building had allowed them to erect cells about seven feet high. The ceiling of the cells was made of chain-link fencing with large openings, fencing exactly like that they used for the fences around the presidio. From the ceiling to the roof of the building there was enough space for the guards to walk on top of our cells and keep complete surveillance over the prisoners in isolation.

The doors of the cells were covered over with sheets of steel welded to the bars. The only opening was a narrow space at the very bottom of the cell door, close to the floor, and to one side, where the steel plating didn't reach. That was the hole through which the mess plate would be passed to us.

In one corner of each cell, in the center of a slight depression, was a hole that served as a latrine. A piece of bent tubing above it was our shower. The control knob itself was outside the cell, and the guards on duty controlled it. The cells were completely empty, so the granite floor was our bed. Each cell measured about seven feet long by six feet wide. Years later, I would be in many other punishment cells, and these on Isla de Pinos were the largest of all.

I was sent into cell 1, Boitel into 3, Ulises into 5, and Brito into 7, so there was an empty cell separating each occupied one. Lieutenant Paneque and two guards took charge of me.

"You have to take off all your clothes. It's an order from upstairs." He said this without his usual arrogance and despotism. He couldn't stop worrying about the possibility that we would accuse him. I think he must have decided not to bring up the subject directly because he was always accompanied by other soldiers. His superiors weren't allowing him to be alone with any of us even for a moment. After I found out what had happened, I grew certain he was being watched, and that it was only because he was a member of the Party that he hadn't been jailed at once. They were just waiting to interrogate us.

I began to take off my clothes, sitting on the floor. The men who had captured us hadn't even bothered to search me, so I still had the knife strapped to my leg with rubber-band "garters"; I was also wearing under my shirt the T-shirt with the bottles of vitamins, the water-purifying tablets, the matches, and all the rest.

They didn't even let me keep my underwear. I sat there, completely naked, in the darkness of the cell. It was cold, and I was suffering from the throbbing pain in my leg. The swelling was black. When the soldiers had left our cells and closed the main barred gate that opened into the outside hallway, Boitel called us and asked us what cells we were in. There was no confusion for me because I was in the first one. Ulises was the only one who didn't know exactly which cell he was in. He hadn't thought to look at the number painted in black above his door.

I don't know exactly how much time had passed—an hour, maybe— when they brought us food. I will never forget it. There was white rice and tinned Russian beef with sweet potatoes. It wasn't the food the Circulars were given, of course, but rather the food the soldiers themselves ate. After the meal, several officers in uniform came to each of us. They threw clothes in and ordered us to get dressed, they were going to take us out. Leaning on Brito and the wall, hopping along on one leg, I crossed the interior patio, and we went into the main room of the building.

They had set up long tables with typewriters. Dozens of soldiers made way for us. The whole off-duty population of the garrison and their officers were packed into the room. A middle-aged woman was sitting before one typewriter. She was the judge of Nueva Gerona, and she was going to read the charges against us. To an untutored spectator, this could easily have appeared to be a perfectly correct legal proceeding. (And indeed the reading of charges was performed, but we were never taken to trial. One day the sentence came to us from the tribunal. It had sentenced us to ten years more in prison for the crimes of breaking our original sentences and damage to state property. This last charge against us reflected the crime of cutting the bars of the windows.) Commander Gálvez, the local chief of the Political Police, and other officers in civilian clothing who had come from Havana questioned us at length.

The men from the Political Police tried to get us to tell them how we had obtained our uniforms, the hacksaw blades, and the other equipment. Our answer was always the same: the fat common prisoner, the one called Chito, had been the link who had provided us with the necessary materials. They knew as well as we did that no such person existed, but there was no way to shake us from that response. The interrogation began to get complicated when they asked us how we had gotten out of the presidio. None of them believed our detailed explanation of how we had gone out through the guardhouse. It really seemed so impossible to accept.

"We know there are soldiers who helped you men in this escape attempt of yours," one of the civilians, a Political Police agent, said. "And we know more about that than you think we do. You were taken out and left outside the security cordon, out of danger," he added.

Boitel and I, who were sitting next to each other, simply looked at each other. We didn't want this to get so involved that we would wind up in a situation we had never intended and that really didn't interest us in the least. Implicating a nonexistent Chito hurt no one; now it was obvious that our interrogators believed guards had aided us, and that meant *innocent* men were being implicated.

There was a great expectancy among the soldiers that surrounded us; they were hanging on every word, almost hypnotized by the course things were taking.

The discussion grew heated. Our explanation was always the same—we had gone out through the guardhouse.

"You know all these details—the guardhouse, the ditch behind it, all that —because you can look out the window of the Circular and see it. Dozens of prisoners could give us the same description."

That seemed a perfectly logical assertion, so they kept going over and over those moments, until at last I remembered the large iron gear wheels hidden among the weeds in the yard, over which I'd almost fallen when I was pretending to urinate to give Boitel time to find the ditch. There was no way to make out those wheels from the Circular. I described them to the officer. He looked at me skeptically, called over another of the civilians, and they left the room. Soon he was back. He had been in the guardhouse yard and could see for himself that the wheels were there. Only then did they believe the story we were telling them.

We learned later that the lieutenant in charge of the searches, a man called Tareco, or "Odds and Ends," another of those bullying types the prison was full of, was sent off to a work farm, sentenced to ten years in prison for laxity in pursuit of his duties in the searches. They held him responsible for our smuggling in what we needed for the escape. They never did learn how we managed to do it. Only now, after more than twenty years, are the facts being brought to light in this book.

Guards returned us to the cells and stripped us again. They didn't close the cell door, and that detail caught my attention. I was sitting on the floor; outside I heard the voices of several approaching soldiers. Three or four of them, or maybe five—I'm not sure how many—appeared before my open cell. Now that the interrogations and all the paperwork were finished, they were going to settle accounts with us, collect what we owed them for having tried to escape. Since the light bulb in the hallway was at their back, I didn't realize they were armed with thick twisted electric cables and truncheons.

"Stand up! We're going to make sure you never even *want* to try to escape again!"

My stomach tightened more than ever before. I felt such pressure in my chest that I could hardly breathe. In my months of prison I had learned only too well what these reactions were—they were fear, terror, and in only a few seconds the vision of what was about to happen passed through my mind.

They were already beating my friends. I heard the dry thud of the blows on their naked bodies and the cries and curses of the guards.

"Stand up, faggot!" the guard shouted again as he raised his arm. Suddenly, everything was a whirl—my head spun around in terrible vertigo. They beat me as I lay on the floor. One of them pulled at my arm to turn me over and expose my back so he could beat me more easily. And the cables fell more directly on me. The beating felt as if they were branding me with a red-hot branding iron, but then suddenly I experienced the most intense, unbearable, and brutal pain of my life. One of the guards had jumped with all his weight on my broken, throbbing leg.

I could not sleep that night. My back burned and stung as though it were on fire, and the pain in my leg was almost enough to make me faint. Thus, Lieutenant Tarrau's threat had been carried out, the threat he had made only a few hours before in his headquarters office, that we would pay. . . .

20 / The Ho Chi Minh Pole

The next morning, they welded the doors shut. Lieutenant Cruz, head of the Political Police, told us Castro had personally ordered it done. We were told we'd stay in those cells not for months, but for years.

The military doctor was a Communist who tried to look like Lenin, wearing the same kind of goatee. He was more than six feet tall, had very white skin, and was heavy. His name was Lamar. He wore the uniform of a doctor, but he was a sadist. When I asked him for medical care, he looked through the peephole, stared at my leg, and told me he hoped it turned into a good case of gangrene, "so I can come in myself and cut it off."

That frightened and worried me. I was afraid I would get an incurable infection. My leg was still very swollen and inflamed, and all around the ankle and the calf, the swelling had taken on a blackish color and was shiny from being so stretched and swollen.

Absolutely no one could enter that hallway. The Security Corps was carrying out an investigation aimed at discovering and detaining all our contacts and collaborators. They brought in Oruña and Sierra from Circular 3, the two prisoners who had been in charge of the radio. They had been betrayed by another prisoner. The arrival of Oruña and Sierra allowed us to find out all the things that had happened after our escape.

I couldn't stand up, so I moved about sitting down, dragging myself along on my buttocks. The situation grew more difficult when they named as our personal guards the soldiers who had been on duty at the guardhouse the night of the escape. The guards overseeing the punishment cells, then, were guards who were being punished themselves. The fury and sadism of those men defies description, especially the tall blond young man who had been on duty at the machine gun, singing campesino songs—he considered us responsible for his disgrace.

This guard found himself a five-gallon pail, like those used to wash the floors, and took it in to the common prisoners to urinate and defecate in. When he had it about half full of filth and urine and dirty water, he added a little water to it and climbed up to the chain-link ceiling of the cells. Since I hadn't been able to sleep the night before because of the cold, I had taken advantage of the relative warmth of noon to lie down in one corner to try to sleep a little. I was exhausted not only by sleeplessness but pain as well.

The shock of the cold was what woke me. I was bathed from top to bottom and sitting in a caramel-colored, foul-smelling puddle. Down my face and neck were sliding pieces of excrement. I was the first of us prisoners to receive the impact of that bath, and it took me so off guard that I opened my mouth in surprise. Chunks of excrement fell into my mouth. The guard was above my head, on the other side of the chain-link. I saw the enormous soles of his boots. He was looking at me with loathing. He did not say a single word. Neither did I.

With my index finger I flicked some remains of the excrement off my shoulders and thighs, and I dragged myself over to the latrine to turn on the shower. It was turned off from outside. I called the guard. He didn't answer. Then I shouted to Boitel and the others and told them what had happened. They began to scream, "Water! Water!" The blond guard, the same one who had thrown the excrement on me, came into the hallway and ordered us to shut up. He said there was an order from higher echelons to give us water only to drink, and that only at mealtimes.

A little while later another soldier arrived with a wrench and closed off the taps located in the hallway, out of our reach, putting as much force into the wrench as he could. For more than three months the taps were closed. In all that time, we were not permitted to bathe, even once. There were only those baths of urine and shit that the guards bestowed on us from the ceiling.

The filth dried in my hair and on my body. The terrible smell of it filled the cell.

There are certain things one never thinks about when one reads or hears about a prisoner confined in a cell under the conditions we were kept in; there are things that are simply inconceivable outside a jail. And among those things are a man's bodily functions. We had to relieve ourselves there, in that hole in the ground in a corner of the cell. But when we were done, there was absolutely nothing to clean ourselves with, no water or soap or paper or even a piece of cloth. We had to use our fingers for toilet paper— there was no other way.

Boitel was shouting and arguing with a guard. I didn't know what it was all about.

"Come down here and do that, you coward. You people are despicable! You just do it because you've got that uniform on. Otherwise, you wouldn't dare!"

"What's happening, Boitel?" Ulises asked.

Boitel told us he had been jabbed with a pole. Actually, I didn't understand what he was talking about until the guard walking along the roof of the cells came to mine. He had a long wooden pole, rounded at the end, and I immediately understood what had happened.

Boitel had been sleeping, and the guard had slyly stuck the pole through the holes in the chain-link ceiling and poked him with it to wake him up. From that day on, the "Ho Chi Minh poles" would be used to torture us and send us to the verge of madness. There was no way to escape them, since the guard, up on top there, dominated the whole cell, and he could prod us whenever he wanted. The end of the pole was blunt and didn't wound us, but it hurt, and it didn't let us sleep. That was what they wanted.

There was only one guard who didn't prod us, and when every three days he came on duty in the area, we could sleep six straight hours. But as soon as his relief came, the new man went up onto the chain-link ceiling, pole in hand, and started prodding us. Then he went down; in an hour he came back up again, and once more, the sudden awakening.

I was utterly exhausted. The lack of sleep and the tension were seriously affecting me. I sought God then. My conversations with Him brought me a spiritual strength that gave me new energy. I never asked Him to get me out of there; I didn't think that God should be used for that kind of request. I only asked that He allow me to resist, that He give me the faith and spiritual strength to bear up under these conditions without sickening with hatred. I only prayed for Him to accompany me. And His presence, which I felt, made my faith an indestructible shield.

They continued slopping the pails of urine and excrement over us. In the cold winter mornings, they would also throw freezing water at us. That was unpleasant, but at least it cleaned some of the excrement off the cell floor. Little by little, the latrine, without water to flush out the fecal matter, grew full. As soon as night fell, cockroaches took over the walls and floors and crawled all over my body, and their ticklish creeping often made me jump awake.

In the early mornings the sergeant of the watch came in. He went from cell to cell and shined a flashlight inside to be sure the prisoner was there. I thought it was very peculiar that I hadn't seen Little Prick even once during all those days we had been in the punishment cells. He was the soldier we had met on the little walkway in front of the hospital the afternoon of our escape, and he must have realized later that those two pairs of men he saw walk past him and even say hello were the escaped prisoners. If his superiors found out that he had seen us, that he had been face to face with us without suspecting anything, he would surely find himself in big trouble. I figured it was precisely for that reason that he hadn't showed himself around us; he was probably afraid of how we might react, or that we might say something incriminating in front of another soldier. So I set myself to watching for him. Lying on the floor, I could see a little stretch of the hallway and the entrance gate. Early one morning he finally came in. I called to him, and he stood there petrified. Since he was alone, I softly insisted that he come over.

"Please, Sergeant, it's all right. Come here." My voice was an almost inaudible whisper.

With great difficulty I stood up behind the iron plate over the bars of the door, and when Sergeant Little Prick came over, I spoke into his ear.

"Don't worry, Sergeant. We haven't said anything, and we don't intend to, about the fact that you saw us the afternoon of the escape. So if you're worried about that, you can rest easy. We don't want to do you any harm."

The sergeant's face was glued to the peephole in the cell door. I could see by the ghastly light of the hallway light bulb how his face relaxed.

"Thank you, son. . . ." And he left, but a few minutes later he came back. The morning was bitter cold. Under his heavy military overcoat he was carrying a thermos of hot chocolate. If I had been a rich man with money in the bank, I'd have paid thousands of dollars for every drop of that life-restoring liquid. It was, in fact, like sips of life—it warmed me, it gave me the sense that I could never need anything else again.

"Thank you very much, Sergeant. I'd appreciate it if you'd give a little to my friends, if there's any left."

There wasn't enough for everybody, but every time Little Prick was on duty, he figured out a way to get a little hot chocolate in to us.

When the investigations were completed, the security measures in the area of our cells were lifted and the empty cells were filled with other prisoners sentenced to solitary confinement. The guards continued torturing us with the Ho Chi Minh poles to keep us from sleeping. We could sleep only for short intervals or when it was very, very late at night and the guard dozed off—the guards' sadism didn't go so far that they would sacrifice their own sleep just to poke at us. But toward five-thirty in the morning, they would be up on the ceiling again. The relief came in about six, and they did a little warm-up and stretching with us.

I fell into a deep sleep whenever there was a chance. The need for sleep kept accumulating, and one of the most wished-for things in life became sleep—you wanted to sleep for whole days at a time. After the guards crossed the ceilings of the cells, I knew I would have a few minutes, or perhaps even a few hours, of rest, and I would sink into such a deep sleep that only the prodding of the wooden pole could wake me. It was on one of those occasions, when I was sleeping so deeply, that a rat entered the cell. These rats—as in all prisons, a starving multitude—always find a way into the cells, often by coming up through the drainpipes of the toilets if they're not covered over.

My inert body must have given him courage. Vermin intuit when it's safe to approach their prey. I don't know whether he sniffed around my feet, which was the part of my body closest to the door, first, or whether he slithered straight up to my hands and began to chew on my fingers, gnawing at them voraciously. Something must have startled him momentarily; perhaps I moved and he jumped away. But he came back. It was the guard who saved me. The rat was between my thighs, ready to devour my genitals. The guard yelled and stamped on the screen wire above and poked me. The scene he was witnessing horrified even him. The rat fled, I woke up, and that was when I felt the pain of the bites I bore on the middle finger of my right hand, in two different places. The two wounds were bleeding, which was bad enough, but what if the rat had rabies? I was aghast.

The guard came down to the peephole of the cell door. He was shocked. I showed him my bleeding hand and asked him to report that I'd been bitten by a rat, so I should be given rabies shots. I don't know whether he did; all I know is that nobody ever came to see about it. The only thing I could do was urinate on it—that was a cure the campesinos used. A few days later a thick scab had formed over the bites and a little pus had collected.

There was a prisoner named Valdés who was a stool pigeon for the garrison and had been expelled for that very reason from Circular 3. After his expulsion he lived in the punishment block, and he was a sort of factotum and "pet" of the garrison. He was the one in charge of passing out the food, taking care of the cleaning, and beating the prisoners in that area, always with the backing and protection of the guards. Several common prisoners worked under his orders. Valdés was a homosexual, and besides his other "duties" he took part in rapes of young men who were held there in the punishment pavilion. He was also illiterate—he couldn't read a word.

The first time he entered our block he picked up the wooden pole and poked Boitel, and because of that there was a tremendous row among the guards themselves. We were victims for the sole and exclusive use of the soldiers, something like big game that Valdés didn't have a license to hunt.

I don't know whether it was on his own initiative or on instructions from Lieutenant Pomponio, who was his protector, but Valdés began to urge us to send a note to our friends in the Circular. He kept telling us he had a way to smuggle notes in to them.

We got bored with that song and dance. Finally, I told Boitel I was going to give him a note to deliver.

"You're crazy! He'll turn it over to the soldiers!" he warned me, thinking I had lost my mind.

"Yeah, that's why I'm going to do it, and you'll see—he'll stop this nonsense once and for all."

When I told Valdés I wanted to send a note, he ran out like a shot and within an instant he was back again with a notebook and pencil. The message wasn't very long. It said, more or less, "The bearer of this message is an informer to the garrison. Proof that he is a stool pigeon is that he will turn this note over to one of you." I carefully folded the piece of paper. I knew Valdés couldn't read it. When I gave it to him, he asked for the notebook and pencil back, but I had already torn several sheets of paper out of the middle of it, which I folded up and hid behind the lock of the cell door, between the lock and the steel plate.

He rushed off to turn in the note. I imagine that when the soldier read it, he must have either laughed at Valdés or berated him—at any rate, at lunchtime Valdés came back to the cells in an uncontrollable rage. He flung the mess plate at me furiously. It was boiled macaroni, freezing cold. When I put the first spoonful into my mouth, I spat it out instantly. Valdés had poured kerosene on it. He did the same thing with the others' food. And from that day on when the food for us arrived, Valdés dished up four plates, went out and set them down in the yard, in the cold, so they could "cool off," and then poured kerosene on them. Our complaints and demands to the soldiers did no good; Valdés kept ruining our food, until I made up my mind to put the situation before Little Prick. I don't know exactly what he did, but the food never came with kerosene anymore.

As the weeks without bathing went on, a dark, greasy, scablike layer of filth formed over every inch of my body. My underarms, groin, and scalp almost drove me mad with itching; a pimply rash broke out on my head. A fungus infection began to spread—the filth that covered my body was an ideal medium for fungus and bacteria.

They brought us water at lunchtime and dinnertime in a little can that had contained preserves. To get water between meals or at any other hour than mealtimes, you had to call the guards a thousand times, yell and set up a row. If you did all that, sometimes you managed to get another little bit of water.

My greatest concern was to avoid contracting hepatitis. I knew the dangers of a lack of hygiene. Fecal matter piled up in the corner of the latrine, and thousands of slimy little maggots which crawled up the walls and slithered along the floor of the dungeonlike cell began to breed in it. I never touched the food with my hands. At first they sent in a spoon with the plate of food; we had to return the spoon with the plate. One day Ulises tried to keep his, thinking they wouldn't come into the cell to get it, and in fact they didn't. They simply told him they wouldn't give him any more food until he gave back the spoon. So then he had to turn it in. The next time they brought food, they didn't give anyone a spoon. So we had to eat with our fingers, but since I didn't want to pick up the macaroni or mush or bread with my dirty, excrement-covered hands, I would pick up the plate from underneath, put the edge of it between my lips, and tip it slowly into my mouth. I ate like that, like a dog, putting my snout into the plate. All that saved me from complete animality was inventing interior worlds which I would fill with the images that flooded my mind when I closed my eyes: light, air, inextinguishable suns, horizons that no barbed wire could ever bound, stars, flowers, and a thousand pleasant sounds, all of which came back to me from the world I had almost forgotten—birdsongs, waves crashing against the rocks, the swishing of the branches of trees. All I had to do in the darkness of that fetid cell was close my eyes, and I recreated the Biblical miracle of calling forth the light within me. Then, I was out of my jailers' grasp, beyond their farthest reach. I felt free. I could wander across meadows and coasts, live in a secret universe in which religious faith blended with imagination and memory.

21 / Diehards

At the end of the corridor of our cell block there was a large room. The soldiers decided to change the way new prisoners were introduced into the Circulars. Now they were first deposited in the big room, isolated, to be terrified, to be beaten, and at the end of a couple of months of that, to be transferred at last to the circular edifices. When the first group arrived it was a great event for us—our first contact with comrades coming in from Cuba. They came from the prison at La Cabaña, and they brought information, news.

Among the newly arrived prisoners was Paco Almoina. We had never been really introduced, but we knew each other from the time before I was imprisoned. He had been president of the National Institute of Tourism, a position which was almost a ministerial post. Our acquaintance was due to a national tourism plan which was being financed with money from the Caja Postal de Ahorros, where I was working. Paco, who had been a fighter against Batista's regime, was one of the first to unmask Castro's deceit. His high position within the government didn't keep him from entering a conspiracy against the new dictatorship, once again throwing himself into the struggle for the freedom which the triumphant Revolution had promised and immediately denied. He had been tried and sentenced to death and had awaited his execution for weeks, until the death sentence was commuted to thirty years in prison.

Whenever the guards left, the men in the big room at the end gathered at the door of the room to talk with us. My cell was only a few yards from them.

Paco gave me a half-used tube of mentholated toothpaste, which I applied to my groin and testicles. It cooled and alleviated the desperate itching from the fungus.

The arrival of the group in the next room caused the visits of the prison officers to become more frequent. For the headcounts, two per day, several officers were always in attendance. Political Commissioners also came in, since the detainees there were *plantados,* that is, diehards, recalcitrants, prisoners who had rejected Political Rehabilitation.

One afternoon Lieutenant Pomponio, head of Internal Order, commanded the prisoners to call out "Attention!" when he entered, as common and rehabilitated prisoners had to do; but the diehards refused. There was a stalemate, and then the anger mounted on both sides, until finally the garrison was called in and tried to force the diehards to obey, but the prisoners still refused. The garrison began beating the prisoners, and several men were wounded by bayonets. From our isolation cells, we yelled at the guards to stop; we called them murderers and cowards. To a certain extent we were safe from their blows because our cell doors were welded closed, and if a guard from upstairs on the ceiling used the pole to prod us, we could snatch it away from him.

The day after these events, a common prisoner came in and cut through the welds with a blowtorch. They put on a padlock with a stock around it that closed with an enormous bolt. That way the guards could get into our cells and beat us when they wanted.

One day Pomponio came in to count the men in the big room. His little son, a boy of eight years old, was with him. Suddenly I heard a lot of shouting and screaming. I dragged myself over to the cell door and saw Pomponio run past, shrieking as he spit and wiped off his face with a handkerchief. "The garrison! Call out the garrison!"

He was hysterical. His olive-green uniform and face were splattered with a whitish powder he was trying to brush off with his hands and the handkerchief. Somebody had thrown a bag of *gofio de trigo* at him, and it had burst right in his face. When I saw that, I was terrified. I knew the reprisal would be brutal.

The guards, with Pomponio heading the pack, ran like demons into the passageway. They were in combat formation. I heard the sound of the bayonets and truncheons striking the heads and backs of the offenders, and the prisoners' cries and curses. The first guard who came out when the beating was finished was Pomponio, followed by his son carrying a wooden nightstick. What would happen a few years later to that little boy, into whose hands, instead of a kite or a top, they put a truncheon to beat human beings with?

We were still naked, always naked, and the winter was hard on us. We were getting into the coldest months of the year. It was during those days that a new guard arrived, a man named Juan Rivero, who was to rise rapidly through the ranks because of his sadism, finally coming to hold the position of Chief Director of Concentration Camps. Ulises had met him years back when he was a bodyguard for some official who lived in the Marianao section of Havana. It was perhaps for that reason that Juan Rivero behaved decently toward us. During his turn on duty there was never any physical mistreatment.

Because my cell was so close to the barred entrance to the block where Paco Almoina and our other friends were held, the authorities took me out and transferred me into one of the farthest cells, number 10.

The inflammation in my leg had gone down quite a bit, but the fractured and dislocated bones had knit badly and my foot was permanently turned inward, visibly deformed. We never, my friends and I, stopped asking for medical care, but the reply was always totally negative. The fungus went on spreading across my body, and my greatest fear was that it would get into my eyes. The only remedy I had was applying toothpaste. The restriction on water was still in force, and we hadn't been able to take a bath for months. My body grew blacker and filthier every day.

I then came down with an intestinal infection of some kind and ran a very high fever. I had constant diarrhea and quickly became dehydrated. I hardly had the strength to talk, but my friends began to demand that I be looked after. At last the guards gave in, and I was carried to the hospital.

During that period the doctors in charge of the various wards of the hospital were prisoners. If it hadn't been for them, we would never have had even the slightest medical care.

Dr. Armando Zaldívar was the chief of the ward to which I was sent. Zaldívar was a young doctor who had taken his degree at a Spanish medical school. He was a practicing Catholic, and he had come back to Cuba with the triumph of the Revolution. He soon learned that the country was headed towards Communism, and he didn't waste a moment in putting his stethoscope aside and taking up a rifle. He joined the anti-Castro rebels in the mountains of Escambray. Captured and sentenced to thirty years, he had already spent several months in the prison on Isla de Pinos.

My appearance shocked everyone who saw me. The first thing Zaldívar did was order his assistants to cut off the mane of hair that had been growing for months. It covered my ears and almost reached my shoulders. They shaved me too. Meanwhile, they prepared a bath. I was in very bad shape, and my mind was clouded with fever, but I remember that with the top of a tin can, cut in half and used like a scraper, they scraped off the crust of filth that covered my body. This crust could be peeled off like a scab or like the rind of a fruit. We could hardly believe our own eyes.

Several five-gallon cans of water were needed for that first bath. Peeled, bathed, and shaved, I was a new man—and then I lay in a clean bed. I felt as though I had been set free. Leaving the punishment block for the hospital or the Circulars was, incredible as it sounds, almost like freedom.

With intravenous glucose solutions and antibiotics, my intestinal infection soon cleared up. When I was a little recovered, Zaldívar had some wooden walkers made for me to lean on. It was impossible for me to walk without some support, since I couldn't put any weight on my ruined foot. While the walkers were being constructed, I used a crutch.

The contact with my friends was almost like a tie to the outside world, beyond the presidio. They had news, since the hospital was a sort of clearing-house for information; prisoners from all the buildings were sent there, and of course they traded news and gossip. Through Raúl López, a pilot in Batista's army, I managed to get a message out to my family. My reception was affectionate and warm. It seemed that no one could do enough to help me.

Zaldívar managed to have an X-ray made of my foot. That was how I learned how much damage the fall, and the guard who had jumped up and down on my leg, had done me. The fractured bones had knitted out of place and formed a knot. I also had post-traumatic arthritis and articulation problems in my ankle. Nothing could be done there.

In order to hold me a few days more in the hospital, since Headquarters was pressuring them to return me to the punishment cells, Zaldívar conceived the idea of encasing my leg in a cast and putting me in traction with steel pulleys. He himself put the plaster on me, from my calf to my toes. When this hardened, he cut through the underside with a pair of shears, down to the tip of my foot, and took it off. I could put on this plaster boot very quickly whenever officers entered the ward. When they came in to count us, they would see me with the cast on and my leg suspended in the air by the pulleys. As soon as they left, I would take it off.

One night, Lieutenant Tarrau entered unexpectedly. He was looking for me, but since it was dark in the ward and we had mosquito nets over our beds, he had to have the lights turned on and ask where my bed was, all of which gave me time to put on the cast. He came up to me, lifted the mosquito net, and stood there looking at me with hatred.

"So, you tried to escape on me!" He nodded his head several times, like a veiled threat, and turned and walked out.

He repeated that visit several times. He spoke to Zaldívar and tried to get him to release me, but Zaldívar refused, each time saying that *he* wouldn't do it, that if Tarrau wanted to, it would be Tarrau's responsibility.

The medication for my fungus, applied several times a day, was slowly producing results. Clean new skin was emerging in the areas previously infected. I could brush my teeth, for the first time in several months, with a toothbrush.

The oppression against our ward was growing increasingly intense, to the point that at last Headquarters ordered us returned to the punishment cells, regardless of our conditions. Those that were staying in the hospital prepared some bags for us to take back—mine had a little chocolate and powdered milk, some sugar, a bottle of iodine to fight the fungus, some matches, a little can of a Sterno-like substance with a wick, some soap, and a few other things. It was almost inconceivable that the prison authorities would allow us to take the bags into the cells with us, but our friends insisted that we try.

All you had to do was cross the street to enter the punishment-cell blocks. I hopped along, leaning on the wooden crutches to help me walk. The common prisoner who was at the entrance to the cell-block hallway snatched away the burlap bag with the articles I was carrying. He did this in the guard's presence, and told me I couldn't take it in. But that same night, he brought it back to me. If he hadn't been so quick, the soldier would have confiscated it. Once I had the bag inside, the various guards assumed that it had been authorized.

In those days the cells were full, and therefore, so we wouldn't have to be mixed in with the other inmates, I was put into the cell with Boitel. We talked a lot, for hours and hours. A thick beard of more than three months' growth fell to his chest. His hair was long and tangled; it covered his ears and the back of his neck.

Once it got to be eleven or twelve o'clock at night, we set ourselves to heating the chocolate over the improvised stove. It was a labor of Titans, and it took hours. We had already confected a "choo-choo." This was a long strand of burlap fibers twisted together with a heavy object tied to one end. We would stick our arms out between the bars under the steel plate covering them, and pitch the heavy object down the hallway. The weight would drag the burlap rope down to the next cell, where the next prisoner would catch it, haul in the line, and continue throwing it down, in his turn, to the other cells. The choo-choo enabled us to pass cigarettes, matches, and, that night, a little plastic container with a sip of hot chocolate for each prisoner. That was quite an event.

Boitel was accustomed, as I have mentioned before, to going to sleep late and getting up about midmorning. I, on the contrary, went to bed early and got up early. Therefore, when the headcount officer would pass, I was always awake.

One day they handed down a new disciplinary order—all the men in isolation had to stand inside the cells as long as the headcount lasted; we could no longer sit or lie down. Before, the soldier performing the count would look through the peephole in the door and could see the prisoner. It didn't matter whether the prisoner was on the floor asleep, standing, or sitting—the purpose of the headcount was to assure Headquarters that the inmate was physically present.

But now, Headquarters wanted to make things tougher. Before, the isolated prisoner was treated like an object, or even as though he didn't exist at all. They threw us into one of those cells and took us out months later, bearded and filthy. Now they had new plans for the prisoners. They were going to bend us to their will.

The next morning when the officer stopped at our cell Boitel was asleep and I was sitting with my back leaning against the wall.

"Stand up, you two!" But neither of us stood. The soldier shouted again, but when he realized that did no good, he marched away.

The next day Lieutenant Pomponio, to whom the guard had reported that the men in one particular cell would not stand up, appeared with another guard. The guard pushed the barrel of a rifle through the top of the bars, pointed it at the ceiling, and fired it. The blast woke Boitel up, and he jumped to his feet.

When they repeated this the next morning, we were awake but we pretended to be asleep, and the noise of the shot didn't take us by surprise. With one stratagem after another, one psychological adjustment after another, I readapted myself to the life of the punishment cells.

23 / Our First Victory

They put me in a cell alone again. The months passed slowly. Being closed up was dulling my senses. We shouted to talk to each other, but that took an exhausting effort. Dozens of prisoners came into the punishment block and left again. We were the only ones who were still there, week after week, month after month.

Ulises was the only one of us with a cellmate, a sailor named Santiestéban, who had been in the cell block for months. The rest of us were in solitary.

The inflammation in my leg had gone down almost completely, and it was gradually returning to its natural color. Nonetheless I still could not stand on it, and had to use either crutches or walkers to walk.

We were all becoming weak and debilitated, and the time had grown terribly heavy. It appeared that Lieutenant Tarrau's prophecy that we would spend years in those cells was going to be fulfilled. We were desperate, and yet it seemed we had nothing to lose, so we decided to go on a hunger strike to demand our return to the Circular. This reprisal for having tried to escape had become unbearable.

I was chosen to be spokesman for the hunger strike; that is, I would be the only one who had any dealings with the soldiers. The others would not intervene. I informed the headcount officer of our decision, giving him to know that we would not take any food until we were removed from solitary confinement in the punishment-cell block. We would only drink water.

At that time I had absolutely no idea of how the body and mind reacted in such a situation. I thought you could die after five or six days without eating. I didn't move, I just lay on the floor all the time, to conserve my energy. The first day passed. Then the second.

On the third day Lieutenant Cruz, chief of the Political Police on the Island, came to visit us. He called Boitel, but Boitel told him to speak to me. Cruz asked me why we didn't want to eat, even though he knew our reasons perfectly well. Nonetheless I explained it all to him; I told him that the punishment had exceeded all precedents and that we were not going to just stay there, forever, until we rotted.

He took off the bright-red beret he was wearing that day, scratched his head, and said to me, "Twice while I've been in Havana they've sent me here because of you four men—first you escaped, and now this little strike of yours. . . ." And he walked away.

By the fourth day the sensation that my stomach was empty had disappeared. Physically I felt healthy enough, but the notion I might die of hunger filled me with fear and anxiety. I thought I was in danger of dying at any moment. If someone had told me that there had been strikes of nineteen, twenty-five, thirty-six, and even more days, that Boitel ten years later would go more than fifty days without eating, and that Olegario Charlot would die after sixty-five days, I simply would not have believed him.

Since no one in authority had come to us, it looked to us as though it didn't matter to Headquarters very much whether we lived or died. Boitel got the idea of speeding things up, so we could find out what the attitude of the soldiers was toward us and how tough the authorities really were prepared to be.

We decided that one of us would pretend to faint. The others would call out, and we'd see what happened next. To give it more realism, the fainting man was to strike his head as he fell. Since hitting yourself might not work, or, if it did, might be very risky, someone conceived the idea that Ulises and Santiestéban, who were together, would cast lots to see who hit whom. Santiestéban won the "right" to hit Ulises.

He hit him with his fist near his temple, and that was the blow that Ulises showed as a consequence of banging his head as he collapsed.

We began to shout in mock alarm. The whole cell block joined in the deafening shouting and crying for a doctor. They took Ulises off to the hospital.

Sergeant Naranjito stopped in front of my cell. His ever-present cavalry saber was hanging at his belt. A few days before he had talked to me about the strike and even admitted that he thought the time we had served there in the punishment cells was excessive. This time he brought us some elating news. He spoke with a slight nasal twang.

"Valladares, there's a mutiny in Circular 4. They say it's in support of you. And tomorrow they're going on a hunger strike in Circular 2, too."

Our hopes were lifted. An hour later, they brought a medic from the Circular, López de León, to look at us. Headquarters had caved in under the pressure from our comrades in the Circular, who were demanding that the authorities tell them the state of our health. But the Circulars didn't want the report of just any soldier—they wanted another prisoner to tell them. That was the first time that had ever happened.

López de León went down the row of our cells. It was he who told us that Headquarters had informed the Circulars that we were to be taken out of the punishment-cell block the next day.

The easy victory of that first hunger strike inspired Boitel with the idea of organizing a general strike in which all the political prisoners on Isla de Pinos would participate. There were around six thousand men at that time, and we agreed to work toward Boitel's purpose when we returned to the Circulars.

Very early the next day, Dr. Lamar, the man with the Lenin goatee, entered the cell block. He insisted on speaking with Boitel about the conditions for ending the strike. Boitel told him the only person authorized to have any dealings with them was me—no one else. The authorities had already given the order to take us out, and we knew it, but Dr. Lamar didn't know we knew. He wanted to negotiate—if we called off the strike, they'd take us back to the Circulars. But our refusal to suspend the strike was flat and final. I told him we would only consider our vow unnecessary after we were outside those walls. I informed him, moreover, that Boitel was in very bad condition and needed immediate medical treatment.

A few hours later they took Boitel to the hospital too.

When the soldier who came to get us tossed a change of clothes in to me and told me I was going to the Circular, I experienced one of the greatest joys of my life. Getting out of there was like getting out of hell itself.

So that we four would never be able to plan another escape together, we were dispersed among the four Circulars, one of us to each. Ulises went to number 3, Brito to number 2, Boitel to number 1, and I to number 4, which we had originally escaped from.

Then on the two crutches I cast a last glance at the hallway, at the cells of the punishment-cell block. I had suffered greatly there, but at least it had given me a more realistic sense of how much I could endure. I had made a singular discovery—pain can also be a spur to struggle.

24 / General Strike

felt a little dizzy when I came to the walkway. Two guards were escorting me. I had been locked up so many months, unable to look out at a distance, that something had altered inside me—it looked as if the enormous structures of the Circulars and the mountains to my left were falling in on top of me, rushing toward me, closing in on me in constant wavelike motions.

I stopped, closed my eyes, and shook my head a little to see if I could clear it and make that strange sensation go away.

"Let's go! Speed it up a little!" It didn't seem to matter to my guards that I had to use crutches to walk. I couldn't walk any faster, and I told them so.

I went on slowly, without thinking about the soldiers and their rush— they had ceased to exist for me. The ninety or a hundred yards that separated me from the Circular was an unforgettable journey. I breathed greedily, filling my lungs with fresh air scented with pine. I reveled at seeing the light again. The sky was intensely blue and clean. There was not a cloud in sight.

The year before, I had walked that route dressed as a soldier, attempting to escape. Now the return trip kindled many memories of that fateful afternoon. My head reeled with them.

They saw me almost immediately from the Circulars, and the windows filled with faces. My comrades began to shout. They waved their hands and handkerchiefs in warm affectionate welcome.

We stopped in front of the main gate. The guards escorting me turned over the transfer and entry papers to the ones in charge of the Circular and marched away from me.

A soldier unlocked the padlock, and as he swung the gate open the heavy lock and the rusty hinges of the door creaked.

The prison yard was full. As I entered, the men broke into a thunderous ovation and shouted *Viva*s that echoed in welcome. It was so moving to see them cheering me so sincerely that I could not keep back the tears. I was embraced and clapped on the back from all sides.

I don't know how many times I told the story of how it had all happened. I talked so much that I lost my voice. To begin with, I went to live in the Cruz brothers' cell on the fifth floor, but a few days later I moved into cell 35 on the same floor, a cell not so crowded. I lived with Chaguito the racing driver, many times champion in Cuba and abroad, the man who had been the lookout for our escape.

In the days after my return, I caught up on everything that had happened during my absence. The explosives were still in the basement, and the munitions experts from the Political Police inspected them periodically. But at least in our Circular, there was the minimal sense of security that came from the fact that we had deactivated the detonators. Our groups of lookouts were still organized, and there was no way the technicians in charge of blowing us up could do it without being detected when they entered the area of the buildings, no matter the hour they chose.

An interior transfer had been effected in February. They put Benito, my future father-in-law, into Circular 3. Boitel, Carrión, and some other good friends were transferred to number 1.

The number of books in circulation astounded me. As we had been authorized three volumes per prisoner per month, there were hundreds and hundreds of books in the building. To get around the prohibition of books not printed officially by the National Press of Cuba, family members had become real artists at disguising forbidden books and clever at sneaking them in. Therefore, you might see a book on Marxism become, after the first few pages, *Latin America: A Continent in Eruption* by Eudosio Ravines. The family members would find a government publication the same size as the book they wanted to smuggle in and would put on its cover and the first few pages. They did the same thing with magazines from Communist countries such as the Soviet Union, Poland, and so on, and managed to smuggle in under their covers *L'Express, Time,* and other publications from the free world. The guards who inspected them were usually very low-ranking and hardly knew how to read. When they saw a cover with the hammer and sickle or the little logo of the National Press, they let the text go through unexamined. In the cardboard boxes used to send authorized articles, prisoners' families would smuggle in the pages of a Bible. They hid the pages between the two layers of the corrugated cardboard, which had been taken apart and glued back together again.

Years later, more competent personnel from the Political Police would come in sporadically to look over the books and magazines, and they would discover the trickery and take the texts away with them.

But no matter how much some things had improved, still there was an air of great discontent in the Circulars, even among the most resigned prisoners. Always, in every human group, there are those who will swallow anything, those who simply keep their mouths shut and in violent epochs will allow themselves to be slowly killed, availing themselves of neither the poor relief of protest nor the more drastic possibilities of rebellion. But even those men were sick and tired of this. The moment comes at last when even the most docile of men feels his patience exhausted.

I could see that the situation was ripe for declaring a general hunger strike and demanding humane treatment, medical care, letters, sun, adequate nourishment. I talked to the Major of the Circular about this and met with some friends to talk about the conclusions that Boitel and I had come to after the success of our strike in the punishment cells. The Communists, who were accustomed to being the ones that held hunger strikes, didn't know yet how to break them, so before they learned how to react, we could win the first great battle of the political contingent in the prison. From the moment of my arrival, I dedicated all my time and energy to convincing my comrades that the time was ripe, that we shouldn't let it slip by. Little by little, even the most reluctant men grew sympathetic to the idea.

Boitel was now in Circular 1. So that we could communicate with each other, we recruited two telegraph operators. A blinker was constructed from a metal canister. We cut out the bottom and made a sort of window shade to fit it, and with a rubber band and a few pieces of wire, we had the mechanism to open and close the aperture intermittently for the dots and dashes of Morse code. The light for the blinker was furnished by a little kerosene lantern set inside the canister. We would sit up on the fifth floor late at night and transmit our messages back and forth.

The food grew worse day by day, and all of us were growing weak from lack of proper nourishment. One noon they brought in the lunch tanks and the men in charge of serving the rations stirred the water around, hoping there might be some solid food at the bottom. But there was nothing there. It was just hot water with a little grease floating on top.

So prisoners began to shout for the "lunch" to be sent back. The spirit was ready, and the strike erupted. But there was an element of violence in it, because some men were so overwrought from the anger and frustration that had been building up for months that they screamed in protest from the windows that opened onto the main gate. Cries escalated to action, and they threw a glass jar at the roof of the guardhouse at the gate. One of the guards raised his machine gun and fired. The burst of fire spattered on the bars of the window and left one of the Rivero brothers wounded in the neck. Two other prisoners were wounded in the chest, but fortunately the shrapnel passed through without hitting any major organs.

At the same instant that the guard's shots rang out, the prisoners began to throw more jars at the main gate. Retaliatory machine-gun bursts aimed into the prison yard followed the first. But that did not keep prisoners on every floor from wrapping pieces of cloth around heavy objects, setting the cloth afire, and throwing them down to the prison yard. The flames from the burning cloth blocked the gate. The medic López de León took a gallon bottle of alcohol out of the dispensary and threw it from the second floor into one of those bonfires. The alcohol exploded and created a conflagration that raged all the way up to the first floor. Suddenly the guards began to scatter in all directions, abandoning their posts and yelling that we were all crazy. They were terrified—they'd realized that only a few yards from the blaze there was a huge cache of TNT.

When the fire died down, the whole battalion of the presidio massed before the Circular.

We cleaned out the entrance and brought down our wounded to be taken out to the hospital. We told the officers that we were declaring a hunger strike and that we would send our demands in writing later.

At that moment one of the Circulars was having a visit, and all the family members and prisoners were inside the dining hall, where they heard the shots and the shouting. I ran upstairs as fast as my bad leg would allow me to the fifth floor and my cell. There René, Chaguito, some others, and I found four sheets and sewed them together as fast as we could. There were still a few hours left before the visit ended. We took a mixture of Mercurochrome, Betadine, and water and mixed that with crushed pencil lead, and I painted a sign on the sheets: WE ARE ON A HUNGER STRIKE.

We used pieces of twine to hang the sign outside across the windows of the fifth floor. When the visitors began to leave, they saw it and took the news to Cuba the next day.

Circular 1 immediately joined our strike, as did Circular 2, but only some of the prisoners in Circular 3 took part, since a group of prisoners that had been there since 1959 did not want to join the movement. The next day the guards brought the tanks with lunch, and it actually looked appetizing. As we did not allow it inside the Circular, the guards left it there at the entrance where we could see and, worse, smell it. The vats contained soup with rice, and there was even some meat and green peppers floating on top. They were going to use food like that, never before seen in the presidio, to weaken our resolve and break the strike. No Circular except Number 3 accepted the food.

One of the guards told the gatekeeper of our Circular that the Political Commissioners were stirring the guards up against us. So, to neutralize the Political Commissioners' campaign, I painted another sheet, this time addressed to the guards, which said: SOLDIER, MILITIAMAN, WE HAVE NOTHING AGAINST YOU. WE ASK FOR HUMANE TREATMENT. We hung that banner on the side fronting the guardhouse, so the guards would be sure to see it.

Prison Headquarters called all the Majors of the Circulars together for an interview with Tarrau and some other functionaries. When our Major came back, he told us Headquarters had flatly refused to give in to any of our demands. If we unconditionally gave up the strike, they would send for the Majors again later, at which time the Majors could put our demands before them. Otherwise, no concessions, no negotiations at all.

Our answer to that was for all of us to gather in the prison yard. We descended with mattresses, sheets, and cots and put all the men in bad health, whether chronically or because of current conditions, and all the old men to the front. I painted another sheet, this time aimed at Headquarters: OUR ANSWER: MEN PREPARED TO DIE. Our decision to resist was in fact final, irrevocable, as though we thousands of men had been one. The Communists kept bringing tanks full of theretofore unheard-of food—chicken in delicious-smelling sauces, salads, even desserts—and left it all just on the far side of the main gate. Since we were on the ground floor in the prison yard, those tanks were very near and very tempting—we could see them, smell them, and that was torture indeed. But we resisted.

In Circular 1, Tony Lamas took his life in his hands and climbed the columns that circled the building, on up to the conical roof. The operation took steadiness and nerves of steel. At a height of more than a hundred feet, he then crept along one of the narrow support beams to reach the central point of the roof, where all the supports, like the spokes of a bicycle wheel, converged. Down below there was empty space. The slightest dizziness— and he was on a hunger strike—meant falling to certain death on the ground. When he reached the central point on the roof, he had to crawl even higher, where there were some wooden transomlike windows, to complete his mission. At that point he took out a Cuban flag and hung it where everyone could see.

This act had great significance for us. We took it as a communal triumph, because the garrison was never able to get the flag down. There was not a man among them who dared climb up there; they tried several times during the searches, but midway the guards always chickened out. So the symbol of our country remained up there, waving in the air, as though reminding people that the best men were with us, not them. With the passage of months and the battering of rain and wind, it grew faded and tattered.

The strike continued. The strike had come about so spontaneously that the lack of mental preparedness and of medical supplies affected us as much as the lack of food itself. There were only fifteen or twenty intravenous packs in the dispensary, and they were used for the oldest and weakest men and for several of the prisoners who had begun vomiting or otherwise become dehydrated. Some men could not even keep water down. We must have presented a very alarming sight. Since there was nowhere to hang the intravenous bottles, we strung together several lengths of rope that before we had used to pull pails of water up from one floor to another, ran the line from one side of the prison yard to the other, above the first rank of cots, and hung the bottles from the line.

The day after they had said they would not meet our demands, Head-quarters sent for the Majors again. Sanjurjo, at that time Director-General of Jails and Prisons in Cuba, had rushed over from Havana. He interviewed the Majors. He listened to the explanations the Majors gave for the stand we had decided to take in order to achieve our goals. Nevertheless, ignoring the justice of our case, he tried to negotiate with mere promises. Our repre-sentatives' firmness finally forced him to see that we would not compromise, so it was they who had to give in.

We had won.

We were incredibly happy. The victory gave us new life. After so much abuse, such ignominy and misery, the triumph even further strengthened our spirit of combativeness and resistance.

There began to be better nutrition in every sense of the word; we were allowed to receive correspondence once a week and send a letter every fifteen days; water was brought to the prison more frequently; and the authorities provided us a little more medicine and increased our visits to one every three months. Achieving all that from the Jails and Prisons Headquarters con-stituted an unprecedented success.

There were many reasons the authorities had capitulated so quickly. I don't think it was because the government was afraid of us, nor out of any humanitarian motives. They gave in rather because they weren't prepared to confront a strike movement of thousands and thousands of prisoners. Boitel and I had perceived that in the punishment cells: faced with the threat from Circular 4 that the men there would join our personal hunger strike, the authorities immediately caved in. The government simply did not know what to do in such a situation. It was the element of surprise that brought about our triumph. But soon enough they would be ready for such confron-tations, and then we would be the ones who were surprised.

On the other hand, the Communists don't feel obliged to keep their promises, so in a few weeks problems began to crop up. For example, once they didn't bring in our mail, so to try to put a little pressure on them we refused to come down for the headcount until our letters were delivered. We had won a battle, or maybe a skirmish, but the war went on.

25 / La Pacífica:
Our First Great Setback

The year 1962 was one of great events in Cuba. Late in the year there was the Soviet missile crisis on the island, which brought the world to the threshold of atomic war. This crisis certainly was the gravest and most memorable event of 1962, but even earlier in the year there was a high-level military conspiracy aimed at bringing down the government; the Political Police infiltrated and aborted the plan, in which the Army, the Navy, and the National Police were all implicated, but the crisis left its marks. The government's reaction when the conspirators were found out was a true bloodbath. Dozens of detained soldiers were put into the jails at La Cabaña and Castillo del Morro and immediately executed, without trials, sentenced solely by the decisions of the high command of the Political Police. Those without a doubt were the most terrible nights that La Cabaña ever witnessed. Because of that conspiracy, which became known as the August 30th Plot in Cuban prisons, 460 soldiers were shot by firing squads across the island.

All the time those massive executions were being carried out, visits in the prisons of El Morro, La Cabaña, and others continued uninterrupted. That way the government could be sure the prisoners' families would spread the word of the terror of those days to all the rest of the population of Cuba.

When the conspiracy crisis was over, Castro created three different armies—the Army of the West, of the Central Region, and of the East—so that there could never again be a nationwide conspiracy mounted in Cuba. Each of these armies has its own general staff, and they are totally independent of one another. Any contact between them is considered high treason and is punishable by immediate execution.

In the prison itself, 1962 gave us several months of relative tranquillity, until September. They were doing a search in all the Circulars, and the prisoners as usual were taken out into the corrals where the visits had been held before. In Circular 2, they discovered that Héctor González' and Domingo ("Hatchet") Sánchez' cell bars had been cut. Several officers and a Political Commissioner came to the corral gate to call them out, and the two prisoners left. Hatchet went first, Héctor a few yards behind. During the searches you are always alert, attentive to what's going on. I was watching the two men distractedly. There was nothing strange about prisoners being taken out to the punishment cells; it was routine. But suddenly the guards began to beat them. Immediately, as they received the very first blows, prisoners from the Circulars began to yell at the guards. Hatchet was robust, with white hair and extraordinary physical strength. Both he and Héctor immediately bristled against that treatment and returned the blows. A wave of guards swept over them and beat them all the way to the punishment-cell block.

Some of the prisoners from Circular 2 had already gone back in, but another group refused to enter, out of solidarity with the beaten prisoners. They demanded that the prisoners be taken out of the punishment cells.

At that, the garrison called in reinforcements and entered the corral to take out the protesting prisoners by force. A pitched battle of prisoners and guards ensued, with the guards' superior force, of course, once more winning the day. They struck savagely at the prisoners. Impotent behind the bars, we could do nothing but yell at the guards, to try to hold down the aggression.

From Circular 2, prisoners began to throw plates, bottles, and anything else at hand down at the guards, whose response was to shoot at the prisoners. They machine-gunned the windows, and several men were wounded, two seriously, although no one died. Within minutes a new wave of reinforcements arrived and started to use tear gas. Sergeant Naranjito led that second wave; he was the one that threw the first Soviet-made tear-gas grenade at Circular 1. It looked like a tin can.

That same afternoon, as a protest against this barbaric and aggressive overreaction, Circular 2 decided to send its food back. Communications were exchanged between that Circular and the others, and a general protest was declared. At first, no one really thought about a hunger strike, only about returning the food to try to provoke someone in authority at Prison Headquarters to come, so we could discuss the situation of the beaten men held in the punishment cells, try to get them returned to the Circular. However, the next morning, encouraged by the easy victory of the previous strike, we got out of bed on a new hunger strike.

I painted a Cuban flag on a sheet, with the help of Samuel Aguilar. We put it across the big window on the stairway from the fifth floor. There was a piece of black crepe hung on it.

That day passed unremarkably. The next day I still hadn't gotten out of bed when Samuel shook me awake. He was obviously frightened and was clutching the flag, all wadded up in his arms.

"We're surrounded!" he cried, and pointed toward the window.

I jumped off my cot, and when I looked out toward the walkway, the metal bulk of a Russian Stalin tank, its cannon aimed at our Circular, left me stunned. There was another one stationed next to the dining hall. A light mist still hung over the ground, so I couldn't see any farther. The tank seemed to be sitting on top of a dense cloud, floating on top of the walkway. Later that day when the fog lifted I would see two more of them.

"What do I do with the flag?" Samuel asked me.

"Well, go put it up again. Let them take it down."

When the sun dispersed the mist, we could see the gigantic massing of troops the prison authorities had brought together during the night. On the other side of the security cordon the prison was surrounded by troops with mortars, and still more troops were getting off trucks. Several helicopters were hovering over the prison, and it seemed likely the operation was being directed from their vantage point. Inside the security fences, an armored personnel carrier stopped in front of Circulars 3 and 4. The turret gun of a tank swiveled slowly, taking aim on the cells. There must have been at least fifteen hundred troops.

A cordon of guards surrounded each Circular, posted so close to each other that they could have held hands. Every twenty yards or so they set up machine guns on tall tripods. Patrols with German shepherd dogs came and went. Trucks and jeeps in incessant activity kept passing by. This looked like war.

When the four Circulars were completely besieged, Commander William Gálvez, Curbelo, Tarrau, and several high-ranking officers from the Political Police took charge and called the Majors together to inform them they were going to perform a "peaceful" search. That bit of sadistic irony prompted us to baptize that search La Pacífica.

The soldiers started this "peaceful" search with Circulars 1 and 2. It lasted from early morning until night. We watched them take out truckful after truckful of the prisoners' belongings. Circulars 3 and 4 would be searched the next day. All through the night, armored personnel carriers patrolled around the Circulars while the tanks sat there immobile and menacing. Several soldiers armed with B-2 machine guns had been posted in the central tower. Their mere presence there was cause for anxiety. Almost no one could sleep for the tension; we were all waiting for dawn, and with it our turn.

They brought our breakfast earlier than usual. The sun had still not come up, although the sky was filled with light from the east, when guards opened the main gate. A flood of soldiers, one after another, all with helmets and R-2 rifles with fixed bayonets, took up positions next to the wall on both sides of the entrance gate. Another group of soldiers without rifles but carrying bayonets formed a line in front of these first soldiers. In the tower more guards appeared, carrying tear-gas launchers.

Then a platoon of officers entered. They were yelling orders and threats through a megaphone, telling us to strip and put our hands on top of our heads and come down to the prison yard. By this time guards had taken over the floors and were dealing out beatings left and right.

They herded us little by little between the two wash areas. Anyone who lowered his hands was beaten until he raised them again. The stragglers on the floors were hunted down and beaten. When we were all downstairs, more than a thousand of us, the guards began shoving the men on the fringes of the milling crowd of prisoners, prodding them with bayonets and the toes of their boots and yelling at them to turn around. The order was for us to form into files, each man standing with his chest, genitals, and thighs pressing against the back and backside of the man in front of him. That caused a furious protest, and the reprisal was instant, brutal, and merciless. The guards unleashed wave after wave of blows with their bayonets on the backs and heads of those at the rear of the file.

They took out some prisoners, and eight or ten guards grabbed them, spread-eagled them, and lifted them off the ground. They threw the prisoners to the ground face down and spread their thighs, and other guards rammed the barrels of their rifles between the cheeks of the men's buttocks. Not a few prisoners were forced to drink filthy water from the puddles scattered across the prison yard. The guards simply held the men's heads in them until they had to swallow.

We were so squeezed together that we must have looked like one compact mass of flesh. Men at the rear of the files could not lower their arms, for fear of being beaten yet again. I was packed in toward the middle, so the multitude of men kept me out of the direct reach of the soldiers. Many of us covered our genitals with our hands so we wouldn't have to push them against the next man.

There was one straggler who jumped over the railing on the lower floor and landed on the shoulders of the men below him. He begged them to make room for him, so he could get down, but it was virtually impossible. That poor man crawling on top of the other men, asking them to make room for him, made a grotesque, absurd vision.

We stood there for more than twelve hours. Several men fainted. They didn't fall, they *couldn't* fall, they just stood there unconscious, held up by the surrounding bodies, with their heads leaning on the shoulders of the man in front.

The guards threw all our belongings into the prison yard, everything we possessed except our beds. Books, food, soap, razor blades, socks, underwear . . . they destroyed whatever they could. They pulled the heels off our shoes, they stomped on any eyeglasses left behind in the cells and reduced them to shards. All drinking glasses, jars, bottles, and even toothbrushes suffered the same fate.

There has never been, in the twenty-five years of existence of the Cuban political prisons, a search to compare with that one. There were worse massacres and beatings, yes, with deaths and serious wounds from bullets and bayonets, but never such an organized and heartless destruction as *La Pacífica*. Moreover, the stage was set for our total massacre if we rebelled against what they were doing. An article published in the old official organ of the Communist Party, the newspaper *Hoy* (*Today*), proves they were willing to justify our mass murder. The article falsely claimed that the counterrevolutionary prisoners held in the prison of Isla de Pinos had mutinied. We had supposedly intended to take over the Island, and five hundred of us had died in the attempt. That was September 11, 1962. The High Command of the Political Police with the personal approval of Castro directed and ordered that search.

Our defeat was total and devastating. When the search was finished we immediately began to try to help the men who had been wounded by bayonets and kickings. We made a report of those who were seriously enough injured to need immediate medical attention in a hospital as well as of those who needed tests to determine how much internal damage the bayonetings and beatings might have caused.

When I went back up those stairs filled with naked prisoners I was overcome with despair. I had a foreboding that after that, the repression would surely grow immensely worse. More than ninety percent of our belongings had been carried off or destroyed. The canvas and burlap of our cots had been slashed by bayonets.

The prison authorities ordered all the cells of the first floor evacuated. They were not to be occupied again. This measure made any attempt to break through the floor and get at the explosives almost impossible. What the measure immediately meant was that the evicted prisoners had to be distributed throughout the other floors, and that obviously made the crowding much worse. There were cells which housed as many as four or five prisoners.

After *La Pacífica*, the weight of the little family package we were allowed to receive was reduced to seven kilos, about fifteen pounds, and could be brought in only every two months. Moreover, it could not contain powdered milk.

I will never forget the food they gave us, at almost nine o'clock that night. Rice and black beans. We had spent the entire day without a bite to eat or even a sip of water. The only thing we had had all day, and that with unwillingness and disgust, was the filth that had fallen on us when the guards upstairs on the floors had overturned the tanks in the bathrooms. When the food finally came I had to use a piece of cardboard for a plate—they had taken my plate away.

26 / A Debate: The Importance of Living, the Crisis of Giving In

ur organization disrupted by the savagery of the search, our study programs ended, ourselves reduced to thinking only about such things as finding a piece of wood, or a nail, or a piece of thread to sew up the slashed bed, all of us felt our days grow long, heavy, and spiritless. But one day it occurred to Paco Almoina and a little group of friends—René González, Ramiro Machín, and some others—to start a club in Paco's cell. It seemed such a preposterous idea, but it worked. We managed to collect several burlap bags that had been thrown out by the owners because they were slashed open, and we joined them all together and made a rug the size of the cell. Then we took the empty cans they gave us to replace the jars and bottles we had been using before and made teacups by covering them with burlap and straw from the bags our families had brought us. The next step was to get hold of some teabags, which came into the prison with some regularity in those days. Then from five o'clock until nine o'clock at night, barefooted (we always left our shoes in the hallway), we would sit yoga-style on the rug and sip tea and have readings from the few books that had been spared in the search. One of the favorites was *The Importance of Living,* by the famous Chinese thinker Lin Yu-tang. It had survived because it had been hidden under a revolutionary cover—*Leftism: A Childhood Disease of Communism,* by Lenin.

We ended our meetings at nine o'clock at night, the hour the cornet was played for lights-out, and each of us went back to his own cell.

Inspired by that reading, we called the time we spent with Chinese philosophy "the hour of eloquent silence." I enjoyed that book enormously; we laughed with the philosopher-thieves or the profound Lao-Tse and the author's own spicy observations. The hours were an oasis of peace, the calm eye in the vicious maelstrom of those days.

The second book we read was *The Prince of Foxes.* We vicariously lived through those adventures of the Duke of Orsini. We took turns reading, but whoever read was always careful to end our get-together at a moment of great suspense in the plot, so all of us awaited the next day's episode like wide-eyed children.

First the defeat of the Bay of Pigs invasion, then the search and its depressing aftermath, not to mention the constant threat of being blown to bits by the explosives in the event of an attack on the country—all these things contributed to the discouragement and frustration of many prisoners. The guerrillas in the mountains had been routed, and there were only a few pockets of brave campesinos still surviving, so there was no real hope for the fall of the regime. There were so many "negatives" in the picture that finally many of the prisoners opted to join the Political Rehabilitation Programs.

Their family situations also influenced the decisions of many of the men. They had joined the struggle against Castro, sacrificing family and home, had risked their own lives, trying with their own efforts to prevent Communism from taking control of the country. But when freedom fighters were detained, the Political Police took revenge on their relatives, looted their houses, in many cases even stripped them of their furniture; and if the family had had a lovely home, they were sometimes thrown out, as happened with my wife-to-be, Martha, when her father was arrested. Since all the furniture was in his name, they took away the television set, the refrigerator, the record player, all the electrical equipment which had become so scarce in the country. They also confiscated the family's savings account.

The Revolutionary Government passed a law which allowed all the property that belonged to men found guilty of crimes against the State to be confiscated. After the confiscation, CDR mobs would picket in front of the homes of the prisoners, as they had done in front of mine. Agents from the Cuban Gestapo, dressed in civilian clothes, led "spontaneous" demonstrations of the people's repudiation of the families of counterrevolutionaries. The family was then marked forever and its members outcasts. The wife and children of a "traitor to the Revolution" were fired from their jobs, mistreated and discriminated against at school.

The children would come home crying from the insults their classmates had yelled at them. They were like pariahs, kept out of all extracurricular activities, and this with the tacit approval of the teachers, who were forced to acquiesce to such practices, since otherwise the teachers themselves would have run the risk of losing their jobs.

The repression of family members condemned them, therefore, to poverty, misery, and perpetual harassment. Their water would even be shut off, as happened to my family. We lived on the second floor; my mother and sister had to go to another prisoner's house to get water, across the street, and carry it upstairs in pails. They suffered all sorts of humiliations, and were the daily butt of outrageous discriminations. For example, my mother was once standing in a long line with her ration card, in front of the store she always went to. When her turn came, the militiaman who was handing out whatever item it was, in company with the president of the Defense

Committee, told her that they were all out of the desired product. My mother knew that wasn't true, but there was nothing she could do. She turned around to leave, and immediately saw them go on distributing the item they had refused her and that legally she was entitled to.

This torment of the families of political prisoners grew more and more severe as the Revolution grew more and more radical. Repression, harassment of all kinds, outrages, hunger, terror—those were the daily facts of life. In the jails the Political Commissioners exploited this situation—after all, the Revolution itself had brought it about as a means of coercing the prisoner. The Political Commissioners would call the prisoner to an interview at which they would paint the prisoner a terrible picture of his home—many times it was through the Political Commissioner that the prisoner first learned about what was really happening, the magnitude of the hardship his family was suffering, because his family would suppress or gloss over that tragedy in the letters they sent or when they visited, so as to spare the man the additional anguish and worry.

The Commissioner, with a kindly, paternal attitude, as though he were really touched by those terrible truths, would go on and on, telling the prisoner about his sick mother who had no medicine, the days his family could not eat, his son running wild for lack of a father's discipline. He would insinuate that all that would change if the prisoner would only cease his rebelliousness. He would urge the prisoner to think about his family, stop being selfish. The Revolution was generous, was always ready to give him another chance.

"Who helps your family?" the Commissioner would say. "Do you think the Yankees send them money? Your family is abandoned to its fate. Nobody cares about them. You were *used,* talked into trying to destroy the Revolution, and now you see it's the Revolution that's concerned about your family, and about *you,* too."

That kind of work was planned and carried out by the Director-General of Political Rehabilitation of Jails and Prisons.

Each man who agreed to enter the Political Rehabilitation Program had his own reasons for doing so, each man's circumstances were his own, and therefore I never felt it was my place to judge another man's decision to join. I knew that a great number of those men would never willingly have compromised their ideals and that they underwent terrible crises of conscience when they defected. They took a step which separated me, but only physically, from very dear friends whom I still love as brothers. It is not every man who sees his road as indefinite resistance, not to mention the involuntary martyrdom that sometimes resulted from such resistance.

Some prisoners used Political Rehabilitation as a route out onto the street where they could continue their struggle. There were cases of men who did that, and they were shot or returned to prison. However, those cases were very few.

27 / The Dark Waning of the Year

In October 1962, even in prison we immediately learned of the presence of Soviet missiles in Cuba. The little radio brought us the news.

The world events of those weeks led to great activity among the soldiers, since everyone knew the country was in imminent danger of being invaded by the United States.

All the land around the Circulars was planted with long, sharp wooden stakes against paratroopers that might be dropped to take the prison. Several batteries were installed and aimed at the Circulars, and technicians made constant checks on the explosives that were designed to blow us up.

Those were indescribably tense days. As we learned more and more about the events taking place, we began to realize that nuclear war was entirely possible. It is common knowledge that the world has never been in more danger of general holocaust than then. If it came about, we would be the first casualties.

Since the country was in a constant state of alert, all the lights were ordered turned off at night. The presidio was completely dark, as were all the surrounding offices and installations, the guards' houses, everything. I have never seen such impenetrable darkness. You couldn't see your hand in front of your face, even if you spent hours in the dark, letting your pupils dilate to their fullest. So to get to the bathroom down the hallways, you had to count the metal railing supports as you groped and slid your hand along. It was so dark that almost the whole Circular would be illuminated if somebody struck a match.

The vigilance groups we had organized to keep our jailers from setting off the explosives hardly slept at all. Our watches were redoubled; the total obscurity made surveillance diabolically difficult.

When Kennedy promised Moscow that Cuba would not be invaded and the crisis abated, toward the end of October, Castro ordered the TNT charges deactivated. Months later the explosives would be taken out—those explosives whose presence had menaced us since April of 1961 would be removed at last.

During this time I began to write Martha secretly. To get the letters out to her, friends who had joined the Rehabilitation Program helped me. They received frequent visits and maintained contacts with civilians who were collaborating with us.

When they began to construct a big shed about ninety yards long, no one had the least idea what was going on. Within a few weeks, the news filtered through that they were going to hold the visits there. They were erecting the shed above the corral located beside Circular 2, and we thought they were building it to give us shelter from the sun and rain. How naive we were!

The shed was divided lengthwise by two fine-mesh chicken-wire screens, set about two feet apart. The day the first group of prisoners were taken out for the visit, there was an immediate protest. You could hardly make out faces through the screens. Children were crying and frightened. They had been told that their fathers were waiting to see them on the other side of the fine-mesh screens, so they tried, but futilely, to make out the features of the faces they loved. This measure, enormously cruel, impeded any family contact. There was not even a mother's, wife's, or child's kiss to warm your days after the visit. We unanimously decided not to accept visits under those conditions. Men in the Political Rehabilitation Program didn't have to have their visits under those conditions. The difference between the two kinds of prisoners was being underscored again and again.

A few months after the invaders of the Bay of Pigs had been tried and sentenced, the Cuban government chose 214 of them to be ransomed. Castro put a price of $100,000 on them. They were brought to the prison on Isla de Pinos and confined in one of the big rooms in the punishment-cell block, under special guard so they would not be able to communicate with the rest of the inmates.

Castro had expressed an interest in exchanging the invaders for tractors and medicine, and the negotiations for this exchange were begun through a man named Donovan, an American lawyer who had experience in prisoner negotiations with the Communists.

One cold morning in December 1962, the invaders left the presidio dressed in dark pants and yellow T-shirts. We were all overjoyed for them —hands and handkerchiefs waved from every window. We were saying goodbye and thanking those who had tried to liberate Cuba from Communism. And too, a little window of hope had opened for us. The precedent had been set for the Cuban government to enter into that type of negotiation. We might be ransomed, too. Twenty years later, that hope of being exchanged is still clutched at by imprisoned patriots.

. . .

Two days after the Bay of Pigs invasion had failed in 1961, the transfer of prisoners from the theater of war to prison in Havana had begun.

Captain Osmany Cienfuegos, his shirt open, his sleeves rolled up, and carrying a machine gun, called out orders. The invaders lined up two by two, surrounded by a heavy guard; they waited for the transports that would carry them to the jails in the capital.

When the trailer truck pulled up in front of them, it never occurred to them that they were all going to be crammed in there. The trailer was completely closed, an ordinary trailer—it still had the number 13 of Expreso Internacional (a private company which had been confiscated by the government) painted on it. By one of those ironies that usually happen only in novels, one of the prisoners who was to get on this death truck was Mike Padrón, the ex-owner of the firm.

The militiaman Fernández Vilá, who was assigned to the National Institute of Agrarian Reform, went down a list of names. He called out 149 prisoners to get on the trailer. The prisoners protested that was too many men, they'd be so jammed together they wouldn't even be able to move. Also, the trailer had no air vents.

Osmany Cienfuegos threatened them with bayonets. They got on the truck as the circle of guards closed in on them.

"We're going to suffocate in there," one of the prisoners said.

"Good. Then we won't have to waste ammunition shooting you," Cienfuegos answered.

The last man to get on was Máximo Cruz.

The trailer with its cargo of men headed west, toward Havana. Inside, the air began to fail. The men desperately hunted little chinks through which air scantly filtered, but it wasn't enough for everyone.

Cuco Cervantes was one of the men in that group. He was a chronic asthmatic; he had even been rejected at first when he signed up to be a member of the invading forces, but he was so determined to fight for his country's freedom that he finally persuaded the recruiters to accept him. Now his lungs desperately needed oxygen. René Silva helped him, holding him up so that his nose would be closer to one of the little holes. The air grew fouler and fouler, and the hellish, stifling heat made the situation even worse. Cervantes collapsed and died. Then René felt himself growing weak; at last he couldn't even stand up anymore. René's body fell across Cervantes' corpse. When the trailer arrived at its destination, nine of those men had died of asphyxiation—Pepe Milián, José Ignacio Macia, Santos Gil Ramos, Emilio Quintana, Moisés Santana, José Viraleyo, Pedro Rojas, Cuco Cervantes, and René Silva.

The Cuban government, to quell the uproar those deaths caused, set free any relatives of the dead men who were still in political prisons. The authorities seemed to reason that that would somehow mitigate the enormity of the deaths by asphyxiation.

That was why Ulises was called out now. René Silva had been his brother. The family had decided not to tell Ulises about it, to spare him that added suffering. So Ulises had no idea that his transfer was not to another jail in Cuba, but rather to the United States.

When Ulises waved at us from the front gate of Circular 3, where a jeep was waiting for him, the sky was gray and cold gusts of wind wailed through the bars of the windows, which by order of Headquarters could not be closed or covered.

We had already reported that Don Tomás de Aquino, an old black man who lived on the second floor, had a very high fever. We asked for authorization to put a sack over the window, since his cell opened to the north and the freezing wind was gusting through the bars. Since *La Pacífica,* when all the materials we had used for curtains and awnings had been destroyed or taken away, the authorities had prohibited us from using those burlap flaps to cover the windows.

All night the north wind blew freezing through the window. When they called us out for the headcount, the gray body of Don Tomás was lifeless. He died from the cold, our doctors told us.

They began to make transfers among the Circulars. Lenin had said that the prisoner should be moved constantly, and prison authorities in Cuba followed his directives to the letter. The objective sought by this is the disorientation of the prisoner. A transfer forces all the plans that may have been worked out to be dissolved and rethought. If transfers are frequent enough, escape plans hardly ever come to fruition.

I left without knowing which Circular I was being assigned to. It turned out to be Circular 1. In the search performed at the entrance gate they went through the few things I still had and took away half of them.

Some friends were waiting for me in the prison yard to help me carry my bed and bags and find some space, which was at a premium. They had invented a way of hanging a third bunk between the two that were permanently attached to the wall, as a burlap hammock might be hung, since that was the only way that four or five prisoners could fit into those tiny cells.

Boitel and Carrión were there. Our reunion was an unexpected bonus. Boitel lived on the second floor with Pérez Medina, a friend from before imprisonment. Pérez Medina was a cousin of Neno, the young man who had given me the crucifix and driven a truckful of troops off a cliff.

I found a place in cell 53 on the second floor, with Wilfredo Nova, one of the best poets in the prison and a loyal, delightful friend. That Circular, which we jokingly called Generals and Doctors—parodying the title of a famous novel—was made up of people carefully selected by Prison Headquarters. In this Circular they had concentrated all the professionals—university people, students, leaders of anti-Castro organizations, politicians, former high-ranking officers of both Batista's and Castro's armies, important functionaries from the two governments, and other people considered dangerous by the regime. The purpose of this selection was to distance the thousands of prisoners in the three remaining Circulars from those the government called *cabecillas,* which means "pinheads" and "hotheads" as well as "ringleaders." So the word then summed up everything the authorities thought of us, showed both their contempt and their fear. We were the ideologues.

From the intellectual point of view, that time in Circular 1 was for me the Golden Age of the Presidio of Isla de Pinos. The cunning of our families in smuggling books in to us right through the searches gave us an abundant supply of reading matter covering all knowledge. The cultural activities, with all those books, became truly outstanding, given our other circumstances. We wanted to put some language courses together, and within a week we had made dozens of manuscript copies of textbooks. There were not enough notebooks to go around, though, so when we finished one, we erased all its pages with the sole of a tennis shoe and reused the notebook as many as five times.

Nonetheless, dogged attempts were being made to undermine prisoner strength and morale. They began to call out groups of prisoners from all the Circulars; they were to go to Prison Headquarters. Every day they called twenty or thirty. Almost always they were the same men—leaders of counterrevolutionary organizations or prisoners who were somehow important because they seemed to represent a position or were respected by other prisoners.

The object of the interviews was to offer the prisoners Political Rehabilitation. They were always given the same argument—resistance was futile, their families were abandoned and helpless. The men who agreed to join had to sign a little form renouncing all their beliefs and adopting Marxism as their new philosophy.

It so happened that hundreds of prisoners who had sought to join the Rehabilitation Program were not called. Only some of them were taken. We didn't know it, but this was a deliberate strategy of culling. Men not accepted were considered by the recruiters to be innocuous inside the Circulars. The authorities thought, moreover, that weeding out the *cabecillas* would leave the less educated, less "dangerous" prisoners, lacking leadership, easier to manipulate, easier to induce to join Political Rehabilitation. The authorities were attempting to achieve several ends with this one strategy: to snare leaders of organizations, prisoners whose decision might, according to Headquarters' view, decisively influence other men's attitudes; to keep out men they thought unimportant; and psychologically to break down the rest. A tangled, ugly web. . . .

But if there is any ideology based completely on a misunderstanding of human behavior and the workings of men's psyche, their motivations, that ideology is without doubt Marxism, and so the authorities' calculations went astray. Though this mistaken strategy was followed faithfully for years, time would show that every man's conscience, system of values, and personal pride were what led him to resist. No man needed another to show him the way.

Our food was reduced to the minimum, especially after Hurricane Flora, a storm which battered Cuba terribly in 1963, leaving hundreds of people dead and the whole province of Oriente leveled.

Men from Prison Headquarters came into the Circulars asking for our help. They asked us to donate food and blankets. Because many of our families lived in the disaster zones, and moreover out of simple human solidarity, we made our donations very willingly. It was moving to see prisoners who didn't have even enough for their own elementary necessities giving the little they possessed—blankets, a T-shirt, socks—to alleviate the suffering of the people who had been ruined by the hurricane. Several trucks with our donations were dispatched from the presidio. It was a terribly cold winter that year. I, like almost everyone else, had donated my only bedcovering. Later I got a burlap bag and sewed it to a few pieces of plastic, which at least gives some protection because it doesn't let heat escape. And with that improvised bedspread I would cover myself at night.

Incredibly, Headquarters notified us that we had donated our lunch for three months to the victims of Hurricane Flora. At nine o'clock in the morning they would bring some tanks of hot greasy water in which a few pieces of macaroni would be swimming. Immediately we started calling it "tube soup." In the afternoon there was a little bitter rice flour and a piece of bread.

There had never been so much hunger in the prison. There were men who devoted all their time to hunting sparrows, which flocked in and around the prison. It was sad to see men goaded by hunger spending hours with slingshots watching out for little birds.

Wild doves too would peck around under the cell windows in the afternoons. I was one of the men who set up traps to catch them. The snare would be a strong thread with a piece of grain tied to it, with a hook, manufactured inside the prison, stuck to the piece of corn or rice. Other men had complicated nooses. I never managed to catch a pigeon that way.

Cats would come into the Circular at night. Soon we were constructing traps to catch them. And cat became a much-sought-after and most delicious delicacy. The first time I ate one, I smacked my lips over its flesh as though it were the most exquisite dish I had ever in my life tasted. If you were lucky enough to have friends who had trapped a cat, they always gave you some of it to eat. As I've said, my first step in overcoming the scruples

I had been lugging about with me all my previous life was eating grain and broth with maggots and worms, so eating a cat was no great sacrifice. I knew that there were countries where cats were raised for food. What you ate was simply a question of habit.

From the first floor, a group with a lot of initiative planned to capture one of the little pigs of a litter being raised by one of the soldiers. These little pigs ran around loose all over the prison. The men made a rope, sacrificed pieces of corn on the cob to lure the shoats, and managed to snare one. They knew it wouldn't fit through the bars of the window so they made a savage decision. The animal squealed and shrieked like the very devil, but as soon as it had been hauled up to the window, hands reached out and slashed its throat while another pair of hands held a burlap bag out under the animal, to catch its blood so it wouldn't be wasted. At the same instant, in perfect synchronization, men began slicing and cutting it up. The work went incredibly rapidly. They cut it into pieces that fit through the bars and in moments it was inside, completely jointed.

28 / Some Men Freed, and
Some Who Were Tried and Sentenced

The little group of Americans held on Isla de Pinos had found out that Donovan, the lawyer who had been instrumental in the exchange of the Bay of Pigs prisoners, had come to Cuba again, this time with the hope of reaching some agreement in the negotiations for them. The Swiss embassy, in charge of United States interests in Cuba, had visited the Americans and told them how the negotiations were going.

One day the guards called them. But Vidal Morales and Rafael del Pino were left in the Circular. They were stunned, crestfallen. They were both Cubans with American citizenship, and they knew Castro's hatred for his enemies.

One afternoon while he was lying on his cot, Vidal Morales was called. He jumped up and, surrounded by friends, collected his few belongings. An escort of guards took him to the building the other Americans were being held in. Director Tarrau, bemoaning the fact that Vidal had been called, told him he'd been saved at the last minute in the negotiations.

So there in the Circular was the only American citizen, Rafael del Pino, excluded from the exchange, by Castro himself. That was April 13, 1963. Vidal Morales said that number was beginning to have special significance for him. On the 13th of December they had arrested him, he was tried on the 13th of March, and on another 13th he was taking the first steps toward freedom. Thirteen wasn't always an unlucky number.

From the cell block the prisoners were transferred to La Cabaña, where they were locked up in an isolation cell. On April 21, Donovan came to visit them to tell them they would be leaving with him for the United States. At the last second, Jack Besaldo, who had served ten years, and Johnny Spiritu were added to the group. But when the prisoners were taken to Political Police Headquarters to be given civilian clothes, Spiritu was taken away, and they never saw him again.

At ten-thirty in the morning, a Red Cross plane took off from the

International Airport at Rancho Boyeros, headed for Homestead Airbase in Florida.

When they were aloft and the friendly stewardess, Kay Burnet, told the emotion-filled passengers that they could unbuckle their safety belts, she passed around champagne for a toast, and Donovan, looking down toward the coast of Havana falling away behind them, told them, "We're over international waters now. You're free men." They all cheered and applauded, and more than one pair of eyes brimmed over with tears.

On their arrival in Florida, Dr. Dean Wyantbales of the U.S. Public Health Service examined them with the aid of Dr. Bighinetti of the Red Cross. Three of the American passengers breathed with special relief: The whole negotiation had been carried out especially for their sake, to keep them from falling into the hands of the Soviets. Carswell, Dunbrunt, and Karansky were their names, at least at that point. They were agents of the CIA whom the KGB had been looking for with special zeal for years and who had slipped through their fingers again.

Month after month passed, but the decision not to accept visits with those metal screens remained unanimous.

Martha and I continued to write each other, in spite of tremendous obstacles. We were writing with invisible ink, a very simple but very effective ruse. Since Headquarters allowed us to bring in school notebooks, I sent Martha instructions for preparing the invisible-ink solution and using it to write me. The ink can be made very easily by adding a little manioc or cassava starch to boiling water until the liquid becomes about the consistency of very thin paste. She used that ink to write me letters in harmless-looking notebooks. Her pen traced out the letters in a soft shine which disappeared very quickly as it was absorbed by the paper.

I received those notebooks, which appeared fresh and new to the authorities. To bring out the writing I would put a few drops of iodine in a little water, wet a piece of cotton with this "developer," and run the moist cotton over the paper. Martha's precise, clear letters jumped off the page. She became a real expert at this writing. It occurred to her to get a brand-new fountain pen, never filled with real ink, and to fill it with the starch solution so she could write more quickly and not have to keep dipping a pen into the ink.

Every two months I would receive one of those notebooks, completely filled with her writing. Every page was a great joy to develop. When I needed to send her a message and keep it secret I used the same method. Sometimes I would even send the letter through the search. I had an infallible method —I would take a big sheet of lined paper, write in my secret message, and on top of it would write her a letter in ordinary pencil or ink, praising the good treatment I was receiving from the authorities. That was enough to ensure that the letter would be sent without fail.

She told me she used two methods for developing the message. One was with iodine and the other was with heat. I couldn't always obtain manioc starch, so sometimes I wrote her using aspirin dissolved in water. Since salicylic acid reacts to heat, you can bring out the message with a flame, or even a hot iron. There was also a medicine called Panomin, an antispasmodic the dispensary always had a good supply of, that I sometimes used for ink. And when none of those alternatives was available, I used something always available in great quantity—urine.

My correspondence with Martha was my most important occupation during that time. Thanks to our letters we grew to know each other better and better. Martha was no longer a little girl; she was now seventeen, and the two of us invented through our letters a wonderful future that we would share with love and hope. Our friendship filled both our lives with tenderness and faith. We began to feel we had been friends forever, more like two people very dear to each other who just hadn't seen each other for a long time than like people getting to know each other. For me, the letters were a sweet, firm support. I had not declared how I felt to her, but even without those words I felt there was someone who was thinking about me, waiting for me, besides my family.

Her father, Benito, had been put into Circular 1 also, and although we couldn't share a cell, we both lived on the second floor.

The change widened my circle of friends, and I spent several very pleasant weeks. At night a group of friends would get together in my cell—ex-Commander Claudio Medel, Carrión, Neugart, and I—and we had some good times talking about literature, history, and philosophy.

Medel had an amazing memory. He sometimes gave brilliant lectures on military history, and we were always ready to listen. On one occasion, for the benefit of the Americans present, he gave a talk in English on the American Civil War, and the Americans said they'd never heard a lecture so detailed and complete even in their own country. They probably didn't realize that Medel had given those same lectures when he was a professor at the Academy of Advanced Military Studies and that he was the author of half a dozen books which had been published in the United States and were considered to be among the best in the field. His specialty, actually, was Napoleon; he was the organizer and director of the Napoleonic Museum of Cuba, owned by the millionaire sugar magnate Julio Lobo.

Medel was a veteran of the Second World War. He had been a B-26 tail gunner, but he had always been an exceptional scholar. His command of French brought him an unexpected promotion when a high-level military mission from France arrived in Cuba. He was the only person on the General Staff who spoke French, and when Castro's Revolution triumphed, Medel was still on the General Staff. He had no problem, since the "bearded ones" were in need of his talents and abilities. Raúl Castro himself sought out Medel's company often. When the first great conspiracy was uncovered in 1959, the conspiracy called the Trujillist Plot, Castro cleaned out the

Army by jailing the conspiracy's leaders and expelling many other soldiers under suspicion. Medel was among the conspirators, and when Raúl Castro found out about his involvement, Raúl went to see him and told him, "Medel, you're a great traitor!"

"A very modest one, Commander, a very modest one," was Medel's answer. And that anecdote became one of the most famous of the many to enter the history of that conspiracy.

Boitel slept in a hammock, and we would get together every day in his cell. Many times we would discuss the possibility of a new escape attempt, but we never could work out the logistics for it.

That summer, an unusually hot one, several whirlwinds occurred on Isla de Pinos. These whirlwinds are a sort of small tornado with very powerful winds. In Cuba they're called "clouds' tails." One of those tornadoes carried off several sheets of roofing from the Circular and left a hole three or four yards wide in the ceiling. Because there were no fiber-cement sections to repair the hole, our jailers just left it gaping. They knew, of course, that it would be impossible for us to descend from the sixth floor along the outside wall of the Circular without being seen by the guards, so they didn't worry very much about it.

Sun came in through the hole, and the area underneath it became a kind of solarium. However, curiously enough, most of the men weren't interested in getting any sun. Only a few men went there with any regularity. Augustín Piñera, an ex-captain who had been a pilot in Batista's dissolved air force, was among them, and he and I forged a deep friendship in the solarium.

Piñera was a victim of the first of Castro's great crimes and abuses of authority. I am referring to an action whose monstrousness the press of the world picked up in the year of the takeover, 1959—the *cause célèbre* was called the Pilot's Case, and it should have been enough in itself to alert the world to what the future path of the Revolution would be.

On January 1, 1959, the day Batista fled the country, a group of combat pilots, some of those who had participated in the anti-Castro guerrilla operations in the Sierra Maestra, fled with their planes to the Dominican Republic or Miami. The liaison and transport pilots, instructors, and mechanics and ground personnel had no reason to flee, so they stayed at their posts.

Castro himself called them all to a meeting and told them the aviation sector would not have any problems. He told them he knew that those who had fled were the ones that had attacked his troops, that the rest, those who stayed, were loyal, and that he was now going to need them, since he intended to bombard the Sierra Maestra with toys for the campesinos' children. But he never did use them for that. The man who did, on February 14, bombard the ranges of Escambray with clothing and toys for the campesino families was Commander Eloy Gutiérrez Menoyo, the legendary hero of that zone, where he fought boldly against the Batista forces.

And then, unexpectedly, all the pilots on the Columbia Military Base, where the Army Air Force was headquartered, were arrested. The authorities told the mechanics that they would be witnesses at the pilots' trials. A revolutionary who had been exiled in Mexico, Antonio Sánchez Cejas, was named by Castro himself to be official investigator of the case against the pilots.

The day they transported the accused men to the city of Santiago de Cuba, the wife of one of them tried to speak to her husband. Sánchez Cejas grabbed her by the arm and shoved her away; she fell. When the woman's mother went to help her up, the officer stopped her. He told her her daughter could get up by herself. The young woman insisted on seeing her husband. Sánchez Cejas threatened both of them, mother and daughter, and said that if they didn't leave of their own accord he'd throw them out. So they had to go away. The wife had bruises on her legs and mouth from the fall.

And this was the man the government named prosecuting attorney for the trial. It was to be his first case, and he planned to make a brilliant debut.

The government ordered an immediate and summary process. Sánchez Cejas got all the family members of the pilots together and told them he wanted them to know that the death penalty was the normal sentence in these cases of ex-soldiers in the Batista army and that all the men would be executed by firing squad, so the families might as well get used to the idea. He figured he had already won the case.

The family members went to Monsignor Pérez Serantes, the man Castro had asked for help when the assault on the Moncada barracks failed in July 1953. Castro sought the monsignor's protection and intercession with Batista to obtain certain guarantees if he voluntarily turned himself in to the authorities. (In the assault on the Moncada barracks, a group of Castro's troops burst into the military hospital where wounded and sick soldiers were convalescing; several defenseless sick men were stabbed in the back as they lay in their beds. Some of them had just undergone surgery and were still under anesthesia.)

The pilots' families, with the intervention of Pérez Serantes and a priest named Chabebe, managed to get the trial postponed, thereby gaining enough time to secure lawyers to prepare the defense.

The president of the tribunal assembled for the trial was Commander Pena, leader of the 18th Column of the Rebel Army.

Once the mechanics were transferred to Santiago de Cuba for the trial as witnesses, they were included in it as parties to the crime. Sánchez Cejas charged the men with genocide, a criminal offense that does not appear in Law No. 1 of the Sierra Maestra Code drawn up by Commander Sorí Marín. The pilots were being tried under the laws of that code, though, and the tribunal was to find the guilt or innocence of the parties only by its dispositions.

The only thing Sánchez Cejas managed to prove was that in the entire course of the war a mere eight people died in air attacks. The tribunal itself was well aware of the fact that many of the bombs dropped by the accused men had not even carried detonators—on purpose. Many pilots supported Castro and dropped bombs that would not explode so that the Castro rebels could use the TNT the bombs carried for their own purposes!

The prosecution's witnesses were demolished, and not only by the defense, but by logic itself. One man testified that he had been hit in the chest by five machine-gun bullets fired from a B-26 bomber. That perjuring witness didn't know that B-26 machine guns used .50 caliber shells and that no one could survive being shot with them. It was proved that he had actually been struck by spent rifle shells.

Another prosecution witness, a woman, testified that she was attacked by a Seafury airplane, one of the fastest prop planes in existence. Nonetheless, the woman identified the pilot, named Campbell, and pointed him out at the trial.

Daily, the prosecutor made heated radio speeches attacking the pilots. He also used the newspapers *Sierra Maestra, Revolución,* and *Surco* for his propaganda. He published articles calling the pilots cold-blooded murderers.

At six-thirty on the afternoon of March 2, the tribunal handed down its sentence, which was read by Commander Felix Pena, the president of the tribunal:

> This tribunal, conscious of the responsibility it bears to the Revolution, to the people of Cuba, and to history, with the full conviction of the nobility of its action, inspired by the same democratic principles which honesty, love, fairness, and justice have inspired in this revolutionary movement, a worthy example for all the peoples of North and South America and the world . . .
>
> Finds: that we must and do hereby absolve each and every one of the accused parties of that crime, and only that crime, with which they are here charged, at the same time ordering on the strength of that finding that they be set free, dictating to that effect all the orders necessary to implement this resolution, as well as the notice of same to each and every one of the parties.

Sánchez Cejas, the prosecutor, reacted immediately. He spoke with Raúl Castro, who was being kept up to date on the trial. Sánchez Cejas then went to radio station CMKC and broadcast a long harangue against the tribunal and the pilots who had been found innocent. At the same time Communist mobs started rounding up the people of Santiago de Cuba to join them in the streets in protest against the tribunal's verdict.

As soon as Castro found out about the result of the trial he sent instructions to the Military Chief of Santiago de Cuba, Commander Piñero, alias

Redbeard (now head of the Americas Section of the Party Central Committee), to prevent the pilots from being set free.

Captain Pepín López, who was in charge of the custody of the pilots, received the order not to set them free, an order given to counter the "failure" of the tribunal. Years later Pepín López escaped from Cuba, and he carried the order with him as proof of what had happened.

That same night, Castro appeared on television on Channel 6 and spoke to the people:

> The verdict of acquittal handed down by the Tribunal in the trial against the pilots will be appealed, since just as a war criminal who feels his sentence is unjust has the right to appeal, so the Prosecutor's Office, which represents the people and the Revolution, has the same right, when the verdict is unjust.
>
> It was a grave error on the part of the Revolutionary Tribunal to absolve those criminal pilots of any wrongdoing. . . .
>
> It would be the height of naiveté for a people and a Revolution to set free precisely the most cowardly murderers, men who have proved themselves the servants of tyranny. The Revolutionary Tribunals need no further proof than the cities and populations devastated and the dozens of corpses of women and children blown to pieces by machine guns and bombs from those planes. Could we in good conscience give these wretches the chance once again to pilot bombers against Cuba, once again to write their sinister history of mourning and tragedy from some airbase in Santo Domingo or one of the other countries in which tyrants guilty of monstrous crimes have taken refuge?
>
> The Revolution was not fought for that, and those of us who are at the head of it will not permit such a mistake to be committed. This is a question which concerns the security of every citizen. Therefore we feel obliged to intervene in this matter. We cannot keep silent before such danger. The people of Santiago de Cuba should put their minds at ease—the verdict will be appealed and a fair and impartial Tribunal will judge the facts again. . . .

These words spoken by Castro decided the pilots' fate beforehand. Everyone now knew, even before the new trial was held, that they would be found guilty. For Castro, a lawyer himself, the sanctity of a fair and impartial trial signified nothing. Those are fantasies as far as tyrants are concerned.

The real consideration which made Castro want them jailed had been revealed in his speech. They couldn't be found innocent because they would be free to fight him again; they were young officers, educated in and graduated from schools in the United States, and they were not going to follow him

along his Marxist path. They were potential and extremely dangerous enemies. The colonels and other older officers, mature men, sometimes more
than sixty years old, the superior officers of the High Command, were
investigated and sent off to their homes. Castro wasn't afraid of them; they
were too old.

Castro named a new tribunal made up of public servants absolutely
trustworthy in their loyalty to him alone. It was presided over by Commander Manuel Piñeyro, and it condemned the pilots to thirty years, the mechanics to ten. The sentence included forced labor.

I met those pilots, and some of them became very good friends of mine.
Besides Piñera, there are Estévez, Campbell, the Bermúdez brothers—well,
really all of them.

The defense lawyers from the first trial, Peña Jústiz and Arístides D'A-
costa, were thrown out of the Army and fired from their teaching positions
at the Universidad de Oriente. Peña Jústiz wound up in prison, where he
met with the men he had been defending. I met him too. He later died as
a result of his imprisonment. Félix Pena, president of the first tribunal, the
man who found the accused men innocent, and Judge Advocate Paruas
requested Commander Yabor, also a member of the tribunal, to present their
resignations to Urrutia, the President of the Republic. Their resignations
were immediately accepted.

A few days afterward, Commander Félix Pena turned up dead in his car,
with a .45 caliber bullet lodged in his heart. There were several explanations
for his death. One was that he had committed suicide because he was
ashamed of the injustice he had perpetrated in the pilots' case and had been
humiliated at the hands of Castro. Another explanation was that he had
been murdered in such a way as to make it appear a suicide. The only thing
for sure is that that same night Fidel and Raúl Castro, visibly high-spirited,
went to a baseball game. They were conspicuous by their absence from the
funeral, nor did they even send a note of condolence to Commander Pena's
mother.

With the judicial monstrousness and travesty that the trial of the pilots
signaled, whatever injustice, whatever judicial "irregularities" that had been
committed by the government of Batista were now equaled by the Revolution's. Nevermore would those who supported the Revolution and censured
and decried the crimes and abuses of the Batista regime have any moral basis
for their criticism.

29 / Forced Labor

It was Piñera who initiated me in star-watching and the study of astronomy. I spoke to him about some of my readings, and he convinced me I should learn about the sky. On clear nights we would go up to the sixth floor and the hole in the roof. There was also a window that opened onto the east; we waited for the rising of the constellations Orion, Canis Major, Leo. During the day I studied astronomy books. Little by little I came to know the stars—Sirius, Arcturus, Rigel then became part of my world.

Malnutrition was taking its toll. Inmates began to faint during the head-counts, and quite frequently during the day there would be cases of men fainting or collapsing from fatigue. This situation was constantly denounced by the prisoners. The prison's Chief of Medical Services was a soldier by the name of Alvarez who had been to Algeria on an Internationalist mission and who instead of a stethoscope always carried a pistol; he would shoot toward the Circulars just for fun. Every effort we made to improve the situation met with his total unconcern.

One day the Chief of Medical Services of the Ministry of the Interior, at Isla de Pinos on an inspection visit, came to our Circular. One would naturally assume him to be a doctor, but he wasn't. He had been a traveling salesman for medical-supply companies. This man, "Dr." Herrera Soto-longo, a Spanish Communist, had fled to Cuba because of the civil war in Spain, and thanks to the solidarity of the Cuban Revolution with Spanish Communism, he had become Chief of Medical Services of all the jails and prisons in Cuba. And you always had to call him "Doctor" or he wouldn't answer you. He knew nothing at all about medicine, of course, but he was a man the Leader could trust. We placed our grievances before him—the need to examine the sick and wounded, better medical care, and the like—and miraculously the authorities began to do blood tests on groups of men.

One of the inmates who worked in the hospital would go to the Circulars and the prisoners would stick their arms out through the bars. The first results were alarming—two and a half or three million red corpuscles. A count of between four and five million red blood corpuscles is normal. There were cases with as few as two million. These men were carried to the hospital on stretchers so they wouldn't have to walk.

Prison Headquarters was alarmed. They consulted with Havana, and then they just stopped the tests. It had been almost two years now that proteins and vitamins had been utterly lacking in our diet. The health of numberless prisoners was ruined.

In the little "care" package that our families sent, only flour, roasted cornmeal, and candies could be included, plus any powdered foodstuff that was not milk or chocolate. I recall that my mother made me some little cubes that looked like candies. She made them at home out of eggs and beef liver dried in the sun, powdered, and thickened and bound with sugar. They tasted terrible, but they were protein. The inspections didn't catch them, so I received some protein every sixty days. Moreover Martha had somehow gotten hold of some vitamin tablets and ground them up and added them to the *gofio de trigo*. It became an obsession with me to try to avoid suffering the ravages of vitamin deficiency. I devoted all my wits, all my energies to achieving subsistence nourishment.

In Cuba the acquisition of powdered protein or other dehydrated food-stuffs was simply impossible—they did not exist. Yet because of the general malnutrition among the prisoners, after some years, for the first time the authorities softened a bit and gave us canned goat meat. It was stinking meat, and it filled the whole Circular with its rank odor, but I devoured it with delight.

Later they allowed us one boiled egg three times a week. Sliced cucumbers began to appear. Here was some improvement. But it wasn't motivated exactly by humanitarian concern—we couldn't be weak and anemic for what they had planned for us.

It was about this time that Manolo Ray, who had been Minister of Public Works in Castro's first government and was now a leader of one of the largest anti-Castro movements, announced from exile an invasion of Cuba. On May 20 I and a number of other prisoners were taken out of the Circulars and transferred to the punishment-cell block, where we were put into two large rooms, one on each side of a smaller room which opened onto the bathrooms. We were there as hostages. The head of the garrison, Captain Morejón, came to tell us straight out that when the first shot was heard, we would be executed. They placed a machine gun before the only entrance to our room, so we were prisoners within the prison.

We had to find out what was happening. One wall of our room, with its high windows, opened onto Circular 3. We decided to try to set up communications with that Circular.

We placed two beds, one on top of the other, under the window. Rogelio Villardefranco and I climbed up to the window. Villardefranco was an experienced, fast telegraph operator. We signaled several times until the men in Circular 3 saw us. Immediately they went to get one of the telegraph operators in their Circular, and we set up communications. Every afternoon we climbed up to receive the news bulletin. Villardefranco received and I copied it down on a piece of notebook paper which I titled "Now You Know!" As a masthead I drew a very stylized newspaper boy running down the street with newspapers under his arm.

Once a guard saw us. Captain Morejón came into the room and called for silence and began very calmly and composedly to explain that there were rules in the prison which prohibited citizens detained there from climbing up to the windows. But the longer he talked the angrier he became, and he finished in a vulgar harangue full of the grossest threats. As he was leaving, he yelled from the barred door, "I'm giving orders to shoot to kill the faggot that climbs up to that window again!"

But we took precautions and kept climbing up and peering out. We couldn't bear to suspend those communications.

We were there for exactly one month. On June 20 they ordered us to get our things together. Boitel, Fernando Pruna, and I left together. We were taken to Circular 3. There were 150 of us that time, but within three or four weeks, there was another transfer, this time general, massive. It took one entire, exhausting day. Hundreds of prisoners with all their belongings went from one corral to another, from the Circulars to the corrals. They were shifting us around according to a selection they had made of men for some special plans they had. Those of us who were in Circular 1 got back together again now in Circular 4.

Everything was now ready for the beginning of the forced-labor program, the greatest outpouring of violence that had ever been seen in the history of the presidio of Isla de Pinos. It would only be surpassed years later in the blackout cells of Boniato Prison. The commencement of forced labor was preceded by a wave of terror and repression aimed at intimidating us and breaking us down. The directors of the Ministry of the Interior had already accepted the fact that they would have to kill many of us.

The plan was called Camilo Cienfuegos. Camilo Cienfuegos was one of the commanders who had fought with Castro in the guerrilla forces, a militant in the Popular Socialist Youth Party (JSP), a name used by the Communist Party since 1944. Cienfuegos disappeared mysteriously in a flight from the province of Camagüey to Havana.

On August 9, 1964, the formation of the first forced-labor squads was begun in the buildings which at that time housed the political prisoners called *plantados,* or diehards; that is, those who would not join the Rehabilitation Program under any circumstances or after any sort of "persuasion." With no motivation whatever, without any justification, the garrison broke into Building 6 blindly wielding truncheons, bayonets and rifles, and electrical cables. They invaded the high floors beating the prisoners and destroying everything they found in the cells. Within five minutes there were dozens of wounded and bruised men.

The guards saw the terror they inspired, and it spurred them to greater and greater violence. They were drunk with it, it became a means of pleasure for them. They took great and cruel, almost sexual, delight in their power. Lieutenant Porfirio García, head of Internal Order, directed the search personally, bayonet in hand. He hit anyone he wanted, without a second thought, and his men imitated him brutally. Lieutenant Porfirio plunged his bayonet into Ernesto Díaz Madrugada, just above the groin, perforating his bladder. Then as Ernesto was falling, Sergeant Matanzas, Porfirio's sidekick, stabbed him again, finishing him off. They stabbed him again and again as he lay on the ground. Then they grabbed him by the ankles and dragged him down the stairs. His head banged against the stairsteps, and blackish blood gushed from his mouth. He was already a corpse.

The murder of Ernesto, the first casualty of forced labor, was committed in cold blood, to make us see that the same thing could happen to any of us; they wanted us to realize that our lives were worthless to our attackers.

Circulars 1, 2, and 3 and Building 6 were already going out to work. We hadn't been called, and some of the men thought that since in our building there were "classified personnel"—students, professionals, and those who had the most political clout—we would be exempt from forced labor. In our Circular there were also old men and men with physical handicaps, and that strengthened the theory that we would simply be spectators of the tragedy the rest of the prisoners were acting out.

Another play, this one a despicable, shameful farce, not a tragedy, was acted out, and all of us witnessed that one in great anger. A group of men who had gone into the Political Rehabilitation Program in order to earn favors from the enemy weren't satisfied with their own collapse; they decided to lure others into the program and belittle the holdouts. On their own initiative they wrote and staged a play which they titled *Freedom in Three Steps*. The plot painted men like us who had decided to resist entering Political Rehabilitation, to remain in the Circulars, as "antisocial elements, criminals, drug addicts, and homosexuals"—the utterly depraved, in the words the Communists would use to refer to us in their defamation campaigns. The play made excuses for the fact that its authors had taken the first step—accepted Political Rehabilitation—by saying that it had been impossible to live with us.

That shameful spectacle debuted in the dining hall of the prison on Isla de Pinos. And it went onstage before an audience of prisoners, including women, brought from all over Cuba expressly to see it. It was a tremendous hit. The Ministry of the Interior even had the play performed throughout the country; it played in theaters in Havana and even on television. Meanwhile the government's repression left a trail of hundreds wounded, bruised, beaten, and that first death.

Lieutenant Porfirio finally came to our Circular and instructed the gate-keeper to tell the men whose names would be called to come down immediately. He was carrying lists made up by Headquarters. These would be the work gangs. Each gang, which the authorities blandly called a "block," was composed of four squads, and the squads in their turn were made up of about fifty prisoners.

I was called and assigned to block 20, with most of my friends, with the exception of Boitel, who had been put in with the students. Carrión, Pruna, Gustavo Rodríguez, the pilots, and some two hundred other men made up block 20.

At that time I was sharing a cell with Richard Heredia. In the first days of our detention Richard and Carlos Alberto Montaner had tried to dig a hole through the wall of the jail at Political Police Headquarters.

Trouble occurred while we were still inside the Circular, in the prison yard. Some men from the fourth floor began to yell "Murderer!" at Lieutenant Porfirio. He turned around and complained to the gatekeeper, but the men upstairs went on yelling.

He *was* a murderer; he had killed Ernesto. But he didn't like to be called one. He went to the gate and ordered the guards called out. In five minutes, troops armed with rifles with fixed bayonets, Captain Morejón leading the charge, ran up to the gate like rabid dogs.

The prisoners began to sing the national anthem. Those of us in the prison yard would be the first to meet the garrison's attack. I could see myself cut to ribbons; I was scared. Pruna and Carrión were standing beside me. I told them we ought to move closer to the central tower, where we had a better chance of protecting ourselves. We couldn't leave the prison yard or go up to the other floors or run inside the walls.

Lieutenant Porfirio was bellowing and ranting because the garrison had come with their bayonets fixed to their rifles instead of carrying them like knives. Fixed bayonets at close quarters were difficult to manage, and since the prisoners might get hold of the rifles and use them against the guards, the guards couldn't enter the grounds.

He had the padlock opened. We were terribly nervous and tense, ready for the beating we knew was to come. But Captain Morejón entered alone. The notes of the national anthem ended, and the voice of Mario Gavilán rang out from the fourth floor:

"Captain, the only thing that we've done here is sing the national anthem, and no Cuban can possibly be offended by that, no matter which side he's on!"

A silence charged with foreboding and fear had fallen. There was a moment of hesitation in Captain Morejón.

"All right," was all he said.

He turned and marched away. That day, thanks to Gavilán's calm, very opportune intervention, we were saved from another beating.

Rivero Caro, a lawyer and journalist, was one of the first to decide not to work. And he informed the officer organizing the work gangs of his decision. The officer took note of his name and that of Alfredo Izaguirre, who had been the youngest newspaper editor in all of North and South America, a member of the Interamerican Press Association (SIP). He was in charge of the daily *El Crisol* in Havana, which had been nationalized by the government. Alfredo had participated in several actions against the Castro regime. He came and went many times from Cuba clandestinely; he planned an attempt on Raúl Castro's life. Later he planned an attack on the American naval base at Guantánamo, an entrenchment on the south coast of Oriente province, which he had hoped would be interpreted as an act of revenge on Castro's part. He wanted to provoke the armed intervention by the United States, which he hoped would put an end to Castro. But State Security discovered the plot and Alfredo was arrested. He spent many weeks sentenced to death. Every night he thought he would be taken to the firing squad. But the fact that he was a member of the Interamerican Press Association caused Castro to change the death sentence to a thirty-year term in prison.

The operation planned by Alfredo and coordinated by the Central Intelligence Agency was called Operation Patty. The Cuban Political Police called their retaliatory action Candela, or Operation Firestorm. Because of the far-reaching implication of this case, the Cuban authorities made a movie about the operation, which featured the sagacity of the organs of State Security. The movie bore the title *Patty and Candela,* and it was shown in all the movie houses in Cuba. However, the master stroke of propaganda backfired. Alfredo, who was supposed to be the villain of the piece, the man who had tried to destroy the Revolution, who had been sent by the CIA, who had been a tool of the Yankee capitalistic society, was immediately perceived as the hero, since most of the people sitting in the movie theaters shared his desires and hopes for freedom. (I had occasion to be witness to this phenomenon years later. In the hospital of Combinado del Este prison in Havana, all the nurses wanted to meet Alfredo; they had unfeigned admiration for him and everything he represented.) The Political Police withdrew the film from the movie theaters.

The first man they called out for having refused to work was Rivero Caro, and along with Alberto Muller and his brother, he was carried off to the punishment cells. These two latter men would join the work gangs later, not without first being beaten and forced to work.

They beat Rivero Caro. Then they dragged him out to work, only for a few days, alone, right around the Circulars, digging in the ditches parallel to the security cordon fence. Then they locked him up in the cells. Long afterward, almost two years later, when they transferred him to the prison at La Cabaña, his back was still marked and scarred from the beatings he had received. It looked as if he had been burned.

Alfredo Izaguirre talked to me about the logic he had followed in deciding never to work. He reached the decision calmly and rationally. He knew he was exposing himself to mutilation or even to being beaten to death, but his decision, once made, was irrevocable.

When they put him into the punishment cells, he was left alone for two or three days. At the end of that period Lieutenant Porfirio, Sergeant Matanzas, and several armed guards came to get him.

From the Circular, we watched Alfredo led by that platoon of men to the back of the main guardhouse, where a ditch carrying sewage ran. They tried to give Alfredo a can to clear the excrement that had accumulated along the edges of the ditch. Alfredo refused even to touch the can.

Lieutenant Porfirio explained to Alfredo that the only thing he had to do was squat down and move the can around a little—that would satisfy them. It was a question of principle for the soldiers. They were trying to break down his resistance, to make him back down, to make him give in, to force him to give up, contradict himself. But it was a question of principle with Alfredo as well. We watched him from the Circular. Not even bothering to speak, he shook his head no.

They bashed him in the head with the can. His head began to bleed. Then they began to beat him savagely. The blade of a bayonet slashed his forehead. Sergeant Matanzas had narrowly missed killing him.

After the first broadside of blows, Lieutenant Porfirio again urged him to cooperate; he tried to convince him that the best thing for him to do was agree to work, even if for only one minute. But Alfredo's attitude had become even more stubborn, if that was possible. So they beat him again. They stopped and even promised him they'd take him to Cuba, which for a prisoner on Isla de Pinos was one of the most wished-for things that could happen. But Alfredo, his face bloodied, kept saying no. They kept beating him, stopping occasionally to see if he would give in. But it was all in vain. Enraged, furious, they jabbed and pricked him with the bayonets and beat him with their rifle butts until Alfredo lost consciousness. They picked him up by his hands and feet in a dead faint, bleeding profusely, threw him into the back of a jeep, and drove him to the punishment cells. From Circulars 3 and 4, dozens of eyes followed what was happening. As they took him out of the jeep, he began to come to. They threw him on the floor of a cell, and a few minutes later Dr. Agramonte, a tall heavy black man, the new military doctor for the prison, appeared. He was accompanied by a very short man, who knelt down beside Alfredo. Alfredo had been dumped face down on the cell floor. The short man yanked him up and held him erect against his knee. He looked over the bayonet wounds. He felt for a pulse, but there was none. They stripped him completely, leaving him wearing only his boots. Alfredo could hear them but he didn't have the strength to speak. "We've got to take him away immediately," the short doctor said to Agramonte. They put him on a stretcher and covered him with a sheet, with just his boots peeking out a little. As they carried him into the hospital, people who saw him come in thought he was dead.

They examined Alfredo. His nose was broken and he had dozens of wounds and bruises all over his body. One of the bayonet wounds was in the crease under his buttock, where the thigh and buttock join, and since when he was lying face up the wound was concealed, it escaped the medical inspection.

He was given intravenous saline and glucose. When he was moved to a bed for the IV, the wound in his buttock opened and began to bleed profusely. Blood soaked through the mattress and started to drip onto the floor. By the time someone came in and discovered the blood, Alfredo was in a coma; he was bleeding to death. They gave him emergency transfusions to replace the blood he had lost, and they managed to save him.

Fifteen days later, Alfredo still couldn't raise himself from his bed. The savage beating had left him with large bruises and broken blood vessels all over his body. There were purple circles under his eyes from the inflammation of his face and the bruises from his broken nose. Still in that condition he was put back into the punishment cells, without any other medical attention.

Alfredo Izaguirre was the only prisoner I know of who never performed any forced labor for his jailers—not even a minute's. It is fitting that his name go down in the history of the Rebellion of the Cuban Political Prisons.

30 / The Quarry

The members of gang 20 were called out to be issued working clothes. The next day, we were told, we were going out to work.

The sky was still dark when the gatekeeper shouted for us to get up. There was only a faint glow in the east. After we'd been counted we went down to the prison yard to get our breakfast, which consisted of a little hot water with sugar and a piece of bread a little bigger than an egg, but not much.

Almost all of us were keyed up and expectant. The change of routine, even though it meant going to work, was really something. It was a great event to leave the confines of the prison. The gangs from Circular 3, which were now leaving before we did, told us that prisoners were carried all over the island to work—planting and harvesting citrus fruits, fertilizing fields, cleaning out overgrown areas.

They ordered us to form up outside by twos. Each gang had one foreman and a squad leader for each squad. These men were armed with pistols and a bayonet at their waist or in their hands. Casares, one of our men, knew the leader of the squad I was assigned to, since they both belonged to the same religious brotherhood. Regardless of his supposed religious beliefs, the guard would become one of the most repressive and bloody of the soldiers. We called him Pedro of the Evil Word and Deed, because he himself would always say that he was "always doing evil."

The squad leader called roll not by names but by our numbers. When he had finished, Escambray, the leader of the entire gang, gave orders to move out. We walked toward the main entrance. There the trucks that would transport us to the work area and the troops that would escort us were waiting. There were hundreds of guards, some of them with packs of German shepherds, like Nazis.

They performed another count behind the trucks before we boarded them. Then the convoy drove off, escorted by a truckful of guards. On the cab of that truck, there was a Czech-made B-Z machine gun aimed directly at us.

We turned off toward the left, toward the town of Nueva Gerona. Before we crossed the Las Casas River, we turned again and took the highway that led to the airport. A few years back I had made that trip, escorted then, too, by guards, although the atmosphere had been even more hostile and repressive than now. At least now I could look around without fear. The time before, even that was prohibited.

We passed the airport. To the right there were miles and miles of mango fields. That was Castro's very own idea. Millions of pesos were spent on that plan, and it turned out to be a complete disaster. The land wasn't right for that kind of crop, but none of the agronomists who were advising him dared contradict the dictator. Only a few of the trees ever bore any fruit. Exactly the same thing had happened with that mad campaign of his for planting coffee inside the cities. In parks, in vacant lots, in private gardens and yards, and on balconies and terraces—you had to plant coffee trees anywhere there was a square yard of dirt. Castro announced that there would be a virtual cornucopia of coffee, coffee for everyone. Coffee trees were planted in a belt all around Havana. On one occasion, exuberant over the brilliant scheme he had conceived and put into action, the Commander in Chief sought to impress a group of foreign diplomats he was meeting with in the middle of what was called the Havana Cordon. With evident self-congratulation he showed them the newly planted green belt of coffee trees. But an English diplomat, assigned to the Food and Agriculture Organization of the United Nations, told him flatly that they would never harvest a single bean. That was his expert opinion. Castro reacted as though the man had slapped him. There ensued such an argument that the other diplomats had to step in to calm the situation.

The expert from the Food and Agriculture Organization was right. No one ever drank a drop of coffee made from those plants. And the matter was never talked about again. It was considered taboo in Cuba. But whenever that English diplomat ran into Cuban delegations in London, he would always ask them, with a sarcastic grin, how the coffee was coming along in the Havana Cordon.

The trucks went down a red dirt road bordered by young trees. There was a civilian, the manager of the state farm, waiting there. The guards got off the truck, went through the windbreak of trees, and opened out into a circle that surrounded us completely as we got off the trucks.

The work assigned us was fertilizing—by hand, of course—the pieces of land planted in pangola, a grass used for cattle feed. They handed out burlap bags with shoulder straps. The sacks of fertilizer were piled up all along the field. It was our first day of work, as it was for the guards as well, so things were almost unbelievably disorganized.

As we advanced along the field, the cordon of guards advanced with us. We prisoners always moved inside a large circumference of rifles, bayonets, and dogs, always on flat land stripped of trees, so that any attempt at escape would have been suicide.

From the first day, it seems we all decided on a policy of passive resistance; we'd quietly sabotage what they ordered us to do. It had rained for several days before that first day, and the ground was covered with puddles. When the guards weren't looking we would empty our sacks of fertilizer into the puddles, and the water would swallow it without a trace. Somehow or other, a case of machetes disappeared into the cracks in the ground. With the fertilizer that we "spread" in that work session, twenty or thirty times more ground might have been fertilized.

We went back at sundown without any incident. The next day they took us farther off, to a place they called El Bobo, near the north coast of the island. There were mango trees planted in that area too, and the work consisted of weeding around the trees with a hoe, making a circle of mounded dirt.

One of the ways we resisted was simply by not hurrying, doing everything very, very slowly. Two prisoners were assigned to each tree. Gustavo Rodríguez and I had fallen behind. Pedro the Evil One kept trying to hurry us along, but we held to the same rhythm, so finally they took us out of the group and moved us to another place.

We spent almost the whole morning on one tree. The foreman of the gang, Escambray, had been alerted to us, and he came over toward us. He was already swishing his bayonet through the air, and we could tell he was itching to give us a beating with it. Gustavo was closer to him than I was. He saw him coming and turned to face him, taking a position of self-defense by gripping the hoe with both hands as though he were gripping a rifle for a bayonet fight.

Escambray stopped. "Drop that hoe." Gustavo didn't move. "Drop it."

"I'm not going to drop it, Sergeant."

Escambray saw that Gustavo wasn't going to let himself be beaten without putting up a fight. Several seconds of tension passed. Neither said a word or moved. Why didn't Escambray take out his pistol and shoot Gustavo? I've always wondered. Escambray would later be known as one of the most violent guards on Isla de Pinos. But that was only his second day of work. Maybe *that* was why he didn't shoot Gustavo.

The third day, they sent us to the quarry. There the head of the garrison of guards was a very tall, thin soldier as black as night, named Holé. He was the son of Haitian parents.

Lieutenant Pomponio was waiting for us. He had been made the foreman of our gang. He came directly to me and took me out of the ranks. He led me over to Holé:

"This is one of the ones that tried to escape with Boitel. So find him the biggest sledgehammer you've got. Tell the guards to shoot to kill if they see him getting close to the fence."

Holé studied me for a minute. "Come with me," he said.

We went to the tool shed. He looked around and handed me a twenty-five-pound sledgehammer. I could barely lift it, but I put it on my shoulder and walked down the dirt road leading to the work area, following Holé. A wall of granite rose along the left-hand side of the road facing the ocean. This was a natural barrier. Then there was a semicircular cyclone fence which enclosed the whole quarry area. There were guardhouses with machine guns every fifty yards.

Explosives had been used to sheer off and break up the granite cliff. Great boulders were piled at the foot of the bluff, as well as smaller blocks which we were to break up into yet smaller pieces with our sledgehammers. In the area there was also a sand quarry and a room with lime, into which they would stick prisoners they wanted to punish. The prisoners would come out almost blind, their hands and feet burned from the lime. There was also a mill for crushing rock and a dining hall.

Fernando Pruna had been one of the first to take up arms against Castro in the mountains named Sierra de los Organos, in the western part of Cuba. With him went Nena, at that time his fiancée, her father, and a group of followers, among them the American Austin John. As soon as they made their presence known, contingents of Castro troops went out to hunt them down. Capturing them wasn't difficult, since the Castro troops outnumbered them tremendously, and after several skirmishes they were captured in a fierce fire fight. Pruna was sentenced to death, but he was spared the firing squad thanks to pleas for clemency made to Castro by several student organizations in U.S. universities where he had studied. Those things were still possible in 1959. A year later, Commander Blanco, who had directed the operation in which Pruna was captured, was also transferred to the prison on Isla de Pinos, but by that time Blanco was just another prisoner. He had opposed Castro. Now Pruna, ex-Commander Blanco, and I were in the same group, all of us hefting our sledgehammers.

Every man with a sledgehammer had a helper who carried a long iron bar, pointed at one end. His job was to use the iron bar on cracks in the rocks. My helper was Peñita, one of the Air Force pilots.

The sledgehammer is a tool which, like all tools, you have to know how to use. None of us there had ever so much as held one before in his life. One of the foremen, who was assigned to the troops in the quarry, came over to us. He was limping visibly.

"You mean to tell me you've never broken rocks before?"

"No, sir, never."

"Well, then, you'd better learn. Here, hand me that sledgehammer. I'll show you how. And then I don't want to hear anybody say they don't know how. Here, everybody's got to produce."

He pushed up his sleeves, slid his holster around on his belt to his back, and gripped the sledgehammer. "Now, watch," he said. "The first thing you have to look for is the seam in the rock. Look, here's where it changes color. You have to hit that seam." And it was true. The bottom of the boulder had one dark zone and another lighter, with the seam he had spoken of running neatly between them. He raised the sledgehammer. In his hands, it seemed to weigh nothing at all. As it rebounded off the boulder, he used its momentum to help him lift it over his shoulder again. When he hit the rock two or three times, it fell open along the seam. Then he hit it several more times and broke it into smaller pieces.

When he left, I tried to imitate him. I needed to learn how to do it the way he had, since I knew I wouldn't tire so quickly if I could get the knack of it. At first I couldn't make the hammer bounce off the rock the way he had. The problem was that when I dropped it on the rock, I was gripping it tightly by the handle and the vibration of the shock ran like an electric current through my arms. I finally realized that I had to loosen my grip on the handle a bit when it struck the rock; it would bounce off easier then, and it took much less effort to raise it again. Within a few days I was getting pretty good at combining the work with the sledgehammer with the iron bar.

The enormous boulders lying at the foot of the quarry had been drilled, so that dynamite sticks could be inserted into them and they could be blown into smaller rocks. It occurred to Tony Copado to block the holes with clay. When they rang the lunch bell, the infantry soldiers would go over to the boulders to put in the charges. They discovered they were all stopped up. Holé ordered us to form up and started threatening us. He insulted us, he called us every name in the book, and he swore he'd beat us to a pulp if anything like that ever happened again.

We didn't have the protective equipment that workers ordinarily wear in quarries. We had no boots, no protective goggles. The shards of rock went through our pants like bullets and embedded themselves in our legs. And the glare of the sun on the rocks was blinding—you really need special lenses for that kind of work.

Gustavo and I were working as a team again. When the foreman came by, we would work. As soon as he went off a little way, we'd stop. But as time passed they invented new procedures to keep our production high.

Manzanillo, the foreman who had taught us how to use the sledgehammer, and another guard they called Black Dog began to systematically beat us. The object was to terrorize us. First thing in the morning, they began bludgeoning us, beating us with bayonets, and demanding that we break more rock. They ordered the men in the sand quarry to get out more sand and the stone carriers to fill the trucks faster. When the trucks roared up to be filled, we would make long lines, a human chain, from the area where we were breaking the rocks to the loading point. We passed the pieces of rock from hand to hand. The first man would bend over, pick up the stone with both hands, and with a little rolling motion pass it to the man beside him; that man passed the stone to the next man, and so forth down the line. Anyone watching from a distance would have thought he was watching some strange ballet. Sometimes the sharp edges of the rock would cut your hands, but the chain wouldn't stop for that, and soon we would be passing gray granite rocks darkened with blood. If you dropped one of the stones, the rhythm of the work would falter and the foreman would run over to you and beat you with a bayonet. Bending over like that, with your arms hanging down and rocking like a pendulum to pass the stone from one man to the next, caused terrible back pains. There was hardly time to stretch and get a little relief. If the foremen surprised us at stretching, they would jump all over us. "Keep it moving!"—and they would whack us with a bayonet.

Eloy Gutiérrez Menoyo had been born in Spain and had spent his childhood in Barcelona. His father was one of the founders of the Spanish Socialist Party. His brothers were all dead. One of them had died in the Spanish Civil War, and another, Carlos, had died in Cuba, in the most heroic action of the Revolutionary War, the assault on the Presidential Palace, whose objective was to kill Batista. Castro and his movement had nothing whatever to do with that action.

Eloy's family had fled Spain during the Civil War and taken refuge in Cuba. Eloy had always been a fierce opponent of dictatorial regimes of any kind, so he joined the rebels in the mountains of Escambray and founded the Second National Front, of which he was commander in chief. He led the bloody fighting against Batista's army and on Batista's flight from Cuba came down victorious out of the mountains. In that zone he was the indisputable leader, a hero, and he had the sympathy of every peasant there—but Eloy had fought to establish a truly democratic system in Cuba, not another dictatorship. Therefore when he saw that Castro was becoming a tyrant, he fled the country; a while later he came back with a small group of armed men who tried to reach the mountains to continue the struggle. But he was trapped, captured, and sentenced to thirty years in prison. He was there with us in the quarry.

It seems the soldiers had gotten instructions from Curbelo, the Political Police representative on Isla de Pinos. We had all seen Curbelo's jeep drive into the quarry that morning, and then Curbelo speaking with the Political Commissioner and the foreman named Luis. Our hard-won intuition told us something was going on. Sure enough, in midafternoon they called Eloy out. He was loading stone, piling it exactly the way the soldiers had told him to do it. The foreman Luis and another guard who only a few days before had been in charge of the quarry flanked him as he walked toward the exit along the dusty yellow-earth road. They came to a halt almost directly in front of the guardposts at the entrance.

Fernando Pruna was turning back to his carpentry—he was repairing the handle of his sledgehammer. He had watched Eloy and the guards without even suspecting what was about to happen, or that he would be the closest witness to it—hardly thirty yards separated him from the three men.

Luis took out his bayonet behind the unsuspecting Eloy's back and hit him. Eloy turned like a mad bull. Pruna froze. The foreman stabbed at Eloy several times, trying to stick him with the point of the bayonet, and that was when the other soldier, who had never struck anyone until that moment, took out his bayonet as well and began to beat him. Eloy was cornered. It was an instinctive move on his part to raise his arms to ward off the blows.

We all stopped working when we saw the guards attack Eloy. Some prisoners shouted. Guards took the safety off their machine guns, getting them ready to use against us. Pruna didn't move; he just stood there, watching that bestial spectacle.

After a while Eloy did not even raise his arms to protect himself anymore. Pruna counted 122 blows.

Eloy swayed and staggered. Besides beating him, they were now stabbing him. He fell, weak and fainting, to the ground. They kicked him then. Luis called the dump truck from the stone mill. A prisoner in the Rehabilitation Program was driving it; he was so nervous that he didn't manage to stop the truck next to Eloy, who was lying at the two foremen's feet on his back in the yellow dirt road. Instead, the driver passed him by and then had to back the truck up, almost running over all three of them. Luis and the other soldier picked up Eloy's unconscious body; they seized it by the arms and legs, swung it to give it some momentum, and threw it into the truck. Then they got into the bed of the truck and told the driver to take off. The truck jerked so, it was only a miracle that kept the guards from tumbling out.

The driver thought they were going to the hospital, but Luis yelled at him to turn down the hill toward the squad breaking rocks in the south part of the quarry. Black Dog was down there. They threw Eloy out of the truck and left him to Black Dog.

When we saw that we didn't know what to do. We didn't understand. But we soon found out. Eloy began to regain consciousness. Black Dog told him to stand up. And when he was standing, the foreman took his bayonet out of his scabbard and began beating him sadistically again until Eloy fell, once more unconscious, to the ground. Then Black Dog sat down on top of him, lit a cigarette, took a deep puff, and raising his head to the sky, blew the smoke slowly out. . . .

A deathly silence had fallen. Not a shout, not a sigh was to be heard, not like at the beginning when men were shouting at the guards to leave Eloy alone. Terror floated ominously through the air. Eloy regained consciousness a while later, and again Black Dog beat him senseless. That went on several more times. Because of those beatings, one of which burst an ear-drum, Eloy suffered afterward from constant dizziness.

His recovery took weeks. He was almost unrecognizable, with his face swollen and covered with a purplish-black bruise. The wounds made by the bayonets left marks on his back which two years later were still perfectly visible. One of his retinas was damaged, but they still don't know how serious the damage is, since to find that out you have to have specialists with the proper equipment. As I am writing this story, Eloy and dozens of other prisoners are finishing three years in blackout cells, naked, totally incommunicado, without any correspondence, and under an absolute stricture against any medical care whatsoever. To get medical care, you have to join Political Rehabilitation.

31 / The Brother of the Faith

We had to form up in front of our cells for the morning headcount at five o'clock. A little while later, the foremen of the gangs started coming, and they would tell the gatekeeper which gang to call down. The gatekeeper called attention, then he called out the number of the gang and ordered it down to the prison yard. As other foremen came in, the same orders were called out. The soldiers expected us to follow these orders immediately, but the simultaneous exit of a thousand men was impossible, and some men didn't come down right away. The squad leaders would get furious. To solve the problem, Headquarters ordered everyone, without exception, to come down to the ground floor immediately after headcount. No prisoner was allowed to stay on the floors, not even if he was sick. They would bring in breakfast, which had not varied in the slightest, except perhaps for its temperature—the sugar water might have been a little hotter than usual. We lined up for this meager breakfast by gangs, and when the foremen came, if the gang that had been called out still hadn't had its breakfast, it simply lost its turn. So we often had to run out without breakfast or gulping down our last bite of bread.

All it took for the officers in charge of the Circulars to call out the guards was for a few prisoners to hold back on the floors. That was when the beatings started. The guards would rush in armed with bayonets, truncheons, and chains, and anyone they caught on the floors would be beaten senseless.

These beatings by the garrison began after Captain Morejón said he'd give a gold medal to the man who could stand up for one year to the forced-labor plan and still not get down on his knees and beg to join the Political Rehabilitation Program. Captain Morejón lost symbolically. Out of the hundreds of prisoners who had signed up to join the Political Rehabilitation Program, a great many changed their minds and decided to become diehards, *plantados,* when the beatings started. Not only did they suddenly rediscover a certain amount of their lost pride and self-respect; there was also a "peer-group factor"—they weren't going to let anybody think they'd joined just because things were getting tough.

The forced-labor plan had one consequence the experts in human behavior in the Ministry of the Interior were unprepared for. The presidio banded together in an almost monolithic way. Faced with the aggression of that common enemy that beat, harassed, tortured us, a total identification occurred. We became "aware," and every time they beat another man, it was as though they were beating you. Every time they murdered one of us out in the fields, it was a brother they were killing, and our very hearts bled. Anguish and horror brought us closer and closer together.

The violence redoubled; it seemed we had no respite at all. One very early morning, well within the limits which they themselves had set for us to come down to the prison yard, two completely covered military trucks, those that nobody particularly notices, stopped in front of the main gate, and dozens of guards, armed with anything that could be used for a beating, entered the Circular. But from the moment the first guard jumped out of the truck, the alarm had sounded, and hundreds of us managed to reach the prison yard by the stairways or by dropping from the first floor to the ground over the parapet. The first floor was only about five feet off the ground.

The guards were already occupying the stairways which led from the ground to the second floor, and the gauntlet of blows was terrible.

Mohamed and Botifol were two of everyone's favorite men in the presidio. Mohamed had been jailed as he was finishing his studies in medicine. Botifol was a stock farmer from Camagüey who had come up in the ranks of the Partido Auténtico. Now both of them were trapped up there somewhere. They tried to reach the stairs before the garrison cut off their escape, but they couldn't.

Howls of protest and anger filled the Circular. The guards were making a butcher shop out of the stairways. There was a hail of blows with chains, bayonets, and truncheons. They were breaking heads and arms.

Mohamed and Botifol stopped on the second floor, terrified. They knew what awaited them. Even though they were both intelligent men, in those moments an animal terror possessed them. And suddenly, a squad of maddened furious soldiers caught sight of them and began to run toward them. Mohamed and Botifol didn't hesitate a second. They didn't seem to care that they were on the second floor. They plunged, blind with fear, over the parapet, thinking perhaps that they would fall safely. The impact broke their ankles. In fact, that was the least that could possibly have happened to them; God had protected them. It was a suicidal jump.

That Saturday the platoons of prisoners came back to the Circulars at dusk. There were thousands of prisoners corralled by rifles and bayonets arriving in silence from the forced-labor fields. They made jostling, compact ranks of hunger, of sweat, of exhaustion. They were dirty, some of them barefoot and others with their clothing hanging from them in tatters. Their backs and shoulders were bowed and bent as though they carried all the weight of bitterness and human misery in the world on their shoulders. The muddy roads and highways leading to the jail on Isla de Pinos, and the roads inside the prison barbed wire itself, were full of the long columns of men winding to their cells from another wearying day's work in mosquito-infested swamps, in quarries, in the fields of citrus trees our blood fertilized. More than six thousand political prisoners were now lodged in that gigantic concentration camp.

Some of them had already entered the buildings. You could hear the foremen's and squad leaders' voices yelling at them to move along. But the prisoners, undernourished and bent with fatigue, could only trudge heavily, slowly. The shouting was normal to them, nothing special, the everyday litany of month after month, year after year. Then the guards would unleash a hail of bayonet or truncheon blows over the heads of the men at the front of the lines, and the file of men would move a little faster. Gang 26 with its four squads came slowly along the highway which ran parallel to our building. They didn't walk, they dragged themselves. They hardly had the strength to lift their feet. The guards yelled at them to speed it up and threatened them with machetes and bayonets. The prisoners made an effort, but the escorts wanted even more, and they began to beat them. "Speed it up, you sons of bitches!" they shouted as they vented their fury. The blows of the machetes and bayonets on the prisoners' backs sounded like low thunder. The file began to break up, but the guards chased the men down, striking out blindly. The first prisoners made a superhuman effort and almost ran to dodge the blows. Suddenly one prisoner, as the guards rained blows on his back, raised his arms and face to the sky and shouted, "Forgive them, Lord, for they know not what they do!" There was not a trace of pain, not a tremble in his voice; it was as though it were not his back the machete was lashing, over and over again, shredding his skin. The brilliant eyes of the "Brother of the Faith" seemed to burn; his arms open to the sky seemed to draw down pardon for his executioners. He was at that instant an incredible, supernatural, marvelous man. His hat fell off his head and the wind ruffled his white hair. Very few men knew his real name, but they knew that he was an inexhaustible store of faith. He managed somehow to transmit that faith to his companions, even in the hardest, most desperate circumstances.

"Faith, brother," he constantly repeated, and he left a wake of optimism, hope, and peace. All of us called Gerardo the Brother of the Faith. He was a Protestant minister and had dedicated his life to spreading the word of God. He was his own most moving sermon. When he came to the prison of La Cabaña, thousands of prisoners were squeezed into those *galeras.* There was simply no space. Men slept on the floor, in corners, under beds. And the fear of death permeated our nights, for those were the nights of the firing squads. We never knew if we would ever again see our friends who walked off to the tribunals. Bullets killed so many Cubans who stood up to the dictatorship; the centuries-old moats shook with the brave cries of "Down with Communism!" or "*Viva Cuba Libre!*" But at those instants of almost unbearable anguish and dread, the Brother of the Faith would say that the prisoner they had shot was a privileged man, that God had called him to His side.

He helped many men face death with strength and serenity. He came and went constantly among the groups of men, trying to instill faith, trying to calm their spirits, trying to give support.

When they opened the *galeras,* he would go through them, looking for sick men, and whether the sick men wanted him to or not, he would carry off their dirty clothes. And you would see him down there in the prison yard, with a piece of burlap bag or plastic tied around his waist like an apron, standing over mountains of dirty clothes, bent over the washbasins with sweat pouring off him.

He would get us out of our cots to go to the prayer meeting. "Get up, you lion cub! The Lord is calling you!" It was impossible to say no to the Brother of the Faith. If he saw that someone was pensive and downcast, he would say to him, "I want to see you at the prayer meeting this afternoon," and you had to go. His sermons had a primitive beauty; he himself had an extraordinary magnetism. From a pulpit improvised from old salt-codfish boxes covered with a sheet, behind a simple cross, the thundering voice of the Brother of the Faith would preach his daily sermons. Then we would all sing hymns he wrote out on cigarette packages and passed out to those of us at the meeting. Many times the garrison broke up those minutes of prayer with blows and kicks, but they never managed to intimidate him. When they took him off to the forced-labor fields of Isla de Pinos, he organized Bible readings and choirs. Having a Bible was a subversive act, but he had, we never knew how, a little one which he always carried with him.

If some exhausted or sick prisoner fell behind in the furrows or hadn't piled up the amount of rock he had been ordered to break, the Brother of the Faith would turn up. He was thin and wiry, with incredible stamina for physical labor. He would catch the other man up in his work, save him from brutal beatings. When one of the guards would walk up behind him and hit him, the Brother of the Faith would spring erect, look into the guard's eyes, and say to him, "May God pardon you."

There were more than a thousand prisoners in that building. We all had great admiration, great affection for the Brother of the Faith. Whenever the guards broke in to beat the stragglers out to work, there, always encouraging us, cheering us up, was the Brother of the Faith. "Don't tempt the devil, brothers," he would call out to the tardy men. While we stood in the long line for "breakfast"—the never-failing sugar water—many times the

Brother of the Faith would tell Bible stories or make us laugh with his original and highly personal disquisitions on sin and men's conduct. "Don't ever forget that I lived in sin and knew temptations," he would tell us. His constant labor was to teach us not to hate; all his sermons carried that message.

My gang worked only at the quarry. The other gangs would be moved all across the Island, planting citrus trees, gathering the crops, maintaining the plantings, cutting hay by hand, and doing all sorts of other farm labor.

In the quarry the guards grew more and more cold-bloodedly brutal. It may be that they got bored. Watching over us as we worked must have been monotonous. Anyway, they would invent all sorts of cruel new amusements. One of the guards had a horse he rode around the area. Whenever he wanted to liven things up a bit, he'd spur his horse to a gallop and, swinging a machete around wildly, strike out at prisoners' backs, like one of those cavalry soldiers cutting down Indians—in this case, unarmed and unable to defend themselves, or certainly unwilling to defend themselves, since that would mean certain death. With the force of the rushing horse and the blow, you were almost always knocked to the ground, and the guard would guffaw loudly at his triumph in bringing down his enemy.

The quarry was the work area nearest the prison, only five minutes away from the Circulars. Still, we were always carried there on trucks. Many days, before the sun had even come up, we were on our way. However, as a sort of compensation, we were also the first gang to return.

When we were all at work, the Circular was like a huge empty coliseum. Only the sick men and a cleaning crew stayed behind. That was the best time to take a bath, because when the other men came in, there weren't enough showers. I always had a long, relatively luxurious bath when there was some reason for me to stay in the building. Then I would go up to my cell, usually to sit down next to the window, where there was light, and study. At night I would go on studying by the light of a tiny lamp I got fuel for by stealing a little gasoline from the tanks of the trucks. I had a little bottle tied to a cord that I would drop into the tank when the guards' backs were turned and some of my friends could keep watch. A little gasoline today, another little bit in a couple of days, and I had enough light to study by.

My friends kept telling me that I was going to go blind. But I wasn't worried about that. I got my hands on an illustrated geology textbook and studied it passionately. Often the next day I would test what I'd learned from the book by looking for examples in the quarry. And I think my attitude toward learning from every situation was a great help. For me, the rocks weren't just rocks. Not that they came alive, but I knew that feldspar, mica, and quartz were among the kinds of rock that composed that granite I was smashing. The world of stone fascinated me. Some of my companions would be curious when they saw me carefully examining a piece of stone. I showed them that in marble and granite you can often find little glints or veins of gold, as of course you can also find iron pyrites, "fool's gold," which is much more attractive to the man who knows nothing about what gold itself looks like. Gold was present in the stone at the quarry, but in such tiny quantities that it wasn't commercially feasible to mine it. I recall that Campbell kept little grains of gold in a matchbox; he planned to melt it down one day and make an engagement ring for his fiancée.

Whenever I thought I'd be able to get them through the search, I took back little samples of minerals with me to the Circulars so I could study them at leisure in my cell. They always searched us as we entered the presidio. At first it was a quick pat-down, so you could easily smuggle through a little rock you had hidden in the crotch of your underwear. I also made myself a little bag I hung inside my pants from the waistband, over my pelvis. That was more comfortable.

Prison Headquarters told us one night that we could receive our visitors in the dining hall, without the hated screens and fences. They were also authorizing our visitors to bring us a sort of care package with whatever foodstuffs they wanted. We would have one visit approximately every forty-five days. You can well imagine the joy that news gave the Circulars. Some of us had gone years without having seen our families, and that promise of finally seeing them was almost too wonderful to be true. I thought about my parents, my sister, and about Martha, whom I'd be seeing after years of frequent clandestine correspondence. We had grown so deeply attached that everything in us cried out for a meeting.

The authorization for the food package was an intelligent step on the part of the authorities. They used us like slaves, and our families would feed us. The country had already instituted rationing cards for food staples and other necessary items, so what they could bring us would represent an enormous sacrifice for our families. They would have to keep food back, out of their own meager quotas, or else buy food on the black market at exorbitant prices, and that at the added risk of being jailed for the crime of "subversion of the economy," which had been forbidden by law on pain of three to six years in jail.

If in those periodic roadblocks the government set up on highways, searching buses and other vehicles coming from rural areas, they found some citizen with a few pounds of meat, he would be charged with subversion of the economy, and if that person turned out to be a family member of a political prisoner, the authorities' fury against him grew even greater. This happened, in fact, to Luis Zúñiga's brother. They searched Luis' brother's house and found letters from Luis, in jail on Isla de Pinos. They also discovered a can containing twenty chorizos, a spicy sausage which is a staple of the cuisine of Spain and all of Latin America. Since the quota of chorizos was one sausage per two people per month, and they weren't always distributed, no one could justify having in his possession a whole can of them, unless a family of forty people lived in the same house. Luis Zúñiga's brother was saved from being accused of having stolen the sausages because the can was from Spain, and he could prove that it had been a gift from a friend of his who was a diplomat. Nonetheless, for having twenty sausages he was accused of the crime of hoarding, which had also been prohibited by law, and they jailed him.

The visits were organized by gangs. They began at Circular 3. Our date was set, and at last the day of the visit arrived, the first visit in two years and some months.

They took us out to the dining hall to search us. Several platoons of guards were waiting for us. The search was distressing. You had to strip completely, leaving your clothes to one side. They went through it down to the last stitch. We had to open our mouths so they could look inside, and if they noticed that a prisoner had false teeth, they made him take them out. They could also oblige us to raise our testicles. A guard would crouch down and look up to make sure that we had not hidden any little piece of paper there. They were obsessed by the idea that we might smuggle out a denunciation, a letter, which might have the force of firsthand testimony. We could take absolutely nothing to the visits except an aluminum cup.

At ten in the morning, the procession of family members appeared on the highway. Our encounters were charged with high emotion. The pitiful embraces, the tears and the joy all mixed in those moments. My family arrived. My father was the only one who let a tear fall; my mother and sister, always stronger at those moments, showed their relief and happiness by kissing and hugging me, both of them at the same time. Only three family members per prisoner could come in, so Martha had to come in with the family of a friend of mine.

I still remember how she looked. More than three years had passed since we had seen each other for the first time. The teenage girl who had so impressed me then had now become a lovely young woman. When she arrived, we looked into each other's eyes, neither of us speaking. She blushed deeply. We had not really been apart since that September 5. We knew that we were now united forever. Words are unnecessary when the communication of spirits says it all.

Our talk consisted simply of holding hands and walking into a fantasy world that sprang from the love we felt and shared. Everything around us disappeared—the people, the place—and we were like the first pair of lovers under a wide blue sky filled with a light that would never fail. In that world we would live forever, leaving cells, locks, terror, anguish, and sadness behind.

But the next day I went off to the quarries again. And that experience was made even more bitter because after the visit, the food went from bad to worse. Now it was a greasy broth with rotten sweet potatoes floating around in it. On one occasion when Director Tarrau came in with a group of officers on an inspection of the plant where cement blocks were made, the mess was being served at that very moment. Cepero walked determinedly toward the group, carrying his lunch. He halted in front of the director and the officers and held out his plate with that broth in it. Time seemed to freeze; nobody moved. We expected the guards to leap onto Cepero and beat him and drag him out out of the director's presence. But it didn't quite go that way.

"This isn't enough food for men who work as hard as we do. It's not even enough to survive on."

Lieutenant Tarrau impassively looked at the plate and then at Cepero. "We know that. That's why we give it to you." And he turned his back and went on talking to the other officers, showing them how the machinery for making blocks worked.

Not a day passed that someone didn't receive a beating. They gave Lito Riaño a hundred blows with a bayonet, counted out by men who stood there and watched the attack.

Sometimes you could escape the grinding, soul-battering drudgery for a bit. The shoes they had given me fell apart. They had been ruined by the rocks. But of course I had helped wear them out by rubbing them on the wall of the cell. It was a typical prisoner's patient labor. So one morning I told my squad leader that my shoes were worn out. I showed them to him. That was how I became part of the group that stayed behind in the Circular, not going out to work. I took full advantage of those days. The enormous silence allowed me to study the whole time. The authorities had so far not considered taking us out to work barefoot. . . .

32 / Sewage

Or so I thought, until that morning when all of us who habitually stayed behind were called out to the prison yard. A small group of sick prisoners, wrapped in blankets and shivering with cold, or their breathing labored by asthma, were forced to go form up outside the building. Then, when the military leader of the Circular had taken all the platoons out, he ordered the sick men back inside, to stand with those of us who did not have clothing or shoes. I waited there with the rest of the men. I amused myself during those minutes observing Saturn, which came out every morning about that time. Gang 20, to which I belonged, went out last to the quarries.

There were about eighty of us formed up in that contingent. Some of us had on only underwear; some were wearing sandals, but most of us were barefoot: men who were staying behind knew that neither shoes nor clothing had arrived in the warehouse yet, so some of the sicker men had given their shoes to healthier men, workers. Only two percent of the prison population could stay behind, not go out to the work fields, on account of sickness. If there were thirty sick men, we had to select the twenty to remain in the building and the ten who, sick or not, would go out to work. They would be dragged out if necessary, but they had to leave the building and go to work.

It struck me as strange that they had not yet ordered us to go back to our cells. That was when a platoon of guards arrived led by Juan Rivero. He had been one of our guards in the punishment cells. Rivero was one of those soldiers whose rank goes to their heads—he was made head of the punishment-cell block and then head of Internal Order and then director of his own concentration camp. He stood there a few moments looking at us, sneering. When the inspection was over, he called the head of the Circular over and asked him for the list of the sick men who had formed up in the front rank, just at the little roadway which led off to the main entrance of the prison. He examined the list and made a gesture with his head. The leader of the Circular ordered the sick men back inside.

Another platoon arrived then, brandishing bayonets, and we were ordered to line up two by two. From that moment on, you could feel the hostility. We marched off toward the main exit of the prison. The guards escorting us on each side were wielding their bayonets and shouting and threatening us. We walked by the soldiers' houses and the Headquarters buildings. We went on through the barbed-wire gates at the main entrance, and turned to the right, toward the east. Moment by moment the violence grew.

They had already beaten several men, and those heading up the files were shoved along and told to march faster. The walk was trying, because most of us were barefoot. The thorns and burrs simply wouldn't allow us to walk as fast, let alone as comfortably, as the guards with their boots on.

That area was totally new to us; we had never worked there. I was slightly familiar with it, though, from the time we were making our preparations for our escape attempt. I had taken notes on it as I studied it through the telescope. Over that way was where the "Turd Bowl" was located, a ditch where all the sewage from the prison emptied, not only sewage from the prisoners but also from the Headquarters installations, the military housing, the shops, the hospital, the barracks, and all the rest—the excrement of some eight or nine thousand people. When we were studying the possibilities for our escape, at one point we considered using the sewers, and I investigated the ditch. At the opening of the sewer a man from inside the Circular could crawl through the pipe, but farther on it narrowed and a man's body wouldn't fit. The people who built the prison had even thought about the possibility of a prisoner's trying to escape that way one day.

In spite of the fact that we were headed directly toward the ditch, it never occurred to me that that might be our destination. When we came to a stand of undergrowth, a little reddish-earth path appeared. Another platoon was waiting for us there, armed like the others with rifles and fixed bayonets. They joined the cordon. The look of this began to worry me. The shoves and the blows on our backs and heads continued. Lieutenant Juan Rivero was marching out in front with two sergeants and a soldier who was not wearing a cap. By the quality of his uniform, we all knew that he was an officer from the Political Police. I felt an almost uncontrollable dread.

We were already accustomed, like Pavlov's dogs, to react to known stimuli. A search was terrible, but we knew what was going to happen. We knew we might be beaten on the stairways as we were leaving, as we were coming back in, but we were prepared for whatever came. Not now. Now we were completely in the dark about what was happening and what might happen.

We crossed the little creek. Murmuring pines surrounded us. The ground here was very rocky. At intervals little islands of sharp spiky rock seemed to float along the surface of the ground. The rocks, called "dog's teeth" in Cuba, were made of millions of microscopic crusts of plankton. We would try to avoid them, but they grew denser and denser. It was becoming almost impossible now to find footing free of those rocks. We finally came to a barbed-wire fence. The first men who tried to get through it by holding apart the strands and crawling between were beaten to keep them from doing that. The guards wanted us to vault the fence. That meant we landed with our bare feet on the other side of the fence, on top of the sharp rocks. The whole purpose of that was to injure the soles of our feet, to make us cut our feet to ribbons on the rocks.

For some men the pain of a rock piercing their foot was so great that they staggered and fell to their knees, and when they stood up again, their knees would be bloody too. The second a prisoner fell, the guards started brandishing their bayonets and yelling at him to run. I caught hold of one of the fence posts and jumped over holding on to the wood to soften my fall. I didn't calculate how near the fence that would make me land. As I landed on the other side, my right ankle, whose bones had been out of place since I was injured in the escape, gave out on me. My left knee buckled. I swiveled involuntarily and crashed into the barbed wire. The barbs ripped into my knee, tearing my pants leg and the skin, and left scars I still bear. Then the guards made us run.

If the rest of the men felt as I did at those moments, they were terrified. A thousand ideas added fire to my terror. I thought we were going to be machine-gunned, since we were outside the prison grounds—far from the prison, in fact. It would be easy enough for the guards to say that it was a mass escape attempt.

Blood from my knee stained my pants, and the stain was growing. When we came to the sewage ditch, our feet were bruised and mangled, many of us had, as I did, scratches and scrapes, and we were exhausted and terrified. What we saw then, though, practically made us retch. The ditch was six or eight yards wide at its widest point. On its surface floated islands of excrement. Above the shit were clouds of green flies. The smell of sewage, of those disgusting miasmas, filled the air.

The squad leaders, at an order from the officer from Political Police, attacked us. They shoved us with their hands and rifle butts and forced us to wade into that horrible ditch. I fell into the sewage headlong—someone had pushed me from behind—and I could not keep the filthy water from filling my mouth and eyes. The pretext for that torture was that we had to clean the bottom to keep the canal from becoming obstructed. In some places the water reached as high as a man's chest or even his chin, depending on his height. The bottom was irregular; there were sharp drop-offs, so that you'd suddenly sink over your head if you took a wrong step. You had to pick something up off the bottom—a rock, a little trash, anything even if it was just a little handful of mud, and take it over to the side of the ditch where the guards were waiting to beat you. The uncomfortable position they had to stay in, squatting down, and the fact that we prisoners had only our heads sticking out of the water meant that the guards would hit us in the face, necks, and on our shoulders. Many men were bleeding from the cuts and wounds.

The scene was indescribable. If you didn't plunge in deep enough, you'd be pulled out onto the bank and beaten. As long as we were out in the middle of the ditch, it wasn't so easy to hit us with their bayonets, so some of the soldiers found long sticks to hit us with at a greater distance. Other guards, wanting to join in the fun of the punishment, threw rocks at us. Then the order to advance toward the narrowest part of the ditch came. It was precisely there that a layer of excrement covered almost the entire surface, damming up the water. The water was flowing sluggishly through a small opening. We waded forward through that sea of shit. Every time we submerged, we had to push aside the excrement so we could get our heads above water. Our hair was full of it. Our ears and the wounds on our feet and those caused by the garrison's bayonets were open doors to infection and contamination. It delighted the guards to see us plunge our heads into those filthy waters. They never let a chance go by to poke us with a bayonet or push our heads down into the water with their boots. Nothing after this can be worse, I thought as I begged God to give me strength to resist, to endure. They had already struck me several times, and the cuts on my knee were burning, irritated by the fetid water.

We were so black that from a distance of only one or two yards, you couldn't recognize even your best friend. We looked as if we'd been dyed in a tank full of ink.

Toward noon, they took us out of the ditch. I felt I'd passed a new test —that had been a bestial punishment. We prisoners looked at each other in silence. We were battered, unrecognizable men covered with filth and detritus. The sun burned down, and our hair and clothes, matted with excrement, started drying out. The guards were taking a little rest. We had to stand in the sun.

Juan Rivero and the officer from the Political Police were strolling nearby contemplating our state with undisguised satisfaction. They gave the order to march, and we marched off, some of us limping, others leaning on friends' shoulders. It was a parade out of some surrealistic vision. Thirst had made my throat scratch, but when I recalled the gulps of filthy water I had swallowed, I felt nauseated. I wanted desperately to get back to the Circular and take a bath and quench my thirst. We were exhausted, almost at the end of our physical strength.

But they weren't leading us back to the prison. We were heading away from it, toward the coast. They gave the order to halt in front of a well where we could get some water to drink. But not a single one of us moved, and we were very thirsty. It was a spontaneous reaction of repudiation, of rejection. The soldiers insisted, and even brought over a can filled with several gallons of water. No one drank. Thinking that perhaps fatigue and the gnawing hunger of months and months might be used to humiliate us still further, Juan Rivero said that he was going to bring us lunch. But we weren't having any of that, we weren't going to eat in that state of filth. One of the prisoners answered him, "Juan Rivero, down with Communism!"

The defiant prisoner hadn't finished his sentence when the entire garrison fell on us, beating us with rage and fury. And they ordered us to double-time back to the lake the ditch emptied into. That stretch had an indescribable brutality about it. Our legs, swollen by hours in the putrid water and then standing in the sun, would not obey. Anyone who fell was savagely beaten. Almost dragging ourselves, putting forth what was for us a titanic effort, we arrived. The little lake was a bowl full of excrement. The ground it was dug out of had excellent drainage, so it absorbed almost all the water, and what was left was a gigantic deposit of shit. But it was not just human excrement. There was also the filth of five hundred or so pigs from a hog farm nearby, which gave off an unbearable stench. There were also bloody cotton wads in it, the sanitary napkins of the women guards, and bandages that had almost certainly come from the hospital, and all sorts of other filth. There the swarm of flies made a constant almost musical background buzz.

Mario Morfi had been beaten more than almost anybody. They had flown into a rage with him, and Juan Rivero had given orders to beat him again and again. So when Morfi entered the lake after those long hours in the ditch, he came down with a cramp. His exhausted legs wouldn't respond, and he began to sink into the shit. He tried to grab on to some support, which did not exist, to stay afloat, but it was no use. He called to his nearest comrades to help him. The closest men tried to help, but the guards were still incensed with Morfi and they flew at the other prisoners to keep them from reaching him. They yelled at the prisoners to leave him alone, he was all right, he was just faking the cramp so that he could get out of work. I cannot remember witnessing a more horrifying scene in my life than that one. I was some fifteen yards away from the sinking man. All we could do was watch him slowly going under. The guards had loaded and cocked their rifles. They threatened to shoot anyone who tried to get close enough to help Morfi. He kept sinking—down to his shoulders, his chin, his nose. Almost involuntarily, almost without realizing what they were doing, his friends standing closest by, even under threat of being shot by the squads, started running to help their comrade drowning in the filth. Morfi had lost consciousness; nothing but the top of his head was above water. Calimano and Kelo got there first. Others followed. The guards didn't fire, but they did beat the men who ran to his aid. Morfi was pulled out of that sickening quicksand-like lake, and they carried him away, along with another prisoner wounded in the leg by a guard we called Mosquito—for his skinniness and long legs.

Morfi was dazed and semiconscious. He had still not recovered when he was thrown into a truck which had come to bring food to the garrison. We persuaded them to let another prisoner, Franco Mira, one of the Bay of Pigs invaders who died a little later in jail, accompany the wounded men to the Circular, in case they needed any help on the way. Franco tried to give Morfi a little water, to see if he would regain consciousness, but one of the guards kicked away the jar and cried, "Let the son of a bitch die! That'll be one less of you bastards to take care of!"

We stayed about two hours more up to our necks in that shit. And then they marched us back. I cannot recall a longer or more painful march or a return more fervently desired. All I was thinking about was taking a bath and disinfecting my cuts and wounds. I knew the danger they posed, since they had been infected by sewage and shit.

It was the last hours of afternoon. Our wounds, covered with excrement, dried. The excrement in our ears and hair dried too. That poisonous water produced infections in our eyes; there were several cases of hepatitis, and a whole series of digestive disorders. Morfi got an ear infection from all the filth in his ears. His eardrum perforated, and he had problems with balance for the rest of his life.

When the three prisoners arrived at the Circular, at first no one recognized them. The men there had to get very close to them to distinguish their features under the black layer of filth. What had happened? How had they gotten into this disgusting state, with this matted hair and this filthy clothing? The three prisoners were bathed and taken care of, and they told about the ditch and the lake. It had been almost twelve hours since we had left the Circular, and no one had had the least idea where we had been taken. The Circular, as a man, was waiting for the rest of us to return. The halls were full. When that parade of us battered men, exhausted, dragging our feet, trudged into the prison yard, our companions began singing the national anthem. Some of the eighty men had still not come through the entrance gate when the garrison, infuriated by our reception, gave us a farewell beating. I was one of the last men, and the point of a bayonet pierced my left wrist when I tried to ward off the blow. No one anticipated the garrison's reprisal against us for singing the national anthem—they turned off all the water until the next day. That meant we couldn't take a bath.

Only two days later, a truckful of shoes arrived, and all of us who didn't have them were issued them immediately. Prison Headquarters instituted a control over the issue of work clothes by keeping a card on each prisoner which showed the date of the dispatch of the articles. This was supposedly to keep us from tearing up our clothes and the like. They had already put that measure into effect in another Circular, but the cards showed clothes and boots supposedly issued to the prisoners which the prisoners had never received. So when they presented us with those cards for us to sign, we refused. The first man they tried to make sign the card was Rolando de Vera. They put him in the basement and gave him a beating, but he still didn't sign. They carried five or six more men down there and beat them, but those men wouldn't sign either. That made the authorities finally give up. Two years later it would be discovered that the leaders of the gangs falsified our signatures, thereby stealing thousands of items—books, blankets, and clothing—which brought a very high price on the black market.

The violence of the garrison now led by Captain Morejón left a wake
of dozens of wounded and beaten men every day in every Circular.
The searches, performed only as a means of constant terrorism, became ever
more frequent and brutal. Squad leader Almanza poked out one of Domingo
Fernández' eyes with a bayonet. Marcané, one of the most furious and
bullying of the soldiers, broke a bayonet over Rafael Márquez' back. When
he began to beat Rafael, he went completely out of control. In fact, there
was hardly any such thing as control anymore.

At the main gate of the Circular one day, even before we had been
counted, squad leader Pedro the Evil One began to beat Eulogio Cantero.
They shouted at him from the Circulars that that was enough, to stop, but
the prisoners' cries made the guard even more angry and he kept beating
Eulogio, like a man possessed. He screamed and bellowed, which even
Eulogio didn't do. Hundreds of prisoners watched the barbaric scene. Some
of us counted 120 blows. That same day squad leader Escambray, head of
gang 6, came earlier than usual to get his prisoners. They all noted that he
seemed to be in a terrible mood that day. When he got them to the work
area in the middle of nowhere, miles from any populated areas or even a
house, he seemed to be inspired by a cruel idea. He ordered all the men to
form up and, surrounded as they were by a circle of bayonets, to strip. And
he made everyone in the gang work stark naked.

Ricardo Vázquez and Israel Abreu, my friend and workmate in the
Ministry of Communications, decided in the face of this dreadful wave of
violence not to perform any more forced labor, and they declared a hunger
strike. The authorities beat them furiously for several days.

"Something's gone wrong," the authorities must have said to themselves.
They were incapable of understanding that a human being is more than a
machine. They couldn't conceive why those hundreds of prisoners, who a
while before had actually been applying for the Rehabilitation Program,

were now adamantly refusing to go into it under any circumstances, especially once forced labor and the wave of repression and beatings had begun.

And the conclusion that the authorities arrived at was that they needed
even more repression, more terror, so that everyone, en masse, out of sheer
desperation, would enter the Rehabilitation Program. But that did nothing
but make the resistance more solid and unified, make the prisoners' rejection
of and contempt for such a merciless and inhuman enemy grow even
stronger and more intransigent.

Political Commissioners were going out with the forced-labor work
gangs. Our Commissioner was replaced, and one morning the new one, who
had just graduated in the latest group of Commissioners from the Ministry
of the Interior, arrived to go out to the fields with us. His name was Leonel
Urquiza. He was very young, about twenty-three years old, and he didn't
look like the ones before. He had been raised in a middle-class family, had
been a good student, a boy with a real thirst for knowledge. He was curious
to get to know us, to find out what made the political prisoners tick. Why
were we, according to what he had been told, the worst of society, the most
abominable? In the courses given by the Ministry of the Interior, they had
told him that the political prisoners were cold-blooded murderers, vicious,
desperate men, capitalist exploiters, pimps and procurers, and of course, to
a man, agents of the CIA.

Just as in Russia during the first years of the Bolshevik Revolution, in
Cuba the Political Commissioner was the highest authority and the soldiers
were subordinate to his decisions and teachings. The first thing that this
Political Commissioner did was get on the truck with us, an unprecedented
thing to do, since the Commissioners always traveled with the garrison.
Nothing like that had ever happened before, and it was very uncomfortable
for all of us. We were used to being able to talk and make jokes during our
trips, gossip about the latest news, but we couldn't do any of that with a
soldier among us. We clammed up—we had to keep the integrity of our
common interests. He saw that, but it didn't make any difference to him.
At lunchtime, traditionally the Commissioner stayed with the other soldiers,
but Urquiza came over to us. I was sitting in a little group made up of
Celestino, Carlos Betancourt, a very dynamic, combative journalist, Dr.
Súarez Matta, who died a little later from lack of medical attention, and
Buria, one of the pilots. We always had lunch together, under some tree if
there was one, or out in the open if not.

The Commissioner asked if he could sit down with us—and he kept
doing that every day. He was a young man with a passion for culture, for
philosophy, and for the arts. Our approach was not to virulently attack the
regime, but rather to show him that in the first place we were not what he
had been told we were. Then he himself confessed to us, "They told me
before I came here that I would find criminals, drug addicts, empty stupid
men with no ideals. But it hasn't been that way. I've seen revolutionaries

who helped the Revolution come to power, students, professionals, campesinos. You men are not what they told me you were."

That statement from him implied many things. First of all, he was becoming aware that he had been duped. So we decided that we would exploit that first chink in his armor, show him yet other tricks that had been perpetrated on him.

Dr. Súarez Matta, in those brief moments we had to eat, would talk philosophical or historical matters, and the Political Commissioner was an avid listener. He heard ideas the mention of which—the thought of which —was prohibited in the society he represented. He often brought the newspaper *Granma* with him. It was the official organ of the Communist Party of Cuba. And he would ask us to give him our reaction to things it printed. We would show him the doctrinaire objectives of the newspaper and the fact that the news was not really informative. Then at night he would listen to the news on foreign radio stations and the next morning would tell us what he had heard. Since we too had a radio, we could confirm easily enough that he was reporting the news back to us unexpurgated, that he was not a plant from the Political Police.

That young man's liking for us was obvious. He always sought us out, he loved to talk and to ask questions. We warned him that he had to be careful about the way he talked when he was with the men of the garrison.

He was the person in charge of bringing our letters to us, and he did it when we were in the fields. As a proof of his respect, he didn't open our group's letters. Moreover, he offered to smuggle some correspondence out for me in particular, as a special favor. Nonetheless, others among the two hundred prisoners of the gang felt great hostility for him. We could not divulge the work we were doing with him, we could not tell the other prisoners we were trying to convert him, for security reasons. He was the supreme authority over the work gang. When trouble seemed to be headed our way, he would call us aside and tell us what was going to happen—for example, if one of our men was going to be taken away for a beating from the squad leaders. In many cases the Political Commissioners, who seemed the most humane and peaceable men within the prison system, were those who selected the prisoners to be beaten. He told us that himself.

One day they took our whole block out to an area near the coast which they had cleared off in preparation for planting pangola. There were hundreds of acres of a fine whitish sand. The trucks couldn't get out to the area, so we had to march along a road the bulldozers had just finished making. Our work consisted of scattering handfuls of the grass that had gone to seed, then covering the ground over. A tractor would then come in and turn the earth so the seed would sprout.

The sky quickly began to cloud over. Heavy rain clouds rose up on the horizon and tumbled together, and the gusts of wind and the turbulence of the clouds made the sky look as though it were boiling. The rainstorm broke like a torrent. Within seconds we were soaked to the skin. We huddled together in groups as the guards made a circle around us. It rained for almost two hours. The truck that was to bring lunch couldn't come because one of the bridges on the highway had been washed out by the river. So, at four o'clock in the afternoon, we began to march back to the prison. We had been lashed by the wind and rain, our clothes were dripping wet, we were cold, and we hadn't eaten a bite all day. On both sides of the road the water stood in great puddles. Two tractors had bogged down in the mud. We ourselves had to wade through ankle-high or even calf-high water, while the guards picked their way along the highest parts of the road where dirt had been piled up by the tractor-graders.

Leonel, the Political Commissioner, was walking with the prisoners slogging along. I recall that I picked some wild lilies and put them in my shirt pocket. I'd try to smuggle them into the Circular. We were weak and exhausted and soaked from head to foot, so someone started singing. Others joined in, and soon we were marching along, singing our battle hymn. As we sang, we felt renewed, reinvigorated, and we even walked faster. The soldiers now actually had to almost run to keep up with us. It went that way for about five minutes, until the leader of the gang, a man named Richard, ordered us to stop.

"Halt! Halt!" he shouted, running toward the front of the column. The garrison couldn't keep up with the group of starved prisoners. "What's going on with you men?" he shouted at us. "Are you trying to wear out the guards?" We were prisoners, many of us middle-aged or beyond with white hair, we were exhausted by the work they made us do, we were starving, but we had that vigor and energy which is born inside a man and which has nothing to do with the calories that he consumes. The rain couldn't dampen our spirits!

Leonel couldn't keep himself from asking with a certain admiration, "Where do you men get the ability to stand up to this? What keeps you going?"

"We have an inexhaustible supply, sir, an imperishable source. That's what constantly feeds us. It's love," I said, and gripping the bunch of lilies, I added, "These flowers are much more powerful than bayonets. They came before bayonets, and when bayonets have disappeared from the face of the earth they will still exist."

Leonel looked at me. I think he understood my message.

That afternoon must have been decisive for him. When he got back, a letter from his family was waiting for him. The government had taken his father before a labor assembly for not having gone to a Sunday work outing of "volunteer laborers," and they had declared him a nonperson. His father had been a laborer in a factory in Guanabacoa in Havana. The decision about his father must have been what finally decided the matter for Leonel.

In a meeting with the other Political Commissioners he stood up to the plans for repression which were being fomented and he committed the grave error of defending us prisoners from a humane point of view. A few hours later he received orders not to leave the area of the prison. But still, even though he was under arrest, he came to the Circular. He ordered the gatekeeper to call me out, and in a matchbox, so the escorts if they were looking wouldn't notice, he gave me a letter. In it he told me of his disillusionment with the system he had always defended before and of the way he now saw the situation.

We never saw him again. We did learn that he was taken to trial, accused of "ideological weakness" because he had allowed himself to be confused by the enemy, found guilty, and sent to jail. Years later Carlos Betancourt ran across him in the prison at Guanajay.

The Political Commissioners assigned to our work gang afterward never tried to talk with our little group.

Repression grew much worse for us after what had happened with Leonel. They divided us into two groups of about a hundred prisoners each, and a man named Ventura came in as the head of the gang. He was a real sadist, a thief who became a scourge not only to the prisoners but also even to the truck drivers and the few campesinos who still kept a few chickens or pigs. Ventura never came back to the prison with empty hands. He'd as soon steal wood or posts or planks as produce and chickens from the State or from private citizens. If he saw a pig, he'd say it was wild and run it down and catch it and beat it to death and carry it off with him. He transported all his booty in the trucks. He would stop in front of his house on the road to the south and drop off what he pillaged. There wasn't a single day that Ventura didn't beat some prisoner as well. He often said that if the regime should ever change, he knew that under a democracy he'd only be sentenced to a few months of jail for beating prisoners.

We were standing out in the open one cold, gray morning, in line waiting to be counted. Ventura began to deal out blows with the flat of his bayonet. He got angry at Manino and started to jab him with the bayonet. But Manino jumped back with feline agility and slipped away from the sure stabbing. His reflexes saved his life. The point of the bayonet wounded him in the chest right above his heart. Half an inch closer and Ventura would have killed him. The squad leader called roll hurriedly and we marched off to the trucks.

The squads and platoons of Building 5 and some prisoners from Circular 1 filled the roadway. There was the same hullabaloo as always. The soldiers were yelling at the drivers, at the prisoners, and the columns of prisoners were jumping onto the trucks. Every once in a while you could hear the dull thud of the blow of a bayonet, or you would see a guard pushing some prisoner with one hand while he wielded a machete or a truncheon with the other. But that was an everyday occurrence. Every morning we went through the same thing. We hardly paid any attention to it anymore. Sometimes they beat the man standing next to you as you were boarding the trucks, or while the squad leader walked down the files counting the men he would slap somebody with a bayonet or smash him with a truncheon and the ignominy would not even merit any special comment. We would get onto the trucks and the conversation would go on as though nothing had happened. It was as though we all expected those despicable things to happen.

Our platoon was sent off that day to clean some large pastures covered with weeds. From the moment we got off the trucks, the squad leaders started beating us and the threats rained down on us. The security cordon was tighter than ever, and we were working within a circle of threatening bayonets. They lined us up in single file, and at a signal from the squad leader we raised our picks and dropped them and bent and pulled out the weeds by the roots. Not a single prisoner's voice was heard. Nothing but the squad leaders', who kept yelling at us to work faster. Soon they began to bring their bayonets down on our backs. The guards were furious, and they ran up and down the long line, stopping to hit somebody every few feet. There was enormous tension. I felt the same as always, that knot in my stomach as though my intestines had been filled with cement. I knew it was a symptom of fear. I tried to control it; I breathed deep and tried to think about something far from there. The picks rose and fell slowly, taking out the divots of earth and leaving the roots of the weeds exposed. The points of the picks and the edges of the shovels were so polished from use on the farms and the sun was so glaring that everything looked like silver. We were working in silence, but all at the same rhythm, almost in slow motion, constantly resisting. Perhaps that tenacious opposition is what keeps a man from feeling that he is a slave. Luis Laberto, one of the youngest of the prisoners, was working beside me. He wasn't yet twenty-five years old, but he had been beaten furiously in the previous weeks and he was terrified.

"Armando . . . " I looked at him out of the corner of my eye. He was barely six feet away from me, and after he pulled out a big wedge of earth, with a bunch of weeds, he came a little closer.

"You've got to help me. I can't take this anymore." His voice sounded desperate. "Run your pick through my foot. They'll have to take me to the dispensary and I can spend a few weeks without having to come out here to work." I realized that Luis Alberto was about to break. His voice trembled as he pleaded with me. I tried to calm him down.

Many prisoners would ask one of their workmates to wound them with a machete or a pick or a hoe. They pretended it was an accident so the wounded man could take off work a few days or a few weeks, depending on how badly he was injured.

"Calm down, Luis Alberto. We've been through worse things than this, and we've taken it. Don't let yourself fall apart because of this depression.

It's temporary, it'll pass. Remember, if you do this to your foot it can leave you crippled forever, and you're young. Look how we all stand up to this —and there are some men here old enough to be your father. Get hold of yourself."

We heard the squad leaders' yells and some bayonet blows, and we stopped talking. We concentrated on our work. The squad leader passed a good way behind us. Luis Alberto started pleading again.

"Next time he's going to beat me. I'm sure he's going to."

"Get to work. Think about something else, Luis Alberto. You're letting your nerves get the best of you. We're all in the same boat as you, and we keep going. You're no weaker than anyone else. Try to get hold of yourself. If other men can stand up to this, you can too."

The curses and threats of the squad leaders grew closer again, so I concentrated on my work. I raised my pick, and as I was going to drop it, a little behind me, toward the left, I heard a dull plaint, like a groan that was almost a shriek. Luis Alberto had run his pick through his own foot. The point of the pick had gone all the way through his boot, passed through the bones in his foot at about his instep, splintering them, and had come out through the bottom of his foot. Luis Alberto fell to the ground writhing in pain. He had let go of the pick, but it was still stuck in his foot, and it quivered and bobbed around grotesquely.

I saw many cases like Luis Alberto's. For many men who were terrified and beaten down by the forced labor in the fields, wounding themselves seemed to offer a way out. They simply lost control of themselves, they seemed to snap. Coming to that decision to wound yourself, and then actually doing it, implied a long process of internal struggle. The first time the idea came up, it would be rejected, since the instinct of self-preservation would still be stronger than the need for rest, release. But a man's internal resistance would grow more and more strained, and one day under the beatings or the murders in the fields, it would simply snap.

On the sixth floor there was a prisoner who helped men who wanted to break their arms. A whole technique for that grew up. The arm would be wrapped very tightly in towels and placed between two pieces of wood. The "bone-breaker" would raise a wooden club and hit the arm. The bone would break with a muffled, deadened snap without breaking the skin, although sometimes it was necessary to hit the arm several times before it would break. The victim would writhe in pain, grow pale, and break into a cold sweat. Some men who had spent weeks of dread, thinking about the moment, would break down psychologically at the last moment and fall into a kind of lethargy, as though they were in the middle of a nightmare. They realized the magnitude of what they had done and would promise themselves never to do such a thing again. Other men, on the contrary, would do it again.

Faced with those self-inflicted injuries, the garrison decided to take even those men with broken arms out to work. There was one prisoner in Building 5 who responded to that by breaking both his arms. The squad leader, who felt that the man was making a mockery of his imprisonment and the forced-labor plans, did what no one expected—he took him out to work with both arms broken. He knew he couldn't work, but he beat him with a bayonet. The next day when the squad leader called the man out, they had to carry him in a wheelbarrow they used for carrying out the trash—he had broken both his legs as well. So they simply couldn't take him out to the fields.

The beatings, the terror, acted as the last straw for many men who had old, festering psychological traumas, and the dread and horror drove them mad. Going out to the field to work, after all, might mean death from the beatings, not to mention the beatings themselves and the mutilations. Those poor men's imaginations invented a thousand ways to avoid forced labor, because they felt they were keeping themselves alive that way. Besides breaking their arms and legs, many men drew out the liquid around their kneecaps with a hypodermic needle. Others injected petroleum into themselves or rubbed stinging nettles and other plants on their skin until they swelled up like monsters. Some used bees—they had the bees sting them on their members or their cheeks and their whole faces swelled up almost unrecognizably. There were also some men who kept little cloth bags of salt they would rub their skin with. The action of the salt made horrible sores on their skin, and they kept the sores inflamed so they wouldn't heal.

Around that time the military doctor who visited the Circular was Dr. Agramonte, as I have mentioned before. A sick prisoner had to have his permission to remain in the Circulars. By order of Headquarters, only twenty men could stay in the Circular sick each day. The men in charge of reporting them were our doctors, who lived with us. And how were we to choose from among eighty or a hundred sick men those who could stay behind and those who had to go out and work? What the prisoner-doctors decided to do was report everyone and force the soldiers to make the selections. Therefore it was Agramonte who made the final choice. He would come into the Circulars and sit at the little dispensary desk. The sick men would stand in line in front of the desk. He would see them one by one, though he hardly looked at them, and select the men who were to stay, more or less at random. Other times he simply laughed at them all.

One day a man with an injured hand stood before him. Agramonte told him there was nothing wrong with him that would keep him from going to work. The prisoner protested; he said he was really sick.

"Listen, for you to stay here inside, you'd have to cut off one of your fingers," Agramonte answered, and he called up the next man.

Not long afterward, the prisoner came back. Dr. Agramonte saw something in the man's expression which frightened him. The prisoner raised his closed fist, opened it, and dropped on the desk before the horrified eyes of

Dr. Agramonte the thumb of his other hand, which he had somehow sawed off. "There's the finger you asked me for."

The doctor stood up pale and trembling and began almost hysterically to scream at the man, "You men are all crazy! Crazy!" And he was still screaming that word as he ran away.

Dr. Agramonte never came into the buildings again. From that time on, he did his work at the main gate, on the outside of the bars.

34 / Concentration Camps and Murders

The Ministry of the Interior's predictions, that we couldn't stand up to a whole year of that work without begging on our knees to enter Political Rehabilitation, were never fulfilled. We had actually earned the gold medal Captain Morejón had promised us, and not just one prisoner, as he had said, but rather thousands and thousands of us.

Their failure made them unleash an even more desperate wave of violence. But in step with the insane fury of the soldiers, a deep consciousness was growing inside us, an inflexible determination to resist, not to give in. We grew harder and harder, convinced that we were a symbol of resistance for the entire country. They couldn't make us give up or give in. It was not a dark, fanatical resistance, but light and premeditated, the product of our very beings, of faith and love of God and of freedom.

Those values are inexhaustible sustenance for the man who holds them. And I did not have the resignation to accept docilely, as an inevitable fate, whatever came. I knew, I was convinced, that this was a difficult stage on a voyage, like a storm which surprises the ship on the open sea, but which I, like that ship, would pass through. Getting through it, leaving it behind, overcoming it, depended on the serenity and firmness with which I held to my personal beliefs.

On the Island they began to build three huge concentration camps. One of them was on a farm called La Reforma, another on a farm called Mella, and the third, in the south part of the Island, in the Valley of the Indians (Valle de los Indios).

When we passed through those areas in forced-labor transports, we would see how the work was progressing. The government had plans to evacuate the prison on Isla de Pinos, disperse the prisoners to the concentration camps or enroll them in the Rehabilitation Program, and convert the prison into a museum, since Castro had been a prisoner there for several months. But he had been a prisoner not in the Circulars, not even in a cell, but in an area of the hospital reserved exclusively for him, with all the amenities—daily visits, sun, books, an open space in the yard, and other luxuries inconceivable to us.

Fidel Castro admitted as much himself. Here is an excerpt of a letter written by him on April 4, 1955:

> I get sun several hours every afternoon, and Tuesdays, Thursdays, and Sundays in the morning too. A big empty yard, completely closed in by a gallery. I spend many very pleasant hours there.
>
> I haven't told you I fixed up my cell on Friday. I washed down the granite floor with soap and water first, then some marble dust, then with Lavasol, and finally with more water, with creolina [a disinfectant like Lysol] in it. I organized my things—now absolute order reigns. . . . I'm taking two baths a day now, "on orders" of the heat. I feel so good when I've bathed! I take my book and am happy for some moments.
>
> I'm going to have dinner—spaghetti and squid, Italian chocolate for dessert, with fresh-brewed coffee, and an H. Upmann No. 4 to finish off. Don't you envy me? They take care of me, everybody does his little bit to take care of me. . . . They won't listen to me—I'm always fighting with them so they won't send things in to me. When I'm getting my sun in the morning in shorts and I feel the breeze off the ocean, I feel like I'm on the beach—and then off to a little restaurant. They're going to make me think I'm on vacation! What would Karl Marx say about such revolutionaries?

In another letter written in June of that same year, Castro says:

> They opened my cell up into another apartment four times bigger, with a big patio open from seven in the morning till nine-thirty at night. Prison personnel do the cleaning, we sleep with the lights out, there are no headcounts or formations all day, we get up whenever we want to—I didn't ask for these improvements, it goes without saying. Plenty of water, electric lights, food, clean clothes, and all for free. No rent. Think things are any better "over there"?

Rehabilitated prisoners and several squads from our Circular worked at La Reforma camp, which was built in the typical style of concentration camps. The barracks were located at the center. They were made of block walls with roofs of fiber-cement panels. Around them were two tall hurricane fences with concrete posts curved outward and strands of barbed wire strung along the top. The guardposts had spotlights and machine guns.

The concentration camps were located in very strategic places from the point of view of forced labor, in the areas where most work was needed. That way prisoners didn't have to be transported all across the Island. But in their plans the Party didn't take into consideration the fierce resistance of the prisoners, who were determined not to enter the Rehabilitation Program. The prisoners had decided that the government would not have prisoners who worked like slaves.

On January 9, 1966, the leaders of the gangs met with Tarrau at Prison Headquarters. The meeting lasted only a few minutes. They discussed the reasons the counterrevolutionary prisoners gave for not going into the Rehabilitation Program and formulated a plan to force us to enter. The method they decided on was an operation of real terror. The heads of the gangs received bloody orders; they were given free rein to kill prisoners in each gang.

That news reached us immediately, but no sooner than we felt the violence itself. The soldiers' beatings became systematic. The squad leaders of block 18, Luis and Guesternay, were possibly the most sadistic of all the soldiers who passed through the prisons. They were always drunk, and when the trucks took prisoners into the fields, far from highways or roads, they would order the prisoners off and have them surrounded by the garrison, who aimed their machine guns at them while other guards beat them. In their brutal zeal, those two guards committed such vile acts as forcing the prisoners to pull weeds with their teeth and to eat dirt. They were always trying to make us rebel so they'd have an excuse to kill us. If prisoners protested about some act of aggression, the escorts in the cordon might simply open fire. Eddy Alvarez and Danny Crespo, in block 31, were killed just that way.

Three examples will show the extent of the violence and cruelty the guards could engage in with impunity. The head of one of the squads, a man named Arcia, wanted to humiliate Julio Tan, so he ordered him to pull weeds with his hands. Tan refused. The squad leader, bayonet in hand, attacked him and wounded him. Julio, trying to escape the blows of the bayonet, fell to the ground. Behind him, another of the guards hit him with a hoe. That was the moment Arcia was waiting for. He plunged the bayonet into Julio Tan's thigh and moved it around in a circle to enlarge the wound. Julio bled to death within minutes.

Diosdado Aquit had picked up his plate and was standing in front of the trucks as he did every afternoon. The cordon of guards was very close by, ready to get onto the transport after the prisoners had been counted and had boarded their trucks. There was a strong gusty wind blowing. Aquit's hat blew off his head and fell a few yards away. He asked the squad leader for permission to get out of line and pick up his hat, and the soldier told him to wait a minute, he was going to do the count, but when the count was over, Aquit could go get his hat. The squad leader began the headcount, came to the end, turned around, and signaled the prisoner to go pick up his hat. Aquit left the line, took two or three steps, and bent over, but he never straightened up again. From the back of the line, one of the escorts had emptied his AK rifle's magazine into Aquit's back.

"That'll teach you not to get out of line without permission!" he said, gesturing at him with the still-smoking barrel.

Robert López and I had been together since 1961. He was an idealistic young man, freckled, very pleasant. He declared that he was on a hunger strike. He said he wouldn't work anymore, he wouldn't take the beatings and harassment any longer. When the guards agreed to take him back to the Circular, everyone thought he would go into the hospital. But the convoy went on toward the punishment cells, and they threw Roberto inside. They cut off his water so as to make his agony even more painful.

Captain Morejón went into his cell and asked him what it was he wanted. And Roberto told him that the only thing he wanted was some flowers put on his grave when he died. The men who were in the next cells could very clearly hear everything that was happening.

Roberto spent weeks on the hunger strike. His thirst made his ordeal even worse, and certainly hastened its outcome. As he was dying, he kept crying out for water. The men in the adjoining cells called the guards and asked them to bring him water, but instead, the guards took out the prisoners who were yelling and gave them a beating with thick braided electrical cord. All morning you could hear Roberto calling out for water.

Finally two or three of the guards opened the gate to the punishment-cell complex. They went all the way to the back, where Roberto was lying on the floor. They stopped only when their boots were almost touching the prisoner's cadaverous face. "You want water?" one of the guards said. "Well, drink piss!" And he pulled out his member and urinated on Roberto's face, in his eyes, in his gasping mouth. The next day Roberto was dead.

We also suffered tortures that were not intentional. At the front of the prison grounds, to one side of Prison Headquarters, there was a group of houses which prison officials and their families lived in. One of the houses belonged to Dr. Condy, the director of the hospital. He lived there with his young, very imaginative wife. This young woman was in the habit of offering us nocturnal entertainments, and the prisoners had to actually mount a campaign to put a stop to her spectacles.

Almost every night when her husband went out to meetings and assemblies, she would turn off all the lights in the house except the ones in her bedroom. The bedroom window, wide open, directly faced the prison buildings. She would then sit in front of the mirror with her back to us and begin to take off her clothes, slowly, as if she were a striptease artist. Completely naked, she would turn and pose before the mirror, then begin to comb out her hair. Her long hair fell almost halfway down her back, and she would smooth and caress it with provocative gestures. She would raise her hair with her brush, shake her head, and let the hair fall again. Then she would pose before the mirror again. She would put her hands on her waist or slide them across her breasts and thighs, caressing herself voluptuously, and she would rhythmically sway in a lascivious dance.

What was going through that woman's mind? She knew that hundreds of eyes were devouring her from the prison windows, that the looks charged with desire were drilling through space, the looks of men who had spent years without any sexual contact with a woman. Perhaps in her lustful dreams, she saw herself possessed by us in an indescribable orgy.

We mounted a campaign against the woman's provocations; we reported her to the guards. Soon the guards came, and that window was never opened again. Some days later the doctor and his exhibitionist wife were transferred.

A group of prisoners discussed whether they should work anymore, and they came to the conclusion that it was better to get two or three tremendous beatings in a row rather than one every two days or two weeks. But out of the thousands of prisoners who were taken to the fields, only eight or ten were brave enough to accept the consequences of refusing to continue to work. One of those was Pilotico. The beating they gave him was unprecedented. Years later his back was still one huge scar, as if they had held red-hot irons to his skin. Only those of us who saw and knew what had happened could believe it; men who found out about it later could hardly imagine that the scars on his back had come from beatings.

Boitel also decided not to work anymore. After one beating, he declared himself on hunger strike, and they took him off to the hospital. There they tied him to the bed with rope, and several soldiers and male nurses, prisoners, force-fed him with rubber tubes they ran through his nose down to his stomach. He spent several months like that, until he was transferred to the punishment cells. There the authorities had brought together a group of men who had refused to work—Izaguirre, Rivero Caro, and Nerín, all three of whom had spent more than a year in solitary in those dungeonlike cells.

Of course, many other prisoners were sent to those cells, too, to be punished for real or imagined breaches of prison discipline. Hundreds of prisoners passed through them. It was the repression capital of the prison. From the minute you arrived, the guards surrounded you with electric cables hidden behind their backs. They asked you which cable you wanted to be beaten with. There were two, the "skinny" one and the "fat" one. The first was actually thicker. At any rate, the guards wound up beating you with both of them—and with machetes as well. If the guards were in a bad mood one day, they'd cheer themselves up by taking the prisoners out of their cells and beating them. As the beating went on, their fury seemed to dissipate.

Paco-Pico was in one of those cells. He had had constant problems in his work gang because he was rebellious and stubborn, so he was put into solitary confinement. As dusk fell one day, one of the guards opened the gate and told him to come out of his cell. The other prisoners thought the guards were going to give him one of the scheduled beatings. Paco-Pico stepped out into the hallway. From a few yards away, another guard aimed a rifle at him. I doubt that Paco-Pico ever even suspected that that scene and the dark mouth of a rifle would be the last things he would ever see. The first report echoed all through the building, and that report was followed by another. Paco-Pico fell to the ground.

The guard who had opened the gate was very nervous, and he told the squad leader—Arcia, the same man who had killed Julio Tan—that he was going to call the hospital to take Paco-Pico away.

"Not yet. Let him bleed a little more," Arcia answered.

Minutes passed, and they stretched into hours. A pool of blood grew under Paco-Pico's chest. When the garbage truck stopped in front of the punishment pavilion, they threw on the garbage cans. Then they picked up the body of Rolando Movales, nicknamed Paco-Pico. It was already rigid and cold.

"He's as stiff as a board," said one of the soldiers. They threw him onto the truck on top of the trash, and they drove his corpse to the hospital.

In winter we shivered with cold. They didn't give us any heavy clothing or permit our families to send it to us. We had to wrap ourselves in old burlap sacks sent over from the warehouse. These sacks were sort of raffled off, and therefore only a few lucky men got them. In the fields the rain soaked us through to our skin. Many men could not stand up to the weather, the swamps, and the grinding work. There were many cases of tuberculosis, pneumonia, and that sort of wearing disease brought on by lowered resistance. The guards and squad leaders would stroll around all wrapped up in military capes and overcoats while we would be trembling from cold in the rain, and yet we couldn't stop working. The knee-high mud, the plagues of mosquitoes seemed to eat away at us.

When we came to an area infested with mosquitoes, we knew what would happen. Every time we went to the fields, as we got off the trucks the heads of the gangs would line us up and count us, and then we had to wait until the cordon of guards was in place. Those "special" times, then, in a low, swampy area with lots of mosquitoes, the head of the gang would invariably give the same order: "Leave your shirts here." They made us work without shirts so the mosquitoes could get at us more easily. To protect ourselves as best we could, we carried slivers of Russian soap with us, a terribly smelly soap we would rub ourselves down with, always taking care that the squad leaders didn't see us. When the soap mingled with sweat, a sort of pasty froth resulted and worked pretty well at repelling mosquitoes. But other times not even that saved us. There were always cases of malarial fevers and other illnesses we couldn't identify.

The prisoners who worked in shoes with holes in them were attacked by chiggers, little insects related to mites. They're tiny red bugs which embed themselves in the skin, under the toenails, and if left untreated become infected and form cysts full of pus. They're very painful and they itch like the devil. We would try to combat them with almost-boiling water or with gasoline. We were also infested with ticks. These tiny little animals got into your armpits, your crotch, even your eyelashes and all the hair on your head. There are still prisoners who suffer from illnesses transmitted by these little ticks and from the larger wood ticks. One of the ways to combat the little creatures was shaving your whole body, including your eyebrows, your genitals, and your head, so that they wouldn't have a single hair to hide themselves in.

There were some prisoners almost blinded and some blinded completely in one of their eyes by toxoplasmosis, an illness caused by a fungus which attacks and destroys the retina. Antonio Domínguez got this disease.

Long lines of injured men would form up in front of the dispensaries in the Circulars. There were men bayoneted in the fields, or whose heads had been split with rifle butts. The prisoner-doctors would patch up the injuries as well as they could, and the next day the men would have to go out into the fields again. Those prisoners shot at work were taken to the hospital building. Some, like Napoleoncito, whose femural artery was grazed by a bullet, were somehow, miraculously, saved.

We always carried a little cotton and some bandages to the fields with us, a sort of first-aid kit of the most rudimentary kind. One of us would be in charge of carrying it, and we would euphemistically call him the gang's medic. We were only allowed to use the bandage material for emergency medical care—to stanch wounds with, for example.

Every effort to get the Commission on Human Rights of the United Nations even to consider our denunciations was fruitless. We sent that organization detailed information about the tortures, the murders, the plans to blow us up with the explosives installed in the Circulars, but it did nothing. The prestigious Commission on Human Rights had deaf ears and blind eyes for what was happening in the Cuban political prisons.

Exactly the same thing happened with the International Red Cross. Talking to it about violations of human rights in Cuba was like talking to a post; it refused to listen. Cuban political prisoners simply did not exist. Why get upset about them, then?

Years later the Red Cross came to believe what it had been told. The United Nations as a whole and its individual nations know about the horrors of the Cuban jails, but they don't dare condemn Cuba in their annual assemblies.

35 / "Dirty Tricks" on Both Sides

Celestino and Buría invited me to join an escape. They knew about my previous attempt, and they wanted to try another. This time the escape would be made from the fields where we went out to forced labor. It wouldn't be easy, but it wouldn't be impossible either. The important thing was to have an alternate—Plan A and Plan B—so we'd have a better chance of getting away. We weren't going to try to get off the Island immediately, because that actually presented the greatest risk. We would fake that last stage of the escape, while actually remaining in hiding. Then, when the search had been called off, once they thought we had gotten away, it would be easier to get off Isla de Pinos.

Everyone knew that the common prisoners who had escaped years ago from the dairies or other work centers and gone into the pine groves or swamps usually wound up giving themselves up to the authorities because they were starving to death. The campesinos had been so terrorized that you couldn't just knock on somebody's door for food or aid. The authorities made sure of that.

I told my comrades that the only way to survive was not with food stores cached someplace beforehand, but by eating whatever came to hand—crickets, lizards, frogs, snakes, and the root vegetables that we knew were edible. I proposed that we begin a training period. We'd start by eating insects. At first the idea seemed extreme to them, but in the end they went along with it—although Celestino and Buría didn't actually start immediately. I did, however. I had read that in some parts of Asia the people ate crickets and considered them a delicacy. The crickets on Isla de Pinos were big and juicy. I began preparing myself mentally, and one morning I decided to eat my first raw cricket. Before throwing it into my mouth, I crushed its head so it wouldn't bite my tongue. For all its being my first one, it didn't taste too bad. A week later I was eating thirty or forty insects a day. I had all my friends in the gang hunting them for me.

We were cutting elephant grass, a tall, canelike grass that reaches more than six feet high. My gang was stuck in the stands of this grass. Since early every morning we went to the same place, I laid a few burlap sacks across a piece of sandy ground. Crickets by the dozens took refuge under the sacks, so I had my own cricket farm. (As a boy I had gathered crickets that way to use as fish bait.) Some of the men, simply for the spectacle of seeing me eat them, would go out and find crickets for me too. They thought I wasn't quite right in the head. But even a few weeks earlier when we were working in the pangola fields, Obregón and I had begun to eat the grass. We would pick out the juiciest stalks and chew them for a long time. We looked like ruminants, every day chewing a cud of that plant. I had read an article about the nutritional value of pangola in a cattle-raising text that Alfredo Sánchez, my cellmate, had. As a sort of joke, Obregón and I told the rest of the prisoners that if they wanted to be as strong as a bull they should eat not the bull but what the bull ate, and many of the men grew fond of the weed and chewed it as we did.

I went from eating crickets to eating lizards and frogs, then little snakes, and I considered the clean tasty flesh of the *majá,* a relative of the boa which reaches several feet in length in Cuba, a delicacy. I also ate, among other things, raw tubers, birds' eggs, and the sprouts of elephant grass. Anything that walked, flew, or swam was edible. In the fields where cattle grazed, I would steal the molasses they put out in the cattle troughs. That represented calories, and I needed them. My iron stomach took it all very well, miraculously enough. I decided the place to test whether I could eat what nature offered was before the escape, not after, since that way if I should get sick, I could go to the hospital or get help from the doctor-prisoners in the Circulars. It turned out that nothing ever happened to me.

I substituted food I ate outside in the fields for some of the food they brought to the prison. I also increased the number and kinds of insects that I would eat. Sometimes I ate grasshoppers, larger than crickets and very abundant in the fields, although they had a strong sharp taste.

Work in those fields consisted of using a machete to cut the stalks of elephant grass and then loading them onto the trucks. The plant is covered with a fine fuzz that gets into your clothes and all over your body and produces terrible itching. Socarrás and I were loading the trucks, but we weren't doing it fast enough for the squad leader. He punished us by taking us off that detail and setting us to cut the grass. They designated a special guard to keep threatening us and pushing us along. This soldier's hair was yellow, he had no teeth, and he always wore red knit gloves. He carried a machine gun and a machete. All afternoon, until they gave the order for us to get our things together for the return, he kept harassing us, but especially Socarrás, trying to get him to run away so he could machine-gun him. But we didn't set foot from the place they had assigned us. We let other prisoners know about the situation.

The next morning the toothless guard with the red gloves was waiting for us again. On the way to the fields he gave us both a beating, and from the moment we arrived, he was threatening that he would *really* beat us if we didn't work faster. He kept harassing Socarrás until finally he pushed him with the barrel of the machine gun. I yelled so our comrades would know what was going on, and that defused the situation a little.

It must have been about ten o'clock in the morning. We had five minutes to eat a little *gofio de trigo* which our family members had sent. On the Cuban prairies there lives a small snake called *jubo*. I caught one about a foot and a half long and held it so only its head peeked out of my fist. It was lashing my forearm frantically with its tail. I shook the glove off my right hand and gripped him with both hands.

"Look what we've got for coffee break!"

"You're going to eat that snake?" Socarrás said that to me as a kind of joke, because of my decision to eat any animal that crossed my path, but I answered him in perfect seriousness, "I certainly am."

The guard watched me curiously—the last thing he expected to see was what followed. With a quick movement, I placed the snake's head between my teeth and bit down forcefully. One bite broke its spine and split its flesh. Then I chewed off its head with my front teeth. Blood gushed from the body and splashed all over my face. The guard ran off yelling for the leader of the gang, and I spit out the head and laughed and threw away the body, which was still writhing.

The terrain of the central part of Isla de Pinos is made up of ferrous rock. Even little round pebbles are covered with a sort of rust. There are horrific electrical storms in that area of the Island.

We were cutting big spreads of pangola with our machetes one day when the sky darkened and booming thunder heralded the lightning storm. Then, as the thunder came closer and closer, rain began to fall furiously. A stroke of lightning broke one of the fence wires, and another ran along one of the wires like a fireball.

Many of the guards threw their rifles as far away as they could, since they thought the metal would attract lightning.

Very close by there was a little wooden chapel, now old and unused, which the old proprietor of the farm, a man named Cajigas, had built when his son was killed in a plane accident. Inside, Cajigas had set up an image of the Virgin of Santa Barbara, though the Revolution had pulled it down, so all that remained was the pedestal and the niche. Before the Revolution, if someone in the area died, family members and the campesinos from surrounding parts, who believed in Santa Barbara, would often bring her flowers. Santa Barbara was in some ways a much more African, animistic "saint" than a Catholic one.

We took refuge in that chapel, and Guilio, the military squad leader, came in with us. He was young, tall, and heavy. Only ten or twelve of us could fit. The rest of us had to stay outside in the torrential rain. Guilio seemed very, very nervous. He kept wiping his face with a handkerchief, and his hands were shaking. He could hardly speak. His bottom lip trembled visibly. He was terrified, and it was obvious enough to us that it was the lightning crashing all around us that frightened him. At every crash or flash of light, it seemed the walls of the little chapel quivered. Celestino Márquez and I began to talk so the squad leader could hear us. "It's really dangerous to have these machetes inside here with us. Iron attracts lightning." We hadn't finished the sentence when Guilio ordered us to throw all our machetes out of the chapel. But the lightning kept flashing and booming all around. It was really quite an impressive show.

The squad leader was pale, and he couldn't hide his terror. So we went on talking, just to see what would happen. "Well, without the machetes inside, it's a *little* safer to be here. There's no metal to attract the lightning. The only thing left is the squad leader's pistol," Celestino said. So, very nervously, Guilio asked us if we really thought his pistol was dangerous. "Of course it is," Márquez responded. "I was in the Army, and they always told us to get rid of our weapons in situations like this. I remember in San Antonio de los Baños, at the military base, one of my friends was fried to a crisp by a stroke of lightning because he wouldn't take off his pistol." Márquez hadn't finished speaking when the squad leader had his belt and pistol off and was holding them at arm's length. He called the head of the gang from the door and threw the pistol to him to take care of. That poor man with his atavistic terror of lightning was like a hunted animal. The incredibly violent bolts of lightning came one after another, and the ground and walls seemed electrified. We went on talking. "They built this chapel to Santa Barbara. She's the patron saint of lightning, you know. That's why when these storms come, people that believe in her always pray to her. Maybe the Virgin is upset because her statue was torn down, and she's taking her vengeance now."

Those words filtered into the squad leader's mind. He knew about the beliefs that his own parents and grandparents had held, and that he himself had grown up with, but since now he was in the Young Communist Movement, he had renounced those beliefs, at least theoretically.

"I think we ought to get out of here," he said finally, very nervously.

"No, outside it's even more dangerous. Besides, Sergeant, man can't escape the anger of nature and God when man has offended them." And at that very moment, a blinding flash of lightning fell almost at the door of the chapel and filled the air with an overpowering smell of sulfur.

"There's nothing we can do," Celestino said with a note of lugubrious resignation. "The only way we can save ourselves is to put ourselves in God's hands. That's the only way."

Another flash of lightning, and another. We thought Guilio was going to take off running, crazed with panic.

"Outside you could get killed," Celestino went on. "We can only save ourselves by praying, since this is punishment from Santa Barbara. Let's pray. There's nothing else we can do!"

"Our Father, who art in Heaven . . . " Another flash of lightning, and Guilio, almost unintelligibly, as though he were muttering, stammering, joined our prayer. . . .

The searches when we went back into the prison were superficial. Generally they were no more than a quick pat-down, although there were some squad leaders who took great care that no prisoner brought anything in from the fields. What we usually tried to bring in were pieces of wood to make a fire with and heat up some sugar water or *gofio* during the winter.

The wood would be prepared in the fields, in little flat, short pieces. Men would tie the pieces to their legs, up almost to their testicles, or to their backs under their belts. Of course, we risked reprisals if they caught us at it, but in reality some squad leaders didn't even bother to search for it, or looked aside if they saw it, and let us bring in pieces of wood as long as we did it discreetly. In other blocks that wasn't possible.

Sometimes we would hide what we wanted to bring in at the mouth of one of the drains around the Circular. The next day, the men who cleaned around the outside would pick it up and bring it in with the cleaning utensils.

There's a funny story about that sort of thing. The head of Circular 2 thought he was infallible at keeping prisoners from bringing in anything undiscovered. One afternoon Captain Morejón, right before the prisoners who were being searched as they entered the Circular, told this soldier to keep his eyes peeled for contraband. "There's not a prisoner that can get anything by *me,*" the head of the Circular answered.

"Why, if you're not careful, these men will drag a sack of fertilizer in right under your nose and you'll never even know it."

The soldier smiled smugly, but we prisoners accepted the challenge Captain Morejón had set for us. That sack of fertilizer would show up, inside the Circular, or bust.

But how were we going to get it in if it weighed a hundred, two hundred pounds? The squads spreading fertilizer took charge of that. First they emptied out one of the fertilizer sacks, but they opened it only two or three inches, very carefully unraveling the seams sewn in at the factory, and emptied the contents through that small opening. They carried the empty sack to the door of the Circular and left it there, and the cleaning squad brought it in and took it up to the sixth floor. That's when an army of ants went to work. Hundreds of men brought in fistfuls of fertilizer in their pockets, in their little sacks, in matchboxes. Little by little we filled the sack. When it was full we closed it using the same little holes that the thread had gone through when it had been sewn up in the factory. One week later it was discovered in a search. The garrison was thrown into consternation; nothing else could be talked about for days. The soldiers and the Political Commissioners came out to the fields to try to find out how we had done it. But they never did; and in fact, I'm telling the secret for the first time here and now.

We were finishing up the details for the escape. We found a huge map which measured almost three yards square. The squads used it when they divided the land up into smaller fields for fencing. The map didn't even fit inside the cell. Since there was no way to unfold it completely, we divided it into eight sections.

The second part of our escape plan had a variation: an escape from the Island to the nearby cays. For that, we planned to make a little boat out of two palm trunks lashed together with wire. The palm tree that grew in that area had spreading fan-shaped leaves, though it didn't have a very thick trunk.

To get the palm trunks that we needed, we found a very fast, silent way of cutting them down. On an abandoned range where tank warfare had been practiced, we had found some buried communications wires. There were thousands of yards of very fine steel wire, some of which we smuggled into the Circular coiled around our waists. With this wire we made a very efficient cutting instrument. We would take three or four strands of the wire and braid them together like a guitar string. Then we would tie the ends together tightly and attach them to two small pieces of wood like bobbins, about the thickness of a cigar. You could saw this braided steel wire vigorously across whatever you wanted to cut, and it would cut through anything, even steel. The wood of the palm trunks was like soft clay to it. We tested it in the fields. It took less than a minute to cut through the trunk of a palm tree, and since the cut was so fine, if there was no breeze to move the tree, the trunk would remain erect as though it had never been cut at all.

When one day the gatekeeper, holding a list, ordered the whole Circular silent, I had not the remotest idea of what was about to happen. I heard my and many of my friends' names called, including my close friends Pruna and Celestino, and then immediately the order to get everything we owned together, with the exception of our beds. We were being transferred.

There was something out of the ordinary in that transfer. We'd never heard of the officers who had signed the list, and it didn't seem to be an internal transfer, because of the hour they were carrying it out. Many of us thought they might be taking us to the concentration camp in Valle de los Indios to the south of the Island, since it was rumored that the most difficult prisoners were being transferred to that camp.

We went out, calling goodbyes and being embraced by our friends. Buría had not been called. Once again a transfer had destroyed escape plans.

36 / Back to La Cabaña:
The Same Old Routine

We were led to an area over by the electric plant where they searched us and took away all but a fraction of what we were carrying. Then some trucks arrived. They took Boitel out of the hospital and some other men out of the punishment cells, among them Izaguirre, Rivero, and Nerín, so we were right about the "most troublesome prisoners," but they didn't drive us to the concentration camps at the south of the island. On the contrary, the speculations about our transfer took a turn toward optimism —President Johnson had asked Castro to release political prisoners to the United States at about the time of the exodus from Camarioca, that port on the north coast where Cuban exiles in Miami went to pick up their relatives.

The trucks took the little road that ran next to the fence on the east of the prison. From the jail windows, handkerchiefs and hands were waving goodbye, and cries of joy rang out. There were about 150 specially selected men in our group. There had only been one other exit like that—that of the Bay of Pigs invaders when they were ransomed.

When we came to the bridge across the Las Casas River, the procession of trucks turned to the right and stopped on the pier. It looked like a full-scale military operation; extraordinary security measures were in effect on the pier. The entrances were blocked with patrol cars, and we saw soldiers armed with submachine guns posted on the roofs. The ferry was waiting for us. That was when a jeep arrived with Húber Matos and Cruz, one of the old officers who had been sentenced with Húber Matos. And that event was very strange indeed. For the first time, ex-Commander Matos had been taken out of incommunicado and was seeing other prisoners. The possibility of a prisoner trade looked more and more credible. In that comparative handful of men, the authorities had collected those prisoners who most stood out for one reason or another—leaders of movements, prisoner representatives, the most stubborn and unyielding *plantados*. Castro might well want to get rid of us. The presence of Húber Matos was a sort of confirmation of that theory, for he was the most isolated, best-protected, and best-known prisoner in all of Castro's jails.

We boarded the ferry and sat down in the passenger salon. From the place I was sitting, near the bow, I could see the machine gun that was trained on us. The whole deck had been taken over by soldiers and agents of the Political Police in civilian clothes. They kept Húber apart from the rest of us, on the second deck of the ship.

The ferry had to be towed to Batabanó, a port to the south of the province of Havana, since its engines were damaged. When we left the mouth of the river, a patrol launch slipped into our wake to escort us. At the bow, the soldiers uncovered a 20mm gun; on the roof of the bridge there was a machine gun. The soldiers were barefoot and shirtless. The sun neared the horizon, and dusk began falling. The sun was an enormous red globe which dyed the waters purple. It was a beautiful afternoon. The mountain ranges of Isla de Pinos looked like the bluish humps of enormous dinosaurs, and among them you could make out the lights of the prison. A gray haze enveloped the cylindrical piles of the Circulars.

For those of us aboard, the vision of the distant prison was overwhelming. The sun sank into the ocean, and we sank as well into thought. The rushing of the open water along the sides of the boat, rolling out into an embrace of spray, was lovely. Not a voice was to be heard.

Like many other men, I thought we were going to be ransomed. Many efforts had been made in that direction. Constant rumors over the years reinforced that hope, but many times the rumors had been spread by the authorities themselves. They did it to raise the prisoners' spirits, so they could watch them drop again when the rumor turned out false. These sudden changes produced depressions which ate away at you, undermining your psychic reserves. The sudden highs and lows left marks of disorientation and dread. But now something different from anything that had ever been imagined before was happening—we were leaving Isla de Pinos.

Pruna, Luis Pozo, and I were sitting on the same bench, and a little beyond was Boitel, whom I hadn't seen for more than a year. Several of his friends were talking to him. When he was alone I went over to him and we talked about the most important things that had happened since we had last seen each other. Boitel was very thin, but he still had that same old energy and enthusiasm, which was so contagious.

The voyage lasted some twelve hours. It was about sunrise on the morning of May 29, 1966, when we arrived at Batabanó. There the security measures were even tighter. The roofs of the warehouses and the intersections had been turned into nests of machine guns. Dozens of soldiers made two files down which we marched off the boat in little groups of eight or ten men.

English Leyland buses were waiting for us. We got on. The back seat was completely taken up by armed guards carrying Czech submachine guns. When we were all seated, four or five soldiers took up positions near the driver and aimed their rifles at us. The seat next to the emergency door was also taken by a guard. The authorities had taken such massive security measures so no one could attempt an escape. Five or six buses made up the motorcade which departed slowly in a beehive-like flurry of military vehicles and officers shouting orders to the drivers.

In our bus, the idea of a prisoner trade still held, and we knew that within an hour it would be proved right or wrong.

When the buses, escorted by patrol cars from the metropolitan police and Political Police, took the Vía Monumental toward the prison of La Cabaña, our hopes for ransom began to fade, and as we turned now unequivocally toward the horrific fortress, other worries and fears erupted in our heads.

Still, going back to La Cabaña from Isla de Pinos was the greatest hope that any of us had had when we would go out to the forced-labor fields, since we never knew if we would return alive from the violence of the guards and squad leaders.

The garrison of La Cabaña was waiting for us. They were ferocious-looking.

We walked across the moat where the riddled wooden stake stood against the backdrop of sandbags—Castro's slaughterhouse, as the whole country called it, the fateful firing-squad wall.

They put us into the corral where the prisoners had their visits. It was divided down the center by two fences of thin wire mesh, like those they had put up in the prison at Isla de Pinos. Many guards were waiting to search us, among them several women soldiers. We had to strip in their presence, menaced by the bayonets and the threats of the guards. It was an embarrassing situation. The women looked brazenly at our nakedness. One of the prisoners in our group was a mulatto we made jokes about because of his enormous penis. When one of the women soldiers saw it, she called out to the other women to look at it, and they shamelessly cracked filthy jokes about our comrade.

After that search, they left us with hardly anything. We only had a change of underwear, a pair of socks, the aluminum cup, and some items of personal hygiene. They took everything else away from us. When we went into the prison yard, we were applauded from the *galeras*. Those of us coming from Isla de Pinos were received with real admiration. Prisoners in all the jails knew about what was happening there and about the heroic resistance the prisoners were offering the barbaric plans of the government.

We were sent to *galera* 7, the last one, the smallest one, the gloomiest, the most isolated, the blackest and worst of the whole prison yard, where the government had a group of ex-soldiers that had been sentenced to death. Where hardly eighty men fit, squeezed tight together, 225 of us were "housed." The bunks, stacked four and five high, almost grazed the ceiling. In the center was a passageway so narrow that only one person could get down it. In the space between one group of bunks and the next, you could only enter sideways.

The lunch hour had already passed—they served lunch at nine o'clock in the morning. But then breakfast was served at four o'clock. It was always warm sugar water and a piece of bread. At two o' clock in the afternoon they served dinner. The rest of the time you spent with your stomach empty, until the following morning. The food had never been so scanty, nor had the authorities ever used food so markedly as an instrument of repression, as at that time. The hunger suffered in the prison of La Cabaña was incomparable to anything that had been suffered before, even on Isla de Pinos.

When at about two o' clock in the afternoon we were sent to the "dining hall," a structure the authorities had improvised in the prison yard by putting several long tables under a fiber-cement roof, our comrades who wanted to wave to us flocked to the bars of the *galeras*. Bernardo Alvarez was in *galera* 12. I raised my hand when I saw him, but one of the guards jumped at me and knocked my arm down with a bayonet. I couldn't even lift my arm to wave, nor could we say a word to our friends. Nonetheless some of us did it, and the guards began to pull us out of the files at bayonet-point and take down our names. They said they were going to suspend our visits. But we prisoners wouldn't give them our real names— we gave them invented ones, or even names of famous people. Some said they were Leonardo da Vinci or Albert Einstein. The guards carefully wrote the names down; they had never heard of any of those men.

I have never forgotten that meal. It was three spoonfuls of rice with some chicken bone, utterly without meat. When I say three spoonfuls, I am not estimating. It was exactly three—I counted them. And a piece of bread, and that was it. I had never seen such a tiny ration.

There was a guard who counted off two minutes by the clock. At the end of the two minutes, you had to stand up, whether you had finished your so-called meal or not—but at least for the rice that was more than enough time.

You were forbidden to carry the bread back to the *galera*. If you didn't know about the rule and were caught carrying the bread in plain sight, you had it taken away from you. Everything was aimed at making us feel the pinch of hunger, since what did it matter to them whether we carried bread back to the cell with us to eat later?

When I got back, I sat down and thought the situation over. There were many prisoners who became very upset over the restrictions on our food, but the authorities didn't care whether the prisoners got upset or not. That was the whole point. I realized that it was by means of hunger that they were now trying to manipulate us, humiliate us, reduce us to simple hungry animals, and so I decided that the next day I would impose strict discipline on myself. I would further strengthen my will against the authorities' harshness.

That afternoon there were hurricane-force winds and a torrential rain-storm, which were the forefront of a tropical storm. The next day it went on raining, and there was no lunch or dinner. At nightfall it had begun to clear off, and the platoon of guards and several officers stopped next to the cell bars and ordered us outside for a headcount. They told us to form up in twos, which we did. Then they opened the gate and ordered us to double-time out of the galleries, through a double file of guards. Suddenly the guards, who were armed with bayonets and wood and iron truncheons, attacked us and screamed at us to run. Running the way they wanted, at double-time, through the whole prison yard, was one more humiliation they wanted to impose on us. There was a wall about a foot high at the door of the *galera* which had been erected to keep out the water, since when it rained that part of the prison yard flooded. When we went in and out we had to step or jump over that retaining wall amid a hail of blows. Not all of us managed to get over the obstacle; many men fell headlong and were beaten with nightsticks by the guards.

The authorities made running at double-time a matter of principle, as did we in resisting it. We refused to run. That decision would cost us many a beating. They performed the headcount twice a day—at dawn and at dusk. Eugenio de Sosa lived in the first tower of bunks next to the bars, and it was he who let us know that they were about to begin the headcount, when the officers in charge of it entered the main gate. He also alerted us when the troops arrived for the searches. We were all now feeling tremendous tension, because we knew we would be beaten savagely every time we went out of or came into the *galeras*.

We were so hungry that our stomachs felt as if they were gnawing at our spines, so we invented ways of getting around the guards' vigilance and taking our bread up to the *galeras*. Somebody got the idea, for example, of hiding it inside his shoe and smuggling it in that way. It was a little piece of bread, rubbery and elastic. Men would also carry it in a little bag hung under their testicles. Then, about nine o' clock at night, when they were hungriest, they would put a little salt on it, the only thing we had if we had anything at all, and would eat it so salty that it would drive them to drink quarts of water. At least the water helped fill you up.

I soon put into practice my decision not to allow myself to be manipu-lated by their control of our food. When I sat down to my three spoonfuls of rice, I pushed one spoonful off to the side. I then ate the other two. Celestino and Pruna would tell me I was crazy. I told them it was a way to test my will and strength of character. If the authorities gave me only two spoonfuls tomorrow, I'd leave one of them uneaten. I felt I had won a victory. From that time on, I always had food left over.

The days they gave out cornmeal mush, the food was more like torture.

They served the cornmeal practically boiling hot, so when it had just cooled enough or you'd blown on it so you could put a spoonful of it in your mouth, the two minutes were up, and you had to stand up and leave the dining hall with your stomach still empty. Since you could take your cup with you to eat, I immediately solved the problem of the hot mush. I simply poured some water into the steaming mess, stirred it up a little, and ate part of the soup.

In the dispensary there was a dental chair and a dentist. But it was as though they didn't exist at all, because there was an order not to fill cavities for any prisoner. The dental equipment was used only for the soldiers.

The military chief of the dispensary was officially a doctor, an eighty-two-year-old man named Blanco who had been expelled from the College of Physicians many years ago, before the Revolution, because, the story goes, he had been involved in the death of a patient on whom he had performed an abortion, which was what he really did for a living.

The Revolution "rehabilitated" him. He always wore an olive-green uniform and cap, which gave him something of the look of a train conductor. He had an unlighted cigar butt always stuck in his mouth. He went to the dispensary only once in a while to sign papers. The person who actually ran the dispensary and who was always there was an old guard named Fundadora, a skinny bilious man with a face pockmarked by smallpox.

Carlos had a cavity in one of his molars, but what could he do to get it filled? Fundadora was the only one who could give the authorization, but he was a crude, despotic, self-important little man. Other prisoners had tried to get him to authorize a filling, but they had never had any luck. Carlos decided to try a new tactic.

The first thing he did was find out all he could about the man. Fundadora had been in the laundry business. He had gone into the Ministry of the Interior in 1959 and had been a guard since then. He had had a white lab coat made for himself like the ones real doctors used, and he strolled through the dispensary keeping an eagle eye on everything that happened, poking his nose in and offering opinions on what the prisoner-doctors were doing. They were all terrified that the ridiculous old fool would keep them from their visits or even send them off to the punishment cells. Twice a week we could go to the dispensary. They would give out an aspirin or some infusion for a cold and a few tablets for asthma. The day Carlos' turn came, he got a jar of tonic and two tablets of aminophylene for his asthma. He then walked directly over to Fundadora, who was standing next to the entrance, and drew himself up before him.

"Excuse me, Doctor, would you allow me to speak with you for just one moment?"

The guard's face was transformed. His fatuousness wouldn't allow him to see that Carlos was making fun of him. He had called him Doctor, and that made him as happy as a child. His voice was very hoarse. He hawked and asked Carlos what it was he wanted. I had to turn around; I was choking on my laughter.

Carlos told him he didn't trust the instructions for taking the medicine that the medics had given him. He asked Fundadora if he would just confirm that this medicine was right for him, and tell him the best way to take it.

"Well . . ." And Fundadora looked carefully at the bottle as though he were studying it. "Take one teaspoonful when you go to bed, and if you feel stifled in the morning, take another," he told him.

Carlos thanked him and left. Two days later he went back to see him.

"You have no idea how much good the treatment you told me to follow has done me. I'm sleeping better than ever, thanks to what you told me. I knew you had more experience than that medic, and you knew these medicines better than anybody here."

The man's absurdly inflated vanity went on rising.

"I've been in and out of this dispensary for several years now," Carlos went on, "but really, it's never functioned as well as it does now. Since you've been in charge, things have really improved. It's obvious that you're a man who knows how to give orders and command respect. The order and discipline here are really something!"

That was just too much for the poor man.

"Well, I've always been that way," he said and smiled smugly. "Because I like things done right, and people who work with me have to learn to say 'How high?' when I say 'Jump!' "

Carlos kept this act up for several days, praising Fundadora's knowledge and feeding his ego. One day he took the plunge. He was going to try to get what he was really after. When the old man said hello and asked Carlos how he felt, Carlos put on a face of great pain and told him he had hardly slept at all last night.

"Did you finish the bottle of asthma medicine?"

"It's not that. It's that I have a cavity in one of my molars and it's been driving me crazy. I've been asking them to take care of it for me, but they told me it had to be authorized by the Ministry of the Interior. Imagine! How will I ever get the Ministry of the Interior to give me permission?"

"Who told you that? What do you think *I'm* here for? That's absurd— the Ministry of the Interior! *I'm* the one who gives permission here!" And he called the dentist over, a prisoner who practically idolized soldiers, to the point that he constantly humiliated himself.

"Fix this man's tooth right away."

The dentist was dumbstruck.

"Move! Are you deaf? Didn't you hear me?"

The afternoon of one particular headcount was unforgettable. The garrison had beaten us as we had come out of the cells. Candedo, the man who was running out beside me, stumbled as we crossed the foot-high doorsill, and his hand found nothing to grab to catch himself. So although we stopped for only a second, that was enough for the guards to rain blows down on us. I have the marks of that beating on my head still, another souvenir.

The garrison, as I have mentioned, had received orders to make us double-time all around the patio. They showed their power over us that way, but we had already decided not to obey. Several officers and the two guards of the prison yard began beating the first men in the file with their bayonets and ordering them to the main gate. The rest of the file entered the *galera.* Then the lieutenant who was head of Internal Order closed the gates and thirty-five of us were locked in the patio. A general battle between the garrison and us ensued. Toledo, whom we called Muñeca, "Doll," was in front of the *galera* that the dispensary was housed in. He was a small man, but he was very brave. He was fighting all alone against five or six guards who had him cornered between the wall and a huge tank of water. Lieutenant Lirbano exchanged some blows with him but then backed off. Muñeca was a real fighting machine.

The Bayolo brothers were also struggling with some other guards. Castroverde pulled a piece of wood off a desk and leaped to the attack. The garrison siren was already sounding and the guards on the roof shot bursts of machine-gun fire into the air to alert the other guards to the urgency of the situation.

The yelling and screaming from the other galleries didn't stop for a second, nor did the siren, and suddenly the garrison reinforcements rushed in through the main gate.

Orosco, a prisoner who had entered the country clandestinely, wanted to keep the panic from getting worse, so he started yelling at us to back off, but not to run. He had been an officer in the Army and knew the importance of not panicking. We slowly backed off to our *galera.* Orosco kept yelling for nobody to run. Beside him Pepe Márquez was walking. I was trembling with fear and panic. In front of *galera* 8, I lost control, and in fear of my life, I took off running with some of the other men.

Dozens of guards, some barefoot and shirtless, but all brandishing weapons, filled the prison yard. Leading them, dressed impeccably, was an officer from the Political Police.

Furiously, raging, the guards were beating us. In that deluge of blows with chains, bayonets, and nightsticks, and in fear of being run through with a bayonet, we kept retreating toward the back of the prison yard, which grew narrower and narrower until it formed an angle in front of our gallery. There, squeezed together into a terrified little huddle of men, we were even better targets for their fury.

The officer from the Political Police ordered them to stop the beating and delivered a harangue to us about the power and strength of the Revolution. Then he ordered us taken to the punishment cells.

When we came to the punishment cells, they put us all in together. We were squeezed in so tightly that the guards could hardly close the cell door. We couldn't even sit down. They kept us that way all night. Our ankles and legs swelled. We didn't sleep a moment. We kept thinking that at any second we'd be taken out into the neighboring cells, which were vacant. But the guards didn't do that. We spent two and a half days on our feet.

Water was strictly rationed in La Cabaña, and we had to stand in line to receive the ration we were allowed, one liter per day per person. That was all the water we had both to drink and for our personal hygiene. A soldier was in charge of supervising the doling out of the water; he controlled the flow from outside. Twice a week they would send in a couple of pailfuls for baths.

The garbage cans overflowed in the prison yard. There was a constant stench from the garbage, and all around the garbage cans there were maggots and putrefying matter. Flies buzzed around by the thousands. Whenever there was a breeze, dirty toilet paper blew all over the prison yard.

We were so crowded into the cells that we couldn't get down off our cots. The vaulted ceilings oozed water constantly; the moisture stains on the ceilings grew gray and green from mildew. It was worse during the rainy season, since there was a constant drip over some of the cots. You could make a kind of canal out of pieces of plastic—a sort of rain gutter to draw off the dripping water so that it would run down the walls and onto the floor.

There was a group of soldiers from the Batista regime in that *galera*. They had been sentenced to death and had been awaiting their execution since 1959. The night of January 29, 1967, the guards took out Elizardo Necolardes, who had spent eight years in the jail, and shot him before a firing squad. That created great depression and consternation among the other men who had been given a death sentence, since they foresaw their own executions following immediately. We found out later that on one of his trips to Oriente province, as he was giving a speech, an old friend of Castro's had declaimed to the audience that Necolardes, who had been a Batista politician in that area, was still alive. Castro had turned to one of his aides and ordered Necolardes shot at once.

The lack of winter clothing caused us to shiver with cold. The prison was right on the shore, so we were lashed by the frequent cold fronts coming down from the north; the windows of all the *galeras* opened onto the north, of course. The thermometer would drop sometimes to thirty-five or forty degrees. Once again I found a burlap bag, which I lined with pieces of plastic. I sewed it up especially well along the edges so I could keep the bedbugs out. They were thriving in that gallery, and they liked to hide in burlap.

The visits during that time were allowed every three months, and they were held through two screens of fine metal mesh, like those the authorities had tried to impose on Isla de Pinos. I never went up to the fences, since

Headquarters had forbidden me, as they had so many others, to see my parents for six months. We were allowed one letter every three months, as well. They used our correspondence as another means of manipulating us. On occasion they would tell a prisoner he had two letters—one from his wife and one from his mother—and he had to choose which one he wanted to get. Whenever they gave me one of my letters, I never read it immediately. I would put it on my bed and open it the next day. I always tried to exercise my will in matters such as that, to counter the authorities' psychological warfare with strategies of my own.

37 / The Struggle
Against the Blue Uniform

The day the news came to us that they were finally dismantling the prison on Isla de Pinos, we were all overjoyed. That was toward the beginning of March 1967. After they had shipped us *cabecillas* off to La Cabaña, the authorities figured the men who remained there had lost their leaders and would be easily transferred into the Rehabilitation Program.

So they began the final offensive. They murdered many prisoners, mutilated dozens, wounded hundreds in one last effort to break the resistance of those heroes, who stood up to it all with incredible stoicism. The authorities were employing all the resources at their command.

After they had physically "softened up" the prisoners, they began taking them out of Isla de Pinos and scattering them throughout the country, to the concentration camps the prisoners themselves had in some cases helped build and to closed high-security prisons. The authorities sent them as far as possible from their families, into remote areas. The purpose of this operation was to weaken the strongest points of our resistance; if their new plan was to work, prisoners had to be broken.

When the prisoners arrived at their new destinations, they were given a new uniform. It was blue—the same uniform that the common prisoners and rehabilitated prisoners were wearing. Men who refused to wear the blue uniforms were beaten by experts in hand-to-hand combat sent from the Ministry of the Interior. In Pinar del Río province on the main island of Cuba, in the three concentration camps Sandino 1, 2, and 3, the methods used were more brutal than in any other prison. The guards placed hoods over the prisoners' heads, tied ropes under their armpits, and dunked them in wells if they did not agree to wear the uniform. They burned them with lighted cigars, they yanked them about by the hair, and they beat their heads against the wall until they fell unconscious to the ground. Then the guards dressed them in the blue uniforms and tied them up with ropes. In two days, having given them no water or food, they untied them. And if a prisoner took off the uniform, they beat him again. They had no respect even for old or sick men. The men who stood up to all the tortures and still refused to put on the blue uniform were driven naked to the provincial prison located at kilometer 5.5 of the highway which runs to the little town of Luis Lazo, in Pinar del Río. There, in a special pavilion with cells along each side, they collected all the prisoners from the various concentration camps throughout the province—Taco-Taco, Sandino 1, 2, and 3, El Brujo, and so forth. That was the reason they called the prison at 5.5 the Naked City.

The director of the prison, Lieutenant Edmigio González, stuttered. His nose had been broken once, flattened against his face, so they called him Pug. This man was well known by all the prisoners in Cuba for his ruthless ferocity. He often said that Fidel Castro was in charge of the area from Havana to Oriente province, but in his province, Pinar del Río, it was Pug that gave the orders, and he would say the nickname himself. But if any prisoner dared mention the nickname and Pug found out about it, he would beat the prisoner senseless.

He often would have a prisoner brought to his office, and he would tell him he knew that the prisoner called him Pug, but he wanted him to say the name to his face. Naturally, of course, the prisoner would say absolutely nothing. Pug would insist, he'd threaten the prisoner, he'd order the prisoner to say the name, and then he would begin to beat the prisoner frenziedly. "Say it! Say Pug! Say it, say it!"

Within a matter of just a few weeks there was not a single political prisoner left in the old prison on Isla de Pinos. Lieutenant Tarrau, the prison director, in recognition of his work in directing the violence, torture, and murders at that prison, was promoted by the express order of Fidel Castro to membership in the Central Committee of the Communist Party. He was given the rank of commander, and he was named Chief of Political Instruction for the Ministry of the Interior. He represented the moral conscience of the elite of the Revolution. He was the man who incarnated the norms of behavior of a revolutionary.

But Tarrau liked his alcohol and his young women. And so the old satyr caused a scandal in the sumptuous neighborhood of Miramar—he would go swimming naked in the pool of his mansion with several young women, who sometimes got drunk and ran out into the street. One particular incident could not be hushed up—the Political Police for obvious reasons tried to whitewash the incident, but Tarrau received a reprimand. The scandal was not in accord with his rank, and the bacchanals had to be held with complete discretion from then on. But Commander Tarrau kept running wild through the streets in his Alfa Romeo, a gift from Castro himself; he would constantly be seen all over Havana with young girls. One scandal, with an underage girl, was the last straw for Castro's patience, since it sullied the public image of the Party. Tarrau was expelled from the Central Committee, stripped of the rank of commander, and relieved as head of Political Instruction of the Ministry of the Interior. He was sent to plant pangola grass in Camagüey province. The same thing happened with the notorious Efigenio Amajeiras, the first Chief of Police under Castro. He smoked marijuana and was known all over town for his debauchery. He was thrown out of the Party for a scandal which included dozens of revolutionary officials who didn't know how to be discreet in their "entertainments." Among those was the current Cuban ambassador to the United Nations, Raúl Roa. The scandal and subsequent purge was called the Dolce Vita Case. Like Tarrau, Amajeiras was punished by being sent off to plant grass.

Once Tarrau was out of the way, Pug took charge and became the most feared and repressive director of prisons in the entire country. One promotion quickly followed another. He had turned the jail called 5.5, in Pinar del Río, into his private fiefdom. On one particular occasion the political prisoners in one of his cell blocks had a tremendous argument with Pug because they refused to put on the blue uniform of the common criminals. Pug ordered walls a foot and a half high raised before the bars at each end of the cells. Then soldiers came with hoses and flooded the *galeras*.

"If they don't get dressed now, my name's not Pug."

He kept the prisoners in that lake for several weeks. They had to stay up on their cots; they couldn't come down since they were practically living in a swimming pool. Since the toilet and urinal were underwater, it was impossible to use them, so when the prisoners relieved themselves, the excrement floated around the cell.

Some of the political prisoners who were being forced to wear the blue uniform organized a resistance front in the concentration camps. Their work was extremely courageous. They did so much damage (from the authorities' point of view) that they were separated from the other prisoners and sent to closed jails and held incommunicado, and reprisals were taken against them.

In the prison at La Cabaña the change of uniform was accomplished without recourse to violence. Those of us who refused to put on the uniform were stripped of all our belongings, including the clothing we had worn up until that moment, a khaki uniform, and we were transferred to several widely separated *galeras* completely empty of furnishings. This occurred in the last days of July 1967. There were more than three hundred of us in each *galera*. When it was time to go to sleep, we did not physically fit on the floor. We had to lie down absolutely cheek by jowl with our cellmates, and even so we had to take turns so that all of us could sleep. About thirty men always had to stand up at the entrance gate.

With those of us who had been in the prison at La Cabaña now in separate *galeras* and reduced to undershorts, the last group to wear the old khaki-colored uniform had been eliminated. A few days later in *Granma*, the official organ of the Communist Party, there was a news item that carried photographs of the Circulars on Isla de Pinos. The article said that the counterrevolutionary prisoners were now on rehabilitation farms all across the island. It also declared that there was only a small group of recalcitrant prisoners still held in closed prisons. No mention was made of turning the prison into a museum, however.

All of us were to accept the blue uniform; if we did, we would instantly disappear into the mass of more than 100,000 common prisoners then being held in Cuban prisons and jails. The government intended to simply make the category "political prisoner" disappear, have us taken for common criminals. It didn't seem to matter that we hadn't joined Political Rehabilitation. Thousands of men in blue uniforms as well had refused to join. They rejected the plan, kept up their combativeness; but the fact that they were held in remote areas, in the concentration camps, euphemistically called "farms" by the Communists, made the publication of those lies possible. The fact that everyone wore the same color uniform made the lies difficult to disprove.

A few days later the authorities began an offensive based on a more positive approach. They offered all sorts of enticements to make us rebels get dressed again. They promised to transfer us to prisons near our family homes, reduce our sentences, locate us on *real* farms, give us forty-eight-hour passes so we could go home, and make all kinds of other concessions. As the days passed, many men who saw no other way out of the situation decided to put on the blue clothing. When this happened, the authorities took them away immediately and put them in La Cabaña. Then they set the prisoners to talking with their friends, to try to convince them how useless it was to reject the uniform. Not all prisoners allowed themselves to be used for that proselytizing, of course, but still, little by little, the number of those of us who were still without clothing was being reduced. Those who decided to leave our group did it almost entirely within the first few weeks. Among those men was Alfredo Carrión. He had always wanted to try to escape, and he saw in the blue uniform his chance. Many of those who got dressed at La Cabaña were sent to a concentration camp called Melena 2. Carrión somehow got himself sent there, and he signed up as a volunteer to go outside the prison grounds to work. He and Lino López Quintana had planned an escape, and they dedicated all their time and ingenuity to the scheme.

A squad of prisoners would be taken out in a trailer pulled by a tractor. Behind it came a truck with the guards. For several weeks Carrión and Lino studied the route. They scrutinized the countryside—the fields planted with sugar cane and all the roads crossing through the area. They observed that on one of the roads they took, there was a curve where the tractor as it turned raised a cloud of dust that enveloped everything and severely reduced the visibility for the guards in the truck behind. Carrión and Lino threw themselves out of the trailer at the precise moment the tractor turned that curve. The reddish dust was a dense curtain that kept them from being seen by the guards. They hid among the weeds in the ditch until the truck had passed, and then they struck off into the cane fields.

When the trailer came to the field they were to work in and the guards counted the prisoners, there were two missing. Immediately the alarm was sent out, and trucks loaded with troops dispersed down all the roads and surrounded the area. Soldiers were posted at all the crossings; reinforcements were called in from the nearby village of Melena del Sur. Dozens of militiamen arrived immediately with barking dogs, and the search for the missing men began.

Carrión and Lino felt they had a better chance to escape individually, so they had agreed to separate. Even so, the cane fields were crawling with guards. Carrión and Lino were trapped. Carrión managed to get out of one of the planted fields and into the next one before the soldiers took over the access roads. And when he got to the other side of that second field, he managed to get into the next road as well. But a militiaman posted behind one of the bushes along the roadway saw him creep out, looking cautiously, furtively, all around. Carrión didn't see the militiaman, so he thought the road was clear. The militiaman set his R-2 rifle in the fork of a tree, took careful aim, and with complete ease shot Carrión. Carrión fell to the ground. He was wounded in one leg, but he didn't move. He was very intelligent; he knew that if he moved they'd shoot at him again. The only way to save his life was to lie there quietly. He heard the militiaman coming closer. He heard bootsteps crunching the leaves of the dry cane stalks, and he heard them stop behind him. Carrión didn't turn over, but he called to the militiaman not to fire, that he was wounded. And then he heard the reports of the rifle at point-blank range. The bullets passed completely through his body.

That same night, with a group of friends in a bar in the little town of Melena del Sur, the militiaman, known as Jagüey, told the whole story of the escaped counterrevolutionary and how he had asked him not to fire. "Imagine, and me just itching to try out my R-2 for the first time!"

Lino López was beaten by the soldiers when they captured him. He was a cousin of Commander Sergio del Valle—at that time the Minister of the Interior, now Minister of Public Health and one of the highest leaders of the Party. Later Lino disappeared. The Political Police told his family, after months of their trying to find out what had happened to Lino, that he had died in a mine explosion as he was trying to escape through the American naval base at Guantánamo. But why did they never bring the family his corpse? Lino's disappearance is still shrouded in mystery.

Carrión's family was luckier. They received a telegram from the Ministry of the Interior informing them of Carrión's death. The authorities would later say that he had tried to assault the garrison of the prison.

The authorities informed the family that there would be a funeral and that the body would be available for viewing one hour before the burial, but when the family arrived, the Political Police had taken over the building and placed guards at the door. An officer took Hilda, Carrión's mother, and his fiancée, Margarita, aside to warn them that if the guards heard a single sob, they would carry off the corpse immediately. They didn't want any whining. They also forbade them to see the corpse, which had been riddled with bullets. For the whole duration of the wake, there was a soldier stationed next to the coffin. The wake didn't last an hour. Fifty minutes after the family had entered, the authorities took out the coffin. A tall mestizo soldier, wearing the olive-green gabardine used exclusively by the Political Police, got in next to the hearse driver, and a car filled with soldiers followed the hearse. At Colón Cemetery the burial was over in seconds. The authorities didn't allow a single word to be said over the body by the twelve or fourteen people gathered there. As soon as they put the marble across the vault where they had interred him, they told all the people they had to leave. The women wanted to say prayers, but that was forbidden also. The guards ran them off. One guard remained posted there. My wife-to-be, Martha, and the fiancée of Oscar Fuentes, another prisoner who had been a friend of Carrión's, hid in the cemetery chapel, from where they could see the vault Carrión's remains lay in. They watched the guard for some time. When they finally gave up and decided to leave, at nightfall, he was still standing there.

Given all the men who had gone into Rehabilitation, we could all now sleep on the floor. There was plenty of room, in fact. That year the cold fronts from the north arrived earlier than ever, and freezing blasts of wind, or so they seemed because of our lack of clothing, swept through the galleries. But prisoners always find something even where nothing seems to exist. Some men managed to find a piece of cardboard or a scrap of black greasy paper from the kitchen, and they would cover their legs with it, or place it between their bodies and the cold granite floor. At that time the authorities instituted searches each day at dusk to try to find those pieces of paper, cardboard, and the like. They thought that we would never manage to get through a winter without clothing, and they were smugly waiting for us to give in. Even the soldiers on post were talking: "We'll see what you guys do when it really gets cold."

And it did get cold. When they took our clothes away from us, they had put us into three *galeras,* and another four or five remained vacant. That had been during the scorching tropical summer. Now that winter was coming, they spread us out through the empty galleries, so we would feel the cold more bitingly. They had left those galleries empty on purpose.

You simply couldn't sleep. The wind blew all night long. I recall that through a friend who was in the Rehabilitation Program and worked in the dispensary, I got my hands on a roll of toilet paper. I was sleeping as close to the wall as possible. I got the idea of rolling myself up in toilet paper, around and around my body, mummy-style. It is incredible what a sense of well-being that light covering of paper produced in me—it was as though

I had pulled on a pair of wool pants. But that only lasted for two nights. They discovered me and took away the toilet paper as they had everything else.

The soldiers would call out prisoners at random to try to get them to dress. They would argue, falsely, that they had run out of the old uniform, that there were no more in the warehouses, and that no more were being made—so they had to issue the blue ones. They would say that agreeing to put on the blue uniform had no political implications, but not even they themselves believed that.

At that time the director of the prison at La Cabaña was Lieutenant Justo Hernández de Medina. He showed himself to be a very clever, politically astute man from the moment he arrived, and moreover he had orders from the Ministry of the Interior to keep systematic beatings to a minimum. Hernández declared that he was opposed to torture and that he felt that no prisoner should be mistreated. But for him, only beatings might be considered a violation of human rights; keeping us completely incommunicado, denying us any mail, visits, books, keeping us naked and underfed, making us sleep on the floor, and effecting psychological tortures on us were not violations.

One of the first of his innovations was sending someone to get the prisoners and take them to his office, where he would "talk" with them. He was especially interested in learning why we rejected the blue clothing, and he enjoyed arguing in favor of our accepting it. He told me on one occasion that the Revolution was making great progress, and he invited me to go through the city of Havana so I could see for myself that a lot of things had improved.

"Look, Lieutenant," I answered, "let's suppose that you people have achieved a standard of living higher than in any capitalist country, where everything exists in abundance. I would still be opposed to your system because my arguments are ideological, not material. I oppose the whole system because of the freedom it denies, not because of the consumer goods it lacks. That's why the progress, the achievements of the Revolution, have no real meaning for me."

The Ministry of the Interior was resorting to any tactics it could think of to make us get dressed. In accord with that, the situation in the concentration camps, where the blue-uniformed men were transferred, improved noticeably. Repression there seemed to have been put on hold. The authorities allowed those men frequent visits, and several of the men who had taken on the new uniform were even released, but all this was no more than a bait they dangled in front of us to try to get us to wear the blue. They went on bringing back to La Cabaña some of the men who had left so that the men could tell their friends how well off they were there, in contrast with our own situation.

And the truth is, we were almost dying of hunger and cold. I had managed to communicate several times with Martha, thanks to the men who were working in the dispensary, but very sporadically. One morning the prison director sent for me to tell me that Martha was standing at the main entrance to the prison, at the head of a delegation of family members of prisoners. They were making a fuss and haranguing the soldiers because of the means the Ministry of the Interior had been using against us. He said that if she ever came back or if anything like this ever happened again, they would throw her in jail. He told me to find some way to get that message to her.

What had actually happened was that the authorities had said earlier that they would allow our families to bring us a blanket and wool underwear. Relatives who knew what kind of cold we were suffering showed up the next day with the clothing, but when they arrived, it seems the authorities had not said a word about the matter to the soldiers on guard, so the guards didn't know what to do. They asked Headquarters how to deal with the situation, and the director himself came out and flatly denied permission for the winter clothing to come into the prison. Martha argued with him, and that's when he threatened her and accused her of being the leader of the group. Then he came to see me, to tell me he had threatened her with jail.

At that time food had decreased to an absolute minimum. At lunch there was a little cornmeal broth and one single leaf of lettuce per person. Mohamed and Misthray began to show effects of vitamin deficiency. In fact, there were many cases of conjunctivitis and other vitamin-deficiency diseases.

We came into possession of some lists of the food we prisoners were theoretically receiving. The menus were made up in Prison Headquarters. Such things as macaroni, meat, salad, bread, and sugar appeared on the list, whereas what we were actually getting was that nauseating cornmeal broth, a piece of bread, and a small leaf of lettuce.

The bulletin board in the kitchen was covered with those fantasy menus. Anyone who came to the prison and looked over the menu for the month's food would no doubt think that we prisoners were the best-fed people in the country. What really happened with that food was that it was "diverted" to the guards' kitchen. And if there were anything left over, the soldiers carried it off to their own houses. Castro said in a speech before the Central Committee that theft was an institution that undermined the foundations of the Revolution. It was also the order of the day in the prisons. The leaders and directors stole cases of tinned Russian beef, cooking oil, jellies and preserves, and all sorts of other things from the warehouses. And the phenomenon was not peculiar to La Cabaña; it was a constant in all the jails and prisons across the island. While I was in the prison at Boniato, every afternoon I would watch from my cell as a sergeant we called Nice Guy would throw preserves, fish, onions, and all sorts of other things into a five-gallon tank and then put a piece of plastic on top of it and fill the top part of the tank with leftovers, which he said were to feed some pigs he had at home.

As winter deepened it became even colder. In Cuba, though one might not think it, the temperature can fall to forty or perhaps even thirty-five degrees. But even the cold could not break our resistance.

During that winter, Prison Headquarters thought up some new trials for us. One of them they put into effect at the jail called 5.5 in Pinar del Río, Pug's feudal estate.

Prisoners there were completely naked. When they came out of their cells to clean the passageways, some of them out of modesty would keep pieces of paper like a breechcloth over their genitals. But every four or five days there was a search which deprived them even of those minimal coverings.

The authorities decided to put these prisoners into cells with five or six common criminals of the worst kind, prisoners hardened by years in jail, and to create thereby a climate of violence in which the only law would be the law of the strongest. When they put a political prisoner into one of those cells, the soldiers would tell the common prisoners that they could do anything with the newcomer they wanted to. No problem.

That was an open invitation to rape, among other things. But that method failed also. Most of the common prisoners had, more than respect, admiration for the political prisoners because of their attitude toward the garrison and the whole system. In the entire history of Cuban political prisons, there was only one instance in which common prisoners participated with the garrison in beating a group of political prisoners. That was in the jail at Guanajay. Years later those common prisoners who had taken part in the beating were killed, one by one, by other common prisoners who had found out about what they had done and who took revenge for it.

One morning the guards called several of us out. The officer from the Political Police who had come with the two guards to get the prisoners told the head of the *galera* not to save any lunch for them, they weren't coming back. In the afternoon, they took another five men out of our *galera* as well as other prisoners out of other cells. We couldn't figure out why they were making those transfers; we had no notion what strategy it reflected. We did hear, about five minutes after the prisoners were taken out, the sound of the police mobile cell that was used to transport us. Then began the rumors, fueled by the garrison itself, that the prisoners taken away had been issued the blue uniform and that those prisoners who didn't put it on were being transferred to an inhospitable cay off the south coast of the Island where they had to find their own food and live in the open, harassed by mosquitoes. We even heard the rumor that they were being sent to the Soviet Union. All that time they kept carrying out groups of men who did not come back. Silvio Martínez and I were called out together. The uncertainty, the thousand questions we had had for days, now took on immediacy, and we were very apprehensive.

They took us out of the cells, and in one corner of the prison yard two barbers practically scalped us with electric shears, cutting off all our hair except a tuft right above the forehead. The freezing wind gave me goosebumps all over my naked body. We left through the main entrance escorted by guards armed with AK rifles and fixed bayonets. They put us into the corral where they held the visits. A few minutes later they signaled us to start walking.

Along the sides of that roadway paved by slaves two centuries ago, guards were standing at attention with battle helmets, rifles, and fixed bayonets, one every ten or fifteen paces. My mind was racing. I tried to make it go as fast as it could, since not knowing what was to come, and of course always expecting the worst, you must keep yourself as alert as possible.

That morning of October 5, 1967, everything was gray—the sky was gray, the very air was gray. We were now approaching the Headquarters buildings, and a door opened, from which emerged the director. He told one of the guards to put Silvio in a room off to the left and me into one to the right. When I entered I took everything in with one glance—there were two chairs, a little desk with some Marxist pamphlets, and, on a little wooden box, a pile of blue uniforms. There was also a boarded-up door. I was sure that they were spying on me from behind the door, through the cracks. There was another box overturned and some uniforms strewn in a corner, mixed with more pamphlets, which indicated to me that there had been struggles there.

I was sure they would come in to beat me and forcibly dress me, since that possibility had also been rumored. But I had prepared myself for that, so it wouldn't come as a surprise to me if it happened. Assuming that I was being watched through the chinks in the boards across the door, I decided to try to look tranquil—a feeling I was far from experiencing at that moment. I sat down on one of the chairs and opened one of the pamphlets. I couldn't tell you what it said. At that instant of danger which I felt as an almost physical presence, I gave myself up to God, and I felt a warm wave spread over me, comforting me inside, and I was filled with courage for whatever would come.

I heard voices, and immediately the door opened. My mother and Martha were pushed into the room. I remember wishing that the earth would open under my feet and swallow me up. My first reaction was to embrace my mother to hide my nakedness. Martha was my fiancée; we lived in a sort of wonderful idyll, but that despicable act of unexpectedly confronting me, naked, with Martha made me furious and at the same time embarrassed and ashamed of my nakedness.

Immediately the director, Lieutenant Lemus, head of Jails and Prisons, and a Captain Ayala, from the Political Police, entered. The Political Police

officer was tall and gray-haired. They tossed me a blue uniform and told me
to get dressed. They said if I did they'd give me a forty-eight-hour pass to
go home with my family.

My angry reply was that they were immoral blackmailers and that I was
not going to put on the blue uniform. I told my mother and Martha to leave
immediately and tell other men's relatives not to come, not to allow themselves to be used by our jailers.

Martha and my mother had been notified by telegram to come to the
prison, that they were being authorized a visit. I kissed each of them as they
left. The minutes of our visit had been very short, but they had seemed
eternal to me. When they had gone, Lieutenant Lemus shouted at me
indignantly. He asked me what I thought my attitude was going to get me,
how I could go on being so rebellious.

"I don't think anything, Lieutenant. I simply act the way I think is
right."

"Liar! You men think that if you reject the government's clothing, you
can blackmail us and get yourselves sent to the United States!"

"What you think about my attitude doesn't interest me, Lieutenant."

"Get him out of here! We'll see whether he gets dressed or not!"

They took me out of that little room and led me across the street, where
they put me into another room, which had a judo mat on the floor. I saw
men there who had disappeared since the day the military had begun this
particular operation. They had gone through the same thing I had. But not
all of us had resisted the shock, and quite a few had taken on the blue
uniform. There was the case of one prisoner in whose dossier appeared the
name of a girl who had really been only a friend. Nonetheless they made
her come into the room where he was held naked. Those repressions always
had their effect on some prisoners. And the group of diehards kept growing
smaller. . . .

I sat down on the judo mat with the other men. In one corner there were
some chairs and empty wooden boxes piled up. The place had been quickly
set up for us, since actually it was part of an area with offices. There was
a hallway, at the end of which a guard with his back to us was posted. Beside
him was the door to a bathroom; the door made a lot of noise when it was
opened or closed.

The office door in the hallway intrigued me immediately, because according to what the men who were there said, a couple of times a day the soldiers
came in through it. I examined it and realized that it wouldn't be difficult
to force the door. We quickly organized ourselves. Two or three of us made
a little group as though waiting our turns to go to the bathroom, so in case
the guard turned around, that little group would block his vision. Then,
when they slammed the bathroom door, I would force the other door and
the sound would be blotted out.

We did that, and I quickly entered the office. There were several desks. I quickly started going through the drawers. They contained foreign publications obtained by the families of the prisoners from embassies, but those publications never reached us. There were also some letters. I remember that one of the magazines had a story about Stalin's daughter, who had fled the Soviet Union. But the most interesting thing to me was the orientation pamphlets, which were used for training the Political Commissioners in ways to sap the resistance of the relatives of the prisoners. I discovered a report which discussed the existence of a group of counterrevolutionary prisoners, us, against whom all forms of physical and psychological pressures to force them to go into the Political Rehabilitation Program had been tried, to no avail.

There were some other very interesting pamphlets which completed my booty, and at a prearranged signal, I left the office. We took turns reading that material, very discreetly. In other riflings of the office, we took out books and more magazines and other publications.

The next day they moved us into a larger room so there would be space for the men who kept arriving. The wall at the back of that room was next to prison yard 1, where the rehabilitated prisoners were kept. I had friends there, and knowing that the wall put up by the authorities was made of cement blocks, I began to make a hole with the handle of a spoon, turning it around and around like a drill to perforate the blocks. In just a few hours we had a hole about the diameter of a cigarette at its narrowest part. I looked through, and the first person I saw was Ronald Lipper, the Canadian who years later when he was freed would write a book about his years in prison. With his help I managed to get out a note to Martha.

Two days later they returned us to the prison yard and then called out about fifty prisoners, me among them, and directed us to a prison van.

We were the first prisoners to travel naked all the way across Cuba. Inside four tiny cells in the van we made an exhausting voyage of more than five hundred miles. We urinated and defecated inside the car itself, in cans. That was February 27, 1968. Our destination was the jail at Boniato in Oriente province, at the other end of the island, as far from our families as we could get and still be in Cuba.

When we arrived, the garrison was already waiting for us. They led us into the area where the visits were held and performed a search on us there. They stripped us of our shoes and gave us some crude boots in return. From there we were sent to pavilion 2, which consisted of a hallway with twenty open cells on each side. We could then move around freely inside the pavilion, up to the main barred gate. It was colder than in Havana, perhaps because the prison lay in the hollow of a valley. Bernardo Alvarez and I shared a cell. We had to sleep on the floor, since the cells had neither beds nor cots.

38 / Naked

That same night we found out through some common prisoners that another group of political prisoners were kept in isolation in a ward in the hospital building. Like us, they had rejected the blue uniform. There were about twenty of them, and they were closed up in cubicles where men with tuberculosis and other infectious diseases had been kept previously. With them were men sentenced to death, kept there to await the firing squad.

Their cells were relatively spacious, but they were closed off at the entrance with metal plates and had only a barred window at the rear. The authorities had promised that they would give the prisoners at least underwear to cover their nakedness and blankets against the cold, but that promise was another they did not keep. Some men had already spent months there, sleeping on the granite floor.

On November 13 of the previous year, when the cold was entering in icy gusts through the barred windows, the head of Internal Order, Lieutenant Jauto, showed up to respond to the prisoners' constant demands for the underwear and the winter coverings the authorities had promised.

"If you don't want to be cold, you have to agree to wear the blue uniform. And if you don't like that, you can go on a hunger strike."

He turned around and marched off. The next day the prisoners accepted the challenge. They returned the breakfast sugar water and declared a hunger strike. A few hours later, Lieutenant Jauto returned. He ordered the guards to open the gate and he took away the tanks drinking water was kept in.

"You men can declare a hunger strike, but we can put you on a thirst strike," he insolently sneered.

Three days later, the provincial Director of Jails and Prisons and a delegate from the Ministry of the Interior, Lieutenant Povadero, visited those prisoners to threaten that if they didn't change their attitude and accept the uniform, the authorities would just get the coffins ready to bury them in, because they were prepared to let them die of hunger. The Ministry of the Interior recognized only one class of prisoners—common prisoners —and therefore the men had to wear the designated uniforms.

At six in the afternoon of the same day, some of the prisoners were taken out of their cubicles. Troadio was the leader of the group. He was terribly weakened by hunger and thirst. His lips were cracked and he was completely dehydrated. The men on strike had agreed that if the group was divided up to be taken to different jails, each man would decide what was best for him to do.

Morales, Peña, and some other men remained in the hospital. At the end of five days of hunger strike, a doctor named Rodríguez, who was in jail for a common crime and who went around inspecting the cells, informed an officer named Castillo, the military head of the hospital, that the prisoners were so weakened that the slightest complication at all could bring on the death of any of them.

That same night, several guards entered the cells and forcibly took the prisoners to the dispensary. They tied them to hospital beds and administered solution intravenously.

A change at Prison Headquarters brought Lieutenant García, an old militant in the Communist Party, to the directorship. He visited the strikers and promised that if they ate, the next day he would give them clothing and blankets. They had already gone seventeen days without eating. They agreed, under the condition that they would begin the strike again if he did not keep his promise.

But he kept it. When Lieutenant García went to visit them later, they asked about the men who had been carried away and demanded their return, since the situation had been resolved. The director told them that the other group had behaved more intelligently when they were transported to another prison than this group had—they had gotten dressed.

"I want you men to see how well off they are, so tomorrow I'm going to bring them here to see you. You can talk to them and see for yourselves that it's absurd, useless to resist. The Ministry has decided to use a different uniform, and you men may as well accept that."

The next day the men were taken to Headquarters. J. Vázquez, Argeciras, Pavón, and some other men were there, men who had been sent to the concentration camp called Tres Macíos—"Three Cattails." The story they told of what had happened there was staggering. There were three men missing, who had no doubt been able to resist. But not for very long, since we found out they finally got dressed.

During those days, Rivero Guevara, Trujillo, and eight ex-brigadists from the Bay of Pigs arrived at Boniato. And on February 27, our group from La Cabaña had arrived.

The doctor, a common prisoner named Artemio Rodríguez, casually mentioned that a whole transport of political prisoners had arrived naked from La Cabaña. He did it intentionally so that our comrades, isolated in the cubicles of the hospital, would know. This gave them a tremendous boost. They now knew that they were not alone, and our presence meant they had support for their resistance. Isolated resistance is simply not the same, nor is resistance in small groups, as when you know that there is a large group backing and sustaining you. It doesn't matter that you can't see each other or communicate. It is enough to know that they are there, in the same prison. It was as though we had sent out roots and were connected underground in an act of solidarity.

The group in the hospital were used as guinea pigs for a psychological experiment aimed at breaking them. The authorities sent for their families, and of course their mothers, wives, sons, and daughters begged them to put on the uniforms, obviously afraid that they would become sick or even die. Naturally, before the visit, the instructors gave a political talk to the relatives, telling them that if the prisoners got dressed their conditions would be improved, and they even built up the families' hopes with the promise of setting the prisoners free. But if the prisoners kept refusing to put on the blue uniform, the orientation officers added menacingly, the Revolution would not tolerate more defiance, and what was waiting for them would actually be much worse. The families knew that the authorities stopped at nothing, that for them a prisoner's life was worth almost nothing.

The moving visits full of pleas and tears, the family members begging the prisoners to get dressed, were over in just a few minutes, because the watching soldiers ended the visits as soon as they saw that the prisoners' decision was firm. Nonetheless, some prisoners agreed to put on the uniform. So there were fewer rebels left. . . .

The men from the hospital who still refused the uniform were put into cells under the Headquarters stairway, then at nightfall they were taken out and put into the prison van. There were thirteen of them. Director García entered the vehicle and looked at the men, one by one. He made a gesture at Napoles and ordered him to get off. They put Morales on in Napoles' place. Morales had been left in his cell, but he had had an argument with García once and García had an unconcealed hatred for him. García knew where that group was going, and he wanted Morales to go too.

The convoy departed along the road which led to the village of Bayamo. When they came to this little town they continued southward, toward Manzanillo. At midnight the prison van stopped and Peña, Alcides, Rivero, and some other men were unloaded. They were standing outside the concentration camp of San Ramón, and a reddish light illuminated them. There were about thirty guards, some armed with rifles and some holding gasoline torches that flared in the wind. The leader of the troop was a Lieutenant Beci, a thin black man famous throughout the area for his cruel treatment of prisoners. Whenever they wanted to frighten or terrorize a prisoner in the region, all they had to say was that they were going to send him to Beci.

They walked off along a path through weeds. You could see, far off, the spotlights on the guardhouses and the lights in the barracks. Rivero turned his head toward the concentration camp, and one of the guards slapped him.

They came to a slope. In its side, six tiny cells, like crypts, had been scooped out. They were so low it was impossible to stand erect in them. The guards stood the prisoners in front of the wall of dirt to the side of the little cells. The light from the gasoline torches, swaying in the wind, lent the scene a sinister gloom.

Lieutenant Beci and the head of Internal Order, accompanied by an officer from the Political Police, called Nieves out. "Strip!"

Nieves refused. They called out Peña, Alcides, and Rivero, who also refused to take off their underwear and T-shirts. Then the officer from the Political Police gave an order, and the guards attacked the prisoners. They beat them with their fists, they kicked them, and they pulled off their underwear and T-shirts. Then they put the six of them into one of those tiny cells.

Since it was impossible for all of them to lie down, some of them had to stay seated with their legs drawn up. They were in total darkness. When day broke, the guards brought them their breakfast, which consisted of a piece of bread and a little warm water with a drop of sugar.

The rest of the dungeonlike cells were occupied by common prisoners. The authorities considered those cells so subhuman that the maximum time they kept a prisoner there was one week.

Nieves was the first one the soldiers called out the next noon. They took him out to a swampy stretch of land next to the cells, and ten or twelve guards surrounded him. The same officer from the Political Police who had confronted him the night before asked him whether he would get dressed in the blue uniform, and when Nieves once again said no, they beat him unconscious. Then they dragged him through the mud and put him into the cell again. Next they took out Rivero and the others, one by one. Peña was the last. They beat each one with rubber hoses and bayonets and shut them up in the cells with the common prisoners.

This difficult situation made the six political prisoners decide to go on a hunger strike, but first they explained to the common prisoners that the action was not directed against them. In fact, it would be those prisoners who even further dramatized the physical state of the strikers. After a few days, the authorities returned the strikers to their original cell, which was the only way of stopping the strike. The strike's aims had been realized.

Their quota of food was cut to such an extent that in all the time they spent, only one day were they given a boiled egg. Alcides ate his egg, shell and all.

After sixty days in the cell, they heard a troop of soldiers shouting and cursing at someone. The door of the hallway opened, and in the darkness they could make out soldiers dragging a man along the ground. The soldiers passed in front of them and threw the man into a cell beside them. When the guards had left, they called the newcomer, but got no answer. At dawn, Alcides called the unknown prisoner again. It was Napoleoncito, no less. The guards had dragged him from the prison van to the cells. He was covered with mud, and his whole body was bruised and battered. He told them that in Tres Macíos, too, prisoners were being shut up in cells similar to these, also situated outside the concentration camp.

Napoleoncito, Balbuena, and some others had been stripped of their underwear the same way the prisoners at San Ramón had been, that is to say, after being beaten unconscious. Naked, in the middle of the night, surrounded by about twenty guards, they were herded through some over-grown fields to where the terrible "drawer cells" were located. They were called this for the very good reason that they were long (about five feet) and narrow (about two feet), shaped like drawers. They were the most terrible cells that had ever existed in the history of the Cuban prison system. When Alcides was put into one of the drawer cells he couldn't even lie down; he simply didn't fit into it, and his shoulders were squeezed between the two walls. Those cells had just a hole to defecate into.

The prisoners at San Ramón were in two adjoining cells. Before them there was the little hallway, with an iron door. The floor, slightly sloping, rose up to the back wall.

The authorities stopped the breakfast piece of bread. Instead they gave out two little crackers. There was soup at lunch, and in the afternoon a bitter cornmeal mush made out of corn used to feed cattle. Because of the diet, Morales got diarrhea, which a few days later was bloody. They reported this to the soldier who brought them their mess, but the answer was always the same—they had to get dressed if they wanted any medical care. They spent days squatting on their haunches, and this caused their legs to swell. Trujillo was the first one whose legs swelled, but a little afterward everyone had terrible edema and cramps. The skin was as shiny as though it were about to split and burst.

Since the hole for the toilet was a little toward the back of the cell, when the man farthest from it had to use it, everyone had to move as one compact mass of flesh, in coordination. There is nothing more unpleasant than defe-cating with other people physically touching you, squeezed up against you. The men decided that the last man to use the hole would stay over it until the next man replaced him. They thought that after that, nothing could be worse, until the hole got stopped up and the excrement began to spread through the drawer cell.

They discussed whether to go on a hunger strike. But most of them thought they should wait awhile longer, to show the camp authorities that they could resist however brutal and inhuman the conditions were.

Instead of defecating into the hole in the cell, they began to throw their excrement into the hallway, where it piled up. They also urinated outside the cell. In a little while the stench was so terrible that the guards, who could stand to be there only a few minutes, couldn't control their stomachs and began to vomit. Maggots by the thousands crawled in the corners, in the hole full of shit, and in the pile of excrement in the hallway. They covered every surface. Morales still had bloody diarrhea.

Outside there was a wooden trough, a feeding trough for cattle, where the guards brushed their teeth, and it was that water, full of the spume from the toothpaste, that the prisoners were given to drink.

Blood began to appear in Morales' urine too. The seriousness of his condition made the other prisoners decide to go on a hunger strike, especially when Morales had an attack of arthritis which immobilized one leg and one hand. In spite of his suffering and the fact that he was absolutely cadaverous, the demands that he receive medical attention or at least be taken out of that cell went unanswered. If he didn't agree to put on the uniform, he had no right to any consideration, the authorities said. The only thing they did was take Trujillo out to examine him and get the maggots that infested his hair off him. Morales was covered with maggots as well.

In that environment of rot and stench, with the passageway full of excrement, the guards finally brought in an intravenous kit for Morales, whose condition was deteriorating almost hourly. The jailers didn't want anyone to die. They preferred to keep the prisoners on the borderline between life and death, so that out of fear of dying the prisoners would agree to put on the blue uniform. The solider had to stick the needle into Morales seven times before he found his vein. And the glucose, 1000 cc, was not allowed to drip into the vein; the valve was opened completely and the liquid flowed into Morales as fast as the needle would permit. Morales began to tremble from the effect of the liquid pouring into his body.

Napoleoncito also had attacks of diarrhea, but the only thing the guards did for him was move him into another drawer. Morales remained on the hunger strike even afterward, and once the soldiers saw that his decision was irrevocable, they took him out and forcibly put the blue uniform on him. It wasn't hard for them to do—Morales could hardly move. Even so, they had to tie him up to take him to the prison at Boniato. They put him into a cell with a member of the Communist Youth who had been arrested when he was stopped on the way to Havana with his girlfriend; the police had found four pounds of coffee the couple were carrying to his mother.

Morales, half paralyzed, couldn't take off the pants the guards had put on him forcibly, so he asked the young man in the cell with him to please take them off him, so he could go to the bathroom. The young man helped him off with his pants, and Morales picked them up and threw them out of the cell into the hallway, next to the shirt that he himself had managed to take off. Lieutenant Castillo came in immediately and threatened to return him to the drawer cell.

"You can take me wherever you want to, Lieutenant. I'm not afraid of you," Morales answered.

The other inmates in the drawer decided to go on a hunger strike in support. But the authorities weren't willing to allow that, so they "broke" the strike. The first man they took out was Nieves. They dragged him through the mud and the weeds to one of the guardposts at the concentration camp. They tied him to an iron bedstead there and tried to put a liter of glucose into him. They sewed the needle into his skin. Nieves managed to pull it out anyway, and he threw the bottle to the floor and smashed it. The guards beat him unconscious. He had been on a hunger strike for several weeks at that time.

They also took out Rivero and Alfredo Peña and dragged them through the mud as they had the others. The first days they had done this they threw the prisoner into the weeds and grass face down and several guards immobilized him. One of them would hold the prisoner's head up and clasp it between his knees, put a stick under his nose, and pull it upward. This caused irresistible pain, so the prisoner had to open his mouth. Then another guard would pour bottles of broth down his throat, which the prisoner had to swallow whether he wanted to or not. They repeated that process every day. Then one day they stopped using the stick because it broke some men's noses; they started using a spoon as a lever. They would hold the man's nose and when he opened his mouth to breathe, they would wedge one or two spoons between his teeth vertically so he couldn't close his mouth and then pour the broth down his throat. If the prisoner struggled, he could break his teeth and rip his gums and lips open.

Napoleoncito's condition was growing steadily worse. His diarrhea was uncontrollable. The night they took him out of the cell it was raining in torrents. They dragged him off with them by the arms; his body was naked. He didn't say a word, didn't even moan. He had been wounded in the thigh during the forced-labor days on La Cabaña, and the wound was troubling him terribly. His years of being mistreated were now taking their toll. Four guards dressed in raincoats surrounded him. He looked up at them from the mud he was lying in. A solider put a kerosene lantern down beside him, and the other three held him down. They were going to give him glucose. Napoleoncito counted the times that soldier stuck the needle in his arm trying to find the vein. They stuck him seventeen times.

The men resisted for more than six months. At the end of that time, the authorities realized they could do nothing to break the prisoners' resistance. Every day they had to feed them forcibly. And still some of the prisoners would stick their fingers down their throats to bring on vomiting and expel the broth they had been forced to swallow. So finally the authorities released them from the cells.

The firmness and decision of that group saved the rest of the rebel prisoners from having to go through the same thing. If the experiment had worked and they had given in, if they had accepted the blue uniform, the authorities would have put us through the same treatment—the drawers of the Tres Macíos and San Ramón concentration camps were a horrific experimental plan for the men who had rejected the uniform of the common prisoners. What was truly heroic about the men who had been the victims of that experiment was that they realized that the treatment of hundreds of other prisoners—whether we would have to go through the same experience —depended on their behavior. They were always conscious of that, and the incredibly high *esprit de corps* and the responsibility they assumed helped them all to keep on resisting, even when their physical strength had run out.

Many days before they were taken out, Alcides had become delirious and begun to rave—he didn't know where he was. Rivero, the Protestant minister, called over from his drawer and asked him please not to scream, to try to sleep. When a little while later he was brought to the prison at Boniato, Alcides did not remember, nor does he remember still today, what happened in those last days he spent there. Alfredo Peña, after five weeks of daily pleading, arrived crippled at Boniato. He had an infection in his joints which kept him from walking. We had to take maggots out of his hair. He was literally covered with fungus. Balbuena never returned to normal—the torture of the drawers drove him mad. One day he jumped over the parapet of the central prison yard at El Príncipe Prison in Havana and fell to his death.

39 / At Last, Some (Apparent) Progress

The prison at Boniato is made up of five large buildings, or rather, complexes of buildings. Each complex consists of a long steel-mesh passageway connecting a series of eight perpendicular wings, four on each side. These wings are two-story buildings; they are spaced several yards distant from each other down the passageway. The three yards between the wings on each side are like interior patios, enclosed on the outside end by a tall wall topped with barbed wire.

At nightfall we always beheld an incredible spectacle, the spectacle of the rats and the owls. These prison yards were teeming with enormous rats— so many of them that you had to see it to believe it. There must have been 100 or 150 of them in every patio. In the middle of the day dozens of them would come out and run through the cracks in the prison yard and across the little patches of grass. Nothing kept these rodents from taking over completely but the owls—they at least kept the population down somewhat. Owls are very common in Cuba, and each bird would swallow down several rats every night. No one ever put out rat poison—quite the contrary, in fact; behind the kitchen there were huge piles of garbage which were ideal foraging and breeding grounds for them. Around the edges of the sidewalks running beside the buildings there were hundreds of rat holes.

Every evening the owls with shrieks of jubilee hurtled down on the rats, grabbed them in their claws, and flew back to the roof to pull them apart and eat them. We would watch the hunt from our windows.

A few days after our arrival, the head of Internal Order, accompanied by some other guards, came into our section and went back to a little room toward the back which in the past had been a dining room. He called us all together. When he tried to talk, the words wouldn't seem to come.

"Well, I . . . " And he tried again, but the only thing he managed to get out was a single sentence.

"There's a lot of air here, and air is good for the organ."

We all looked at each other and tried to hold back our laughter. But then he repeated the sentence, and everyone burst into applause, which seemed to nudge him out of his block. Our demonstration of delight made him happy. He was almost illiterate—he could hardly put two words together —but he swelled up his chest and went on with his eloquent discourse, and at that moment we baptized him the Organ, and the name stuck.

The next day the director of the prison and an officer from the Political Police visited us. They didn't speak, they just marched stiffly in, as a show of the power that they couldn't, or didn't want to, hide. They also went into the little room. But when we came in they just sat there looking out the windows unconcernedly, waiting for one of us to say something to them. This was a strategy they used frequently, as a means of showing their contempt for us.

But since no one looked at them or approached them, Director García finally asked where the man in charge of the section was, and when Perdomo, the political prisoner we had selected to speak for us, identified himself to the officer, the man from the Political Police spoke to him.

"There's a disposition from the Ministry of the Interior which states that you men have to dress in a blue uniform. If you do not, you will have to take the consequences."

"Lieutenant, we are not criminals, nor are we in the Rehabilitation Program. International treaties which govern the treatment of prisoners, to which the Cuban government is a signatory, specify that political prisoners may not be forced to wear uniforms, much less if they are the uniforms of common criminals. Here no one will accept your blue uniform."

"You are not political prisoners. You are counterrevolutionaries. In socialist countries there are no political prisoners. That's the first thing you must recognize. And second, *we* are the ones who give orders in Cuba, and we do not tolerate defiance on the part of anyone. You either get dressed or all the severity of the Revolution will fall on you. We will not permit even one more breach of discipline. I want you men to know exactly what you are doing. The uniforms are waiting for you outside."

"No one is going to get dressed, Lieutenant."

"We'll see whether you get dressed or not," said the lieutenant from the Political Police, trying to contain his anger, and with a rictus freezing his mouth into a strange pouting grimace, he walked toward the bars, followed closely by the director.

In half an hour, several platoons took over the passageway which connected the buildings. They arrived armed with machetes, chains, iron and wooden bars, and bayonets, and stationed themselves very close to our section. Then other platoons, armed with rifles, joined them.

From the moment the first platoon arrived, the alarm had sounded among us. We held a quick meeting and decided not to allow ourselves to be beaten without putting up some defense, because we were sick and tired of taking their beatings like little lambs.

The guards were looking toward our cell windows, an unmistakable sign that that was where they were headed. That was when the officer from the Political Police appeared. He spoke with them, but we couldn't hear what he was saying. He was gesticulating angrily, though. When he finished his harangue, the guards marched toward our section. They opened the entrance gate, but inside we had already formed up into a human mass which blocked the entrance and had armed ourselves with the broomsticks and mop handles that we used to clean the floors and the plungers for unstopping the toilets. And so the battle began. The guards attacked us with their chains and truncheons; they tried to penetrate the cell area. Since the gate was only a little more than a yard wide, we could completely block it to keep them from coming through. Onofre, the Bayolo brothers, Ortíz, El Pacífico, Perdomo, and others were swinging and jabbing their mop handles, battling guards who were used to being able to beat us without any resistance from us. They didn't know how to take this counterattack.

The cries and shouts of the officers egging them on didn't seem to have much effect. The guards armed with rifles, coming in behind this first wave of guards with hand weapons, could do nothing. All they would have had to do was fire into us to scatter us completely, but that would have been at the price of killing someone, and evidently at that time they didn't have orders to go that far.

In the heat of the fight, Santiago Bayolo and El Pacífico pushed through the crowd and were fighting outside the cells. The beating they got from the guards was terrible. They buried a bayonet in Bayolo very near his crotch, but miraculously his life was spared. El Pacífico's scalp was split with a blow from a chain, and the blood flowed down his neck and shoulders. From the building in front of ours, where the common prisoners were watching the melee, came cries of admiration. Those men, accustomed to living under the same terror as we did, were watching this unequal battle between armed, trained guards and prisoners defending themselves with whatever came to hand—it was an unprecedented event. The resistance we put up against our jailers drew cries of solidarity from the common prisoners. This was surely the first time they had ever seen such a thing. In reprisal, part of the garrison entered their section as well and waded into them with clubs and bayonets.

We held the garrison off until, finally, they retreated. They carried away two of our men. There was tremendous tension among us, since we fully expected them to return at any moment. We organized a watch to keep guard all night long, and we could hardly sleep from nervousness. They might come back with tear gas or smoke bombs. But the sun rose without incident, and about midmorning they informed us that we were being transferred.

Under heavy guard we were led toward Building 1. Everyone, guards included, was very tense. We were stripped of our shoes and spoons and put into large cells which theoretically accommodated six prisoners; twenty of us were stuffed into them. I was sent into the first cell. A contingent of

officers and soldiers filled the stairways and halls. We could see the lieutenant from the Political Police who had ordered the beating running back and
forth constantly.

The cells had no sanitary facilities of any kind, and the windows had been
blocked up. At the entrance to the section were the collective toilets and the
showers—which, of course, were not working. Beside them a tall cement
tank had been installed, where water was stored. From then on, in order to
go to the latrine, you had to call the soldier on guard. The large room in
front of our cell was emptied. Part of our punishment was being kept
incommunicado.

When the hour to go to bed came, we found that only nineteen of us fit
on the floor, and even then we had to lie down in such a way that not an
inch of space was left between our bodies. We even had to balance our
aluminum drinking cups on the bars of the gate because there wasn't space
for them on the floor.

We had to take turns sleeping. The one poor man who couldn't lie down
had to remain standing in a corner, virtually immobile. The next morning
the guards took Alberto out and put him into another cell, which had only
seventeen prisoners.

The first night I didn't sleep a wink, and I don't think very many other
men did either. The granite floor was cold as ice. Enrique Fernández and
Ramonín Quesada were sleeping on either side of me. Quesada had been a
commander in the Revolutionary Army; he had fought in the mountains
against Batista. I was sleeping toe to toe with another ex-commander,
Ramón Guin, who had also fought against the dictator. At the moment of
writing these lines, Guin is still somewhere in the Cuban prisons with other
commanders who fought for Fidel Castro.

Whenever someone needed to go to the bathroom, it was a real odyssey.
You had to begin by calling the guard posted outside at the main gate.
Jutting out from the other side of the entrance bars was a large piece of
cardboard, placed there to keep us from seeing outside. Generally the guard
pretended that he didn't hear us calling. Some prisoners with colic or
diarrhea, which constantly affected prisoners in Cuban jails, couldn't wait
for the guards to "hear" them, with predictable consequences. The soldiers'
refusal to respond was one of the most constantly humiliating trials the
prisoner had to go through. So, as our response to that, we began to shake
and rattle the bars, run our cups back and forth across them in unison. That
was perhaps the most irritating thing a prisoner could do. It seemed to drive
the guards crazy. The most serious offense in Boniato Prison was making
noise with the cell bars, which of course the soldiers could never prevent
because the whole cell front was barred and it was easy to shake them. As
soon as that unholy symphony started, the guards would run over; that
means of protesting became a weapon we used often.

There were about a hundred of us men. When we got up in the morning, we had to be taken to the toilet. A guard would open the first cell, and we would all go out together to the tank where the water was stored. We could only wash our faces; baths were authorized only for specific days of the week, and they were rotated among the sections.

The authorities soon changed the rules; they had the bright idea of taking out the prisoners in the morning one by one. It was an incredibly provoking thing to do. Guards moved as slowly as they humanly could. The minimum time it took to unlock the cell, take the prisoner out, accompany him to the latrine, wait for him to do what he had to do, and return him to the cell was five minutes. It might take longer. That meant it would have taken eight or nine hours for everyone to go to the toilet one by one. Understandably, this treatment triggered a reaction on our part. We began to urinate out into the hallway. There were those who could not wait and who defecated inside the cell and threw their excrement into the hall. Within a few days the hallway was so nauseating that even the soldiers who had to come in every day and walk the length of the corridor to perform the headcounts or do other jobs grew sick. But they had to take it, or modify the rule they had just put into effect. The disgust reflected in their faces and the stench of the hallway became our allies.

The day one of the guards slipped trying to jump over a pool of urine and fell into it finally brought a solution to the problem. The guards issued an ultimatum to the authorities. They refused to go into that area until it was cleaned up.

The chief of Internal Order, no less than the Organ himself, came to discuss the issue. The prisoners chose me to deal with him. Ramonín Quesada and Alberto Bayolo went with me. As soon as the Organ opened his mouth, all sorts of nonsense came out, the most absurd mixture of pomposities and vulgarities imaginable. Apparently he had recently heard the word "resplendent" and he wanted to impress us with the way he used it.

"It is resplendent upon you men to help us resolve this issue."

The use he put that poor word to made Ramonín burst out laughing. I managed to contain my laughter, though I still don't know how I did it. But the situation was in fact resolved. They promised to take us out to the toilet in groups, and they put five-gallon cans out in the passageway in front of the cells for us to pour our urine into. We used a small can inside the cells like an old-fashioned chamber pot, and emptied the slops into the larger cans in the hall. This can afforded great relief, especially at night, since formerly if someone had to go to the bathroom, everyone would be awakened by the cries of the man calling out to the mock-deaf guards.

The information we managed to get was very sparse. The window of the toilet was blocked with boards nailed right to the window frame. There was, though, a little chink through which I would peek out into the courtyard, and I was delighted to see a man named Jesús whom I had met through my future father-in-law, strolling and taking a little sun out in the patio.

The guard, when he opened the cell, generally did it trusting that all the windows were nailed up. He would close the main entrance gate and leave us out in the passageway, so I could call out to Jesús when I saw him passing close by and estimated that he was under the window. The first time I called him he couldn't figure out who was calling him or where the voice was coming from, but the second time he looked up. Jesús was very spirited, and he said he was willing to help us. I told him what we needed and the way to get it in to me.

The next day I unraveled one of the rags we cleaned the floor with and made a cord with a little ball of soap on the end to weight it. Several of us pulled the board away from the window while others watched to make sure the guard didn't catch us.

Jesús was waiting down below. He tied the little package with the things I had asked for to the cord, and I pulled it up quickly. That was a treasure for me—there was a ballpoint-pen refill, two pieces of onionskin, and a spool of strong thread. If he had been caught doing what he did, Jesús would have been beaten and thrown into the punishment cells for months.

The next day he picked up a letter I threw out for Martha. Once again I had managed to break out of my isolation, and I truly felt I had accomplished something.

We occupied only one section of the cells in that pavilion. The cells in front were vacant. The garrison hung curtains made out of burlap sacks over them so that we couldn't look out through the windows on that side. Otherwise you could have seen the Headquarters buildings.

Enrique Cepero had a plan for an escape. Escape was really quite difficult for us at that time, since we had absolutely no resources. The major obstacle was clothing. We were naked, after all. But thanks to the extraordinary abilities of our group's tailor, Mario Díaz, this first hurdle was crossed; he made two sets of clothing out of some rags and sheets. Pepe Fernández was to accompany Cepero in this virtually impossible long shot. Everything was done to perfection. One of the chains on the front gate had a broken link, and they escaped into the cells at the front of the pavilion when the guards were changing the chain. They got out by cutting some bars, but they didn't manage to get very far; they were discovered by the garrison and taken to the punishment cells. A little while later, Cepero would try to escape again, this time from the jail at Guanajay, dressed in a military uniform which he had made himself. However, within just a few yards he would be recognized and captured by one of the guards.

One afternoon Jauto, the chief of the political commissioners, called me to tell me that my father was now a prisoner, sentenced to twenty years. He told me my father was being held in the concentration camp called Manacas in the province of Las Villas, and that if I put on the blue uniform, they'd take me to see him.

I was dumbstruck by that news. I had never expected such a thing. But

I told Jauto that I wasn't interested in his deal. I had no intention of getting dressed for any reason, any reason at all.

Years later I would find out what had happened to my father. He had a friend named Roberto Herrera, who was detained on the suspicion of conspiracy against the State. My father brought this man's family to visit him, from the province of Las Villas to Havana, where Herrera was a prisoner in La Cabaña. My father behaved more like a brother than a friend with the man. But Herrera went into the Political Rehabilitation Program, and in an act of collaboration with the Political Police he denounced my father. He said he had been in a conspiracy with him in 1960. My father therefore went to prison. He was deeply wounded by this betrayal by a man he had taken to be his friend.

I was terribly worried by the news of my father's imprisonment. A new suffering was added to my existence, perhaps the most troubling of all because it meant even worse poverty, hardship, and harassment for my family. My mother and sister were now alone, helpless, and more marked out than ever because now both my father and I were political prisoners. It was the worst news I had gotten so far in all my years in jail. I felt so sorry for my father, too, a man sick and getting on in years. But there was nothing I could do in the face of this latest setback but roll with that punch as I had with others and try to keep my faith strong. It was one more test, one more challenge to my resistance. Still, I asked myself if my rebelliousness was worth it. All I had to do, really, was say I'd wear the blue uniform and the next day I would be on my way to Havana, and the day after that visiting my family. That would surely mitigate the effect of my father's imprisonment. It would be a great relief to my mother and sister. What about Martha? Would she be able to understand my action, and to accept it? I was sure that she would, that she would accept it to all outward intents—but deep inside, would she really? I had prepared her, since the first day; I had told her very clearly that I had no intention of acting any differently. I had always explained to her not only what I was doing but also why I was doing it. Now, after so much and so long, a change in my conduct might look weak or inconsistent to her.

I don't think one should be dogmatic; I think, rather, that one's ideas and judgments should be flexible enough to evolve. But there are things one cannot compromise or change—one's deepest convictions and ethical values, those principles which, like pillars, sustain a person's self-respect. If a single one of them developed a crack, started to give way, a person's life's edifice could come crashing down about his ears. I felt, when I looked at my situation, that to waver, as my jailers obviously wanted me to do, was to put the internal structures of my life in danger. Still, I did vacillate, and I doubted; but then I prayed to God, and He, whom I never doubted, showed me the right path again—my rationalizations suddenly looked flimsy and transparent, and I began again with new reserves of faith and hope.

Those of us who refused to wear the blue uniform were scattered through all the prisons and concentration camps in the country—the jails at Camagüey and Holguín, at Manzanillo, at Pinar del Río, at Guanajay, the prisons of Castillo del Príncipe and La Cabaña, and more besides. But we had all agreed that we would accept no accords until our jailers brought us all back together again in Havana, so the effort of the Ministry of the Interior to undermine our cause by dispersing us and pressuring each one of us individually was rendered ineffective.

In many jails the authorities employed systematic beatings to force us to dress. They also confined prisoners in dungeonlike cells whose walls and floors were covered with melted asphalt, which left marks on the prisoners' skin for the rest of their lives. The Director of Jails and Prisons, Captain Medardo Lemus, took part personally, along with a heavy contingent of guards, in the clubbing of prisoners in the old fortress of San Severino and in the Aguica concentration camp in Matanzas province. That was where García Plasencia, a prisoner they were beating, punched Captain Lemus in the jaw. They practically killed García for that. As I write this, García Plasencia is still in prison, twenty years later.

Several months passed, and Castro's government became convinced that our position had hardened, especially after the men that had not been entirely determined to stick with our protest had "gone over" and put on the blue uniforms. It had been a victory of sorts for the regime, it's true. Most of the men in the original group had accepted the uniform. That was the point at which they called us out and we departed once more, in the same prison vans, for Havana. The Ministry had ordered that we be brought together again in the prison at La Cabaña.

Moments before we left Boniato Prison, a soldier approached us, looked around suspiciously to make sure none of the other guards could hear, and whispered to us that we were going to get what we had wanted—the uniform we had worn before.

The return trip to Havana, although it was more than twelve hours long and full of discomforts, was a happy one for us, then, since it signified a return to the capital, to sources of information, to proximity to our families. Although we might not be able to see our loved ones, we would know they were close by, just across the Bay of Havana.

In Camagüey another prison van joined us. In it were naked prisoners from another jail.

When we arrived in Havana and were walking through the main gate, a guard gave us underwear and a towel. Almost everyone had been gathered there again—only we and a group from the San Ramón concentration camp were missing. The soldiers treated us relatively gently. Rejoining our old comrades made us all very happy. They placed us in *galera* 13. And they announced a visit from the Minister of the Interior, Commander Sergio del Valle, one of Castro's right-hand men.

He had hardly entered—surrounded by half a dozen bodyguards—when he began to speak. He said the uniform question had been terminated and they were going to give us back the uniforms they had taken away from us. He added that no measure would be taken against anyone who didn't wish to accept the old uniform; any prisoner who remained naked would be granted the same rights as the uniformed prisoners.

But mostly his words seemed false, hypocritical, misleading to us. We wondered why, after keeping us naked for more than a year, beating us, torturing us, they would suddenly be willing to give us back the uniforms they had stripped off us. It seemed prudent for us to think the offer over for a while. There were other matters involved too—for example, the policy on visits, correspondence, medical care, living conditions, and so forth. We'd better wait and think and see what happened. A lot had happened in the past year, and this was all very sudden.

Boitel was one of the proponents of this approach. But most of the men simply got dressed—there were only about 250 of us waiting to see how the Communists' strategy unfolded.

At first the Minister of the Interior himself had said that we could all stay together in one *galera,* both the men who agreed to dress and those who didn't. But a few days later we were separated; those of us without clothing were taken to *galeras* 12 and 13.

The days of the visits were set. We were allowed to make up some shorts and to wear collarless white pullovers to visit our relatives. They set up partitions and made ten or twelve cubicles in the long visiting hall so that we would be able to be beside our family members. My meeting with my mother, sister, and Martha was indescribably happy. They told me everything that had happened recently.

Those visits, after months and months of not seeing each other, and the need to find everything out in a few minutes produced tremendous anxiety. You felt so rushed and hurried. I had had that experience before, and so I had a list of things I especially wanted to know, made up ahead of time calmly and thoughtfully. I used the crotch flap of my underwear as a secret pocket. Using the underwear to smuggle correspondence in and out later became a sort of fad. By that time the authorities' security measures had been relaxed considerably.

We were allowed to go into the prison yard for several hours sometimes, getting sun and exercise. The guards' treatment of us softened a little. But it all reflected a devious strategy to make as little difference between us and the uniformed prisoners as possible; after all, if there was no difference, why not put on the uniform? They needed us to get dressed to be able to carry out their plan to destroy the system of political opposition in the jails.

Soon enough we distrustful prisoners would be proved right.

40 / Martha Arrested: Our Wedding

L iving conditions soon began to deteriorate. The authorities didn't keep their promises of adequate medical treatment, they didn't transfer the mentally ill to appropriate treatment centers, they didn't let us have our mail. We had to send food back because they would send thirty or forty rations too few. Since the authorities wouldn't send in the missing rations, all of us went without eating. Someone suggested a hunger strike in which both we and the prisoners dressed now in the yellow uniform would take part.

To show the authorities that we were firm in our decision, we brought out all the foodstuffs we had inside the cells—a little sugar and flour and a few crackers left over from the packages our families were allowed to bring us every ninety days. We put the food, in little bags, out in a line in front of each *galera*. We only drank water, and we wanted to make sure the soldiers knew it.

In spite of the memories of the traumatic previous general strike we had mounted on Isla de Pinos, we were confident of winning this one. And that firmness of purpose, that decisiveness, is always a key factor in a hunger strike. We all felt we had been tricked and deceived once more by the authorities. Our stoicism had won the battle over the uniforms—we had turned the other cheek to brutal and inhumane treatment, our resistance had forced the other side to give in. Now we felt we had to resort to more active measures to secure humane treatment.

The first two days that we refused to eat, things went well enough; the third day, though, soldiers replaced all the rehabilitated prisoners who usually brought the tanks of food to us. They stood in front of each *galera* with tanks of food and big pots of wonderful-smelling soup the likes of which we had never seen—they thought they would break us with that temptation.

One night about a week later, Lieutenant Lemus, Director of Jails and Prisons, appeared in the prison yard with several officers and called twenty-five prisoners' names off a list. Those were the prisoners the authorities took to be the leaders and instigators of the strike. The Revolutionary Army ex-commanders Húber Matos, Eloy Gutiérrez Menoyo, and César Páez were called, as were Bernardo Alvarez, the Bayolo brothers, Lauro Blanco, myself, and others. Prison Headquarters thought separating us from the rest of the prisoners might break the strike. They thought we were its leaders, but they were wrong. They took us to the main gate. Húber Matos and I were the last two in the group. It looked as though they were going to take us out of the prison yard, but at the last minute there was a change of guards and they led us back to *galera* 18, the last one down the line. It was completely isolated, empty; they left us there.

Starting the next day, a procession of officers from Jails and Prisons began coming into our gallery to discuss the situation with us. They kept insisting they would never give an inch to our demands, because they refused to negotiate under such conditions. We asked them simply to keep the promises they had made to allow us medical treatment, monthly visits, sufficient food for everyone, and daily sun and exercise in the prison yard.

The officers spent hour after hour arguing with Tony Lamas, César Páez, Húber Matos, and me. They did everything in their power to spend as long as they could with us, so as to make the rest of the prisoners suspicious, create resentments, and thereby divide us; but as the days passed and they achieved no results, the authorities began to realize that our determination to go on with the strike was unshakable, and that we would carry it to its ultimate conclusions.

Not a single sick man—and there were many—left the strike. Aldo Cabrera had had two heart attacks, Fernández Gámez had scaly scabs all over his body, Luis Lara couldn't even keep down the water he drank—he vomited almost continuously. Like him, there were many for whom the hunger strike became a double torture. But no one gave in.

Meanwhile, the soldiers kept bringing the big pots of delicious-looking food and setting them down in front of the bars of the cells.

I had managed to get a letter out to Martha, so she was the first person outside the prison to know what was going on. She notified many of the other prisoners' families. They all decided to come, two days later, and stand at the first guardpost at the entrance and wait there until the authorities gave them news of us and the situation. Other wives went to the offices of the Ministry of the Interior, but they always received the same answer from the officials there—as long as we maintained our position, there would be no negotiations.

In the second week, patrol cars full of soldiers blocked the road to the prison entrance; our mothers, wives, and sisters had to stay on the dirt road that connects La Cabaña with El Morro Castle. The women stood outside all day; it rained off and on. No men had come. They knew that if they did they would wind up in jail.

Toward the middle of October the tension and uncertainty led the family members to go to Castro's secretary, Celia Sánchez, to ask her to intercede on behalf of the prisoners. The relatives started to her offices from the prison. So as not to attract too much attention, they went off in groups and met on Calle 23, in the Vedado section of Havana, and from there they marched down Calle K to Calle 19, where Celia Sánchez lived. Some bewildered passersby asked them what was going on. When the women told them, they ran off in terror. All the neighbors shut themselves up in their houses and locked the doors, and there were even some who shouted that they hoped all of us on the hunger strike died.

When the entourage turned down Calle K, a military jeep pulled up. The soldiers advised them to go back to their own houses and said they weren't going to achieve anything by going about it in that way. But the women decided to go on. It was not a classic demonstration with signs and banners, or shouted slogans. It was simply a large group of women walking together in silence.

But suddenly patrol cars, sirens screaming, appeared from all directions and blocked off all the surrounding streets. Policemen jumped out of their cars as though dangerous criminals were committing some violent crime. Young and old women alike were dragged off mercilessly, beaten and kicked, and shoved into the patrol cars.

Martha and another woman had managed to get away, but Martha looked back and saw her friend Inés, Raúl del Valle's wife, struggling with a policeman who had her by the wrists and was dragging her to the car. Martha ran back to try to help, so they arrested Martha and threw her into the same car. The women were taken to the central headquarters of the National Revolutionary Police, at the intersection of Cuba and Chacón streets. The police had them sit down on a concrete bench with some other women arrested in the roundup.

The officer in charge of the patrol cars came in. It was Captain Justo Hernández. He was the same man who when he was director of La Cabaña had threatened Martha with jail. He was hysterical, shrieking and yelling that all the women were agents of the CIA.

Different patrol cars arrived to take them to the principal office of the Political Police, located in the old Villa Marista buildings. Inés, who knew the grudge Captain Hernández had against Martha, tried to hide Martha by standing in front of her, but when they yanked Inés away to put her in the car, the captain saw Martha.

"Look what I found! Now you really *are* going to rot in jail!"

At Political Police Headquarters everything the women were carrying was taken away from them. They even took away Martha's eyeglasses; she couldn't see without them. "You won't need them here," they told her. "There's nothing to see."

They led the women one by one into a little room where several female police officers stripped them naked. When the humiliating search was finished, they were taken to the records section to be photographed, finger-printed, and processed. Then they were separated and put into cells.

A lieutenant went to get Martha and led her to one of the many offices in the labyrinthine building. There seated behind a desk an officer was waiting for her. He began the interrogation by asking her who had organized the demonstration in front of Celia Sánchez' house and why they had gone there. Martha told him that her relatives were dying in a hunger strike that the authorities had provoked by not giving them even the minimum food they needed to live. The officer asserted that the women were organized and paid by the CIA and that everything had been planned and directed from abroad. Martha couldn't help smiling at that, and the soldier grew angry. Then he asked her why she didn't ask her father and me to go into the Rehabilitation Program, since that was the ideal solution to the problem. The Revolution, humane and just as it was, was willing to give all the prisoners, even those who wanted to destroy it, another chance to join the socialist society. Martha answered that Political Rehabilitation wasn't a solution for us *or* for her, that we were not going to deny God whatever the consequences might be.

"Well, you're going to have a lot of time to think about that." Those were the officer's last words. Martha thought she was doomed to spend long years in jail.

They returned her to her cell; the door opened only once more, to pass in a plate of food, but she didn't know how much time had passed, or whether it was day or night. She was taken out again and led in a maze through long passageways and up and down stairs. Another officer was waiting for her this time, a tall young man. He didn't accuse her of being an agent of the CIA; he was very friendly. He began talking about the Vietnam War and about the children who were being killed by the American forces there, and he told her that if she was a Christian, as she claimed to be, she ought to be indignant over the monstrous crimes the Yankees were committing.

Martha told him that according to him and others like him the Americans were responsible for all the evil in the world, but people like him never talked about the way the Communists from North Vietnam were killing innocent people as they invaded South Vietnam. She said that it was never the men that caused the war who died—they sat comfortably behind their desks while the poor wretches they sent out to fight were dying. Then the officer talked to her about the generosity of the Revolution, a revolution which was perfectly capable of helping a counterrevolutionary integrate himself into the society again. He even told her that with the coming of the Revolution the torturing of prisoners had ended. Martha began to laugh in his face. He feigned surprise. He didn't understand what Martha was laughing about. He very subtly tried to get Martha to tell him whether the idea of going to Celia Sánchez' house had come out of the prison; he tried to blackmail her by insinuating that the women would serve long sentences in prison if they didn't talk.

Later, alone in her unlighted cell, she became very worried about Inés and Josefina, Nacer's mother. Again, she didn't know how much time had passed when they called her out again. Once more she went down long hallways and deserted stairs. She was taken to a room where all the women were waiting. There they had to listen to a long speech filled with threats and accusations until finally they were told by the authorities that this time they were going to be freed.

The Political Police telephoned Josefa, Martha's mother, and told her to wait at a certain corner, not to move from it. Very early the next morning, they ordered Martha and Inés to walk to where Josefa was waiting. The three women met in a tearful hug.

The next day the strike ended. At the end of twenty-one days the authorities were forced to give in to the justice of our demands.

They opened the *galeras* and a few men, exerting all the strength they had left, went out into the patio, embracing each other jubilantly. Ambulances arrived to pick up the men in the worst condition, many of whom could not stand, and transfer them to the prison at Castillo del Príncipe, where the National Hospital for Prisoners was located. The ones in least serious condition were given intravenous glucose in the *galeras,* since the ten or twelve beds in the dispensary were full. The doctors and paramedics rushed around like ants; with our group they had their hands full.

As Eloy and I were going back to our old *galera,* Lieutenant Cosme, the director of the prison, intercepted us. He was accompanied by the head of Jails and Prisons. They told us our group couldn't leave the gallery we had been in because we had been classified by the Ministry of the Interior. The authorities were still obviously trying to isolate us.

During the first days after the strike they fed us on broth and puréed vegetables. They called our families to come to the first visit. My good friend Dr. Otto García, a prisoner who worked in the infirmary, found some dark bruises on my body making what looked almost like a necklace across my chest. It was pellagra, a disease caused by malnutrition. But as the food got better, we did too.

Nonetheless, psychiatric care, which we had demanded for the mentally ill, was not offered. Some cases had been reported (among them Rafael Socorro, a young student who went mad with terror in the forced-labor fields on Isla de Pinos), in hopes the men would be taken to a proper hospital. Nothing came of our requests. Húber Matos was the first man out of bed one morning, so he was the one who discovered Rafael's body hanging from the bars. He had hanged himself with shredded sheets. Húber called Tony Lamas and Atilano, and the three of them took the body down as they shouted to the guards to open the cell door. Tony carried Rafael's body in his arms to the dispensary, but he was already dead. That was February 14, 1969, St. Valentine's Day. Outside, in honor of the day, Socorro's mother and girlfriend, along with other relatives and friends, mine among them, tried to get the authorities to allow them to see us. When the hearse passed by, Socorro's girlfriend never suspected that the body of the man she loved was in it.

The months which followed the hunger strike were the most peaceful of our whole life in the prison. But it was only a respite while the military authorities elaborated new plans for what was to be a constant obsession with them—breaking down our resistance, making us cave in, lower our heads, and say, "Yes, Commissar, I have been wrong. I accept Political Rehabilitation because I see now that Communism is the only just system, and it alone can bring happiness to humanity."

Some of us wanted to get married. We requested permission from Ministry Headquarters. It seemed the right moment to do this, given the supposed conciliatory stance of the government at the time. Martha's father and I wanted her to be able to leave Cuba, to go and live with her brothers and sisters abroad. It was necessary for her safety, since she had been arrested and held by the Political Police. Martha, after repeated arguments from her father and me, changed her mind about staying in Cuba and agreed to go abroad. Her family was one of the few that had stayed behind when the lists of applications to leave Cuba were approved. Tens of thousands of people had left for the United States on the so-called Cuban Flights in 1965. From that time on, she could have left.

One morning in a military office we signed the necessary legal documents and were therefore married. That act had absolutely no spiritual significance for us. We would feel and truly be husband and wife only when we were joined in a religious ceremony, before God.

As a special concession to the two couples who had just been married, the authorities were uncharacteristically benevolent—they gave us fifteen minutes in the visitors' hall under the vigilance of the guards. But at least when Martha left Cuba, she would do it as my legal wife. We had talked about how useful her work for gaining my freedom could be abroad. We planned a whole series of activities aimed at creating a public-opinion campaign that would force Castro to free me. She had what it takes—she was a born activist. More than I had ever dreamed, Martha rose to the faith I placed in her.

Boitel and a small group of men declared a hunger strike and were transferred to the ward that the Political Police had under its authority in the military hospital. Several weeks without eating meant that Boitel could no longer fend for himself. His body and its defenses were weakened by previous strikes and by the mistreatment he had suffered during his years in jail. Carmelo Cuadra was suffering too, writhing in abdominal pain. But medical care wouldn't come until the strike ended. The tenacity of the prisoners, though, was stronger than the authorities' pressures.

Three days later Carmelo died from a liver complication. This led the authorities to offer medical aid to the other strikers. That was April 1969.

As the months passed, the authorities began to break the promises they had made in response to our previous protest, and so we went on another strike, demanding humane treatment. Immediately Prison Headquarters isolated our *galera;* they emptied the one next to us because they knew we could communicate through the chinks and holes which the prisoners made in the thick walls.

We had been on strike for two weeks. Every day they brought pots with food, as they always did to break our decision not to eat.

The blue-uniformed prisoners from *galera* 34 had had a visit and had smuggled in letters for those of us on the hunger strike. We had tried to manage somehow to get the letters, but so far we hadn't found a way. One day the garrison opened the doors of all the galleries, and we took advantage of the circumstances. We coordinated a plan to smuggle in a little package of letters for us in *galera* 14. Eloy Gutiérrez Menoyo, Machín, and I set everything up. We knew that the guards had set up ambushes in the storehouse *galera* and behind the tanks of water, to try to intercept us and take away our clandestine correspondence. Raúl Fernández got the package of letters and walked out of *galera* 15 as though he were as carefree and unconcerned as a bird; but suddenly he tossed the package to Eloy; Eloy caught it like a football and passed it to me under his legs when the guards were almost on top of him. I caught the package and passed it the same way to Machín, and Machín lobbed it inside the *galera*. We had moved so fast that the guards running after us were confused. Before their very eyes, under their very noses, we smuggled in the correspondence. They were furious—they held Eloy against the wall with the bayonets of their AK rifles. One of them pricked his neck. But inside the *galera* the men had performed a vanishing act on the cards and letters. There was no way for the guards to retrieve them. Needless to say, the physical effort it took us to get the letters, after we'd been on a hunger strike for two weeks, was exhausting.

The loudspeakers in the prison yard were constantly broadcasting speeches aimed at demoralizing us and breaking the strike. They kept telling us that we would be impotent, that malnutrition would affect our brains, that our bodies would consume themselves and that that, in turn, would reduce the size of our livers, hearts, and testicles. This went on and on. The warnings were always accompanied by moving messages from our families, who were desperately waiting for us at the entrance to the prison.

After fifteen days, one group of strikers, I among them, was separated from the rest and sent off to *galera* 23 in the military section. They searched us and without respect for the fact that we had gone two weeks without eating, beat us and pushed us around however they wanted. We had a little radio that we had smuggled in a while before, and through it we had learned that the whole world knew about the strike. But the efforts of our relatives before the Human Rights Commission of the United Nations, asking it to intervene for us, were once again fruitless.

The guards found the radio in the search, and we were reduced once again to isolation from the world.

The third week passed, and then the fourth, and the desertions began. High-ranking military functionaries visited us daily. Our resistance began to falter. On the thirtieth day of our not eating, drinking only water, they took out Loredo, a Catholic priest. The authorities had permitted Monsignor Azcárate, Bishop of Havana, to visit him. It was a strange visit the bishop had with Loredo. They sat alone on a bench in the little park in the military section.

Monsignor Azcárate told Loredo that our protest was foolish, that we would gain nothing by it, that no one in the outside world knew we were on strike. Azcárate lied knowingly, and the only object of his visit was to demoralize us. We ourselves, before our radio had been seized, had heard the contrary; radio stations in other countries were broadcasting the news of our strike.

Ever since Castro's triumph, Catholic priests had followed the development of the Revolution with great concern. As soon as they saw that it was going down the path to Marxism they denounced it, and from their pulpits alerted their parishioners to the approaching danger. On May 8, 1960, all Cuban bishops signed a pastoral letter condemning Communism. All the schools were seized by the government, including Catholic and Protestant schools, and all religious instruction was abolished. On June 26, 1961, the *Marqués de Comillas* docked at the port of La Coruña in Spain with hundreds of lay and clerical leaders who had been expelled from Cuba. On September 17, 1961, Castro exiled another 136 Catholic priests. The Cuban government's hostility undoubtedly had its effect, because from that time onward the attitude of the Catholic Church in Cuba made a 180-degree turn. The artificer of the new relationship was Monsignor César Zacchi, the Vatican's ambassador to Cuba, who made his first appearance declaring that Cuba was pagan before the Revolution but a believer under Communism.

The youth of the island, in defiance of the regime, filled the churches. Many young people refused to enter the militia and collaborate with Castro. In response to these events a pastoral letter appeared, signed by most of the Cuban bishops, but not by all, since some of them refused to put their name to such a shameful document. In the letter the American blockade of Cuba was condemned and the people of Cuba were asked to work to help the Revolution in pulling the country up from underdevelopment. The letter blamed poverty and scarcity not on the Communist system and its defects but on the American blockade. It was obvious from the way the situation was handled that the leadership of the church in Cuba and the Cuban government were collaborating.

Before the letter was read in the churches, the Political Police in coordination with the Committees for the Defense of the Revolution organized cliques which would go to the churches to applaud the pastoral letter. The Cuban authorities knew about its contents beforehand, but the parish priests did not. The priests received the letter in sealed envelopes, with instructions not to open it until they read it at the principal masses that Sunday. That way, they couldn't prepare replies to it. Not only their parishioners but they themselves were taken by surprise.

The young Catholics could hardly believe what they were hearing that morning. There were loud exclamations of indignation; violent arguments arose in some churches, like the church at Guanabacoa, where the mass erupted into an exchange of blows between the real churchgoers and the Communist agitators who had infiltrated the services. Brother Chaurrondo, in the Church of the Immaculate Virgin on San Lázaro Street in Havana, began reading the letter and then stopped and disgustedly said he wasn't going to read the rest of it. Many other priests did the same.

The Vatican Nuncio appeared in a photograph with Castro and at many parties and meetings. He was forever making declarations. In one, he asked the young people to join the Communist militia and help Castro defend the Revolution against enemy aggression. These enemies were the anti-Communist Cubans who had fled the island and were preparing an invasion to bring down the government, which was exactly what the young people who filled the churches wanted. The most exalted of all the declarations made by

Monsignor Zacchi was the one which painted Castro as a man with deep Christian values. Castro soon gave the Papal Nuncio his own brand-new bus to transport seminarians to farms where they would work "voluntarily" to help the Revolution.

At that time there existed what was called the Havana Cordon. This was a wide farm strip which surrounded the capital, where following Castro's personal directions thousands of fruit and coffee trees and vegetables were planted—with which the Havana population hoped to be supplied. People were sent to this area, as they were to other similar locations, if they applied to leave the country. They had to work there under humiliating, subhuman conditions.

Saturdays and Sundays the government mobilized tens of thousands of people to labor in those fields. The people hated the Havana Cordon; it was maintained by slave labor. Monsignor Zacchi went with Castro to have his photo made as he held a hoe in the Havana Cordon. He declared that the Havana Cordon was "a demonstration of the enthusiasm of the Cuban people."

Miguel Angel Loredo, the Catholic priest imprisoned with us, was arrested in his church in San Francisco. From the moment of his arrest, reprisals were directed at him. He was taken to the forced-labor camps on Isla de Pinos and put to work in the quarries, where he was made to break rocks with a sledgehammer. One morning the guards pulled him out of the group he was in, stripped him, and began beating him with bayonets and cudgels. They left enormous bruises on his face, back, arms, and legs. Unconscious and bleeding from his mouth and nose, he was sent back to the prison.

The news that Loredo had been beaten caused general indignation. He was very well liked among the prisoners. That same day, prisoners secretly got the news of what had happened to Loredo out to his relatives. Soon the news of the event had reached national proportions and even spread abroad. The Cuban leader Carlos Rafael Rodríguez called Monsignor Zacchi to the Ministry of Foreign Affairs. They spoke for an hour in private. The next Friday in the official magazine *Bohemia* there were declarations by Monsignor Zacchi in which he mentioned Loredo. Zacchi said that the Revolution had been very generous with him, had treated him well, since he had not been taken to jail, but to a little farm where he devoted himself to the peaceful work of planting lettuce and radishes. Thus, with this official declaration by the Vatican Nuncio, the truth was completely perverted. When Zacchi made those declarations, Brother Loredo was still bedridden from the blows he had received. In return for his favor, on December 14, 1967, Castro was the guest of honor at Monsignor Zacchi's episcopal consecration; and yet the return of the favor did not end there—months later, when Castro bought a fleet of Alfa Romeos for himself and his aides, he bought one extra which he gave as a gift to Monsignor Zacchi.

After the expulsion of the priests and Zacchi's arrival, never again did the Catholic Church in Cuba raise its voice against the crimes and tortures or demand that the firing squads be abolished. During that time it was not only a silent church, but something much worse, a church of complicity.

Therefore Monsignor Azcárate's visit, with the intention of demoralizing us, did not particularly surprise us.

When someone left the hunger strike, the authorities immediately informed his family. There was a soldier assigned that job. When Martha arrived one morning, the man on duty confused my name with someone else's; he told Martha that I had given in. Martha asked a lieutenant to look for my name on the list. The lieutenant called the Political Commissioner, Patterson. "What's the man's name?" he asked, and he took out his notebook to look for it.

"Armando Valladares," Martha answered.

"Valladares!" Patterson angrily put away the notebook. "That man will never leave the strike. He'll die first; he's one of the leaders."

On the thirty-fifth day of the strike it was difficult to keep the men going. Only a minority of us realized that if we held out for just three or four more days we would win. Other men had a different view of the situation and held to it vigorously. We had become somewhat divided, and at last we arrived at the conclusion that if we did not call off the strike as a sovereign decision taken by us, so that it wouldn't look like we were ending it because of the desertions, the desertions were going to make the decision inevitable. After thirty-six days, we gave up on the strike. The head of Jails and Prisons came with a captain who had been in the little group that had escaped from Bolivia during Ché Guevara's adventure in that country.

"You men have tried to achieve propaganda objectives with this strike. You have attempted to defame the Revolution, because the whole world knew what was happening here. But you will have to pay the consequences," the lieutenant said menacingly to Eloy Gutiérrez Menoyo. And we did. Their fury had no bounds. They carried the men in danger of death to the hospital at El Príncipe. Those who remained in the prison were given some vegetable soup at first, but within four or five days we were getting the same old jail food as always, or still worse than before, and we were not allowed any vitamins or medications at all, nothing to help us recover our health after thirty-six days without food. There were prisoners with cerebral lesions, like Federico Hernández, who were affected for the rest of their lives because they did not receive adequate medical care. We requested medical care for those worst cases. We appealed personally to the military doctor, Dr. Batista, a despotic young man. We told him that his oath as a doctor should prevail over all other considerations, even his allegiance to the Communist Party. But he answered that he was first a Communist, then a soldier, and only then a doctor.

Within a few days a group of prisoners was back again in *galera* 34, held incommunicado. I was among them. My father-in-law, who had served nine years in jail, was set free. All of those of us without clothing were transferred one morning, once again to Boniato Prison.

Thus began one of the most dreadful stages of Cuban political imprisonment. It was marked by its violence, its tortures, and the deaths that resulted from them. The nightmare of the "blackout cells" began.

42 / A Nazi Prison in the Caribbean

f all the prisons and concentration camps in Cuba, the most repressive was Boniato Prison, on the extreme eastern end of the island. Perhaps in the past it had not been so bad for other prisoners, but it has been and will always be for political prisoners. Even today, when prison authorities want to put a group of prisoners through the worst imaginable experiences, when they want to perform biological or psychological experiments on them, when they want to hold prisoners completely incommunicado, to beat and torture them, the jail at Boniato is the installation of choice.

Built at the lowest point in a valley, surrounded by military encampments, far away from towns and highways, it is the ideal location for their plans. The cries of tortured men and the bursts of machine-gun fire are heard by no one; they fade away into the solitude of the place, are lost in the hills and valleys. Relatives are often as far as seven hundred miles away, so they're very seldom standing at the prison entrance asking for news. And if after a long exhausting pilgrimage they manage to arrive at the outskirts of the prison installation, the guards send them back home. The isolation of a jail may be one of its main advantages, and the jail at Boniato is the most isolated of all the prisons in Cuba.

Our trip to Boniato was the worst we had ever made. The police van held twenty-two prisoners uncomfortably, but the authorities crammed twenty-six of us inside.

I was in a cage with three other men. Since we couldn't all sit down at once, I crawled under the wooden seat and curled up. I knocked continually against the other men's legs. I fell asleep with the rocking and rolling of the vehicle and slept until Piloto, nauseated by the smell of gasoline and the rocking of the truck, began to vomit. The only thing to hold the vomit was my aluminum drinking cup, so I gave it to him. About two hundred miles farther on, in the city of Santa Clara, they gave each cage a can to urinate into. I got under the seat again. Urine kept splashing out of the can and wetting my legs from the rough braking and the potholes in the road. Piloto was still very motion-sick, but we didn't have anything to give him to control his nausea. One of the prison vans broke down as we were coming into Camagüey. The trip took more than twenty-five hours.

At last the caravan stopped at the entrance of Boniato Prison. When the door opened, I saw a great billboard saying "CUBA—FIRST FREE TERRITORY IN AMERICA."

They took us out of the trucks and led us to Building 5, Section C. Taking advantage of the tumult of prisoners and guards, I managed to hand a package I was carrying to Enrique Díaz Correa, who had arrived previously and was already inside. Had I not given him the package with the penpoint, a tiny photo of Martha, some small sheets of onionskin, and a jar of ink made in the prison, I would have lost it all in the search, since they stripped us and even looked under our testicles.

A circle of hostile faces and fixed bayonets surrounded us, but there were no beatings. The food that afternoon was served in tins that had contained Russian beef. It was three spoonfuls of boiled macaroni and a piece of bread. That was February 11, 1970.

That day saw the beginning of a plan for biological and psychological experimentation more inhuman, brutal, and merciless than anything the western world had known with the exception of the Nazis' activities. Boniato and its blackout cells will always be an accusation. If all the other human-rights violations had not occurred, what happened at Boniato would be enough in itself to condemn the Cuban regime as the most cruel and degrading ever known in the Americas.

We were locked up in forty separate cells. To go to the latrine you had to call the soldiers. I thought it was strange that we had not been counted at dusk as was usual in the jails. My cell had a burlap cot, but it sagged like a hammock.

At sunrise the garrison flooded the hallway. They came in shouting and cursing. It was the same as always; they had to get all heated up to come in. They beat on the walls and the bars with the weapons they were carrying —rubber-hose-covered iron bars (so they wouldn't break the skin), thick clubs and woven electrical cables, chains wrapped around their hands, and bayonets. There was no justification, no pretext. They just opened the cells, one by one, and beat the prisoners inside. The first cell they opened was Martín Pérez'. I remember his big husky voice cursing the Communists, but without saying a single dirty word. I got close to the bars to try to look out, and a chain blow made me jump back. I was lucky it hadn't hit me in the face.

They opened cell number 3, number 4, number 5. As they approached my cell, I trembled inside. My muscles contracted spasmodically. My breathing came with difficulty and I felt the fear and rage that always possessed me.

Some men, their psychological resistance wasted away already, couldn't contain themselves, and before the soldiers even entered their cells they began to shriek and wail hysterically. Those shrieks multiplied the horror. The soldier that opened the bars to our cell was armed with a bayonet. Behind him were three more, blocking the entrance. I saw only that one of the guards was carrying a chain. They pushed us to the back of the cell so they'd have room to swing their weapons. We tried not to get separated, because we knew that was the most dangerous thing you could do. That was when they would kick you and knee you in the groin. They knocked me to the floor, and one of them kicked me in the face and split my lower lip. When I recovered consciousness my head was lying in a pool of blood. My cellmate was bleeding through the nose and his hand was fractured near his wrist.

Several men were seriously injured. One of the Graiño brothers had his cheekbone fractured by Sergeant "Good Guy"; he spit out broken teeth. He'd been beaten so brutally his face looked like one huge black eye. Pechuguita, a peaceable little campesino from Pinar del Rio, had his head split open; the wound was so large it took twenty stitches to close it. Every man, without exception, was beaten. The guards went about it systematically, cell by cell.

After the beating the officers and a military doctor passed through to examine us. They took wounded men out of the cells, but right there on the spot a medic with a little first-aid cart sewed up and bandaged the wounds. When they finished bandaging us they said, "Don't say we didn't give you medical treatment!" and put us back into the cells, where we waited for our next beating.

I was bruised all over. My face was swollen and bloody. I could hardly stand up for the pain all over my body. They had given me the worst beating of my life. But what had affected me most was waiting for them to come to my cell and beat me. That did more damage to me than the blows themselves. A thousand times I wished I had been in the first cell. That way they would come in, beat me, and go back out again. I wanted it over with once and for all so I wouldn't have to go through that torture of waiting and dreading. My nerves were destroyed by it.

The guards came back in the afternoon, almost at nightfall, and the nightmare of the morning was repeated—beatings, cell by cell, with more wounded men the result. We could communicate with the other sections of the building by shouting back and forth, so we traded the names of the most gravely wounded men.

Odilo Alonso woke up the next morning with his head monstrously swollen; I would never have imagined that anyone could have looked so grotesquely deformed. His ears were so swollen he looked as though he were wearing a helmet. After three days of those two-a-day beatings, many men could no longer stand. Martín Pérez was urinating blood, as was de Vera, and other men's eyes were so blackened and swollen shut by the blows that they could hardly see. But that didn't matter to the soldiers—they beat men again and again.

Sergeant Good Guy, whose real name was Ismael, belonged to the Communist Party. He had a big Pancho Villa moustache. Whenever the garrison came in to beat us, he cried *"Viva Communism!"* madly, over and over. It was his war cry. He would tell the other soldiers to beat the wounded on top of their bandages, so that nobody could say that the soldiers had beaten them more than once. Another sergeant did exactly the opposite— he would beat the wounded men on their bare skin and say with a sneer, "I wanna see 'em sew you up again."

Odilo was getting worse and worse. The blows to his head had affected him horribly. His ears were leaking pus and bloody liquid, and his face was monstrously inflamed. Finally he could no longer stand erect. It was only then that they took him to the prison hospital.

They gave not so much as an aspirin to even the most seriously wounded men. They didn't take any prisoner out of the section unless he was in danger of death. They didn't try to kill us quickly; that would have been too generous a gesture to have hoped for from those sadists. Their object was to force us, by means of terror and torture, into the Political Rehabilitation Program. To do that, they were slowly and inexorably destroying us. They would take us to the very brink of death and keep us there, without letting us cross it. We had even been vaccinated against tetanus, so they could bayonet us, wound us with machetes and iron bars, and break our skulls, sure that at least we wouldn't contract tetanus.

The attitude maintained by our group was discussed in the magazine *Moncada,* the official organ of the Ministry of the Interior, in an article written by the head of Jails and Prisons, Medardo Lemus. He wrote that our resistance was a major block to the plans the government had for enlisting all prisoners in the Political Rehabilitation Program, and that our rebellious- ness and especially our refusal to conform with prison discipline was a bad example for the other prisoners. The authorities therefore saw themselves obliged to separate us from the rest of the penal population.

But men could not stand up forever to the daily beatings, the terror, the psychological tortures, and some took on the uniform. Those desertions caused us great pain. It was as though the authorities were pulling off pieces of our own bodies. I felt diminished every time one of our men left; years of terror, misery, and the dream of freedom had united us.

The capacity to stand up to something like that is very difficult to gauge. Men who had stood up to the Castro dictatorship in all-out combat in the mountains or in the cities, who had gone in and out of Cuba clandestinely on missions of war, who were full of bravery and heroism, could not, unarmed, confront the terror, the lack of communication, the solitary confinement for very long, and they finally gave in. But that might have been better in one sense, because that way our position solidified. Our bodies grew thinner day by day, our strength slipped away, our legs were beginning to look like toothpicks, but inside, the foundations of our spirits, our faith and determination, grew stronger and stronger with every blow of a bayonet, with every ignominy, with every harassment, with every beating.

Every afternoon at dusk the thundering voice of the Brother of the Faith, as we called Gerardo, the Protestant preacher, echoed through those passages, calling out to the prayer meeting. They tried to keep us from our religious practices, to interrupt, silence the prayers, and that cost us extra quotas of blows. The first time this happened the guards unleashed a beating in the midst of the prayer meeting, cell by cell, but as soon as they left the beaten men continued singing, and the other prisoners followed their lead. The guards moved back and forth and handed out blows in what seemed to be a different dimension from the one in which we were praying and singing hymns to God. In the cell in front of mine, I watched guards kicking two prisoners lying on the floor. Those prisoners also began to sing and pray as soon as the guards had left. Now those men over there, who had been singing before, were being beaten. And so the surreal scene went on. Above the shouting and tumult, the voice of the Brother of the Faith was singing "Glory, glory Hallejujah!"

In Building 4 they were renovating the cells, making them even more inhumane and repressive than they had ever been before. Only the drawer cells in the concentration camps of Tres Macíos and San Ramón were comparable to these.

We watched with horror day by day as the construction progressed. We suffered those cells in anticipation. We tried never to mention them. We would look at them in despair, but not a word was spoken about them.

On January 6 we were taken from Block 5 to the blackout cells, as though it were a sinister Three Kings Day present—although by now that day of joy for children had been abolished in Cuba. Almost the whole population of the prison watched the parade of our starving bodies. Our bones stuck out like scarecrows' frames. Some men dragged their legs, others could walk only with help. Men who pushed the wheelchairs of the invalids had to lean on them to stand up. We were human ruins by now, and in a way the torment had hardly begun. But I think all our eyes still glowed with vigorous life; there was a flame, a keenness and zeal in us—our jailers had not been able to uproot that.

The blackout-cell hallway looked like a crypt, with twenty niches on each side. The cells were about ten feet long by four and a half feet wide. In one corner there was a hole for a latrine, and above it, almost at the ceiling, a piece of bent tubing, the shower. The guard posted at the bars could open or close all the showers on one or the other side of the passageway from the outside, with two master faucets.

The leaders of prisons were delighted with the results of their construction. Concentration-camp directors from the province and from other jails came to Boniato. They laughed and smiled with the same pride that philanthropists, men of goodwill, do when they inaugurate a hospital or a school. There was a tone of mockery and sarcastic pleasure in their voices, as though they were savoring beforehand the triumph they had so long awaited. At last the creation of the blackout cells was a reality, for all the Russians', Czechs', Hungarians', and East Germans' combined experience in torture and psychological annihilation was brought to the creation of the blackout cells. Doctors and psychologists from Communist countries, including Cuba, had lent their scientific expertise to the questions of diet, calories, the creation of disorienting situations, the manipulation of wasting diseases, and so forth. When the authorities finished the blackout cells at Boniato Prison, they decided to try out their effectiveness on the common prisoners, so they put in them the toughest, the most ferocious men, the biggest troublemakers they could find, the prisoners who had spent years going from one jail to another. And these men would slice their wrists, swallow nails and pieces of spoons and razor blades, trying to get the authorities to take them out of the cells. The prisoners would rather have their stomachs operated on than stay in the blackout cells. Three months was the longest anyone lasted.

When we were inside the cells, some officers told us about the common prisoners, and they said within six months we'd be begging to be released. The crunching of the heavy metal doors that closed behind us was followed by the sound of locks and chains. We did not know how long we would be there, but we knew some men would not come out alive.

(Now as I write these memoirs, I cannot keep from thinking about the hundreds of my friends and comrades who are still there, now in still worse conditions. Two years ago, to isolate them even more, the authorities erected a wall at each end of the building higher than the roof. Then they strung a fence between the two walls so that the block is now inside a cage. Closed-circuit television is trained on all the passageways.)

Mornings the sun heated up the iron sheets across my window, which faced the east, and the cell became an oven. I sweated torrents of water, and it exhausted me. The sweat and grease pouring out of my body took on a peculiar odor in that closed space and in the darkness—the smell of rotten fish. In the afternoon, the metal sheets on the front of the cell heated up as the sun set. We spent whole weeks without bathing. At their whim or as they were ordered, the guards at the front gate would open the showers from their desk. The water might come at any hour of the day or night. In the summertime they turned on the water when the metal sheets were too hot to touch; in the wintertime they would do it in the early morning. They would come into the long passageway and shout that we had five minutes to bathe, and then when they figured we were soaped up, they turned off the water, and that produced a hellish racket from the prisoners. But the guards would tranquilly go back to the kitchen to chat with the guards from the other buildings. The soap dried on us and made our sticky skin feel stretched and tight, matted our hair. Not only did this new filthiness upset us, the cries for water became yet another torture. That whole inferno, in fact, little by little upset the equilibrium of our minds. That, of course, was precisely our jailers' objective.

We were not allowed any container for water except one, a quarter-liter jar. The latrine hole of my cell stopped up within a few days. Around it the cement depression soon filled with urine and excrement. When it finally overflowed, the entire floor of the cell was covered with that filth. Pepín and I did all we could to unstop the latrine. We stuck our arms into the hole, we used our spoons, but all our efforts were futile. We applied to the authorities to unstop the latrine, but there was no response. When they turned on the water for the showers, we had to stand there in the latrine, where there were already maggots. The shower fell directly into the center of the pool of urine and splashed all over the walls. We lived inside a toilet bowl. The stench was unbearable. Our nostrils were encrusted with filth, as if our noses were constantly stopped up with shit. When the food came we would take the little can in the palm of our hands, as we always did in situations like this, and try as best we could not to touch the food. We didn't even use our spoons; we would pour the food directly into our mouths, as though it were liquid. It was always the same—boiled macaroni, maybe a little spaghetti, bread; bread, spaghetti, a little boiled macaroni.

One night the guards took out four of us and put us into other cells, and in the empty cells they put two prisoners brought in from outside. When the noise of locks and bolts had subsided and the guards went away, we tried to identify the men who had just come in. The men in the cells next to theirs called out to them, but the new men didn't respond. We spoke to them in English and French, thinking they might be foreigners. Nothing. Silence. So we lay down to sleep. The next day we would try to find out who the new men were. They might have been afraid, or have been just a short time in prison.

A horrible scream shook us awake. It echoed down the passageway, which was like an echo chamber. The sound was deafening, and then came howls of laughter, shouts, and incoherent gabble. They had put two madmen into those cells.

Often we'd be violently wakened in the mornings by the raving of those poor wretches. The two common prisoners, lost in the shadows of their own minds, were another ingredient in a plan to unhinge *our* minds. We spent whole nights unable to sleep. The madmen slept during the day and at night wouldn't let the rest of us sleep.

Every two or three days, the guards came in and searched us. The only purpose of those searches was to keep the pressure on, just like the surveillance to remind us that we were watched, so that we would constantly feel the repression. One thing about the searches was almost good—the guards opened several cells at once, so this was an opportunity to see our comrades in the neighboring cells. The guards searched the cells, then they would physically search us, and then we went back inside the cells again.

They always compared the control identification card with our faces. Every hallway or section had a file with our photos, personal data, and the cell number. We had all been photographed before we went into the blackout cells. There was one comrade of ours, a very dynamic, rebellious young man named Alfredo Fernández Gámez, who refused to be photographed. They took him out and beat him unmercifully, and, of course, then photographed him. With these cards they could keep permanent control over us. If the guard was spying on the cell, he knew who he was spying on.

Months passed, and one day a captain from the Political Police visited us. They were amazed at our resistance, and not a little bewildered. So he had been sent to us with a threat. We were standing naked for a search, with our backs to the wall next to the door, when the soldier entered. His face was completely inexpressive, and he didn't walk, he marched, as though he were doing infantry drills. He stopped about halfway down the hallway, his hands behind his back, and he announced to us that the Revolution could not tolerate this irritating attitude of ours any longer. If we did not relent, they would have to be "energetic" with us. He went on talking, saying the Revolution offered us a way out, that we need not fear vengeance being taken against us, but that if we didn't accept their terms there were new plans from the high command of the Ministry of the Interior to be put into effect. They had been very tolerant up to now, but their patience was running out.

"The Revolution does not want to have to exercise all its severity against you, but if you force us, you will never be men again. We are not going to kill you, but we will make you eunuchs. Don't forget what I've told you," he said just as he was leaving. And his words were more than simple threats.

43 / Biological Experiments and Their First Victims

Our diet was designed to try to bring on deficiency diseases and metabolic disorders. Food, consisting only of carbohydrates and a greasy broth, was weighed and measured. Cornmeal, or sometimes a mixture of rice and boiled macaroni, was basically our only source of nutrition. We calculated that we were receiving less than a thousand calories a day. Soon, the results of undernourishment, of eating food completely lacking in protein and vitamins, began to be seen. We grew thinner day by day, hour by hour almost. Hunger made our stomachs gnaw themselves. It was during that time that I began to have dreams of a table set with all sorts of food, a luxurious banquet. Hunger became an obsession, but not a single man of us gave in because of it. The months went on monotonously, with no event to differentiate one day from another, one month from another.

The first cases of scurvy were detected. Scurvy is now a very rare disease. It is brought on by lack of vitamin C. One of its symptoms is a dark rash which appears on the legs and thighs. Bruised zones also appear, as though you had been violently beaten. The gums become inflamed; they grow very red and bleed easily, even at the slightest touch. The teeth loosen and fall out sometimes, and other disorders develop, until finally the sick man dies.

Every day a new one of us told the others that the little black pimples had begun to appear. Some men were already familiar with the disease, so they explained what the rash was. The authorities realized what was happening when we asked them for medical care. Several days went by, and some military doctors came. They examined some of the men, took blood samples, urine specimens, blood pressure, they did tests on the coagulation time of the blood, and they left. They came back later with other, foreign doctors, Russians or Czechs, I'm not sure, who touched the sick men, palpated them, scratched at their rashes, and wrote down data.

I recall that during one of the searches I noticed that the black bruiselike marks produced by scurvy had covered Pepín González Saura's thighs. Arnaldo Arroyo was one of the worst cases. His gums were so inflamed that touching them with his fingertip made them begin to bleed immediately. Arroyo lost several teeth; they just fell out, with no pain at all. Piloto, the man who had vomited in my canteen cup, sneezed one day and two streams of blood gushed out. That was how fragile his veins were. These and other cases made the doctors decide to control the outbreak of scurvy. They didn't really want anybody to die—so soon, that is. They gave us lemonade twice a day, to which they added powdered citric acid.

Estebita made our nights pleasanter by telling us in amazing detail about movies he had seen. He was very short and frail, but his voice was extremely powerful, so even from behind the steel plates of his cell he could be heard by everyone. The place, all closed in with metal doors, really had very good acoustics. Estebita gave such interesting richness to his stories, they were so full of details, that still today I confuse them in my memory with movies I've actually seen.

The authorities never allowed us to have newspapers or magazines, except for copies of the official organs of the Party and *Communist Youth*. We were being "indoctrinated." We had assigned José Carreño, who had been a journalist, to take charge of receiving and distributing the propaganda materials. There were only ten or twelve copies for all of us, and we had to take turns reading them. But Carreño went beyond the call of duty by reading the news and excerpting it and critiquing it, pointing out where the news became propaganda, lies, and indoctrination, showing us the rationale behind everything that was printed. Carreño's daily work was invaluable, because in our cells there were campesinos, laborers, people of little education or political awareness whom the propaganda would surely have confused or disoriented had it not been for Carreño's "news commentaries."

My will to survive grew constantly stronger; my determination had become as steely as my cell walls. In spite of my weakness, I would lie on the floor and move my body to help my circulation. I did yoga exercises in meditation and concentration. I knew that darkness could damage my vision, so I tried to ward off that danger. There were small holes in the iron sheet which closed off the window. Your little finger might fit through them, but not your thumb. They were air vents. In the afternoon when the sheet had cooled off a bit, I would put my face to it, first one eye and then the other, and look through the holes toward the blue sky and the green of the hills. I did these visual exercises daily, and I believe I owe my sight to them. There were men whose vision was permanently affected by those years in darkness. You couldn't see a thing in the hallway. I would put my ear against the metal plate to try to hear whether the guards were walking by, though. The only opening at the door was at the bottom, where there was about a half-inch space, perhaps a little less, between the floor and the bars. If you squeezed down against the floor about a yard from the door, you might see a little piece of the hallway. (It was while lying face down on the floor like that, trying to take advantage of the ghastly waxen light that filtered into the hallway under the main gate, that I wrote the first notes about my ordeal.) The guards would constantly come in and walk on tiptoe, slipping along next to the walls, so they could overhear our conversations. Sometimes Political Police officers did the same thing. Since we knew they did this, between ourselves we used a slang which was a crazy mixture of English, French, and Spanish and words we invented ourselves. There was no way they could understand us.

We never knew who might be walking along the hallways. We would only hear the sound of footsteps from time to time or see fugitive shadows passing in front of the chink in the hinges of the door. They no longer gave us beatings at specific times—sometimes several days would pass without beatings, and then suddenly they would burst in, at any hour of the day or night. So there was no rest. At the slightest noise, you'd jump awake, thinking the garrison was outside your cell. It was better when they were beating us only at the headcounts at morning and evening, because between one beating and the next you knew you could have a few hours of peace. Sometimes their tactics were even more refined—shrieking and screaming, they'd beat on the doors with their rifle butts and weapons, shake the locks and chains, and yell at the soldier who carried the keys, "Open this cell, open this cell!" And then they wouldn't come in, they'd go away, while you sat there in unbearable tension and anxiety. The adrenaline had started pumping and all your body's defenses were at work to prepare you for the aggression. The guards did this frequently, and since sometimes they did in fact come back and beat you, I was always anxious, my stomach was always balled into a knot.

The guards, though, who were simple tools of the authorities, never quite understood these methods, and sometimes even they would chafe and protest—they thought it was all a foolish waste of time. Here was an order that got them out of the barracks they were staying in for nothing; and besides, they really wanted to open the cells so they could come in and beat us up.

Those who did know perfectly well what they were doing and its consequences were the psychologists from the Department of Psychiatric Evaluation of the Political Police. They were the ones directing this ambitious criminal experiment, and we were the guinea pigs. The Cuban authorities entrusted to these men their aim of making us submit, not only to the Political Rehabilitation Program, but to the Marxist doctrine which it taught. If they didn't get what they wanted with this procedure, after years of physical and psychological violence, then the only thing left for them to do would be to kill us.

That had been precisely Medardo Lemus' conclusion. In a television appearance the newspaper *Granma* reported on in the edition of May 17,

1969, Lemus answered a question one of the members of the panel asked him about the means to be taken against the counterrevolutionary prisoners who refused Rehabilitation. Lemus had said, "We have to put an end to them." And he argued for "capital punishment" to do just that.

Resistance has its limits, and they were leading us closer to the edge day by day, hour by hour. Slowly, surely, they were literally destroying us. Periodically they submitted us to interrogations to see how the experiment was going, to see whether it was yielding the results they were hoping for. They insisted that we tell them what times of the day we felt best and worst, what bothered us the most, what we dreamed about, whether we thought about our families frequently. The men who "interviewed" us were dressed not in military uniforms, but in the white smocks of doctors. They were courteous and friendly, and they said they wanted to try to help improve our situation a little, that was why our answers interested them. They wrote them down carefully in notebooks and on tablets. We couldn't refuse to let them take blood samples, since if we did they took them forcibly anyway and we got an extra beating for our trouble.

The lack of vitamins brought on pellagra again. I had already had it once before, and so was familiar with the dark stains across my chest and up across my shoulders like a necklace. Other men, such as Fernández Gámez, had different symptoms—their skin peeled and flaked.

For several weeks the authorities put too much salt in the food, so your throat scratched when you ate. Then they totally eliminated the salt for a while. They wanted to alter the inmates' metabolisms. Men who suffered from kidney disorders and blood-pressure problems were devastated by this treatment.

The absence of protein made us suffer what is called nutritional edema. First your ankles and legs would swell up, then your thighs, testicles, and abdomen, and then your chest and face. The cases in which the inflammation spread above the waist were watched more carefully by the authorities; they knew that if the edema spread to the lungs, the brain, or the intestines, the complications would be fatal. Therefore the men judged by the authorities' criteria to be close to death were taken out and carried to the little hospital, a special place they had set up for us. It was also sealed off with iron plates, and the prisoners were held there incommunicado.

Several doctors and psychologists would be waiting for the sick prisoners. They weighed them first, and then from that moment on they kept the patients under close medical supervision. They did psychological tests and interviews. The mental deterioration of the patients interested the authorities more than the physical. They were very interested to know how and to what extent a man's mind might have been damaged. They performed all sorts of tests and analyses—they carefully measured the food going into the men's bodies and the excrement and urine coming out; they did stool analyses and urinalyses; they took temperatures and blood pressure every four hours. The research lasted four or five days, at the end of which they administered massive doses of diuretics. You couldn't sleep then because you'd constantly have to get up to urinate. You seemed to burst, like a balloon. One of the most serious cases was Carreño. When they took him out of the blackout cells they had to carry him to the hospital naked, because his thighs were so swollen they didn't fit into even the largest size of underwear. At the moment the guards were carrying him off, my door was open for lunch, and I saw him pass by. I hardly recognized him, he was so monstrously swollen. His face, legs, and testicles were grotesque. His appearance horrified me. I was almost sickened. The common prisoner who served the food could not raise his head; the authorities had forbidden the prisoners to look us in the face, so he was frozen doubled over there, holding the serving spoon full of cornmeal in midair until the guard shouted at me and I looked away. When they gave Carreño the diuretics and he urinated all that liquid he had retained, a process that lasted for about five days, he lost fifty-five pounds.

The edema in me began around my ankles and ascended to my thighs and genitals. Even light pressure from my finger on my legs made an indentation that took twenty-five or thirty seconds to fill in again, as though instead of muscles, I had pressed soft dough. Those holes left in the flesh were produced because the pressure of the finger displaced the liquid; then slowly the liquid moved back and the indentation disappeared. If you kept up the pressure for a long time, a larger hole would be produced, almost an inch deep. On some occasions when they opened the cells for the headcount we would show those marks to the soldiers, and the soldiers, even against their own will, were shocked.

They took me to the hospital, too, when my stomach began to swell. I weighed 135 pounds when I arrived, and after I'd gone through the whole process of analyses and questions, they gave me the diuretic. When I eliminated all the liquids I weighed 105 pounds. I had lost thirty pounds, then, in less than five days. I had weighed about 150 pounds when I was arrested. Now I was nothing but skin and bones. Still, I was taken back to the blackout cells again. They had to practically drag me between two soldiers, because I couldn't walk a straight line.

Around that time it was getting harder and harder for me to stand up, and I would stagger against the walls of the cell, unable to control the way I walked. My legs would go to sleep on me, and I felt an intense prickling in my legs and often had cramps. My memory was failing me, and I was undergoing a terrible mental confusion. I lost coordination of some kinds of movements, and often couldn't find words to say what I wanted to say. I fell into a deep depression. The least sound alarmed me, and that in turn made my heart race rapidly, uncontrollably. I could hear the throbbing of my own heart like an incessant hammering. I often felt inexplicable fears, and I couldn't tell what was causing the terror, I didn't know exactly what

I was afraid of. It wasn't of the beatings. It was a fear that went beyond that. I felt weak, and I wasn't sleeping well at all.

When I thought this dread would finally reduce me to a shivering, frightened animal, I prayed to God. Lying in a corner of the dark dungeon, I closed my eyes and prayed to Him. Then a sense of tranquillity began to take the place of the terror and fear and I felt comforted, my faith renewed. I always went to Him in search of support and peace, and I always found it. I began every day with renewed faith and the will to continue on the path I had chosen, and to win.

There was always someone among the soldiers who sympathized with our cause. Obligatory military service sent young men to the Ministry of the Interior who were actually against the system. It wasn't easy to win their confidence, since they had been brought up under a regime which bases many of its repressive actions on informers' reports and which gives the stool pigeon a hero's honors. Nonetheless, I dedicated myself to winning some of those young men's confidence, and I managed at different times to get them to help me break out of my isolation. I would persuade them to send Martha my letters, and to bring me hers. It was with the aid of one of those recruits that the first denunciation of what was happening in the blackout cells in Boniato reached the outside world. It was written in the margin of a copy of the official newspaper of the party, *Granma,* and was published abroad. Many of my companions also tried to gain the assistance of these young guards, and some of them managed to do so. Their success depended on the patient labor of weeks and months, and was accomplished not by bribing the guard with gifts or money which the prisoner's family might give him outside the prison, but rather by appealing to the ideals which every young man has, his conscience and dignity, by making him see that he was helping men who had sacrificed everything so he could grow up in a free society and not under a terrible dictatorship.

My technique consisted of showing them, little by little, the horrors which resulted from the tortures I was undergoing. I would ask them how they could sleep at night after having spent a day like that, how they could hug their children if they had any, or their wives and parents, after having witnessed the way we were tortured and beaten. Little by little they became ashamed of supporting, even if only apparently, a regime such as that one. "But what can I do?" they would finally say to me one day. "A lot," I would answer. "It isn't a question of being an active conspirator. You don't have to be against the regime twenty-four hours a day, but one insignificant act on your part, which involves no danger whatsoever, might save the lives of those of us who are here." And then I'd tell him that I needed to get a letter out, and he would almost always begin to cooperate with us.

For reasons of security I cannot give details here about those who helped me, nor about the techniques we used to get information out and in, nor about how we went about deciding that the man helping us was not an agent of the Political Police sent to infiltrate, because there are still many prisoners who employ those means and I don't wish to compromise them.

The weeks went on, and we were still sealed in our cells. I was nauseated and had frequent diarrhea. Our hair fell out in clumps. Burning sores erupted in our mouths, and our dried-out lips cracked. I could hardly swallow, it was so painful to me. Jorge Portuondo was in the worst state of all of us. There were outbreaks of fungus diseases, too, because that darkness was ideal for its growth—almost all of us had fungus in the moist, hidden areas of our bodies. Some men had already gone completely mad, and would moan and call out to their relatives and friends or break out into tears or laughter. Other men would shout that the Communists were coming in to beat them, but they saw them only in their perturbed minds. Nevertheless, every time you heard those cries of alarm, you would wake up in sickness and dread, because your terror kept asking, "Is it true?" I began to have attacks of asthma. I would gasp for air, I could hardly breathe, but they wouldn't give me any medicine. They wouldn't even allow us to use an atomizer to alleviate the symptoms.

Pepín Saura, René, and many others who suffered from asthma were in the same situation. Only René had managed to salvage an atomizer—which was useless anyway because the authorities refused to give him the decongestant for it. It was terrible hearing those gasps of human beings asphyxiating, desperately trying to get a gulp of air down their obstructed bronchial tubes. They could only emit guttural whistles and wheezes.

When I myself was in the middle of one of those attacks, I always tried to stay calm, and I would breathe slowly, but even so the sensation was dreadful. I thought I was going to die from lack of air. Today I remember all that fear and terror like a bad dream, but it wasn't. I have emphysema; my lungs are fibrous and lack elasticity. The refusal to give us medical care of any kind was final, and all our petitions were useless.

Another torment many of us suffered was being taken to the hospital for an electrocardiogram. The doctors would tell us later, very seriously, that we were suffering from a dangerous cardiac condition. They would terrify us with the news, and then they would offer us medical care, salvation, an escape from that hole where we might die from a heart attack at any moment, in exchange for Political Rehabilitation.

The intention of making eunuchs out of us that had been announced by the captain from the Political Police was carried out with meticulous rigor. We were specters, as skeletal as the survivors of the Nazi concentration camps. All of us had lost thirty, forty, or even sixty pounds, though some men were horribly swollen. There were many who could not stand up. The doctors went through the cells periodically, checking temperature, blood pressure, and pulse, examining the mucous membranes of our eyes and mouths, and asking us questions. And the food was always the same—cornmeal, spaghetti, rice, greasy broth, and a piece of bread.

Estebita couldn't go on telling us the plots of his movies; during these last weeks, his body was so weakened by the living conditions that it had fallen apart, given up responding. He couldn't even stand up. We spoke with the headcount officers and told them about our companion's terrible state of health. They paid no attention. On February 4, 1972, Estebita was found dead at daybreak. Three days later, Ibrahim Torres, our beloved Piri as everyone called him, died too. Their bodies could not withstand the experiments.

We were told later by a common prisoner, Dr. Mastrapa, that the doctors' conclusion was that the cause of death of the two political prisoners was "general weakness," not any specific disease or trauma. After those two deaths, then, the leaders of the extermination plan realized that the worst cases would go on dying; but the objective of all this was not to kill us. Five days later they began giving us a spoonful of sugar. They brought fruit and a boiled egg to us once in a while. That change in our food was meant to build up our weakened defenses a little, but not too much. And it cruelly demonstrated the strict control they had over us.

Castro denied the existence of concentration camps in Cuba, as Stalin had done in the Soviet Union. He denied the existence of political prisoners, of torture, of crimes in the jails. Martha, however, had all the means necessary to help us and to make the world know the truth, and she did. In one of the letters that I received from her, she told me how they had forced her to work for the government for months before they let her out. This was common practice now in Cuba. When you asked permission to leave the country, you would be considered from that instant on a traitor to the Revolution. If you were working, you were fired from your job and immediately transferred as far away from your home as possible, to the most remote part of the country, to do agricultural work. There you'd sometimes spend six or seven months without being able to see your family, because if they were five or six hundred miles away and you had only one day of rest a week, there was no time or money for the trip. You'd live in loathsome, foul-smelling barracks without adequate sanitary facilities, nor were women exempt from this terrible cruelty. You might spend two or even three years like that, and in spite of all, some people at the end were not allowed to leave the country. The situation was denounced, scandals were created in the foreign press, and the Cuban government saw itself obliged to soften the work conditions a little bit for those people who wanted to leave Cuba.

Martha was sent to a marble quarry, where she worked all day long. She was there until she left for the United States.

After the deaths of Estebita and Piri our food continued to improve, the calories increased, and our starving bodies recovered a little. How long would that last? Since I thought not very long, I didn't waste half a bite. I wanted to build up reserves for what was to come. I even ate eggshells to get the calcium they contained, and the rinds of all the fruits, even bananas, lemons, oranges, and mangoes. If they gave us lettuce with the roots and all, I ate it roots and all. I pushed myself to take maximum advantage of that bonanza, and to recuperate as much as possible. One day, when they thought we were a little better, they told us we would be taken out into the prison yard for a little sun. That seemed so incredible, so beyond belief or even hope, that we actually *couldn't* believe it. But we were wrong. They opened all the cells, and for the first time in years we could all see each other. We met in that hallway. It was a pathetic meeting.

Friends embraced, crying with emotion. Some of us looked so wasted, so cadaverous, and our skin was so white, that if it hadn't been for the fire in our eyes, you'd have thought we were all dead. Our eyes were sunken into their sockets, our cheekbones bulged, and our skin either hung or stretched tight across our bones. Roberto Alonso's teeth had become crooked and out of position, and many of Arroyo's had fallen out. I was so sad to see them like that that I almost cried, but suddenly I noticed that the others were looking at me in the same way. I hadn't realized until that moment that I looked as wasted and pathetic as all my friends did.

But not all of us could go out into the prison yard to get some sun. Locked up for years in those tiny blackout cells, some men had lost their sense of balance and were unable to walk a straight line. They zigzagged as though they were drunk, making S's from one wall to the other down the hallway. This phenomenon apparently occurs when you lose the line of the horizon and the sense of depth perception for long periods of time. Their brains had to readapt, little by little, before they could walk again. I staggered a little as I walked, and I went down the stairs clutching the walls. In fact we all looked like eighty-year-old men as we made our way down the stairs. That reencounter with air, with the light of the sun, the sky, was unforgettable—and physically painful for many men. Our eyes had been such a long time in darkness they couldn't take the impact of the glare, and we had to close them. My practice of continually looking out through the holes in the iron sheets kept my pain to a minimum.

Today, even after so many years, I remember that day as though it were yesterday. The sky was blue that morning, and the sun in the center of the prison yard was warm. But as I looked off toward the high hills surrounding the presidio, they seemed to rush in upon me. It was like gigantic waves of rock advancing on me, and I thought they were going to crush me. The same thing had happened years before when they took me out of the punishment cells on Isla de Pinos. I had to sit down on the grass and close my eyes— everything was going in circles around me, I was very dizzy. Only a few steps from me, Martín Pérez was walking around one moment and the next he raised his hand to his eyes and softly fell to the grass unconscious. Then others fell. They could not stand that sudden encounter with the sun and air. Soldiers had to come to help us back to our cells.

That afternoon Martín Pérez began to urinate blood and black blood-clots. The officer of the guard was notified immediately. We thought they'd give him medical aid, but the new attitude of the soldiers didn't go that far. To go to the little hospital he had to accept Political Rehabilitation.

In April 1972, a group of fifty of us were called out to find the prison vans waiting for us. We assumed we were being taken to one of the concentration camps at Tres Macíos or San Ramón, that is to say, to the drawer cells. But we were wrong. The trip lasted more than twenty hours and ended at the prison of La Cabaña. A new return and a new failure for the Revolution, which about a year before had deactivated La Cabaña as a jail and with great fanfare announced that the Capitán San Luis Academy would now be located there. San Luis was one of the heroes of the Revolution; his most outstanding action was beating political prisoners, which he did every time he got drunk.

They took us to a *galera* in the military zone, the same they had held us in during the thirty-six-day hunger strike. It was an extension of the *galera* which served as a military kitchen. The floor of the *galera* was nine feet below ground level. A little window very high up on the wall opened onto the pathway, and through it you could see the soldiers' boots as they passed by. There in a space some sixteen yards long and six wide, they put all fifty of us. The soldiers, many of whom knew us from before, surrounded us and looked at us in amazement. At that time I weighed about 110 pounds. I could tell by the expression on some of their faces that they were deeply shocked. One of the soldiers couldn't keep himself from asking, "Where are you coming from?" They honestly didn't know. When prisoners are trans-ferred out of a prison, the troops there never find out anything about them again.

Early the next morning problems began. We woke up coughing; the *galera* was full of smoke. What happened was that the military kitchen was having trouble with its chimney and part of the smoke had to go out through our *galera,* through the window. It had an exhaust fan which forced the smoke right through our room. They used petroleum for fuel, and a fine, greasy black soot covered everything within three or four days. We had to breathe that smoke whether we wanted to or not. When you put a white rag over your nostrils you took it away black from the soot, and when you coughed and spat in the mornings, there was also black phlegm. We immedi-ately wrote a letter to Prison Headquarters, telling them the exhaust fumes from the petroleum were producing everything from respiratory problems to cancer. We told them we shouldn't be kept there; it was exactly like living inside a chimney—in reality, our *galera was* a chimney.

Lieutenant Lirbano, director of the prison at that time, said he had sent our petition up to the Ministry of the Interior, because without an order directly from the Ministry he couldn't transfer us out of the *galera*. There were many other *galeras* empty at that time, including the one next to ours. Weeks passed and nothing happened. The smoke and soot dried out the mucous membranes of our mouths and throats, irritated our eyes, and kept us completely stopped up. We tried to keep the toxic effects to a minimum by covering our noses and mouths with handkerchiefs. Our physical state was so deplorable that some soldiers actually took pity on us. One of them, whenever he was on guard, would hide extra food for us in the bottom of the bread sack, especially fish and tins of meat. He took this food out of the rations for the military kitchen, at the considerable risk of being caught and winding up in jail himself.

44 / Boitel's Death
and Black September

T hose same days, as we maintained a constant struggle with the authorities of La Cabaña to get them to take us out of our *galera*-chimney, Pedro Luis Boitel was dying in the prison of Castillo del Príncipe as a consequence of a hunger strike he was on, in protest against the inhumane treatment he was receiving. The news leaked out. On May 7, when Boitel had already been on strike for more than a month, Dr. Humberto Medrano published an article in Miami's *Diario de Las Américas* denouncing what was happening. The next day public figures and exile organizations started sending cables to the United Nations Commission on Human Rights and to Red Cross International, asking them to intervene as soon as possible to save Boitel's life. The United Nations kept silence, a silence of complicity.

Boitel had always been weak and terribly thin, and his precarious physical state needed little to grow worse. Even so, he had made a decision not to tell the authorities he was on a hunger strike. The authorities were never "officially" aware of it and therefore had made no move until Boitel was already dying and his comrades told Prison Headquarters. The authorities had of course known all along. The first to go to Boitel was a sergeant, aide to Lieutenant Valdés, head of the Political Police in Castillo del Príncipe. When the sergeant raised the sheet and saw what remained of Boitel, his eyes opened wide. He was stunned. He stepped back a step and then ran out immediately to inform his superiors. That skeleton covered with skin, which only made a few soft moans, was truly shocking. In a while Lieutenant Valdés appeared. He also raised the sheet, and although he tried to mask his shock and horror, his face froze. Someone asked Valdés to get Boitel out of there at once and give him medical assistance to try to keep him from dying. Valdés looked around at the person who had spoken, then he turned his eyes once more to Boitel on the cot and said, "I can't do that. I will tell the Ministry about the state he's in and let them decide, but you can be sure we won't give in to any position of force. We're sick and tired of Boitel and his hunger strikes. If it depended on me, he'd die, and I think that'll be what the Ministry decides, too."

Hours passed and no one came to give Boitel medical care. He moaned constantly. His comrades sat there in silence, conscious that they were in the presence of the death of their friend and that they could do nothing to keep it from happening. The next morning they called constantly, but it was only hours later that the guards took him out. They had evacuated a little cell in the prison behind the room named the Fajardo Room. He wasn't being taken to the hospital. At the door the head of Jails and Prisons, Medardo Lemus, Lieutenant Valdés, O'Farrill, and other officers were waiting. Several prisoners observed the scene from the high windows of the Fajardo Room. When the guards put Boitel inside, the officers put a screen in front of the bars and a sergeant was placed on guard. Everyone could hear Lemus say very clearly to the guard, "When he stops breathing, let me know, but not before." And he walked off with the rest of the officers.

All night the prisoners in the other room took turns watching. In the early morning hours, they heard Boitel's voice asking for water. They saw the sergeant move about uncomfortably in front of the bars. Hours passed, but Boitel never complained again. He had died after fifty-three days on hunger strike. It was May 24, 1972.

Days later Lieutenant Abad from the Political Police went to the house of Señora Clara Abraham, Boitel's mother. She was reading the Bible. A group of soldiers pushed open the half-open door. There was a doctor with them. When Clara saw them she was overcome by one of those premonitions which never deceive the heart of a mother. "My son is dead!"

"Who told you that?" Lieutenant Abad asked her in surprise, thinking that perhaps the news had filtered out. "You're mistaken."

"But what's happened to my son?" the mother insisted.

One of Boitel's cousins was in the house, and the authorities called him aside to ask him to give his aunt the news. But Clara didn't wait. She ran out into the street and headed directly for the prison at El Príncipe. But the guards, who knew her and knew that Boitel had died, didn't let her get past even the first guardpost. Clara refused to go away, so she was taken away forcibly in a patrol car to Political Police Headquarters, at Villa Marista.

Noemí, a friend of hers, went with her. Noemí had refused to leave Clara, although Clara had insisted that she not go with her. Once again Lieutenant Abad appeared at the office.

"We're going to have to give you the news anyway, Clara," he told her.

She was sitting down, but when she heard those words she jumped up, took the lieutenant by the shoulders, and shook him. "What news? Tell me, what news?"

The officer pushed her away violently. Clara fell on the couch and was struggling to get up again when Abad stopped her. "Your son is dead and buried. And don't scream, because you're not in your own house, you're in State Security."

Clara still tried to stand up, but Lieutenant Abad pushed her back onto the couch. She had the strength of desperation, so Abad slapped her and had her put into a cell. Late that night they put her into a patrol car and took her home again. Several guards at the house made sure she didn't leave again. They had also cut off her telephone to keep her from telling other people the news. Members of the CDR, given orders by the police, threatened to turn her in if she disrupted the peace with her crying and moaning.

The next day officers from the Political Police visited her again to tell her where they had buried her son's body. On May 30, Clara tried to go with some mothers and relatives of other prisoners to put some flowers on the grave where Pedro Luis was buried. Clutching rosaries, they walked down the gravel paths of the cemetery toward the area where the common graves were, the same lots in which the men shot by firing squads were laid. But before they arrived, they were intercepted, insulted, and attacked by a group of women armed with wooden clubs wrapped in newspapers. The group of women wouldn't even let the mothers offer a prayer. The women recognized some of their aggressors, even though they were dressed in civilian clothes —they belonged to the garrison of the women's prison.

The news of the death of Boitel, the most rebellious of the Cuban political prisoners, came to us through Dr. Gallardo, a prisoner who visited us often and who later turned out to be an infiltrator from the Political Police. A few weeks later a group of officers were gathered at the house of Alfredo Mesa, an officer in the Ministry of the Interior. His house was near the Casino Deportivo, on the outskirts of Havana. The men had all met there to go out together duck-hunting in the Zapata swamps. As they were getting their shotguns ready, Medardo Lemus was heard to comment that Castro had given the order to "get rid of Boitel so he wouldn't make any more fucking trouble."

Since the smoke kept clogging our noses and lungs, many respiratory difficulties arose, even in those men who had never had problems before. We were always coughing and having headaches. Around that time there was a reorganization of the ministries in Cuba, and medical aid in prisons, which had always been under the Ministry of the Interior before, passed into Public Health. That situation lasted for only a few months—the Political Police would not tolerate their prisoners' not being absolutely and completely in their grasp. Nonetheless, those days of interministry struggle were enough to get a commission from Public Health, made up of civilians, to make an inspection tour. They saw the soot and smoke for themselves, and they took samples of the air. The results of the tests proved the air was not fit to breathe, but we had to wait months more before we were taken out of the *galera*.

Also around that time we received the news that the authorities from the Ministry of the Interior had finally given up "persuading" the diehard political prisoners in the jail at Guanajay and started new repressive measures aimed at humiliating them and thereby forcing a reaction so the soldiers could impose even more merciless disciplinary measures on the prisoners. At their September visit, when their families were already waiting outside, the prisoners were made to strip completely inside the circle of guards for a humiliating search. Until that visit the prisoners had taken off only their pants and shirts, but kept their underwear on. Normally the prisoners were taken out all together to the room where the searches were performed, but this time the guards called out only three at a time. When they arrived, in place of the four or five soldiers usually on hand for the searches, there were twenty-five or thirty. The prisoners refused to strip, and they informed the officer in charge of the group that if those were the conditions of the visit, they'd rather not have a visit. The officer told them that whether they went out or not they had to strip. The prisoners continued to refuse, so the guards began to beat them. They tore their clothing to shreds. Then they took out a few more prisoners and the scene was repeated.

In the buildings the other prisoners began to shout and beat on the bars. Outside the families heard the uproar and the cursing and shouting of the guards and struggling prisoners.

The visit was suspended, and all that day the tension mounted. At nightfall hundreds of guards, armed with rifles with bayonets and tear-gas-grenade launchers, entered the prison yard. The troops were commanded by Medardo Lemus himself. They surrounded buildings D and E, and they began to take out the prisoners in little groups to the visiting room, which was also full of soldiers. There they forced the prisoners to strip by beating them. They beat them with sticks and clubs and kicked them as they lay in pain on the floor. Some men had to be dragged out to the punishment cells. They went on beating them and dragging them until no more men fit into the punishment cells. Early the next morning the prison vans arrived and the rest of the prisoners were taken out. In the visiting room about fifty guards with rubber tubing, chains, iron bars, and bayonets were waiting for them. More than twenty men were gravely wounded, and none of them received any medical attention until two days later when they were transferred to the inmates' hospital in the prison at Castillo del Príncipe. More than sixty less seriously wounded men were taken with the rest of the prisoners to La Cabaña. Clutching the windows, we watched them coming along the pathway behind the prison, dragging their beaten legs, leaning on each other's shoulders, surrounded by a cordon of guards armed with bayonets.

This episode, one of the bloodiest of all, is known among Cuban political prisoners as Black September.

The events at the prison of Guanajay were not by any means an isolated instance, but rather obeyed a policy of repression all throughout the island. In the jail at 5.5 in Pinar del Río they gravely wounded several prisoners. This wave of repression and terror was denounced before the United Nations, but, as always, silence was the only answer.

A delegate from the Ministry, Lieutenant Ramiro Abreu, now head of the Central American Section of the Party Central Committee, paid periodic visits to the prisoners. He was reviewing our files. On one occasion he told me that he'd been working with mine, and he serenely admitted to me that if my trial had been held two or three years later, the maximum sentence I'd have received would have been six years. "Then why did they sentence me to thirty, Lieutenant?"

"Because counterrevolution in those first years was very fierce, very dangerous, and it had to be controlled. We had to defend ourselves, we had to be energetic. We know we committed some excesses, and your case is just one of them."

"But if you admit that the Revolution was unjust with me, and that excesses were committed in sentencing me to thirty years of prison, knowing that I've already served out thirteen years as a prisoner, you ought to set me free. Why don't you?"

"Well, because you're still acting like a rebel. If you went into the Rehabilitation Program, in a few months we *would* set you free."

Years later, many other authorities told me the same thing. They admitted they had been stepping on me unjustly, but they told me all the same that I had to beg their pardon for putting my neck under their boots. They would never get me to do that.

I got a kidney infection about that time. My face and ankles swelled up terribly and I had a high fever. It was difficult to see a doctor and we had only a military medic, so I had to write dozens of letters—to the Ministry, to the director of the prison, to the provincial headquarters and all sorts of other functionaries. I think it was that constant pecking away, like drops of water, that sometimes got results. After all, I couldn't lose anything by insisting, since I had plenty of time. Finally I managed to get them to take me to the doctor and give me antibiotics. But the pain went away for only a few days. I needed a renal examination, I needed to be seen by a specialist. I began to urinate blood.

One afternoon Lieutenant Abreu entered our *galera.* I explained what was happening to me, and to prove it I took an empty intravenous bottle and urinated into it. My urine was bloody. Two days later, three guards with machine guns took me to Calixto García Hospital. I had what they called pyelonephritis, an inflammation of the kidney and the funnel-shaped duct by which urine leaves the kidney. In the general exam they performed on me they discovered polyneuropathy, too, on the basis of an absence of certain reflexes and the presence of disturbances in my locomotion, which I had never given any importance to.*

On May 30, 1973, my birthday, they took us out of that chimney-*galera* at last and led us to prison yard 2, where the political prisoners were kept. They sent us to *galera* 12, where we had a little more space and air. They also allowed us to get a little sun three times a week, but we were forbidden to receive visits or packages from our families.

A good while before, the government had begun a new policy. We didn't know about it in much detail, but apparently it consisted of reimposing new sentences on top of the sentence you had already served if you refused to change your attitude and bow down before the authorities. A year before your sentence was up, you were called to Prison Headquarters and forced to work in a brigade for the Ministry of the Interior, but held to the discipline and conditions imposed by the Jails and Prisons Headquarters. If you agreed to do that, you were transferred to a "work front," where you wore the blue uniform and lived in the barracks of the common prisoner, which you were now considered to be.

If you refused this offer, however, you would never be set free. Therefore, a sentence of six years might become eight, ten, or even thirteen, as happened to Julio Rodríguez Lamelas, who had to serve more "extra" years than his original sentence. The authorities called a sort of kangaroo court sometimes to add the years to your sentence. Other times, as in the case of René Ramos and many others, you received the sentence from a tribunal you'd never seen. Little by little the number of rebels who had served out their sentences but did not agree to the government's conditions grew into the dozens. Each year these prisoners would receive a new extension of their sentence; they would be serving ad hoc sentences of life imprisonment. You could no longer dream of the day your freedom would come. This new measure wiped out that dream completely.

The Ministry of the Interior had gotten frustrated. After having used all the torture, the physical and psychological violence they could think of, not only against us but also against our families, and seeing that it didn't work, after trying for years and realizing that they simply could not beat us down, they got tired of trying. They decided to lock the door forever. Of course, there was no appeal against such a decision, nor any legal procedure which might change it. Revolutionary justice had abolished all internationally recognized jurisprudential principles, which were now called "archaic principles of bourgeois law."

---

*In layman's terms, polyneuropathy is a condition, not a disease, which involves damage to secondary-nerve endings. It may or may not be reversible. The symptoms may include muscle weakness or lack of response, palsy, lack of some sensation, and in some severe cases paralysis and loss of body control.

45 / An Imposed Strike

By way of the visits I established an underground correspondence with Martha. That's how I received her first letter, written on sheets of onionskin in an almost microscopic handwriting, which I devoured with love and dread. She felt very bad. She had left Cuba under pressure from me. I thought, though at the time she refused to believe it, that she might be able to get me out of prison. She confessed to me that she felt useless, that at least while she had been in Cuba she could be on the other side of these walls and moats and share the same sky, the same sun with me. I understood, and I too was sad that she was so far away, but I felt tranquil, because at least she was safe from the repression of the Communists.

Another of my denunciations had penetrated all the defenses of government censorship and was being published abroad. That let people know once again what was happening in the jails.

On tiny pieces of fine paper which came in clandestinely, I wrote Martha several times a week. To get the letters out, I would fold them up carefully like an accordion, which is the way they have the least bulk, wrap them in plastic, and hide them in the crotch of a pair of athletic shorts. I was never far away from those little letters! I slept with them and even took them with me when I bathed, since the soldiers often came in to search the *galeras* without warning and they might discover them.

When I sent Martha a letter with information, a denunciation, or instructions, I made several copies so it would have a better chance not only of reaching the outside, but finally reaching her, since if it was difficult to get through the search system in a jail, it was much more difficult to get correspondence out of the country. We used the addresses of friends of ours in all the nations of Europe and Latin America. The authorities knew that the greatest concentration of exiles was in the United States, so almost 90 percent of the correspondence sent to that country from Cuba was destroyed, and anything sent to Cuba from the United States ran the same risk, but not so for mail to other countries.

We prisoners had two choices. We could keep our letters in hiding places we thought were safe, like holes in the wall or double seams in pillows and beds, or we could carry them with us. I always preferred to carry them with me. That way I could hold on to them until the last possible second. But that meant they always might be discovered in a search, so whenever there was a search I was very nervous.

In our prison yard at La Cabaña there were hundreds of rehabilitated prisoners, almost all of them very young, who had been detained for some political crime. In the other prison yard, with which we had no contact, since it was in another area, there were about eight hundred young men from the obligatory military service, locked up there for military crimes and misdemeanors. In the prison yard we could speak with the rehabilitated prisoners only at a distance, because the authorities wouldn't let them get too close to our bars. The authorities thought our rebellion might infect them.

It might be interesting to draw a brief outline of these young men. Some of them, perhaps sixteen years old, had been born and raised under the Revolution, but they were still antagonistic to the system. In spite of the fact that they were in the Rehabilitation Program these boys kept up a high spirit of combativeness against the regime. Ever since the age of reason, they had learned how to fake, as so many millions of other people had throughout the country. They would go to a mass meeting in the huge Plaza de la Revolución to hear Castro's speeches, the same old songs. They'd applaud him, and then they'd go off to set a warehouse afire or paint signs saying "Down with Communism!" They felt sorry for us veteran political prisoners, but they also had great respect and admiration for us. In order to help us, many of them risked their personal security and their families' visits. They were faithful collaborators. They helped us enormously, and we had, thanks to them, a real network of information all throughout the presidio.

Within a few weeks the garrison's vigilance, which had kept the young prisoners from coming in to our side, had slackened a bit, so some of them took off their uniforms and wearing only underwear managed to come into our *galera*. I talked with them quite a lot, asking them all about what was happening outside the prison. I was interested in where they had come from, who their families were, why they had rebelled against the system, their experiences, their desires, and their demands for the future of the country. I spent as much time as I could talking with them; their lives were so representative of the lives of Cubans under the Revolution, and I found their stories engraved themselves in my memory. I met one young man named Lachi who had tried several times to get out of the country, to rejoin his parents and his sister living in the United States. The authorities did not let Lachi leave with his family because he was of military-service age. But after he had gone through military service, they still wouldn't let him leave. From that time on, he was obsessed with rejoining his family. He tried to cross the waters of the Gulf in a truckbed that had been set afloat. A canvas awning covering the truckbed was his only shelter and a plastic jar of water and a little plastic-covered package of crackers were his entire provisions. About thirty miles from the Cuban coast, almost dying, he was picked up by a Soviet ship.

From La Cabaña large contingents of prisoners were always leaving for the work areas. In 1973 there was a prison population of forty-eight thousand men in the province of Havana, which had a population of two million. The number of prisoners of course includes political prisoners. These men were held in the closed prisons of La Cabaña, El Morro, Guanajay, El Príncipe, Guines, and so forth, in concentration camps Melena 1 and 2 and Quivicán, and in the so-called open fronts, of which there were six in the province. Enormous contingents of prisoners belonged to these open fronts, where they built barns and did other heavy farm work, built houses and other kinds of buildings, schools, and roads. Many tourists and invited guests, among them not a few intellectuals, never suspected that the workers they saw building a road were prisoners. Still, in the April 20, 1973, issue of the official Cuban magazine *Bohemia,* the use of counterrevolutionary prisoners in public works was admitted. The counterrevolutionary prisoners, it was stated, beyond their contributions to agriculture, especially in the sugar industry, had built numerous warehouses, farm buildings, factories, schools, and other projects on which they were still working. Tens of thousands of prisoners, both common and political, cut cane in the province of Havana, under the promise that if they cut so many thousands of tons they could reduce their sentence. They were, generally, deceived. The Communists don't feel any particular obligation to keep their promises.

When the men cutting cane or working at the dairy farms had problems —when they tried to escape, for example, or had an argument with some soldier—their punishment was being returned to La Cabaña. Therefore we always had prisoners coming in, and we knew what was happening in the other jails.

I was still writing, in a sort of frenzy, sending Martha instructions on how to present our situation to the rest of the world, letters to international organizations, governments, and the press. Castro's propaganda and his witting and unwitting spokespeople out in the world drowned out the cries of the tortured men and the clamor of his victims. Cuba was, for most people in the outside world, a kind of earthly paradise, reached by the grace of the Revolution. With their distorted news reports on Cuban reality, the world's press backed the tyrant Castro, and the governments of the capitalist nations of Europe, such as Sweden, offered him diplomatic support, trade, and generous free foreign aid. The Socialist International lent its political and moral support at that time to the dictator, as, twenty-five years from now, it will still be doing, without even blushing.

This indifference on the part of those who should have been feeling solidarity for our sacrifice made us indignant, depressed, and sad. I tried to be philosophical about the fact that at the moment we could hope for nothing from the indolence and insensitivity of the free world, which allowed indignant voices to be heard only when prisoners were mistreated by rightist dictatorships. I knew it would not be an easy task to create public opinion strong enough to do something concrete for our freedom. I had to trust in Martha and my friends abroad and in God to help. But it was *my* responsibility, too, to denounce my unjust imprisonment, although that would be dangerous; they might even kill me. Still I had to run that risk.

When they opened the *galeras* to let us out into the prison yard, some of us managed to get around the guards and mix with the other prisoners. That's how I came to know Pierre Golendorf, a French Marxist intellectual who had come to Cuba and worked for the Cuban government. But Pierre had seen through the falseness of what he called the games of the Revolution and realized that the island was one big farm that Castro ran like a slave plantation. And Golendorf said that out loud; he even wrote it. He wrote in letters about the lie the Revolution had turned into, never suspecting that the Political Police were going through all his correspondence. They accused him, like everyone who stood up to the Revolution, of being an agent of the CIA, and they held him incommunicado to interrogate him. The prosecutor requested twenty-five years' imprisonment for Golendorf, but an investigating officer told Golendorf not to worry, he'd get a shorter sentence, which he still probably wouldn't have to serve completely. Golendorf did get ten years, and the officer from the Political Police didn't trick him—he served only three years and two months. The Political Police could tell Golendorf that beforehand because they had decided on it in the Cuban Lubyanka, which is where for a quarter of a century they have imposed the sentences which condemned men receive at the hands of politicians. The tribunals do nothing but read sentences.

Pierre had been a member of the French Communist Party, and my companions were a little hostile to him because of his background. That didn't bother me; it *never* bothered me that somebody's beliefs were different from mine. I was really very interested in talking with him, and anyway, everyone inside those bars was a prisoner, I thought.

One afternoon, Pierre was washing one of his uniforms in the prison-yard washbasins. I sat down beside him, said hello, and asked him how he had come to the prison. For me what he had to say, the way he looked at this Cuban reality, was very important, very interesting. I tried to draw him out.

"You see, Pierre, what Communism has done in our country," I said to him. "Batista's dictatorship has been replaced by another one, even crueler and more repressive. You, just because you wrote what you saw, have been accused of being an agent of the CIA and sentenced to ten years in jail. This new tyranny is even more implacable than the one before." I told him that under Batista, Communists had even been able to be members of the government. Carlos Rafael Rodríguez, the current Vice-President under Castro, had been one of Batista's cabinet members. And Blas Roca and Lázaro Peña, who were also Communists, had enjoyed all the benefits of the Batista dictatorship even while they were in exile.

Pierre looked very surprised. "I've learned from bitter experience that many things here are not what they seem to be. I thought the Cuban Revolution was the socialist ideal which would return freedom to the people. I came here as an enthusiastic admirer of the revolutionary process. I was willing to give it my best. But I ran up against an implacable bureaucracy with a new power class that eliminated all liberties and that is so unorganized that disorganization becomes a dogma. The country is governed, as though it were a jail, by an implacable dictator who runs everything under the revolutionary phraseology with which he has managed to trick everyone, including me."

"And the most dramatic thing about it is that that trickery doesn't allow us Cubans to find out about the truth of these jails and concentration camps, the torture and the crimes."

"It's true, Valladares, most of the European Left is very pro-Castro, and it seems to them acceptable that certain reprehensible acts occur. They call them legitimate defensive acts, defending the Revolution."

Pierre and I became great friends, and when we couldn't get together in the prison yard we would write to each other. In June 1974 all we political prisoners were transferred to prison yard 1, from which the young recruits held for alleged military crimes had been moved. The *galera* I was sent to was the smallest and gloomiest of all. It was infested with bedbugs and lice. From the ceiling hung little stalactites produced by water dripping through the vaulted roof. The bars at the back of the *galera* had been crisscrossed by dozens of iron bars, welded transversely to make a net. You could hardly put two fingers through the spaces between the bars. The doors of the bathrooms had been pulled out.

That transfer was the beginning of another plan to break down our resistance. At eight o'clock that night we had still not had a bite to eat or a drop of water to drink. And the order was that to be allowed to go to the dining hall, we had to accept a new set of rules—one new rule was that we would not be allowed to take food back to sick men or to the crippled men who could not go to the dining room to eat. They thought that at that hour of the night, exhausted by the move, by hunger and thirst, we would give in. But all the prisoners refused to go to the dining hall under those conditions. That went on for two days running. No one ate. On the third day, the garrison, wearing helmets and carrying rifles, took the rooftops and set up machine guns, and then Lemus, the head of Jails and Prisons, entered the prison yard with his retinue of aides and escorts. He walked up and down and said that if we didn't go out to eat the next day they would declare the whole prison yard on a hunger strike and carry that decision to its ultimate consequences.

For our group, which was the group the authorities hated most because of our intransigence, there was a special cruelty. Since we were just wearing underwear, other prisoners or the authorities themselves had always brought our food to the *galeras*. Now they took advantage of this conjunction of events to force us to abandon our political position, to bring us to such a difficult pass that if we lost this struggle it would mean accepting Political Rehabilitation. Some of our comrades dressed in yellow decided to share our lot, but the authorities told them they couldn't. The garrison gave us an ultimatum—either we give in and go to eat or they would crush us once and for all. Only one man in our group abandoned us after that threat, asking the garrison to give him protection, which they did immediately. They took him to the little storehouse, where the police gave him special treatment while his comrades slowly died.

Some of our friends sneaked food past the soldiers in the dining hall and managed to throw it in to us through a window. For several days we existed like that, dividing fifteen eggs and ten pieces of bread among forty men. Finally they posted a guard in front of the window. On the fourth day of our forced "hunger strike" the garrison came into our *galera* and moved us out into another one, out of the inhabited zone. They stripped us of everything—toothbrushes, cups to drink from, soap, medicine, even the atomizers for asthma. In the *galera* beside us, Húber Matos, Eloy César Báez, Lauro Blanco, Tony Lamas, and other men were held. They called over to us immediately, and we explained our predicament to them. Tony began to make a hole in the concrete-block wall, which was almost two yards thick. In that area, since it was the military area, the dull thuds he made trying to break through the wall didn't attract much attention. And besides, he muffled them by rolling a blanket around the iron bar they were using to break through with.

They finished the job the next day, and they passed sugar water and powdered milk in to us through an intravenous tube. The guards took only two days to discover that opening, and they transferred us again, this time to a *galera* where we had no way to contact other prisoners.

We chose Paco Arenal to speak to the garrison. Every day early in the morning he called the officer of the guard.

"We want to eat."

"Will you accept our conditions?"

"We want to eat without political conditions."

Every day at lunchtime and dinnertime we repeated our request for food.

We never failed to do that. On other occasions we had been on a hunger strike by our own volition. This time it was different; the soldiers were refusing to give us food.

After two weeks of that forced fasting I could no longer walk. The effects of the years of mistreatment and malnutrition, the diseases and polyneuritis I was suffering from, were rapidly aggravated by this latest episode. My mistreated body was failing me. But my rebellious spirit still was strong— I knew I might die, but the possibility didn't frighten me. I believed that if I died it didn't mean the end, but the beginning of real life.

After twenty days Captain O'Farrill, the same man who had taken part at Boitel's death with Lemus and other officials, came into the *galera*. We must have presented a terribly depressing sight, since we were lying around wherever we could, filthy, bearded, and skeletal.

"Why are you men on a hunger strike?" They knew that we wanted to eat, but nonetheless with almost unbelievable cynicism they could ask us that question.

"We aren't on a hunger strike, and you know it. Every day we ask for food. If you want to see for yourself, send for the food and we'll eat it now."

"Yes, you men say that, but we know that all of this has been organized from the outside, from abroad, to discredit the Revolution. There are several CIA agents among you. Naser and Chenequene, for example." We didn't know it, but abroad people knew what was happening to us, so that was the interpretation the authorities gave the matter—it was a CIA plot.

Naser and Chenequene, along with Paco and some more men, were taken out of the group and sent off to a dungeonlike cell with special guards. Meanwhile, our relatives lived for days in unprecedented tension. Mothers and wives collected and begged for news about their sons and husbands.

After thirty days of refusing to give us food, the soldiers began to tell our relatives that some of the men had died, but they didn't give out names. That was the cruelest means they could have chosen to punish our families. There were pathetic scenes at the front gate every time they announced that another of the strikers had died. Some grief-stricken mothers decided to declare a hunger strike of their own; they said if their sons didn't eat, they wouldn't eat either. At the forefront of those mothers was Josefina, Naser's mother. My mother stopped eating too.

Another attempt to try to break down our resistance was telling our parents to write us asking us to stop our rebellion. The authorities would have those letters sent in to us, they said, to keep us from killing ourselves on the strike. Our mothers didn't waver a second. It was a question of the lives of their sons, and they agreed to write. I received a letter from my mother telling me that she was on a hunger strike and that she would die soon if I didn't renounce my attitude. Her letter almost destroyed me—her body, prematurely aged by her sufferings and terror, could not withstand that very long. And what if my mother should die? I asked myself.

The authorities had come to tell several of my comrades that their mothers were dying or had already died. They offered to carry them out for a few minutes to stand beside the deathbed or go to the funeral, but only in exchange for joining Political Rehabilitation. Many, though not all, even though they were sick with grief, refused. I spent two days without sleep. I thought about my mother in her sickness. Did I dare sacrifice her too, she who lived dreaming only of the day I would return to her side? All I had to do was call over the Political Commissioner and tell him that I wanted to leave, and everything would change instantly. I would save my mother, I would save myself, and the whole thing would almost miraculously turn out all right. But then how could I escape my conscience? My self-respect? My inner self? Once again I prayed to God, I entrusted myself to Him and His great wisdom. And as always, He listened. I was to continue the road I had chosen, even though I might be destroyed in the journey. And so my doubts began dissipating.

The visits from the officers continued. To Lemus' ambassadors were added those of the Political Police. A military doctor named Torres Prieto came to examine us. They spoke to those who vomited or looked most seriously ill, frightening them with the announcement of fatal liver or kidney complications, and offering medical assistance if they would give in.

Every day we told them that we wanted to eat. They had begun to refuse us food on June 24. July was already gone and we were at the beginning of August. They realized that our decision would lead to mass deaths. At any moment we might begin to die. Only then, under that pressure, did they decide to put an end to the most heartless measure that up to that moment had ever been taken in the Cuban political jails.

Most of us had to be returned to the *galeras* on stretchers. Immediately several doctors came in to examine us. The diagnosis of my condition was alarming. My reflexes had disappeared. The doctor said I had flaccid paraplegia due to malnutrition. The wasted muscles of my legs were like jelly, and the muscles of my upper body were weakened and sometimes unresponsive. The doctors said that five other men and I had to be admitted to the hospital for physical rehabilitation as soon as possible.

It was difficult even to give me intravenous feedings or medication. My blood was thick and clotted. The food began again, with small doses of sugar water. The third day they gave us cold milk, the fourth day broth, but they never took the IV tubes out of our arms. I thought that within a few days I might begin to feel and be able to move my legs, but it wasn't so. In previous hunger strikes, I had seen this happen to many men who later recovered, but I also had known some, like Liuva del Toro and Pascacio, who had remained in wheelchairs. The mere thought that that could happen to me, that I might be an invalid, horrified me.

The fifth day all officialdom of Jails and Prisons appeared. They entered the *galera* and called Paco Arenal angrily to tell him that those who could walk had to go out to the dining hall and keep all the rules. That was like a cold shower.

"That's like going back to square one, where this whole situation started. And besides, you yourself told us that you wouldn't require us to meet any political conditions. That's why you brought us back," Paco responded.

"We didn't say that. And we never promised anything." They *were* going back on their word. They had intentionally deceived us. After having gone through all that, after the agony of going through a month and a half of not eating, we were spent, all our reserves were exhausted, and they had calculated that we could easily be forced to do what they wanted us to do. They thought we wouldn't have the strength to resist them any longer. And in a way it was true. We did not have the physical strength. But we did have an inexhaustible spiritual reserve that they, who knew nothing about the essential, spiritual part of the human being, never counted on. A murmur of indignation arose from the hospital beds, but they cut it off insolently.

"If you don't like it, you know what will happen, so choose for yourselves. The man who doesn't go along with the way the Ministry runs things will go right back on hunger strike again. So make up your minds."

To their amazement, only two men gave in. The officers were furious. They had never foreseen our reaction to their blackmail. Nilo Muiño, one of the officers from Jails and Prisons, bent over me and yanked the intravenous needle out of my arm. A stream of blood gushed out after it. They did the same with all the men. They threw me onto a stretcher, and two guards took me out. That began the transfer.

46 / In a Wheelchair

he prison yard was full of soldiers wearing helmets and carrying machine guns. They feared the way the rest of the prison would react to this move.

Before we arrived at our new destination, several officers and Dr. Torres Prieto intercepted me. Torres Prieto tried to persuade me to change my attitude; if I didn't, he told me, I would be an invalid for the rest of my life. The officers also tried to convince me. I didn't know that Amnesty International had become interested in my case, but they did.

The return was humiliating. They set me down in the middle of the Headquarters walkway, where they were doing searches and shaving everybody's head. They stripped me completely and seized some letters to Martha and a diary I had kept of the strike. Then they cut off all my hair with a manual hairclipper. Then they sent us to a filthy *galera* with smelly burlap cots and a plague of lice and bedbugs.

That same night they came back to threaten us again. It took them five days to realize once and for all that we would never give in; on the sixth day, August 12, 1974, they gave up. Valdés, the head of the Political Police, told us, trying to justify the way we had been treated, that the Revolution had to shake the trees every once in a while, to shake the capitalists out. That is how he described the decision to let us starve for forty-six days.

Then began the struggle to get medical help. They brought in a commission of doctors from the Neurological Institute in Havana. The neurologists did extensive tests on us, and for six of us their diagnosis was "nutritional flaccid paraplegia." They recommended that we be moved to a specialized hospital. But the Political Police refused, so I began a struggle for medical care which would last years. I wrote the Ministry, the leaders of the Revolution, the Party Central Committee, and what seemed like hundreds of other offices.

We didn't have wheelchairs, so we had to drag ourselves along the floor on wooden pallets. I was twice a prisoner then. I tried to give myself physical therapy. I would lie on my cot and move all the joints in my legs with my hands, to keep them from atrophying completely. I refused to remain an invalid for the rest of my life. My friends helped me by moving my legs, too, and sometimes gave me massages. But that wasn't enough.

Napoleoncito couldn't walk either, but he was getting better. De Vera and I were still in bad shape, though, as were four other men. In a week, on August 19, the guards informed us that there'd be no more broth and purée, we'd be going back to eating boiled macaroni and the tinned meat which was the staple of the presidio. The prisoners called it dog vomit. It came from Holland and was like a soft meat paste, full of fat and starch, put up in 1,800-gram cans by the Homburg company.

There was a Dutch prisoner named Paul Redeker in La Cabaña, accused of being an agent of the CIA. He told us that the meat we ate wasn't for human consumption, that it was made from waste products. But the Cuban government had requested it just that way. Redeker knew all the details because he had taken part in the negotiations. He told us the Dutch had thought it would be used to mix with other materials for animals. You couldn't have found that product on the open market if you tried; it was not sold to the public. It was manufactured and bought especially for the more than 100,000 Cuban prisoners.

Meanwhile, Dr. Humberto Medrano, president of the Committee for the Denunciation of the Mistreatment of Cuban Prisoners, managed to appear before the Human Rights Commission of the United Nations in Geneva. The Inter-American Press Society (SIP) had ceded its turn to him. He denounced the suffering of men and women in Castro's prisons. He turned over to the secretary of the subcommission all the documentation needed to prove the horrors perpetrated in the Cuban political prisons. There were long lists of tortured, mutilated, and murdered men as well as prisoners' letters, smuggled out, telling about the concentration camps, giving their exact locations throughout the island. Dr. Medrano offered supporting evidence from the International Commission of Jurists, the Inter-American Commission on Human Rights of the OAS, the League of the Rights of Man, the International Red Cross, Amnesty International, and other prestigious organizations. All these reports dealt with the violation of human rights in Cuba and the degrading treatment that political prisoners were receiving. The beatings, the refusal of food, visits, and correspondence, and the resentencing of prisoners were all denounced by Dr. Medrano. As he was reading a statement about the men murdered in the forced-labor camps on Isla de Pinos, Sergei Smirnov, the Soviet delegate, interrupted him, shouting that it was a pack of lies. Dr. Medrano answered that these were proven facts. Smirnov insisted that Dr. Medrano give up the floor, and he moved that the report be stricken from the minutes. There was a tremendous argument among the delegates, who debated whether our compatriot Dr. Medrano had the right to go on speaking.

When they returned the floor to him, Dr. Medrano put aside the list of murdered men and began speaking about the women's political prison, which was more cruel and inhumane than the men's, and again a storm of protest errupted.

Smirnov kept shouting, "Comrade President, Comrade President, this is not the place for this type of political expression! This meddling must end!" The Cuban delegate, Hernán Santa Cruz, joined Smirnov in his objection. They asked that Dr. Medrano give up the floor. Some delegates wanted them to give hir. five minutes more, others two. That was when the voice of Dr. Medrano echoed throughout the hall.

"Mr. President, we ask that we be given fifteen minutes more, one for each year of the savage beatings committed against the people, and especially the prisoners, of Cuba." The President, a Rumanian, gave him five minutes. Dr. Medrano asked that the documentation he had presented be officially circulated and that a special commission be named to investigate and analyze the body of proof which demonstrated the constant violations of human rights, the ideological genocide, and the tortures in Cuba.

As it had on May 12, 1972, when it was asked to intervene to save Boitel's life, the United Nations kept silent. The investigating commission Dr. Medrano had requested was never named, the documentation was never circulated—in fact, weeks later it disappeared completely under mysterious circumstances.

All this occurred in August 1974. Meanwhile Castro was still sending his opponents to the firing squads in the jails and still torturing people. And Cuba tried to put a man into the Secretariat of the United Nations Commission on Human Rights.

At that time they sent mail in to us every three months. I could never find out exactly how it happened, but they put in a new military mailman, and one afternoon he showed up with a big package of postcards all for me. He'd seen the postcards at Headquarters and somehow thought I was actually supposed to receive them. All of the postcards were from members of Amnesty International. They came from Sweden, Germany, Canada, and Holland. Somebody had made a huge mistake; I learned that there were people all around the world who knew about our situation, and my case in particular. It was valuable information. And of course it was exhilarating. The next day Lieutenant Ochoa came in very early and asked me to give them back to him for a moment, supposedly to put the stamp of authorization on them. He said he'd give them back to me, as though I could be expected to believe that. I told him I'd passed them out to all my friends in all sixteen *galeras.*

I went on writing the Ministry of the Interior, the Vice-Ministry, and the Red Cross, asking for medical care. I found out that Lieutenant Romero, one of the Political Commissioners, was the secretary of the nucleus of the Communist Party in the prison. We called Romero "Notebook" because he always carried a spiral notebook under his arm, in which he wrote down everything you told him. I called and told him I wanted to turn over a letter to him, as the highest-ranking member of the Party at the prison, and that I would like it taken to Provincial Headquarters. He was alarmed. The idea of a counterrevolutionary prisoner writing a letter to the Party was completely alien to him. He asked me what was going on, but he promised me he'd see to the matter. But I didn't stop writing because of his promises— every day when the headcount officer came in, I gave him three or four letters. At last on November 4 they took me to a neurologist, Dr. Joaquín García. After a long examination and muscle tests, he filled out a certificate for admission to a rehabilitation clinic. He had diagnosed severe degenerative polyneuropathy brought on by malnutrition. He pointed out that only intensive treatment could help me get back to normal.

But that diagnosis wasn't enough for the Political Police. They made me see one of their own doctors, Dr. Luis Díaz Cuesta, head of Physical Medical Services in Havana. His diagnosis was essentially the same, but he pointed out further the atrophy of my leg muscles and a loss of function in my arm muscles. On January 3, 1975, Dr. Díaz Cuesta, too, stated that if I wasn't admitted to the hospital without further delay, there would be a distinct risk that the damage would be irreversible. Friends of mine inside the prison made photocopies of all these diagnoses, and I managed to get them out to Martha, abroad. Years later they would serve to discredit the Cuban government's claims that I was faking my illness.

The bathrooms still had no doors, so we put up some rotten old burlap bags, all patched and sewn together. The flies were a plague which only let up at night. They would light in flocks everywhere; we would burn them by the hundreds with lighted pieces of paper. But the next morning they would fly toward our *galera* from the trashcan on the other side, only a hundred yards away.

In the dispensary, patients on intravenous medication would find a swarm of flies covering the rubber tubing and the bottle. There were no adequate sanitary facilities, just an old bathtub which drained into a can. When the can was full, the water spilled out in a pool on the floor. The toilets overflowed frequently and had to be cleaned out with cans. The stench was unbearable. To unplug the drainpipes, you had to dig up the prison yard and take out wheelbarrowfuls of the filth and trash that had accumulated. Over it all flew the mosquitoes and gnats which would get into your eyes and mouth. There was always diarrhea, and Carreño, Equiliort, Llerena, and other men contracted severe hepatitis. The authorities gave us only one liter of water a day for drinking and all our other needs. That's why when it rained we stuck poles out the window and hung a sheet across them, to try to drain some rainwater into cans. We would pull the corner of the sheet into a can we kept just for that purpose.

We invalids dragged ourselves along on wooden boxes, with the aid of our comrades. Our helplessness was truly depressing. Getting a wheelchair took a bureaucratic tangle of paperwork which might last for years. But we didn't want to wait that long. One afternoon I spoke with Menchaca. He was a Communist, but he was a straight talker and he never made a promise he couldn't keep. He was one of those rare people inside the repressive apparatus who always treated prisoners respectfully. He always behaved very well toward me, never with any cruelty or abuse, something I found very few times in a functionary of the Cuban government. He was the administrator of medical services in the prison. I told him we needed wheelchairs, and that I had friends who could send for them from overseas. The authorities already knew that very well. I told him if the government didn't give us wheelchairs within a week, I'd ask my friends from Amnesty International to send them to us.

A few days later they brought in six wheelchairs for the six of us who were invalids. We didn't have to stay prostrate in bed all the time anymore. And thus began for me a great test of my will, a challenge to my almost hyperactive body, which needed constant activity. I was tied to the wheelchair, but I soon made it almost an extension of my body.

47 / "They Know What They're Doing, All Right"

The heat in the southern part of Oriente province is the most intense of the whole island, and since the jail at Boniato is located at the bottom of a valley, in summertime it's a real oven. The jail was covered with posters celebrating the First Communist Party Congress, which was to be held in September. It was the end of August, and Laureano had been suffering for days from a terrible toothache. A huge cavity had eaten away almost his whole tooth, so there was barely a shell left.

He spoke with the head of the building and with the other officers who attended the headcount, to try to get them to have the tooth pulled, but with no luck. They didn't even give him an aspirin to relieve the pain. The suffocating nights Laureano spent without sleeping because of the torment of the pain kept building up and were driving him to desperation. The lieutenant who was head of the Political Commissioners was sent for, and Laureano's problem was explained. He answered that in order to have his tooth pulled, Laureano had to give up his resistance. He added that we knew that as long as we refused to cooperate we had no right to receive medical attention. Finally, in desperation, Laureano pulled out his tooth with a spoon and a rusty nail. It was a barbaric operation. He destroyed his gums, but he only managed to get out pieces of the tooth. Soon an infection invaded his jawbone. The officer of the guard was called a second time, and he promised to give Laureano a shot to relieve the pain. He said he'd take him to the doctor the next day. But they never gave Laureano the shot.

The common prisoner who served breakfast collaborated with us, and although he was forbidden to raise his head he knew which cell was which. Therefore we had a way of getting around the vigilance of the garrison. He would hide a tiny note, all folded up, inside a crust of bread. The note we received one morning said that the night before, Colonel Ervin Ruiz, provincial head of State Security (who years later when he was replaced by Minister of the Interior Sergio del Valle would be demoted, along with other high-ranking officers), had spent several hours the night before in conference with many other officers and that the posts had been reinforced. Hours passed and they still didn't take Laureano out. But by that time he had a high fever and was running the risk of dying of septicemia. When lunch was brought in, the prisoners rejected it. Lieutenant Elio, head of the building, came to ask why we didn't want to eat, and we asked him in return why Laureano, who was very seriously ill, hadn't been taken out. "You know the conditions we've established—as long as you keep up your rebellion we cannot give you medical attention. Those are our orders."

Juan González, one of our comrades, had been the man designated to speak with the soldiers, so it was he who reported our jailers' latest refusal to help Laureano. We all still had José Ramón Castillo's death in mind, the last of us who, also because of lack of medical care, had died in those blackout cells. Our response was the only one in our power—we beat on the iron sheets of the doors with our pewter spoons and cups and plates. It was a response of impotence and pain. At that very moment there was a visit from the families of the rehabilitated prisoners, and the director of the prison suspended it, saying that the counterrevolutionary prisoners had rioted and taken over the building, wounding several soldiers. He had set it all up very cleverly.

When the relatives of the rehabilitated prisoners were sent out, the garrison, in combat order, marched to our building. The yellow-uniformed prisoners held in the front cell block, in regular cells, saw them coming and blocked the entrance to their hallway with water tanks. When the guards came up the stairs and were about to enter the cell block through the main gate, the prisoners took shelter behind the water tanks and started throwing glass bottles at them. The garrison responded with bursts of machine-gun fire, which blasted holes in the tanks, then they fired three tear-gas grenades, and when the gasping and gagging prisoners came out from behind their blockade, the guards fired again and shot two of them down. Santiestéban crawled out on his stomach and pulled the most seriously wounded of them into a cell. He was bleeding to death.

The soldiers entered the hallway leading to the blackout cells and began to open the doors. As the prisoners came out, they were pushed and kicked down to the end of the hall. There were only five or six cells left to open. The prisoners, beaten, were stumbling and tripping through the hail of blows from sticks and truncheons, bayonets, and chains.

But suddenly, as though to protect them, there appeared a skeletal figure with white hair and flaming, blazing eyes, who opened his arms into a cross, raised his head to the invisible sky, and said, "Forgive them, Lord, for they know not what they do." The Brother of the Faith hardly had time to finish his sentence, because as soon as he appeared Lieutenant Raúl Pérez de la Rosa ordered the guards to step back and as the Brother of the Faith was speaking he fired his AK submachine gun. The burst of fire climbed the Brother of the Faith's chest, up to his neck. His head was almost severed, as though from the blow of an ax. He died instantly. Enrique Díaz Correa, who was beside him, tried to hold up the bloody body, but Lieutenant Pérez kept firing until his magazine was empty. Enrique took nine shells in his body.

Then a real butchery, an organized and systematic butchery, began. Lieutenant Carranza, from the Political Police, fired his rifle, and other guards followed his lead. Roberto Martín Pérez fell wounded, his scrotum pierced by a bullet. Onofre Pérez, Rolando García, and another twenty or so were wounded as well.

Lieutenant Figueroa held the muzzle of his Makarov pistol to Evelio Díaz' head. "Take this, faggot!" he said, and he pulled the trigger. But the pistol jammed, so Figueroa cursed, grabbed it by the barrel, and attacked Evelio with the pistol butt.

Those prisoners still inside the cells were kicked and beaten senseless. Liuva del Toro and Pascacio were pulled out of their wheelchairs by their ankles and dragged along the floor. The guards dragged them down the stairway, their heads banging against every step. Liuva was unconscious when he came to the first floor. Gripping their rifles, the guards ordered the prisoners out of their cells and herded them down to the lower floor. There they hit Posada in the head with a rifle butt, and he fell headlong on the ground. We didn't know it at that moment, but the base of his skull had been fractured. Not a single prisoner was unscathed in the orgy of blood and horror. Naked, cornered like frightened animals and hemmed around by a line of bayonets, more than twenty men wounded by bullets, rifle butts, truncheons, and bayonets were grouped together. Upstairs in the cells the guards were destroying everything, including our clothing. More than an hour passed before they brought stretchers. They brought down the Brother of the Faith and Enrique Díaz Correa and placed them in the fenced passageway between the two buildings. The bright eyes of the Brother of the Faith were now like hard, opaque glass, open in amazement. His mouth was also open. Beside him an almost inaudible moan escaped Enrique. He was still alive, with nine bullets in his body, but he would be saved only by cutting out several organs and a part of his intestines.

Rain began to blow in through the iron fence. Water collected in the canvas stretchers bearing the two bodies, and as it dripped, it was dyed red from the men's blood. That was September 1, 1975, the year of the First Communist Party Congress in Cuba. Two days later guards dressed like prisoners would simulate an attack on the soldiers and the scenes would be filmed to justify their barbarous crime.

The news of the death of the Brother of the Faith had soon spread all over the prison system, and all over Cuba. It even leaked abroad. Before he died, he had repeated those words of Christ on the cross, and all of us, when his blood dried, struggled in our consciences to achieve that difficult but beautiful ability to pardon our enemies. However ferocious my jailers were, with the help of God my heart was filled with the faith that gives a man the strength to go on. And not out of resignation or masochism, but rather out of joy, freedom, and inward peace, because I felt accompanied by Christ through those labyrinths of horror and death, and tried to follow His lesson of forgiving my tormentors.

One of my letters reporting what had happened in Boniato managed to reach Martha. Dr. Medrano and a group of exiles presented the letter before the United Nations. But that prestigious institution didn't even acknowledge receipt of it. It was still deaf and blind to the Castro dictatorship's crimes against Cuban political prisoners.

Soon after we were transferred back to La Cabaña, we were sent to prison yard 2, the same one we had been in before, to *galera* 16, where Bitongo had hanged himself one St. Valentine's Day. But the door into the exterior passageway was not open as before. It was barred now. You couldn't go out into the prison yard and look up to the sky. The soldiers told us that we'd be much better off there because they had "renovated" the *galera,* created appropriate living conditions for us. The *galera* had supposedly been painted, fixed up, and disinfected. It was at night when we first went in, so it was dark. When I had been there ten years before, there had been ten large lightbulbs, since it was the largest *galera.* Now only two were left. It was like a cave.

We settled down the best we could to spend the night, but the bedbugs wouldn't let us sleep. Toward dawn I finally got into my wheelchair and sat there waiting for light.

Common prisoners had lived in the *galera* before us. In all the years I was a prisoner I never saw such filth. The walls were completely covered by a layer of millions of bedbugs and enormous lice and ticks. The toilet facilities, those holes in a corner of the floor, were nauseating. Naser called our attention to them, saying jokingly that the walls were moving. We went to look, and indeed they were moving. There was a writhing wave of maggots with glistening humps all across the wall. A little washing powder was found somehow and the vault was cleaned. The lice and ticks were kept down, at least, that way. There were so many that we made piles of them as though we had swept sawdust up off the floor.

I kept writing the Ministry of the Interior asking for medical attention. At last they took me to a hospital to extract spinal fluid and analyze it.

Lieutenant Ramiro Abreu showed up one day while I was there. He was the delegate from the Minister of the Interior. He spoke with the soldiers a second, and they went away. Then he told me the Revolution knew I couldn't work, but that they would release me in seventy-two hours if I told them, without signing any document, that I accepted Political Rehabilitation. "No one will know about it; we know that makes problems with your friends," he told me.

"I would know it, Lieutenant, and that would be enough." He courteously insisted. He offered me freedom.

"Freedom with strings attached doesn't interest me, Lieutenant, but thanks anyway."

Then they took me to the ward which the Political Police maintained in the hospital. It was an extension of Villa Marista, nothing more; they prolonged the methods of psychological torture and isolation used in Political Police Headquarters. Sick men under investigation are kept in conditions of exceptional repression. It was there that a captain told me I would never be admitted to a civilian hospital because they knew my friends would try to rescue me. Such an idea was clearly absurd.

A neurologist examined me and made the same diagnosis the other doctors had. And since they didn't have the equipment to give me the required treatment there, they were sending me back to the prison at La Cabaña. Then Lieutenant Ginebra told me they were ready to admit me immediately into a specialized clinic, but I would have to accept Rehabilitation first. If I did, the Minister would guarantee that in no more than ninety days I would be released.

"I don't plan to accept Political Rehabilitation, Lieutenant, and as a human being I have the right to receive medical attention without any conditions attached."

"You've heard our last word, Valladares. Think about it."

That flat no, that refusal to give me medical attention, finished off my by then faltering hopes of ever getting better.

Israel, another of the invalids, was given massages by Cáceres, one of our comrades. I went on with my own treatment of moving the joints in my legs. In the wheelchair I could do a series of exercises with the help of my arms, which were improving. Although the exercises kept the atrophy from growing worse, it wasn't enough to make me better. I set up a pulley system for myself out of some strips of burlap that I hung under my ankles and suspended from the cot above mine. When I pulled on the cords I could raise and lower my legs. My muscles were still soft, they had lost their tone.

Living in a wheelchair lent a new perspective to my life. I started describing in verse my impressions and states of spirit, my inability to climb a concrete stairway which any child might step up. One day I showed my poetry to my friend Alfredo Izaguirre, and I told him I was going to try to get it out and have it published. "If you publish this, even if you *are* in a wheelchair the Communists will shoot you in the back," he said.

"Well, if they do, it doesn't make any difference whether they shoot me in the back or in front." And I set myself to getting those poems out of Cuba. I wrote out twenty-one copies, and only one of them, via my good friend Agustín Piñera, got to Martha. *From My Wheelchair (Desde mi silla de ruedas)* was published and translated into several languages. That was the book which made me known in many countries of the world and started the first cracks in the wall of silence and indifference which seemed to have been built around the Cuban political prisoners. The first edition was brought out by Martha with the aid of friends in the outside world.

I knew I was exposing myself to death with the publication of the book, but I had to set an example. Other men had died in these or similar conditions, but they had not been able to leave any other message than their deaths and their rebellion against their victimizers. I wanted to leave a real, ineradicable message. If I died, my verses would be a constant accusation against the criminal barbarity of the Cuban political prison system. It would last longer than simple human memory, which grows cold in time. I wanted my poems and prose writings to make them see what was happening to the prisoners that Castro had taken—forgotten by everyone, the only people in the western world who have had their faith in democracy and their love of God, freedom, and justice tested by more than twenty years of torture. Poetry therefore became a weapon.

A series of circumstances then conspired to help me. After the rigorous investigations it always conducts, Amnesty International adopted me as a prisoner of conscience. They named several groups in West Germany, Holland, and Sweden to work toward achieving my freedom. I learned about the activities of the members of Amnesty International through my clandestine correspondence with Martha. Being adopted by Amnesty International constituted a kind of protection. I believe this greatly contributed to the fact that the Cuban authorities did not physically do away with me in some violent manner. The government knew that all the world now knew that I existed, and not only that but exactly what my situation was. Group 110 in Sweden worked unceasingly for me, and in great part it is due to their extraordinary efforts that I was finally released.

48 / Combinado del Este

n January 1977, the Cuban government opened a large new prison named Combinado del Este, and all of us prisoners were transferred there. Since it was meant to hold as many as 13,500 inmates, the authorities announced once again that they were going to close the old prison at La Cabaña, restore it, and convert it into a museum. But only two years later the jails and prisons of the island had run out of space again and they had to utilize La Cabaña as a prison.

Combinado del Este is a gigantic installation with workshops and factories, among them one which produces prefabricated walls and ceilings. It has a hospital, which Castro visited when it was completed. He studied it for a moment and then suddenly said it ought to have three stories, not two. No one dared explain to Castro that you couldn't just build on another story, that the foundations wouldn't hold it. Instead, they immediately began to build a third story, which they finished in record time. A little afterward the whole back wing sank more than four inches into the ground and the walls all cracked.

In that hospital I was shut up with two of my other friends who were invalids, Israel and Pedro, into a dungeonlike cell at the back of a ward. We could hardly move our wheelchairs around, there was so little space. A short hallway in front of the cell was our only relief from the cramped space, until Lieutenant Armando Valdez, an officer from the Political Police there, gave an order that we were to be shut out of the hallway as well, alleging security concerns as the reason for the measure.

What happened in that hospital is in itself sufficient material for a long book. For the first time they allowed women to see us. There were dozens of nurses in the hospital, all of whom had been carefully selected by the Political Police. They were almost all the wives of militant officials in the Communist Party. The director was Dr. Domingo Campos, a noisy, vulgar man who was terribly abusive even to the male and female nurses.

I tried to explain to him several times how wrong it was to keep us shut up, not allow us to go out into the hallway. All the rest of our comrades kept there could go outside, whereas we, who were in wheelchairs, could not. That was when they appointed Teresa Colunga chief nurse. She was an Internationalist who had performed revolutionary missions in several countries, but she was a humane person. One afternoon she came into that little hole we were locked up in on an inspection visit. Three barred doors had to be unlocked to get in to see us. I was seized with an asthma attack at the time.

"You should go into the hallway and get some air," she said to me.

I explained the situation to her. "I'm the chief nurse here. You can go out, and I'll take the responsibility for it."

The next day, in the presence of the psychiatrist, Dr. Jesús Edreira, Valdez put Teresa in her place; he told her she'd had no right to ignore the orders he'd given. They shut us up in the little hole again. A little while later Teresa was accused of being too humanitarian with the prisoners and was fired from the hospital. Then Isabel came. She was a very beautiful woman with big green eyes and very black hair. She was the wife of an official in the Ministry of the Interior. They made her head nurse of the ward we were in. She was everything a real nurse should be—kind, sensitive, and gentle. But Ana Carelia was made chief of nursing of the entire hospital. She was sent by the Ministry of the Interior. She laid down the law to Isabel. "Here you must forget everything you've ever learned about nursing. These patients are different. You can't speak to them more than is absolutely necessary. You can't give them any emotional support of any kind; that's the way the directors want it. If the prisoners say hello and ask how you are, you are not allowed to respond. You must not allow friendly relations of any kind with them."

Months passed, and every week they announced they were about to inaugurate a new operating room and a physiotherapy clinic with all the necessary equipment. There were still no X-ray machines or a laboratory. They had built a building, but it wasn't yet a hospital.

One day in April, about three o'clock in the afternoon, I was notified that some doctors were coming in to examine me. I was led to an auditorium where five or six doctors of different specialties were waiting for me. The whole general staff was there. Dr. Campos, the director of the hospital, thought they had come to release me, so he was very pleasant with me. My examinations lasted for two days. They even took me to the Military Medicine ward in the Naval Hospital to do an electromyelogram with modern equipment. There was no other such equipment in all of Cuba; this was for the exclusive use of military personnel. Later I would find out that an adjutant commander in the Ministry of the Interior was waiting for the results. It seems that a commission from several European parliaments had come to Havana at the invitation of the Cuban government. Some of the members of the commission belonged to Amnesty International, and the second they set foot on Cuban soil they asked about me. They wanted to see me and continually expressed interest in the state of my health. The Cuban government for the first time saw itself obliged to answer questions about me. Those members of parliament were there, and there was no way not to answer them.

The medical report was an interesting document—instead of reporting on the state of my health it said, "He was sentenced to thirty years in prison for having confected, in accord with other individuals, plans for armed uprising against the State and for performing acts of sabotage, attempts on the lives of leaders of the Revolution, terrorist acts," and a whole list of other things, all of them of the utmost gravity. It went on to say, this "medical" report, that I had kept up a recalcitrant position within the prisons for sixteen years and that I had incited other inmates to follow my bad example. Then it said that I had participated in several hunger strikes and because of that suffered from recuperable palsy of the lower and upper limbs as a consequence of polyneuropathy brought on by malnutrition. This complaint, the report went on to say, "apparently totally limits the movements of his lower extremities."

They admitted the illness, then, but they added that it wasn't as serious as had been thought, and that I could, in fact, walk. When the Cuban government's report was made public abroad, the response from my wife was flat, irrefutable, and corroborated by photocopies of the diagnoses by Cuban specialists which I had managed to get out of the country, and which I had known I would have use for someday. The report, although on Ministry of Public Health letterhead, had obviously been drafted by people who had access to my prison file, that is to say, members of the Political Police. They were accustomed to having their authoritarian, final decisions obeyed without question. They had forgotten that in medicine the words of the diagnosis describe the infirmity very precisely—when a report says "polyneuropathy," "palsy," "paraplegia," and the like, you can't say that the man suffering from those ills walks perfectly.

When my wife brought forth the photocopies of the diagnoses, the Political Police saw that they had been caught in a lie and made to look ridiculous, and they reacted predictably. They came to Calixto García Hospital, interrogated the nurses and anyone else who had had any contact with me, took away files of all the medical examinations, and so forth. And in the prison hospital they did the same thing. From that time on, my hospital records were in their custody. Months later a commander very pleasantly, very casually said to me, "Well, Valladares, a lot of time has gone by since that nonsense about the photocopies. Really, you were much more clever than State Security." He was trying to puff me up. "But just between you and me —I give you my word that I have no professional interest in the matter, I'm just curious—how did you get them out of Cuba?"

I looked at him again, and then all around, and adopted a sort of conspiratorial air. I lowered my voice, and almost whispering I said, "Well, Commander, if you promise that it's just between you and me, I'll tell you." He promised me, a little too eagerly, of course; he was ready to pounce on the information. Then I drew a little closer and whispered, "It was Lieutenant Valdez, the chief of Security at La Cabaña, who photocopied them for me."

The soldier turned about brusquely. A look of anger passed over his face and his eyes flashed, but he swallowed the joke and began to laugh. "I deserve that answer for being so stupid." And he walked away.

At two o'clock in the afternoon the guards did a search during which they even destroyed our shoes and took away our toothbrushes, spoons, pencils, and books. That made me think the commander hadn't taken my joke as well as he'd said he had.

The prison was still not completely finished. Some buildings were still under construction or had been left unfinished, among them the gigantic building which housed the punishment cells, an edifice situated toward the rear of the area, over a hundred yards long and about thirty or forty yards wide. It was to be a one-story building without a single window, and like all the other buildings it would be set up off the ground on short concrete-and-iron pilings. There were ninety-nine cells for solitary confinement, conceived with all the repressive imagination the Political Police were capable of.

The Communists sought an impressive-sounding name for those cells. They called them "disciplinary cells"; we called the building the "Human Rights Building." Since that was the building farthest behind schedule, officials from the Ministry of the Interior demanded that it be finished as soon as possible, and we saw General Enio Leyva, First Vice-Minister, and Colonels O'Farrill and Medardo Lemus file past over there inspecting the work, as well as a stream of majors and captains. The same week the Human Rights Building was finished, its ninety-nine cells were filled with common and political prisoners as well as with men condemned to death, who were taken from there to the moats of La Cabaña. That was still Castro's favorite killing ground. When foreign visitors came, most of them from Communist countries, they were told that that building was the warehouse, and the prison authorities still say that.

At that time two new characters appeared on the scene at the hospital. The first man was now a colonel in the Political Police, formerly an employee of an American oil company which had had offices in Havana. His name was Manuel Blanco Fernández, Mano for short. He was short, fat, potbellied, and red-faced. The old satyr was always chasing the nurses. The other man used the professional name Adrián. He was a thin, sallow man with almond eyes. Within a few days we had found the perfect nickname for him—we called him Captain Liar because he was as lying as he was brutal.

One day Captain Liar told Izaguirre and me that his particular job as a guerrilla in the fight against Batista had been using a knife or bayonet against the crews of patrol cars and taking away their pistols and machine guns. Neither he nor anybody else ever did such a thing, of course, and what's more he said he was all of twelve years old when he did it. According to him, he had dropped out of medical school in his last year—but then a week later he had forgotten that he'd told us that story, and he told us he had been studying law. The next time it was engineering. He told stories of manning spy planes and one-man submarines, traveling all over the world on super-dangerous missions, working for Cuban State Security and the KGB, à la James Bond. One afternoon I thought I'd test him a bit, and I asked him if he'd ever been in Pakistan, Lithuania, Andorra, and other foreign countries. Yes, yes, yes—he'd been to all those places. So then I casually asked him if he'd ever been to that island in the Atlantic off Spain called Atlantis. He thought for a while, rubbed his chin, and then said, "Oh yeah! But just for a couple of hours, on a stopover."

I had to make a superhuman effort not to laugh in his face. This secret superagent made our day—and day after day, too—blithely allowing his leg to be pulled by us prisoners.

But these two characters, working together, soon came to be the most hated and despised of all our jailers. Prisoners, nurses, the hospital personnel, and even some of the soldiers were disgusted and repelled by them.

They threw out or transferred many employees, especially nurses, for befriending prisoners or for not giving in to the two men's amorous overtures. One of the cruel things they did was go to my house and tell my family that Ministry Headquarters had given them orders to start processing my family's request to leave Cuba; of course they had no intention of ever doing such a thing. There was no doubt, though, that the efforts of Amnesty International, the existence of my book—now in a second edition—and the interest shown in me by politicians and intellectuals throughout the world had begun to worry the Cuban authorities. I had slipped through their clutches somehow; they couldn't just kill me and be done with it, because I was now too well known.

I took full advantage of the situation. I redoubled my denunciations, I continued writing letters. I was working on a new book of poetry.

Obviously the authorities wanted to put a stop to these leaks. A friend of the family, Sandra Estévez, was recruited by the Political Police. She was a go-between for my mother and me, picking up letters I had smuggled out to various people in the city and taking them to my mother. Captain Liar's big mouth gave away the game, though. He had to show off how much he knew, and one day he hinted that I was probably going to be carried to a rehabilitation center where no one could visit me, *not even Alicia.* And he smiled and looked at me tellingly. Now, Alicia was the code name I had used for Sandra in my last letter to my mother. When Captain Liar puffed himself up and used the name, I knew the Political Police were intercepting my letters.

I immediately alerted my family that Sandra was working for the Political Police. I told them what they needed to do; from that moment on we would use her as a "disinformation agent" against the very masters she served. I prepared a "big operation"—there was an imaginary friend of mine who'd come to Cuba to give Sandra a miniature Minolta so she could take photos of the jail and of some documents, and also do other things that I asked of her. The authorities were so clumsy that Captain Liar himself would drive Sandra in a yellow Toyota, nice and inconspicuous, to pick up my letters. If I hadn't already discovered the game, one of my relatives who saw the man known in Havana for his almond eyes as El Chino would've soon smelled the rat. My relative saw Sandra and Captain Liar several times driving around to pick up the letters.

I soon led them to believe that I'd finished another book. It was being kept in a house (I didn't say where) and Sandra would pick it up to give my "friend" when he came to Cuba. I sent the authorities on wild-goose chases to nonexistent addresses or sometimes to the houses of people who I'd read in the newspapers were avid supporters of the Revolution. I had them running all over Havana for several months. I smiled at Sandra's notes asking me to tell her where the manuscript was—she kept telling me it would be safer in her hands till my friend came.

The day we decided to expose her, we set a trap. My sister led her to believe they'd hidden one of my letters to Martha behind a certain picture on the wall of my family's house. That afternoon Captain Liar showed up at my house, went directly to the picture Sandra had been told about, and looked for the letter. Two days later when Sandra came, my family confronted her with this indisputable evidence of her collaboration. She broke down and asked us to forgive her. She was crying and terrified. She confessed that Captain Liar had threatened to throw her in jail and send Grasini, her youngest son, to Camilitos, a military school-cum-reformatory, if she didn't cooperate.

Since my house was under constant surveillance I couldn't send anybody from the hospital or any personal friend with messages, or he'd wind up in jail. So I sent my letters to a woman with no link whatever with any prisoners. This woman, who had been a friend of the family for years, would take my letters to my house.

Some of the people in the hospital were helping me. These were people who because of their jobs could come and go as they pleased. The hateful reprisals that had been heaped on me awoke admiration, sympathy, compassion, and the desire to try to help me. Doing things for me was one small way of defying the regime. When I would tell people I'd gone seven years without a visit, that I was forbidden to send or receive letters or cards, they could hardly believe it. Many of them spontaneously volunteered to take letters to my family.

Once I showed one of the nurses a notebook for recording temperatures; I had filled it with drawings, and she and the other nurses went wild—they wanted me to draw for them too. They started visiting with Israel, Pedro, and me. When the Political Police found out that the nurses had in a sense befriended us, they immediately called everyone in the hospital together for a meeting in the auditorium and Captain Liar told them that we were working to undermine morale, that what we were doing was "ideological penetration." He forbade them to go to our cubicle.

Even so, some of them risked talking to us, even helping us. With the passing of the weeks—and seeing our treatment by the authorities—Isabel, that beautiful nurse with the green eyes, and I became friends. They couldn't keep her out of our room—she was our nurse. If a soldier suddenly appeared, she'd stop talking and busy herself taking temperatures or doing other sickroom jobs.

One day Isabel blurted, "Doesn't that man see that he's old enough to be my father? He doesn't even come up to my shoulders!"

It seems Colonel Blanco Fernández had been stalking Isabel from the first moment he'd laid eyes on her. It didn't matter to him in the least that she was a Party member and the wife of one of his subordinates. He hounded her, he tried to make her go out with him, he invited her to go dancing. She was getting fed up with the old man's impertinences.

Meanwhile, in June Martha went to Caracas as the first stop on a long journey that would take her all over the world seeking support for my release. In Caracas Dr. Tebelio Rodríguez introduced her on television. She also met Senator José Rodríguez Iturbe, who was to be one of the most important people engaged in the struggle for my release. He had already written one letter to Castro, signed by a majority of the members of the Venezuelan Congress, asking for my freedom. The former President of Venezuela Rómulo Betancourt also joined the campaign and offered Martha his valuable support and aid. In fact, all the democratic political parties, the press, and other institutions in Venezuela came out in my support. From Venezuela Martha went to Costa Rica.

Amnesty International committees and groups were working continuously on my behalf, as were Per Rasmussen's Group 110 in Sweden. Members of Parliament in Canada signed petitions. The campaign in support of my release was like a snowball. Castro swore that so long as the campaign continued, I'd never be released, and the errand boys from the Political Police kept bringing me the message with the same veiled threats as always.

I made a public response to these threats, in a letter addressed to Martha which said, "You can't drop the offensive. If they tell you they're going to

Ibrahim Torres. A victim of biological experimentation, he died in his prison cell.

Pedro Luis Boitel. A student leader and revolutionary, he was allowed to die while on a hunger strike, by the personal order of Castro.

Clara Abraham de Boitel. She was struck by Lieutenant Abad of State Security when she went to inquire where her son had been buried.

"Cuco" Cervantes. He died of asphyxiation in a closed trailer truck during a prison transfer.

Alfredo Carrión. A law student and a cellmate of Valladares, he was shot in the back and killed after an escape attempt. Lying wounded on the ground, he had asked the militiamen not to shoot him again.

René Silva. A victim of asphyxiation in the same truck as Cervantes, Silva had helped Cervantes breathe before succumbing himself.

Fernando Pruna and his wife. They joined anti-Castro rebels in 1959. Pruna was the closest witness to Eloy Gutiérrez Menoyo's beating in the quarry. They now live in Miami.

Roberto Martín Pérez Rodríguez. One of the longest-held prisoners in the world today, he was shot in the testicles at the Boniato massacre.

Julio Tan. Killed by bayonetting in forced-labor camp.

Román Abraham Aceituno. He was one of the most severely wounded in the beatings at Guanajay.

Eloy Gutiérrez Menoyo. A Spaniard and the head of the Second Front at Escambray against Batista, he was imprisoned because of Castro's personal grudge against him.

Manuel Márquez Trillo. Imprisoned with Valladares for years in the blackout cells at Boniato Prison, he is still in Boniato.

Ismael Domínguez. A cellmate of Valladares in prison hospital, he was also wheelchair-bound.

"Chaguito" González. He gave the "all clear" signal for the escape from Isla de Pinos. He now lives in Miami.

Jorge Portuondo. A squadmate of Valladares in forced-labor camp, he was one of the most seriously affected victims of Boniato's biological experiments. He now lives in Miami.

Oscar "Napoleoncito" Rodríguez. A prisoner in the drawer cells at San Ramón and Tres Macíos, he saved other prisoners by resisting. He lives in Miami.

"Chichi" del Valle. "Shot" by a firing squad with blanks, he was tortured for months and interrogated by Raúl Castro himself. He lives in Florida.

Alcides Martínez. Another heroic drawer-cell prisoner, he was tortured almost to the point of madness. He lives in Miami.

José Carreño. A survivor of the blackout cells at Boniato and of biological experimentation.

"Pepín" Varona. He gave the "raspberry" to Commander Suñol, who had been sent by Castro to threaten the prisoners. He lives in Miami.

Dr. Humberto Medrano. He was the first to present irrefutable proof of torture in Cuba to the United Nations. This same proof later disappeared from official files. He lives in Washington, D.C.

Sergio Bravo. He was shot in the leg in the search following Valladares' escape attempt. His leg was unnecessarily amputated.

Cdr. Jesús Carreras. Shot by a firing squad on the orders of Che Guevara, with whom he had argued.

Cdr. Julio García Olivera. He was in charge of the TNT planted on Isla de Pinos.

Ricardo Bofill. A Marxist dissident and head of the Committee for Human Rights in Cuba, he was sentenced to twelve years for an interview he gave to French reporters.

Cdr. Osmani Cienfuegos. Currently a member of the Party Central Committee, he ordered the prisoner transfer that resulted in asphyxiation.

Lt. Julio Tarrau. The director of prisons on Isla de Pinos, he was responsible for hundreds of mutilations, tortures, and deaths.

Ramón Ramudo. A Swedish-Spaniard and a member of the Swedish Socialist Party, he met Valladares in the punishment cells at La Cabaña. He also knew Robertico, the twelve-year-old prisoner there. He lives in Sweden.

Enrique Díaz Correa. He was wounded by nine bullets when he tried to help the Brother of the Faith. He lives in Miami.

Mario Chanes. One of the leaders of Castro's attack on the Moncada barracks, he is still in prison after more than twenty years.

Alfredo Izaguirre. The only prisoner who never worked at forced labor, he was beaten and bayonetted almost to death for his intransigence. He lives in Miami.

Roberto Perdomo. A revolutionary leader arrested the same day as Valladares. He told the director at Boniato he would never wear the uniform of common criminals—and he kept his word.

Thomas White. Sentenced to twenty-four years for overflying Cuba to drop religious pamphlets, he took photos of Valladares in a wheelchair. He now lives in California.

Benito López, Valladares' father-in-law. He now lives in Miami.

Eduardo Capote. A fighter against Batista. His hands were mutilated by machete blows in La Cabaña.

Dr. Alberto Vivas. He made a fool of the grandfatherly Political Commissioner. He lives in Venezuela.

Dr. Emilio Adolfo Rivero Caro. He was tortured for months to extract a confession and spent years in solitary confinement. He now lives in Washington, D.C.

Celestino Méndez. He planned a second escape attempt with Buría and Valladares. He now lives in Miami.

Carlos Betancourt. A journalist, he was a workmate at forced labor and a member of the group who "turned" the young Political Commissioner. He lives in Miami.

Pierre Golendorf. A French Communist Party member, he was imprisoned in Cuba. He translated Valladares' poetry into French. He lives in France.

Benjamín Brito. A guide in the attempted escape from Isla de Pinos. He now lives in Miami.

Vicente Socarrás. He was punished separately from the others, as was Valladares, in forced-labor camp. He witnessed Valladares' biting off the head of a snake. He now lives in Venezuela.

Mario Morfi. He almost drowned in the lake of sewage. He lives in Puerto Rico.

Orlando Peña. One of the survivors of the drawer cells, he was tortured severely. He lives in Miami.

Rogelio Villardefrancos. A telegraph operator, he helped maintain inter-Circular communications at Isla de Pinos. He lives in Miami.

Angel Loredo. A Catholic priest, he was brutally beaten in the quarries. He lives in Rome.

Julio Rodríguez Lamelas. Sentenced to six years, he was held for thirteen for refusing Political Rehabilitation. He lives in Venezuela.

Carlos Alberto Montaner. An essayist and writer, he attempted to escape with Valladares. He now lives in Spain.

Alicia Gambeta. A young woman Valladares met in the orthopedic hospital. Because of her friendship with him she was denied further medical treatment and expelled from Cuba.

A stupidly forged ID card was presented by the authorities. The color of my eyes was given as brown instead of black. My date of birth was given as my date of entry into the police force. And the date of birth alleged to be mine is given as 1936 instead of 1937. (In subsequent announcements, after it was proven that the birth date was wrong, the authorities simply cut off the offending number.) Finally, my height is given in meters and my weight in kilograms, whereas in the 1950s feet and inches and pounds were still being used in Cuba.

Shortly after, in 1981, in Information Bulletin No. 3, ICAP distributed (and continues to do so) a pamphlet signed by one Luis Adrián Betancourt of the ICAP press office entitled "Desde la silla del engaño" ("From the Deceitful Chair"). It was written to "properly inform the friends of Cuba abroad" about the Valladares case. Of course, the information in the pamphlet contradicts the information on the false ID card. The card clearly states that I joined the police force in May 1958, whereas the pamphlet says that I joined in October 1957.

have me shot and the only way to save me is to stop the denunciations, keep going. Don't stop for anything—for anybody."

Around that time the whole prison was plunged into mourning by the death of Rafael del Pino. Rafael had been one of Castro's closest allies when Castro was in Mexico preparing the Granma landing. They had shared a hotel room. One night Castro confided his plans for Cuba to Rafael, and Rafael was so shocked at their totalitarian aspect that he abandoned Fidel.

Castro never forgave Rafael that "betrayal," so when the Revolution came to power at last, Rafael was jailed. He had been wounded in an exchange of fire with the new authorities and had also been seriously burned. Rafael himself told us that even after ten years in prison Castro harbored the same old grudge against him.

Rafael had to be hospitalized frequently. Once he was in a cell in the Military Hospital recuperating from an operation. He had been catheterized and had an incontinence bag hanging beside him. One morning Castro suddenly showed up, chewing on a big cigar. He was surrounded by his escorts. He looked at Rafael, nodded approvingly, and said, "That's the way I like to see you, Rafael del Pino . . . just like that."

Rafael was the only American citizen that Castro wouldn't release, ever, in spite of the fact that there were no other charges against Rafael than his "desertion."

He was sick, so they told him they'd take him to the hospital, where a cubicle had been prepared for him. But inexplicably, on August 21 they transferred him to a solitary-confinement cell. Zúñiga and some other prisoners were in the adjoining cell. That night they heard several people's voices in the hallway, then an argument and the sound of scuffling. The next morning, August 22, 1977, Rafael del Pino's body was discovered hanging from the bars. The authorities said he had hanged himself with a sheet, but no one ever saw the body. The Ministry of the Interior flatly refused to turn it over to his family.

The heat in my cubicle was stifling, since the prefab walls were lined on the inside with iron sheets and the sun fell directly on the exterior walls for hours during the day. You couldn't even touch the walls—it was like being in an oven. Sweat poured off us. The only way to stand the heat was to get as close to the hallway bars as possible or take refuge in the bathroom. When you washed out your underwear, all you had to do was hang it on the beds close to the walls and it was dry in minutes. I knew the authorities kept us in those cruel conditions because of me, and I felt terrible that my cellmates had to suffer on my account. *They* stood up to *my* punishment stoically, though.

One of my denunciations reached the world outside Cuba, and the Cuban government was inundated with letters demanding humane treatment for me. So much fuss was raised that one afternoon the military chief of the hospital ordered the guards to open our bars. So another battle had been won against the prepotent Political Police, and that strengthened my feeling that if the outside pressure of international opinion was kept up long enough, and grew, Castro would have to release me whether he wanted to or not.

49 / Transfer to Orthopedics

For months Israel and I collected empty ampules, any little pieces of colored paper we could get our hands on, cellophane, anything at all that had a little color or was shiny—from the label off a medicine bottle to a discarded toothbrush to a plastic tube cap. We were going to have a Christmas tree.

Israel made some little people out of cotton balls, and I decorated eggshells and empty antibiotics bottles.

We didn't sleep the night of December 14. Conde, an engineer, and Angelito made a tree out of a broomstick and wire covered with bits of paper, and we all decorated it. It was beautiful. We decorated the room with poinsettias cut out of cardboard and dyed with Betadine.

When hospital Headquarters heard we had a Christmas tree, all hell broke loose. But before Director Campos could take action, dozens of people had come in to see it. Some nurses couldn't keep back their tears; seeing that Christmas tree of ours had brought back memories of the Christmases they had spent before Christmas was abolished by Castro's Revolution.

One of the nurses, Rita, exclaimed when she saw it, "That's the most beautiful Christmas tree I've ever seen in my life!"

The directors of the hospital tried to force me to take it down. I refused, arguing that it was a symbol of my beliefs. I told them we had invested love and a great deal of time in making the tree, and I wasn't about to destroy it. In the afternoon Lieutenant Páez Páez, the head of the Political Police, came around with some other officials to threaten Israel and me. They told us if we didn't take down the tree, we'd go to court on charges of theft; we'd be charged with stealing the State's cotton balls. But we wouldn't take it down, so they took it with them, to Headquarters, very carefully (to preserve the evidence?), on a motorcycle. An investigation was ordered. They wanted to find out who had supplied the broomstick, the wire, the cotton balls; and the Political Police interrogated all the nurses, the doctors, the prisoners who worked in the hospital. The hospital was in a state of siege until the matter was cleared up.

Just a few days after the Christmas-tree incident, Of Human Rights, an organization headquartered in Washington, D.C., which would play a central role in my liberation, got forty-nine United States Senators to sign a letter requesting Castro to free Húber Matos, Angel Cuadra, and me. Secretary of State Cyrus Vance delivered the letter.

It hadn't bothered me in the least when, the first time the authorities had come to take away my wheelchair, they'd given it to another sick man. But the second time, they told me that the wheelchair was common property. I went hours without being able to get out of bed. What's more, one of the wheels came off the wheelchair and the arms were broken. Therefore I requested one from Amnesty International in Holland. Dutch Red Cross negotiated with the director of the Cuban Red Cross, Dr. Luis Angel Torres Santragel. A Cuban ship picked up the wheelchair in Holland and the chair arrived the next week in Havana. A friend told me it was at the Red Cross offices. So I began asking for it.

But Captain Liar's interest in it was piqued, too. He came in one day and brazenly told me the chair had never arrived. I told him exactly where it was, describing the place in great detail. My mother also went to the Red Cross several times to ask them to turn the wheelchair over to me, and each time they had some excuse for her.

One day a man went to my house and told my mother he'd been talking to me and I'd decided to give up the wheelchair, to donate it to the Ministry of the Interior. He showed her a document he said needed her signature. But since my mother had learned to be suspicious of this sort of thing she refused to sign. The man was one of Captain Liar's henchmen.

The wheelchair had been sent care of my mother, so her refusal to sign the document blocked Captain Liar's attempt to confiscate the chair. Faced with that failure, though, Captain Liar didn't give up. He openly threatened my mother. He told her if she didn't sign over the wheelchair, if we kept trying to claim it, State Security would consider that counterrevolutionary activity, and she'd never leave the country. Never. It seems keeping the wheelchair had become a matter of principle for the Political Police.

They knew there was no dealing with me—that I'd never even consider calling off the international human-rights campaign. So they went back to my house to try to persuade my mother to write Martha a letter telling her to suspend the campaign, call off the dogs, as it were, let up on the pressure for my release. If she did, they told my mother, my family would be in the United States by December.

My poor deceived mother, old and full of hope, rose to the bait. But Martha had definite instructions—she wouldn't pay any attention to such a letter even if it came from *me;* it would be easy to forge my handwriting.

She wouldn't act on a telephone call, either—they might be imitating my voice. She would only listen to me about calling off the campaign if I was standing, in person, before her.

Since my mother's letter hadn't helped, then, they came to negotiate with me. They said they wanted to reach some mutually satisfactory solution and that the only obstacle to that was the campaign for my release and Martha's human-rights activity. My response to this ploy was to issue a further series of denunciations to Amnesty International and foreign newspapers and to smuggle out more material for my next book.

They kept pressuring my mother. They offered to let her out of the country so she could call off the campaign. They pointed out to her that she was my mother, that she had more authority to speak for me than my wife. What's more, they said, Martha didn't really want me free, since she was traveling all over the world, living very well at my expense. The police kept telling my mother that if she'd just listen to them, in a matter of six months from the end of the campaign, I and the rest of my family would be allowed out of Cuba. But that didn't work either. I was content, I was in no hurry. In eighteen years I had learned how to wait. I knew the snowball was growing bigger every day and the government would wind up in an avalanche. Time was on my side, and my faith gave me the strength and patience to wait the authorities out.

Sales, Ernesto Díaz, Cuadra, and I had managed to have our books published abroad. The government was outraged by what we were writing. One night Sales, Ernesto, and Fibla were taken to Political Police Headquarters and warned not to go on trying to organize intellectuals' support abroad. Ernesto told them we didn't have to ask their permission to publish our books. And in fact right there in those very cells he composed a collection of poems that he later published.

There was nothing else for the government to do. During one of his visits to the hospital, Captain Liar took out the emigration forms my family had filled out. I asked him what he was doing with them. They were supposed to be in the Immigration Department. He told me State Security was now in charge of such matters, by order of higher authorities. That of course meant that my family's leaving Cuba depended on my conduct. My family were hostages.

That very night I wrote Martha, telling her what was going on and asking her to publicize it. We couldn't let the snowball stop for a second.

Captain Liar devoted himself to going to the houses of many people who were friends of my family, warning people not to have any contact with me, or even to go to my house. He added that State Security knew they had helped get letters to and from me and that they'd be thrown in jail if they did it again. He also visited the families of prisoners who were or had been close friends of mine.

I'm virtually certain that somebody back in La Cabaña had been watching my every move and reporting to the Political Police. I changed "postal routes" often, and some people who had been helping me when I was in La Cabaña, but whom I hadn't employed in months, were visited by Captain Liar, while others I was now using weren't. So apparently the informer wasn't with me now, to give the Political Police up-to-date information, and since they didn't have the gift of second sight they were depending on old information. An incident in La Cabaña took on new meaning now: One day there was a general inspection and search. We invalids were separated from the other prisoners, but the only wheelchair searched was mine. The guards were waiting for me with screwdrivers. They took me out of the wheelchair and went directly to the seat. They opened the upholstery, into which I had carefully sewn letters, photocopies of foreign newspapers, and other documents. There was now no doubt somebody had seen me hide the papers and blown the whistle on me.

This latest Political Police offensive was aimed at shutting off all my routes of communication. It wasn't the right moment to shut me up in solitary confinement, so they used intimidation to reach the same ends. Even Martha's family, friends, and neighbors in Cuba were victims of the threats.

A group of high officials, led by General Enyo Leyva, First Vice-Minister of the Interior, came to the hospital one day. The general asked to see me, and Captain Liar came to take me to him. The general was drunk. This liking for drink, plus certain ideological weaknesses, was to be the cause of his later demotion. Finally he was sent to do farm work in Pinar del Río province.

He greeted me with a smile and, using the familiar *tu* with me, said, "I think that book of yours exaggerates some things, Valladares."

"It's not *my* book, General," I answered, smiling right back. "It's *our* book."

"What do you mean, 'our book'? I don't understand."

"Our book, General, because your side furnished the plot. All I did was write it down."

He laughed. "That's good. . . . The truth is that these"—and he indicated the officers standing all around—"are a bunch of jerks. You managed, right under their noses, to get through all the searches, get around all the obstacles, and get your book out. How long has it been since you've had a visit?"

"Eight years."

"Well, I'll give the order for you to be allowed a visit. Now you see how well we treat you; you can't say we beat you or torture you now. And we're going to take you to a hospital for treatment. Why don't you write a book about that?"

"I will, General, just as soon as the Revolution writes one of its own telling how we were beaten, tortured, and murdered in the forced-labor camps on Isla de Pinos and in Boniato Prison."

The general didn't bat an eyelash. He just said those things had happened years ago because of defects in political programs of the Revolution. Then, taking off his cap, he said, "Look, I'm two years younger than you are, and you look much younger. We can't have treated you so badly."

"The way I am *inside* has a lot to do with the way I look, General. You probably don't sleep as well as I do. That comes from having a clean conscience."

And so our conversation ended, because the general, not smiling anymore, looked at me with reddish eyes, an indecipherable expression on his face, and turned and asked one of his aides something as he walked away.

Days later, in October, Captain Liar came to get me for the so-often-promised transfer.

"He's going to Julito Díaz Hospital," he told my cellmates.

"I'm going to any hospital but that one," I turned and said to Izaguirre and the others. And so it turned out. They took me to the orthopedic clinic in El Vedado.

They had prepared a room for me by blocking up the windows with wood panels. The door was always closed, or in fact sealed, with a soldier armed with a machine gun seated in the hallway. Only one nurse, the head of the ward, was allowed to enter my room. She was absolutely trustworthy; her husband held the rank of commander in the Ministry of the Interior. Still, in spite of the authorities' best calculations, this nurse was touched by my situation. When the authorities discovered that she had some human feeling for me, they immediately took me out of that room and began to harass her. Captain Liar interrogated her and warned her never to have any contact with me again.

I wound up at Frank País Hospital. Meanwhile, the Cuban government set free twenty-eight sick and handicapped prisoners who had been in prison for twenty years. That would have been the perfect moment to release me. I would've been just one more of the thousands of people who left Cuba, my case would have achieved no more notoriety than anyone else's, and I'd be somewhere in the world with Martha trying to get my life together. But the Political Police were always my best public-relations agents—they demonstrated, day by day, the truth of my accusations.

In the new hospital my treatment was changed completely. The hospital equipped a room for me with a physiotherapy table, a Striker frame which tilted and rolled, and a hydrotherapy tank. They assigned Luis Manuel, a member of the Communist Youth and therefore a therapist they could trust, to give me my treatments. Dr. Alvarez Cambra, the director of the hospital, and Esperanza Ortíz, head nurse, both members of the Party Central Committee, attended me.

I could speak with anyone I wanted, I could go out into the grounds and get some sun, and a few weeks later I had a visit from my mother and sister. Given these concessions, I began to think I might actually be set free. Just as I'd done during the worst times, I wrote Amnesty International and other friends and told them about these changes.

One day one of the directors, Colonel Carlos, looked quite pleased to tell me that my name was now on one of Amnesty International's lists. He said I should never think the Cuban government wasn't affected by what that prestigious organization said. So I felt good about my prospects. And my physical condition was improving.

I wanted to find out whether my therapist was an informer for the Political Police, so one day when the guard wasn't in the room and we were alone, I mentioned that offshore radio had reported that my wife had had an interview with the Jamaican Prime Minister, Michael Manley. The next day Captain Liar came in to tell me my wife would get nowhere by seeing Manley. That confirmed that my therapist was reporting our conversations. I tested him one more time to be sure, with a letter I asked him to mail; he turned it over to Captain Liar, too.

Meanwhile the snowball was gaining momentum. The third edition of my book was published. The PEN Club of France took an interest in me and made me an honorary member of its chapter. The new President of Venezuela, Herrera Campíns, included my case on the agenda for talks to be held with Havana and instructed the Venezuelan ambassador to Cuba to get in touch with my family. The Venezuelans had already brought up the matter of my release with Castro once before, but Castro told José Rodríguez Iturbe that I wouldn't be released until I could walk again. Castro would see to it that I was the only prisoner who would never be released from Cuba in a wheelchair.

Of Human Rights had sent a new letter, also signed by dozens of United States Congressmen, requesting my release. Committees dedicated to the same end were founded in several countries in Europe. Castro was furious. He told a group of Venezuelan members of Parliament that the Revolution wouldn't tolerate outside pressure and that I would not be released until the campaigns in support of me were ended.

In spite of these declarations, the Cuban government was obviously trying to negotiate; the Cuban embassy in Venezuela sent Martha a message saying that if she requested it I would be released, so Martha went to Caracas to meet the Cuban Consul General, Amado Soto. She went to the appointment with Amado Soto accompanied by our friend Senator José Rodríguez Iturbe, who next term would be chairman of the Senate Foreign Relations Committee in Venezuela. At that time relations between Cuba and Venezuela were more than a little strained, so when Norberto Hernández, the Cuban ambassador, saw Rodríguez Iturbe in the embassy, he turned on his brightest smile and offered his hand. Hernández was elated by the illustrious senator's visit.

"A great pleasure, Senator. To what do we owe the honor of seeing you?"

"My visit is not official, Ambassador, but rather officious. I have come to accompany Señora Valladares."

The bright smile of the Cuban ambassador flickered and died.

Martha's interview with Consul Soto was brief. He proposed that she publish a letter retracting everything that had been said about me and that she prohibit international organizations, journalists, and intellectuals from discussing my case. In return, the Cuban government would promise to free me within a few weeks. Martha refused his terms.

My treatment continued, full speed ahead. I could already stand with the help of braces to keep my knees from buckling and could hold myself up between parallel bars. In the afternoons, always accompanied by a guard, I went out into the grounds and talked with other patients. I met two young girls who had had polio, Alicia and María Luisa, who made my stay in the hospital a happy, tender time. I made a subversive miniature Christmas tree for them and packed it in a box they opened on the sly in their room.

I was receiving special treatment. I was in the section of the hospital reserved for foreigners and athletes. There were Sandinistas recovering from operations, Angolans, Yemenites. Athletes and foreigners were the only patients allowed such treats as yogurt and butter—in the other wards, where the "pueblo," the "common folk," were, there were no snacks or special food. And we had air conditioning, a luxury no patients but the children enjoyed.

I had been suffering from an asthma attack for two days and I was almost asphyxiated. I really could hardly breathe at all. There was no emergency room in the hospital, so a guard and a nurse went with me to the Military Hospital. The nurse had to keep pumping my chest the whole trip to help me breathe. When we arrived my face was red and I was gasping for air. They immediately put me on a Mark 8 artificial respirator with oxygen and gave me medication intravenously. When we got back to Frank País Hospital the nurse was called on the carpet for having gone with me. It did her no good to say she'd gone for humanitarian reasons. She tried to explain, too, that since it was her shift, the doctor had ordered her to go with me, that in my condition I needed a trained person to go with me, not just a soldier. Dr. Humberto Barrera, a Party official, cut her off: "So he'd have died! Wouldn't've been any great loss, would it, now?!"

In spite of all they could do, in spite of all their predictions that nobody would dare get near the "prisoner," the authorities began to realize that a circle of admiration and sympathy was growing up around me. Nurses, patients, employees, and the children I drew pictures for were my friends.

The antihero became a hero. So Captain Liar went to the children's ward and told the mothers who were there that I'd been sent to prison for dynamiting day-care centers. The mothers laughed when they told me what Captain Liar had said.

To keep this ticklish situation from getting more out of hand than it already was, the hospital directors put me in a room right next to the director's office. We shared a bathroom. That way I could be controlled and isolated. But I would sit in the window of my second-floor room, overlooking the hospital grounds, and nurses, employees, and children would wave to me and call hello; all the children knew my name. On March 2, 1978, Enrique Otero, a Party leader, tried to put a stop to this, too; he called everyone to a meeting in the hospital and told them he wanted those people who were waving to me and greeting me to stop immediately.

But Alicia, my pretty little Peruvian friend, still waved from her wheelchair and said hello, every afternoon. Esperanza Ortíz, the chief nurse, told Alicia I was a criminal.

"I've never known a nicer man," Alicia said. And she kept waving to me. But within a few days Alicia was informed she had to leave the hospital. They notified her family. Alicia was declared to be insufficiently grateful to the Revolution for her care. Before she left, Alvarez Cambra paid her a visit and told her she was not to mention my name outside Cuba.

Customs guards tried to search Alicia before she left Cuba, but following my instructions she refused and demanded to see a member of the Peruvian embassy. She was carrying a letter for Martha, and she succeeded in getting it through.

Not even nurses could come upstairs where I was now confined. Every day the guard brought me little envelopes with the pills I was to take and a list of the times for taking them. They installed an oxygen tent and left ampules of medicine for my asthma, so when an asthma attack came over me I had to break the ampules and prepare the inhalants and set the timer, all the time wheezing and gasping for breath.

Visitors that the directors themselves had authorized were detained by the Political Police, interrogated, and sent home terrified. The authorities postponed my mother's visit for months.

I went on with my treatment, though. They had set up parallel bars and a physiotherapy table in my room. A new therapist was sent, this time a pretty young woman who was a militant in the Communist Youth. They also replaced Captain Liar.

Finally my family were told they could leave the country. But when everything was ready and they had their flight number and their bags were packed, the exit visa was revoked. A few days afterward, Colonel Carlos and Captain Liar's replacement came in to tell me my family would be allowed to leave Cuba if I wrote a letter renouncing my friends abroad and forbidding anyone—individuals, newspapers, and organizations—from discussing my case or publishing my books. I was also to deny everything that had been written or said in my support. I very calmly told them that I would never write such a letter.

"Well, then, your family will never leave Cuba," the colonel told me.

After months of delays my mother and sister were allowed to visit me. When they came to the hospital, my guard was notified and he went down to the lobby. This was a man who often bragged about the beatings he'd given prisoners in the forced-labor camps. Without any rhyme or reason, he told my mother and sister they couldn't come up to see me. He talked to them rudely, he shoved them, and finally shouted at them to get lost. He didn't care that my mother was an old woman, that it had been months since these two women had seen me, or since I had seen them. He said if they didn't leave he'd call a police car and have them arrested. By coincidence there was a foreign delegation in the lobby at the time, representatives of the Commission for the Year of the Child led by Stefanía Abdaba Lim from the Philippines, Sub-Secretary General of the United Nations. This occurred on May 9, 1979.

The Cuban government had now freed more than two thousand political prisoners, with hundreds of common prisoners mixed in among them. And the government was lying, saying that no other political prisoners were included because those who remained in the prisons were terrorists. When the display window was boarded up again, then, we prisoners found ourselves in the same old conditions—a new wave of repression rolled through all the jails and prisons of Cuba. A hundred political prisoners, stripped of all their possessions, were transferred to the blackout cells at Boniato.

But at the same time a man who called himself Commander David began broadcasting over a clandestine radio station, urging resistance and struggle against Castro. Dozens of young people began fighting in underground groups. Anti-Communist and anti-Castro signs and graffiti began appearing in Havana. In Pinar del Río province, nine tobacco-storage houses were burned. Factories and movie theaters were torched in Havana. Anti-Castro leaflets were scattered through the streets. This activity brought on hundreds of arrests. A few months later when I was once again in prison, I would meet many of the people responsible for these "counterrevolutionary" acts.

In the jail in Pinar del Río and in the prison called Kilo 7 in Camagüey, political prisoners were beaten and sent to solitary confinement, left wounded without medical care. On one single night, firing squads assassinated six young men in La Cabaña.

An intellectual congress in Paris named me Honorary President; my good friend from La Cabaña Pierre Golendorf founded a committee for my release, which prestigious intellectuals joined, among them Fernando Arrabal, Bernard-Henri Lévy, Eugène Ionesco, and the actor Yves Montand.

Friends from Venezuela kept up the pressure on the Cuban government; a high-level commission from Venezuela visited my house, and Dr. Rodríguez Iturbe, Leopoldo Castillo, and other officials saw for themselves the Political Police persecution and harassment my relatives were subjected to. They were not allowed to see me, in spite of their repeated requests. But in the talks held with Cuba aimed at improving relations between the two countries, Venezuela made my case a central issue, so much so that months later when César Rondón Lovera, Venezuelan ambassador to Cuba, announced the arrival of a new negotiating committee, Carlos Rafael Rodríguez, ex-Minister in the Batista regime, and now a Minister under Castro, asked Rondón whether Rodríguez Iturbe would be a member of the new committee.

"Of course he will. Why?" the ambassador responded.

"Because instead of dealing with matters of mutual interest, Dr. Rodríguez Iturbe is only interested in one thing. From the moment he sets foot in Cuba he never stops asking, 'What about Valladares? What about the poet Valladares?' I'm beginning to see Valladares even in my soup."

Ambassador Rondón Lovera smiled and reminded Carlos Rafael Rodríguez that I *was* one of Venezuela's interests. "Why don't you release him, put a stop to this unpleasant situation?" he added.

Rodríguez shook his head. "Valladares is Fidel's prisoner. Fidel's the only one who can make that decision."

Meanwhile I never stopped doing my exercises. I had graduated from the long braces to braces that came up only to my calves. I was walking down the parallel bars, doing almost all the work with my leg muscles. In three or four months, I thought, I'd be able to walk without the help of braces or crutches or canes.

In March 1980 my book *El Corazón en que vivo (The Heart in Which I Live)* came out. It was a book of poems, stories, anecdotes, and some documents, and it set off a wave of hysteria through Political Police Headquarters. It was a tough pill for them to swallow. One night Colonel "Mano" burst into my room. There were six or eight other officers with him. One of the officials took photos. Mano was practically frothing at the mouth.

"You're going back to prison!" His lower lip was quivering, his whole body shook with rage. "Let's go!"

I understood—what he really wanted to do was beat me, but they'd given him instructions not to. Otherwise he'd never have been able to control himself.

I moved toward the nightstand to pick up my things, but the colonel stopped me. "You can't touch anything in this room."

"What about the things that belong to me?" I had some underwear and socks and a few other things that I wanted to take with me.

"We'll turn everything over to your family." They wouldn't even let me take my toothbrush.

Surrounded by the angry group of officials, I was taken out of the room. Two of the officials carefully carried the wheelchair. As we went down the stairs, the camera clicked and whirred nonstop. At the back of the hospital several patrol cars were waiting.

Mano and a Captain Lester stayed behind to search my room and take charge of the booty, very desirable articles such as Gillette razor blades, socks, underwear, pullovers (some new), cologne, handkerchiefs, pens, all of which Martha had sent to my mother through some diplomatic-corps friends.

The officials who took me back to prison were very polite, but apart from that no one spoke a word the whole trip. We drove around in circles for about an hour, which I couldn't understand, until a code word came over the radio and we took off like a shot for Combinado del Este.

At the prison, the photographer was waiting for us again. I was taken to a room at the end of the hallway in ward C in the prison hospital. They had set up parallel bars, a physiotherapy table, and—a thing I never thought I'd live to see—the wheelchair from Amnesty International in Holland! The photographer took photos of me beside the wheelchair. At last, after years of claiming it, my constant pecking away at them had forced them to turn the chair over to me.

When they left, closing the barred door that cut off my access to the hallway, the men in the ward came over to say hello. We talked for a good while. Then I tried to get out of the old wheelchair and into the new one and discovered the new one's tires were flat and there was no pump to inflate them with. They had given it to me, all right, and taken my picture with it, but I couldn't use it.

The next day I saw the hospital director, Lieutenant Odisio Fernández, and asked him to send a therapist so I could go on with my treatment. I was happy to be back with my friends, and above all to have the equipment I needed for my exercises. But my enthusiasm suffered quite a blow when Fernández told me Colonel Blanco Fernández, Mano himself, had ordered that I not be given physical therapy. It seems they were trying a new tack; they were going to use the photos to show I refused to do exercises. Back to the old system of reprisals, then; they were exercising their power to perpetrate lies with absolute impunity.

It was at that moment that Castro, angry and indignant that a group of Cubans had forcibly taken asylum in the Peruvian embassy, decided to withdraw the troops guarding that embassy and the other embassies of the free world in Havana. Castro had paranoid fits, which had already led him to declare that the CIA was sending hurricanes against Cuba and bombarding Cuba with fungus and mold that attacked the tobacco and sugar-cane crop. Now he was so sure the embassy incident was staged that he even believed only a few people would take asylum in the Peruvian embassy if he took away the troops. A man could not have been more mistaken—ten thousand residents of Havana invaded the grounds of the embassy within a matter of hours, students, workers, soldiers, professional men and women. Five thousand more were arrested in the streets around the embassy, among them humble campesinos, with a bundle slung over their shoulders, their wives and children following along, who would be arrested when they asked someone directions to the Peruvian embassy.

To top even that public-relations disaster, Castro invited Cuban exiles in Miami to come to Cuba and get their relatives who wanted to leave the island. An exodus of some 140,000 people was the result, and 600,000 more names remained on a "waiting list." But among the first to leave were many common prisoners, since Castro wanted to give the world the impression that the only people out of step with the Revolution were criminals, drug addicts, and the like. The authorities even took prisoners out of jails, made up papers to show they had been in the crowds at the Peruvian embassy, and shipped them off to the United States.

I could see the prison yard of Building 2 from my room, and I watched Lieutenants Calzada and Salcines call prisoners who wanted to leave Cuba and tell them to make a line. Many prisoners left, though many stayed in Cuba for personal reasons—some because they didn't want to leave their families behind forever, and some because they figured this was a trap. Even so, the garrison made other prisoners come out and get into line. Many of the prisoners who had been forced to leave came back in flimsy boats months later to get their wives and children. Some of them wound up in the hospital, where I met them. A year later the Cuban government took them out into the middle of the ocean in rickety little boats, abandoned them with nothing but a couple of casks of water, and told them to head for the United States. Some twenty of those men drowned; only a few made it to terra firma on the Florida beaches, their families still in Cuba.

One event during this period of exodus affected me very strongly. Carmen López was one of the best nurses we had. She was, to say the least, disaffected with the system. So when we heard her voice shouting, "Go, then! Go, then!" louder than anyone in an "act of repudiation" staged by the Party, we were all surprised. She was one of the last people you'd ever think would scream at people who were finally getting their chance to escape Cuba.

The next day it all came clear. It had been a ruse on Carmen's part—she was trying to throw up a smokescreen. But Dr. Margollez saw her at Mariel, told the Political Police, and they stopped Carmen just as she was about to board a boat bound for Miami.

In California, a man named Thomas White was convalescing after an operation for stomach cancer. When he was alone, he'd stand up, pick up his IV bottle, and walk all around the room. He was getting back in shape. He asked to be released, but the doctors didn't think it was time yet. But White knew the day for his last mission to Cuba was coming up, so he just walked out of the hospital.

With his pilot, Melvin Lee, a Vietnam veteran, he took off for Cuba, where he was to drop his load not of bombs but of Christian leaflets. Tom White was going to spread the word of God to thousands of Cuban campesinos.

A storm forced the plane down near a village in the south part of Oriente province, and the two men were captured by the authorities. A few leaflets stuck to the fuselage and scattered through the plane were the evidence for their arrest. After long interrogation the two men were sentenced to twenty-four years in prison for distributing religious propaganda.

When I found out they were right there in Combinado del Este I wrote a note to Tom White thanking him for his truly Christian sacrifice. He belonged to a group called Christ for the Communist World, which refused to let its evangelical work be stopped by any danger. Tom knew about me and the other prisoners through the American media. When he got my letter he somehow found a way to come to my ward to visit me.

I was asleep when I heard somebody calling to me from the barred door. It was Tom White. He told me he'd pictured me as a bent-over old man, white-haired and tottering. I told him I'd pictured him in much the same way. Tom was a typical young American—tall, thin, blond, with bright eyes behind his glasses. He was thirty-one years old, married to a Costa Rican woman; they had two beautiful boys. I was touched by his Christian life, his simplicity, his kindness of heart, his generosity, and his integrity at the most difficult times.

We became great friends within days. We spent hours talking. He had an incredible ability—and his icewater blood helped—to go down to the first floor where sick men from other jails were brought in and to slyly pick up and take letters.

"But that's what I'm here for," he'd say to me, "to infiltrate!" And he'd grin.

When I got a camera to take pictures of my cell, it was Tom who took the pictures. A common prisoner informed on us, however, and the Political Police burst into my cell looking for the camera. They went through everything and finally left with two rolls of unused film they had found. But not the camera. One of the doctors was keeping it for me, and when the search was over he returned it to me—he was worried the police might even search *him.* Then some friends hid it in the soldiers' bathroom. The hospital was declared under a state of siege, all the posts were doubled, and everyone coming in or going out was searched. The Political Police even used dogs, but they couldn't find the camera.

A few days later a common criminal named Hernán, collaborating with the garrison, climbed up on the roof and looked through an opening in the exhaust vent, where he found the camera.

The Political Police went to unprecedented lengths then to try to find the film. They stripped men and women alike, they searched everyone. But Tom White managed to sneak it through all the searches and get it into Martha's hands. And the first photos of me in my wheelchair were published.

It was a hard blow for the Political Police. They returned it to me with interest later, of course. I knew they would, but I was elated—I'd managed to show they weren't infallible.

50 / Hospital Inhumanity

Again I managed to break through my isolation from the world. Friends smuggled out a little poem of mine to Martha, and Martha sent it on to the groups from Amnesty International working on my case. In France the author Edouard Manet arranged to have one of my poems read at a play. The poem, which relates the shooting at Boniato, provoked a great controversy—it tells such a monstrous story that many supporters of Castro refused to believe what they were hearing. The French chapter of the PEN Club awarded me its Liberty Prize.

In Sweden, Britt Arenander, secretary of the PEN Club in that country, publicized my case in great detail with a book titled *The Valladares Case (Fallet Valladares)*. Because of the book and Britt's personal gestures on my behalf, the Swedish PEN Club made me an honorary member.

The colonels of the Political Police were infuriated once more, and once more they made the mistake of increasing the repression against me, thereby giving me even more cause to continue denouncing them.

On February 5, officers burst into my cell and demanded that I go with them to have a conversation with the director of the hospital. I tried to refuse, but one of them twisted my arm. Literally. I decided to go. As I left, hidden photographers from the Political Police filmed me. I discovered them when I came back.

Two days later, February 7, more photographers came to my cell, carrying not only cameras but also strong floodlights. I figured there hadn't been enough light and their pictures hadn't turned out. They took me out into the hallway, but I tried to go back into my room. With all the cameras trained on me, Lieutenant Calzada grabbed the wheelchair by the handles and pulled me back; as I turned to try to knock his hands away, he gave me a karate chop in the neck and I lost consciousness.

My companions told me later that doctors came running and said my pulse was very fast, 160 per minute. Instead of putting me in bed they took me out into the ward. They put an oxygen mask on me and injected some sort of medication into my arm.

When I began to recover, one of the Political Police officers shook me and told me to open my eyes and raise my head. But I was so drugged that I slumped over in the wheelchair, so the officer grabbed one of the spotlights, pulled me up by the towel I had draped around my neck, and said to the others, "Let's see if this doesn't make him raise his head!"

Slowly he brought the spotlight nearer and nearer. The heat was almost unbearable.

"Help me, God!" I cried out internally. I decided the spotlight wasn't hot; it was a block of ice. "It's cold, it's cold," I kept repeating to myself. I made a superhuman effort to trick my senses. I don't know how long it all lasted, but for me it seemed centuries until my torturer finally got so angry at not being able to make me do what he wanted that he jammed the spotlight against my throat. I didn't move. A piece of my skin stayed on the metal reflector.

"Get this son of a bitch out of my sight!"

That was the last thing I heard, and the soldiers' boots the last thing I saw, because I kept hanging my head to the side until they left me in my room and I knew I was alone. The next day I had a huge blister from the spotlight. The doctor who examined me said it was a first-degree burn.

Months later Major Guido calmly told me the burn didn't constitute torture because the officer hadn't intended to burn me, he just wanted to make me raise my head—and anyway the burn was just first-degree. If it had been third-degree, it would've been torture, or if the officer had burned me intentionally.

On March 14 the new director, Colonel Edmigio Castillo, brought in a large platoon of guards and forcibly stripped the yellow uniforms off the rest of the political prisoners. So we were all naked. But the repression went on—those of us who had not worn uniforms since 1967 had our T-shirts, pullovers, and sheets taken away from us, so all we had was one pair of underwear. They refused chronically ill men their medication, even emergency medication, and they broke Roberto Montenegro's nose and split open his eye in a beating in the punishment cells. Ex-Commander Mario Chanes, who had assaulted the Moncada barracks with Castro, been in prison with him, and accompanied him on the Granma landing, was brutally beaten by the garrison and literally dragged to the punishment cells.

Sergeant Medina was as strong as an ox. He didn't have any neck; his square thick head seemed to grow directly out of his shoulders. One day as a visit was ending and the family members were standing, as always, in a long line waiting for the prisoners to be counted so they could leave, a woman called out to her son across a green area. Many prisoners would stand in the windows and wave handkerchiefs to their relatives, so they could wait until the last moment to say goodbye. But this woman was so filled with grief at leaving her son behind those bars and so wanted to stay close to him awhile longer that as she waved her handkerchief and cried, "My son! My son!" she began running toward the building. They could have grabbed her by the arm or even taken her to the hospital and given her a sedative, but Sergeant Medina ran to stop her. She didn't hear him, or perhaps in her grieving hysteria was beyond paying any attention to him. Sergeant Medina caught her, grabbed her by the shoulders, and began slapping her until finally he knocked her to the ground.

A roar of anger broke from the buildings. Prisoners were yelling "Coward!" "Murderer!" Her son threw himself against the bars, trying to get at Sergeant Medina. When the soldiers came, he was so maddened he attacked them. Within seconds he too was beaten to the ground.

Around that time the American movie *Jaws* was a big hit; people were talking about it even in Cuba. We gave Sergeant Medina its Spanish title as a nickname-cum-epithet. We called him the Bloody Shark.

The afternoon of April 2, Sergeant Medina rushed into my cell with some members of the garrison and practically lifted me up, wheelchair and all. He dragged me out of the chair and threw me against the wall.

"I'm gonna pick you up and bounce you off this floor!" he raged at me —and I thought for sure he was going to do just that. They'd come to "search"—they took all my possessions away from me, but they were especially interested in my writings. Five days later Lieutenant Castillo had me taken out of the hospital and put into the punishment-cell pavilion. Once again, they were cranking up the reprisals against me.

The building has three hallways, with cells along only one side. To enter you first have to open a wooden door onto a sort of small foyer or entry, then open the cell door itself. There is a skylight in the high ceiling of the entry. They put me in that first cell, directly off the entry. There was a concrete bench to sleep on, and the latrine was a hole in the floor. (Two days later they gave me a wooden box with a hole in it to use as a toilet.) The wheelchair took up all the free space. At night the room was in total darkness, and as soon as it got dark and all through the night, swarms of mosquitoes seemed to dive for the attack from the skylight above. I found it almost impossible to sleep.

Almost all the sixty-seven men down my hallway had been sentenced to death and were waiting to be shot by the firing squads. They had been accused of both common and political crimes. When I left, only thirteen were still alive, and they were executed soon after.

The men who served the food and did the cleaning were common prisoners. I had always tried to talk to and make friends with those men, especially the young prisoners, some of whom hadn't yet been born when I was imprisoned. The news spread like wildfire through their ranks that I had been sent to the punishment cells. It spread then through the entire prison, because we had organized these young men into groups by building and by floor so they could help us get letters, books, and magazines from the outside and also pass them from prisoner to prisoner.

I spent the second night and many succeeding nights in my wheelchair. I hadn't been able to sleep on the cement slab, I'd been having asthma attacks and I had no medication for them, so I sat up. At last I was so exhausted from sleeping sitting up, coughing all the time, that I had to lie down—my body demanded it, even if I had to lie on what seemed to be a fakir's bed of nails.

The cleaning brigade had managed to get some newspapers in to me; I used them for protection against the mosquitoes. I tossed and turned and didn't sleep well at all.

One night something suddenly caught my eye in the darkness—two bright-green blurs. They were the eyes of a rat. I sat up startled. I immediately remembered that other rat in Isla de Pinos that had gnawed my fingers. Sewer rats are huge. They come in through drainpipes or the latrine holes, which were four inches in diameter in the pavilion. Nothing makes you more nervous than being in a pitch-dark cell with silent, stalking, hungry rats. There's no way you can get back to sleep; you keep jumping awake, thinking they're about to bite you. Sometimes several came in, and if they're really starving they do attack.

I blocked their entrance by stuffing shoes into the latrine hole. I felt better then, almost elated. Sometimes in a bad situation, the least relief, the least achievement, can make you feel infinitely better.

I didn't try to contact anyone then; I knew someone would come to *me.* Your contact should always come to you if possible, not vice versa, and you can never get desperate to break out of your forced isolation or you'll wind up trusting a stool pigeon. It was Eduardo Delgado who contacted me. Delgado had been studying medicine; he and Raudel Rodríguez, who was studying mathematics, had decided to found an organization whose aim was changing the social and political structure of Cuba. They were both post-Revolutionary babies, had been educated along Marxist lines and been members of the Communist Youth, and were now twenty-one years old. They had been sentenced to death. They were in cells on the same hall I was, waiting the result of their appeal. That is to say, their lives were in the hands of the President of the State Council, Castro's hands, and he would order them shot. They sent me paper and a pencil. I found out from Delgado that a Swedish-Spaniard named Ramón Ramudo was held there, too, accused of being a CIA agent. I wrote him immediately; he knew who I was already from having read European news reports.

51 / Robertico

The days passed identically; the only thing that broke the monotony was the transfer of prisoners from the cells to the firing squad.

The violence in the pavilion was wildly out of control. There were sessions of beatings every day, directed by Lieutenant Mejías. They took the men out of their cells into the anteroom at the entrance, so from my cell just a few feet away I could hear the crack of the bayonets and machetes across the prisoners' naked backs. I shuddered at the savageness of the beatings.

One afternoon I heard moans from an adjoining cell, and then the voice of what sounded like a baby. "Get me out of here! Get me out of here! I want my mama!"

I thought my ears were playing tricks on me. I couldn't conceive that a child had been put into the punishment area.

"Get me out of here! Get me out of here! I want my mama! I want to see my mama!" The cries were heartbreaking. There *was* a child in that cell. Days later I found out Robertico's story.

He was twelve years old. Three or four months before he'd been walking down the street by himself when he noticed a car with its windows open and doors unlocked, parked next to the curb. There was a pistol on the seat. Robertico picked it up and was playing with it. Like a cowboy or big-city cop, he'd aim it at imaginary enemies or into the air, to shoot a warning shot. Much to his surprise, the gun went off.

A commander in the Ministry of the Interior, the careless man who'd left his pistol on the seat of an open car, ran outside when he heard the shot. He saw Robertico standing there paralyzed with shock from the pistol shot. He took the pistol away from him, slapped him, and carried him to the police station.

Robertico was sentenced to jail until he had reached his majority. He was sent off to Combinado del Este. Because prisoners are not classified in Cuba, he was put into a cell block with the worst kinds of criminals. Within a few days Robertico had been raped repeatedly. He had to be taken to the hospital with severe rents and hemorrhage. When he was released from the hospital, his file had been stamped with the word "homosexual."

It seems to me there have been few examples of repression of homosexuals in history as virulent as in Cuba. Homosexuals were persecuted, hunted down, harassed. The Revolution unleashed all its fury on them. Men would be arrested in the street solely for the way they walked or for wearing tight pants or for powdering their faces.

They were taken off by the thousands to Camagüey province, where concentration camps had been built called UMAPs, for Unidades Militares de Ayuda a la Producción—in English, "Military Units for Aid to Production." In the concentration camps the regime collected "malcontents" *(desafectos a la Revolución),* Jehovah's Witnesses, Seventh-Day Adventists, Catholic priests and laymen, and gays.

These were forced-labor camps, and the government had decided that the Catholic Church had to send groups of five priests to labor. Among the priests who went there were the current rector of San Carlos and San Ambrosia Seminary, Monsignor Alfredo Petit Vergel; the current Archbishop of Havana, Monsignor Jaime Ortega Alamino; and many other notable members of the clergy.

Pressure was put on the regime from abroad by Jean-Paul Sartre, Gian Giacomo Feltrinelli, Carlos Franqui, and others to try to get Castro to do away with the UMAP forced-labor camps. When he finally did do this, homosexuals were dispersed to jails all across the island, but they were generally put into sections of the jails reserved exclusively for them. I saw these sections myself, in Castillo del Príncipe, in Boniato, and in Combinado del Este.

Robertico was sent to one of those sections even though he was not a homosexual. He was so small and frail that he could slip between the bars. One night he squeezed out of his cell to go watch cartoons on the soldiers' television set, and when the soldiers caught him they threw him into a punishment cell, though they had to take him out three times a week for injections, since he had contracted a venereal disease when he was raped. One of the soldiers told me he didn't even have pubic hair yet.

Every day as it got dark Robertico would get so scared and lonely that he'd start crying. "Get me out of here! I want my mother!" Surely the men in the surrounding cells, some hardened criminals, softened when they heard that poor child's voice. They must have thought of their own wives and children, who might, like Robertico, wind up there. That was no doubt why a roar of indignation rose from the cells the night the guards, made nervous by Robertico's weeping, went into his cell to beat him. Later Lieutenant Mejías forbade the soldiers to beat Robertico with bayonets or chains since he was so little. He said they could beat him only with braided ropes.

· · ·

A few weeks later Lieutenant Mejías informed me I had been found guilty *in absentia* by a military tribunal for writing letters and poetry. I was given an indefinite sentence in the punishment cells. I had managed to organize a communications network between me, my friends, and some common prisoners. But there was no contact between the isolation cells and the rest of the prison, so often I had to wait for communications until a prisoner who had finished his sentence was released from the punishment area. We needed a drop point, too, so we chose the prison dump for a "post office." I could manage to get mail every afternoon that way, when the trash was carried out.

I often received notes from Eduardo Delgado and Raudel Rodríguez, who were still in cells along my hallway. Every time a prisoner was taken to the firing squads, they could feel their turn coming nearer. One day Eduardo's note contained the words, "Dying for your country is only comparable to living for it." And that was true—for them, living had become torture, waiting to be shot, but who knew when? They were living, waiting to die for their country. Eduardo had asked me to write his mother when I got out of isolation, to tell her about his last days. I believe Ramudo took Eduardo's last letters with him to Sweden.

My communications network was functioning very well. Anytime one of Martha's declarations was broadcast, the clandestine radio would pick it up and I'd find out about it. But one day the guards did something unprecedented—they came to my cell, searched it, and took away my pencil and paper, which was not unusual, but then they brought in a carpenter and put a lock on the hallway's wooden door. They'd never done that before. They posted a special guard over me, with the keys hanging on a cord around his neck.

I had managed to salvage a razor blade and a sheet from a prescription pad from the search. I cut a sliver off the wooden seat of my wheelchair, sharpened it, cut one of my fingers, and squeezed out drops of blood onto the sliver. I now had pen, ink, and paper again. I wrote a poem with my own blood. In spite of my isolation, in spite of this latest attempt to keep me incommunicado, and in spite of the potential reprisal, I wrote the poem, and a friend dared smuggle it out to Martha. It was translated and published in several languages. It was the last poem I wrote in prison:

> *They've taken everything away from me*
> *pens*
> *pencils*
> *ink*
> *because they don't want*
> *me to write*
> *and they've sunk me here*
> *in this cell*

but they aren't going to drown me
that way.

They've taken everything away from me
—or almost everything—
I still have my smile
the proud sense that I'm a free man
and an eternally flowering garden
in my soul.

They've taken everything away from me
pens
pencils
but I still have life's ink
—my own blood—
and I'm still writing poems with that.

When Major Guido, a huge potbellied man like a sumo wrestler, Lieutenant Mejías, and some other officers came to my cell and told me to get my things together, I was being transferred, I thought my stay in the punishment cells was over. But as soon as Guido viciously said to me, "We'll see whether you keep writing," I suspected there was still more punishment to come. And I was right.

52 / Ultimate Isolation

When we got to the hospital I noticed nobody was around. Everybody had been shut up, it seems, including the nurses and employees. The hallways were deserted.

There was an iron grating over the opening that was supposed to be the elevator door. They'd been waiting for five years for the bureaucratic machinery to process a requisition for an elevator they'd needed since 1976, but it had never been included in the budget. Patients who had just been operated on had to be carried up and down the stairs on stretchers. The guards carried me upstairs in my wheelchair.

On the second floor we turned left, toward Ward F. It had been evacuated. We walked down the ward to the end, to a room about twelve feet square. It was painted a bright, bright white—walls and ceiling—and there were ten long fluorescent tubes in the ceiling. A bed and night table were the only furniture. Fat Guido smiled. His eyes sparkled. He seemed to be enjoying in advance whatever the repressive brains of the Political Police had invented for me.

I would spend more than a year in that room, and in terms of psychological torture, it was the worst period of my entire imprisonment. But ironically, it was those same terrible months of inhuman treatment that turned the snowball of support for me into an avalanche.

The Political Police wanted to discredit me—they would portray me as a murderer, a torturer, a member of Batista's secret police, glossing over the fact that when I was arrested I'd been working for the Revolutionary government. Before, the Cuban press had made no mention of my supposed profession as police agent and torturer. This was a recent ruse on the government's part. If I *had* been an agent in the Batista government, Castro would have had me shot instantly, as he did so many others, on the mere suspicion of a connection with the previous regime.

This defamation campaign, so typical of Marxist regimes, was coordinated by ICAP, the Cuban Institute for Friendship Between Countries, one of the security agencies of the government. René Rodríguez was its director. He is now accused of involvement in smuggling drugs into the United States.

The campaign began on an old note—they allowed a reporter to visit me, a prisoner held strictly incommunicado. I guessed what was happening as soon as I saw him. I refused to speak with him or allow him to take photographs. He and some officers spent more than an hour trying to convince me it was okay, while my brain was working as fast as it could. I knew this was a trick of some sort, that I'd be quoted as saying things I'd never said, so I tried to figure out how to come out of this as well as I could. Finally I offered to write him a letter and some lines of verse. He accepted. Anyone that reads my letter will immediately see my distrust of the journalist, because its first words are: "You have asked me for an interview for your magazine. I prefer to write it. Any opinion, comment, or interpretation of anything spoken about here will be, except for what is written in this letter, the views of the journalist. Nothing in this letter has been crossed out or erased, and it should be published in its entirety."

I was sure that if some outrageous "facts" about me were printed, my friends abroad would immediately publish an indignant reply. And so it turned out, for the article when it appeared carried a clumsily forged identification card from the Batista police which stated that my eyes were brown, when in fact they're black, and which gave my birthdate incorrectly. And to cap the comedy, my height and weight were given in metrics, whereas before the Revolution Cuba had used feet, inches, and pounds.

A while later in 1981, ICAP began distributing (and still distributes) a pamphlet called "*Desde la silla del engaño*," or "From the Deceitful Chair," an obvious reference to the title of one of my books of poetry, *From My Wheelchair*. The pamphlet was signed by a Luis Adrián Betancourt, of the press office of ICAP, and appeared in Information Bulletin No. 3. Its purported intention was to "properly inform the friends of Cuba abroad" about the Valladares case. In the pamphlet, the information which appeared on the identification card is contradicted. The ID card clearly states that I joined Batista's secret police in May 1958, whereas page 3 of the pamphlet gives the date as October 1957—which was even more impossible, since by that date I wasn't the required minimum age. In later publications, after I'd gotten out of prison and could refute the lies, the ID card always had its right side cut off, so the false date couldn't be seen.

When I say that the greatest promoters of the campaign in my behalf were the colonels of the Political Police, I'm not exaggerating. Their propaganda became a boomerang. Insensitive to and ignorant of human behavior, contemptuous of their own countrymen, who are muzzled by terror and have no recourse against injustice, the Political Police didn't realize that in free countries it doesn't work quite the same way—there are people who are shocked and offended by *any* man's spending more than twenty years in prison, reduced to a wheelchair, kept in inhuman, degrading conditions, held in complete isolation, and not allowed to defend himself. The fact that on top of all that the Political Police were defaming me, saying I was a torturer, a vicious criminal, and a CIA agent and inventing all sorts of other lies, made my situation even more shocking. The Political Police never foresaw the reaction their article about me would provoke. The campaign in Europe solidified. In France the Committee for the Defense of Valladares, at Fernando Arrabal's initiative, published a declaration signed by the Nobel laureate André de Wass, Jorge Semprín, Eugène Ionesco, Bernard-Henri Lévy, Yves Montand, Pierre Golendorf, the poets Philippe Sollers and Pierre Emmanuel, and many other public figures.

As a result of this declaration, Madrid's *Diario 16* requested, in its column "Dissidences," that anyone who wished to join the protest against the Cuban government's defamations should send his or her signature to that publication. Hundreds of people, many of them Spanish-speaking intellectuals throughout the world such as Octavio Paz, Camilo José Cela, Mario Vargas Llosa, Ernesto Sábato, and many others, immediately replied. For weeks letters of support poured into the offices of *Diario 16,* which played a very important role in securing my release.

The French PEN Club handed a letter personally to the Cuban ambassador to Paris. In it, after stating that they had information that I was a victim of torture, PEN members advised the ambassador, "We will await your reply before reporting this information to public opinion, Amnesty International, the Commission on Human Rights of the European Council, and all other international organizations with which we maintain contact."

Meanwhile, the effects of this international campaign were also being felt in the United States, and the U.S. ambassador to the General Assembly of the United Nations, Jeane Kirkpatrick, read a detailed statement on my condition to that world body.

As a reprisal, since they could no longer kill me—it would be too "noisy" —the Political Police tortured me with the most sophisticated methods they commanded, and my family would not escape their rage, either.

When I was alone in the cell, I was incapable of even suspecting how long I'd spend there or what conditions my jailers had designed for me.

The barred entrance opened onto a hallway whose windows had been sealed with planks. I couldn't tell whether it was day or night. The ward was completely empty, so there was no way I could communicate with other prisoners. There was not a single window. The bathroom was inside my room, but when I turned on the taps, no water came out. I called my guard and asked him to turn on the main faucet—I knew how the hospital worked, that you could turn off the water by sections. The guard told me he couldn't do anything except report to the officer in charge of the special guard. That's how I learned I had a special guard force attached to me. By order of the

Political Police, no soldier who was a regular guard at the hospital was to have any contact with me. My guards in the future would be chosen by the Political Police alone, and had to be members of the Party.

I noticed there were no light switches; they'd all been taken out. I called my guard again and asked him to turn out the lights. I wanted to go to sleep.

"The lights can't be turned off," he answered.

I told him I couldn't sleep with ten fluorescent light bulbs glaring in my eyes.

"Sorry—higher orders. The lights can't be turned off."

I realized then that the lights would never be turned off. You can sleep, it's true, in a brightly lighted room, but you don't really rest. A "good night's sleep," the necessary rest, can be had only in darkness or semidarkness. And that was precisely the point—I was not to be allowed that rest.

The heat was almost unbearable because, in addition to the back wall's being heated up by the tropical summer sun, directly underneath my room was the hospital kitchen, where, every morning, oil-fired ovens were lighted. They heated the floor of my room and made it an almost literal hell.

Although the hallway windows were boarded up, the windows in the ward were open, and swarms of mosquitoes invaded the area. There were nights when I killed more than two hundred of them.

The first night I dozed off and on. I'd thought that on a mattress I'd sleep like a log, but the lights kept me awake. The fluorescent glare was so strong that it hurt even to open my eyes, I couldn't look at the walls, either, since the white paint reflected all the brilliance of the lights.

After those endless hours in bed I could tell by the noises from the kitchen that it must be about four o'clock in the morning. I remembered that that was when the cooks came in to start work. There was absolutely no sign of any kind whether it was day or night outside, except those sounds.

They didn't bring me breakfast that first morning. When I asked the guard for breakfast he told me he couldn't leave the ward, I'd have to wait until somebody came. I complained that there was no water, no container of any kind, and that I didn't have any personal articles—no soap, toilet paper, toothpaste, or toothbrush.

They allowed me water only at mealtimes. My requests for a container so I could keep a little water for other times were routinely ignored. I had never perspired so much in any other cell—the sheet and mattress were always soaked, and I was always thirsty. I had no soap to bathe with even if they had turned on the water for a shower. They wouldn't give me toilet paper either. I was kept in those conditions for two weeks.

At the end of two weeks, Major Guido paid me a visit. Of course, he knew what was going on, but part of the game was that I was supposed to report my conditions to him and ask for improvement. So I played the game. In a magnanimous gesture he immediately ordered the guard to bring me soap, a tube of toothpaste, and a liter container for water. He told me he'd give orders to the commander of the special guard to let me have a shower once a day. It was always the Political Police who brought good news; they were the only ones who could authorize anything, from a bar of soap to your freedom—they were the absolute masters of your life.

"You see, Valladares, all these little things can be solved," he said to me with ill-concealed sarcasm.

"So it seems, Major, but I'd like to know the reason for my being shut up this way, like somebody who's just been arrested and is being held for interrogation."

"You know why, Valladares—we have to take drastic measures against you. You keep sending false reports of your treatment out to the foreign press, complaining all the time. We can't allow that, and you won't write anything here. *That's* why. And you're the one responsible for your situation."

"I'm the one guilty for my being in a wheelchair in this room?"

He ignored my sarcasm. "Exactly. You refuse to accept the disciplinary measures that govern every penal institution. And not only here—the same rules apply in jails in capitalist countries, but *there* the rules really are inhumane, because they're aimed at punishment, not at rehabilitation."

"But the disciplinary rules in the jails in free countries aren't intended to make a prisoner renounce his beliefs and adopt the beliefs of his jailers, as here in Cuba, Major. And what's more, there are no political prisoners in free countries—no one's persecuted for his ideas, or jailed for disagreeing with the government, as has happened with so many people here, me included."

"You're mistaken, Valladares. There are thousands and thousands of prisoners in capitalist countries. In the United States the jails are full of Puerto Ricans, Latinos, and blacks who are forced into crime by an inhumane, exploitive society that discriminates against them, makes them second-class citizens, and systematically violates their rights. Those men *are* political prisoners, because they reject an unjust society they wish they could change. Not you men—you've tried to block the progress, the very dreams, of the proletariat."

"It looks to me as if the aspirations of that proletariat conflict with the aspirations of the Marxist dictatorship, because the great majority of political prisoners are workers and campesinos, humble people. They are the ones who have been in conspiracies, those are the people who have rebelled and taken up arms and gone into the mountains."

"Yes, tricked and misled by the lies and propaganda of imperialism, which has used them as tools in its policy of aggression against the Revolution."

Major Guido argued with such spirit that you'd have thought he believed what he was saying. I wasn't the least impressed.

Two weeks later they tried a new policy. One morning they brought lunch no more than an hour after breakfast. Two hours later they brought dinner. When I asked the guard what time it was he told me it was eight o'clock at night. Of course, I didn't know exactly what time it was, but I knew it wasn't eight o'clock at night. Downstairs in the kitchen all the clattering was over by five in the evening, and I could still hear the sound of pots and pans. I realized they wanted me to lose track, or even all sense, of time, so I determined I'd do everything I could to counter their strategy.

I knew they used methods like these in Political Police Headquarters. Besides locking prisoners in dungeon cells where neither natural light nor any sound ever penetrated, the police also administered drugs in the prisoners' food to make them sleep an entire day or longer. Then when it was really night the guard would bring in breakfast. This was harder where I was, since though I couldn't see anything I had outside sounds as references. Soon these sounds were almost like clock chimes for me; I could measure the days and nights by them. And my close observation of hospital routine helped me greatly in this, of course; hospital days were always predictable. I knew that around ten o'clock every morning except Sunday a truck from the central warehouse brought in the supplies for the next day. It always stopped directly under the sealed windows in front of my cell and the driver blew the horn for the prisoners to come unload the groceries.

Another reference point they couldn't keep quiet was the lights-out boomed by loudspeakers on all the guardposts and buildings of the complex every night at ten. Then there was the wake-up call at five-thirty every morning. I strained my ears to hear the conversations of soldiers and prisoners outside and on the lower floor of the building. The prisoners knew I was upstairs, but they could never say anything or call out to me, because the common prisoner in charge of the kitchen, known as Pury by everyone, was an informer for the Political Police. He even slept down there so that he could always have his eye on what went on below me.

The officer of the guard brought in food to both the guard and me. The guard picked up the food at the far end of the ward, locked the door again, walked down the ward to my cell, and passed me my tray. After the first day I always asked him what time it was. But the guards soon stopped wearing watches—they had been ordered not to tell me the time. That didn't matter to me; I kept asking even though they always said they didn't know. That was a little weak, though, so they received new orders—they wore watches, but the watches were set ahead or back. But I saw through that quickly enough and started saying things like "Goodness! I thought it was earlier!" They seemed to think I'd been fooled.

They began to tighten the screws of repression. They wouldn't change my linens even when the sheets were sweaty, greasy, and smelly from perspiration. The mattress was disgusting. Water for bathing lasted only a few moments. The cell hadn't been swept in weeks.

I began feeling dull and lazy. Every morning when I woke up I was tired from the built-up effect of the lights. I squinted continuously; my forehead ached from wrinkling my brow against the lights. And there was no way to avoid them. One day it occurred to me to roll my socks into a kind of visor over my eyes, but I knew I had to take it off whenever I heard the guard coming or he'd take my socks away immediately. Even if he tiptoed, the position of the lights in the hall was such that I could always see his shadow first.

Every morning as soon as I opened my eyes I repeated the month, day, and year. Some prisoners make marks on the wall to keep track of the date, but if they're put in another cell they're lost. So I kept my calendar where they couldn't take it away from me—in my mind. At night I turned the page to tomorrow; I'd say to myself, "Tomorrow will be the so-and-so day of such-and-such month," marking the time from my arrival at the hospital.

I received a visit from Dr. Roberto Puente, subdirector of the hospital and a lieutenant in the Ministry of the Interior. He told me very openly that he'd been sent by the Party on a mission to El Salvador. I knew other staff officers at the prison had been sent to El Salvador, but the boastful way Puente told me made me doubt him. Puente was one of the most sadistic torturers I ever came across in the prisons. He'd keep medicines back from chronically ill men. When a strange virus was causing men all through the prison to vomit blood, he released them from the hospital and sent them back to their unhealthy cells. He refused to let Eugenio Silva and Juan González stay in the hospital intensive-care unit, though Silva had a very serious ulcer, simply because the two men refused to enter Political Rehabilitation.

The purpose of Puente's visit was to assess my psychological state, to see how the "treatment" was working. I recall I asked him the date, though I knew exactly what day it was. I noted that he had taken his watch off and put it in his pocket; the watchband was sticking out a little.

"You don't know what the date is today?"

"No, Doctor, I lost track a few days ago."

He smiled with satisfaction and told me what day it was, but he added four days for good measure.

I talked to him about the lights and their effect on me, which as a doctor he well knew. He told me the lights would do me no harm at all; he always slept with the lights on.

"Well, Doctor, you know there's a campaign by the Revolution to save electricity, and we're supposed to use the fewest lights possible. I hope they don't accuse you of being a counterrevolutionary for this waste of electricity." There was no way to answer such a cynic as Dr. Puente without resorting to mockery and sarcasm.

The weeks passed. From time to time the Political Police performed searches on me and my cell to be sure I hadn't somehow gotten hold of paper or something else to write on. They changed my guards frequently, even though the men had been hand-picked, just to be sure that in the daily routine one of the guards wasn't "infected." Many guards came and went, and one of them got curious and asked me one night why they had me locked up like that. He had felt some twinge of humanity, it seems. Sometimes a guard would get bored at his post, and if he was a talker he'd come to my cell and chat. After all, the guards were on duty for twenty-four hours straight in a little room next to mine; they couldn't leave even for one minute. This was one of those guards. When I finished telling him my story, which he'd followed with some interest, I saw a look of mixed admiration and pity on his face.

"They told me you were a criminal, that you'd planned to dynamite day-care centers and kill the children."

"That's what they always say so you guards will keep away from me."

"Security says we're absolutely forbidden to talk to you."

"Of course, because *this* could happen—I could tell you my side of the story and you could compare the two versions, think about it, and draw your own conclusions. Security doesn't want you to know the truth, so they tell you I'm a murderer."

He was a decent man, like so many other men I met during my years in prison, but he'd been limited by terror. From that night on, that soldier and I often talked.

One morning they started working in the ward. I could hear lots of hammering and drilling. I couldn't see anything, but I soon found out they had built two dividing walls in the ward, separating my cell and the next cells from the rest of the big room. The work was finished in two days, and I found myself more isolated than any prisoner had ever been before. Several days later I heard the sound of nuts and bolts and sheets of metal in the room next to mine. They had brought up gym equipment—parallel bars, tables, walkers—and heat lamps and other physical-therapy equipment.

Dr. Puente and another Political Police officer came to my door. The other officer was Guido's aide, and his perfect physical opposite—thin as a strand of spaghetti, with a bulging, overhanging forehead. He said his name was Beltrán. He was young, very well mannered and kindly. He'd been twelve years old when I was arrested.

"Your very own physical-therapy room is ready. It has all the equipment you'll need. This is so you'll see that the Revolution, without any political considerations, sees a man as a human being over and above all the differences of opinion and belief."

"Yes, Doctor . . . my state, this isolation, the perpetual lights, the daily humiliation, the refusal of a human being's most basic necessities, all that is a confirmation of what you just said."

He turned red. The lieutenant came to his aid; he spoke softly. "No,

Valladares. *We* haven't created this situation. *You* have. You've forced us to take preventive measures. And you're lucky to be a prisoner in a Communist jail, where an inmate's physical integrity is respected. If this were a jail in one of the capitalist countries they'd have killed you already or would beat you."

"I've been beaten, Lieutenant. You mean you don't know about the forced-labor concentration camps, or about Boniato Prison? And those aren't exactly capitalist jails!" I laughed.

That sort of reply always got to them. A Communist always seems to prefer an angry, blurted, uncontrolled manner. The truth, spoken calmly to his face, always exasperates him. As what I'd said was unarguable, the two men turned angrily and walked away.

I thought it was strange that they'd finally agreed to give me therapy and medical care, but I was delighted.

The next day Major Guido, his aide Beltrán, and another officer visited me. They had on the brand-new uniforms worn exclusively by the Political Police, made of the highest-quality cloth and cut well; they were much more distinguished than those of the other State services. In just a few weeks the country would learn to fear the very sight of those uniforms.

"Well, Valladares, since nobody talks about you anymore, since your wife Martha isn't in the newspapers every day or being brought to some microphone to make a speech, we've decided to go on with your physical therapy. If it's taken so long it's because we don't give in to pressure, we don't negotiate under those conditions. The Revolution has defied Yankee imperialism, and, speaking vulgarly, we've taken the ballsy policy."

"Yes," Lieutenant Beltrán amplified, "all things come to an end. We knew the interest of the capitalist press wouldn't last long, they'd get tired of using you as a pawn, to discredit the Revolution. Your friends have forgotten, Valladares, and we're the ones who've come to your aid. We're the ones who're going to give you the medical attention you need."

I knew this decision was by no means spontaneous. Their attitude had been determined by the only thing that makes Communists concede anything to their prisoners—international pressure. The fact that Guido and Beltrán emphasized that nobody ever mentioned my name anymore, that the campaign for my release had fizzled and died, that my friends had forgotten about me, was an indication of precisely the opposite. That was the best news I'd heard since I was put into the eternally lighted cell. And I was not mistaken in my interpretation. I didn't know anything, I had nothing concrete to go on, no details, but I was as sure the campaign was gaining momentum as if I could actually hear the cries for my release.

The first day I was taken for treatment, Major Guido, Lieutenant Beltrán, and Dr. Puente were present. Dr. Puente would hereforth personally direct my exercises, following a plan designed by Dr. Alvarez Cambra. The first session was like a ceremony—the lieutenant and my guard stood in front of the closed but not sealed windows while Guido and Puente stood together and watched the treatment.

I received heat treatments, massages, and passive exercise, and then they put the braces on me so I could walk between the parallel bars. At the end of that first session, which lasted almost the whole morning, I was exhausted. But I was happy, and I determined to use all my physical and psychological strength to recover as fast as I could.

A few days later a colonel came to see me to tell me that I would be receiving better food as part of my treatment. That was the only reason for his visit. The next day something utterly inconceivable happened—they brought me a liter of milk, half a chicken, some fruit, and salad. The miraculous menu was repeated again that evening.

There now remained no doubt that they were going to rehabilitate me physically. I suspected they were doing this to counter the campaign to have me given medical care, but actually it was more than that. Since they had finally decided to set me free, the physical therapy was intended as a way of erasing the traces of the torture that had condemned me to my double imprisonment—jail and the wheelchair. And the authorities wanted it kept secret, because if the outside world learned of it nobody would be surprised to see me get off the plane on my own two feet, not in a wheelchair as they expected.

Havana said I was not crippled. Their spokespeople and agents throughout the world repeated it. It was to be as though I'd claimed they had amputated one of my arms and then everyone saw that I still had both of them. The authorities had always claimed that my condition was reversible, and so it turned out to be. There was no miracle or lie involved in my being able to walk—it was simple manipulation of my muscles through physical therapy. The same men who crippled me cured me.

Castro had told Dr. Rodríguez Iturbe, the Venezuelan Senator and chairman of the Foreign Relations Committee, that I would never leave Cuba in a wheelchair. They were preparing to make Fidel's prediction come true.

In spite of the improvement in my food, the lights were still left on and the searches continued. One day they confiscated a little cardboard box top from a milk carton. The military director of the hospital came to ask me what I wanted it for, and he made another search.

My legs grew stronger day by day. My intensive treatments never let up; sometimes I even had sessions on Sunday. Another doctor from the Political Police, whose name I never learned, came to help in the treatment. The two doctors, one in front and one behind me, pushed and pulled me. More massages, heat, exercises, and walks through the parallel bars. I began to have some control over my movements. But there was great tension during the sessions, and we were almost always silent. The doctors spoke only if they had to give me instructions or tell each other what to do, and then they spoke as brusquely and tersely as possible.

I soon graduated to the short braces again. Several months had passed and I was now walking alone down the parallel bars, though I had to support myself on them.

Every day at the end of the session I was returned to my cell.

To keep my mind occupied and to exercise my vocal cords, I made up talks to imaginary audiences. I would also go over what I knew of academic subjects and improvise lectures on history, geology, and so forth. All out loud—which more than once brought one of the guards over toward my cell, not all the way to the bars but a little way away where he'd spy on me. He probably thought I'd finally gone mad.

I needed to write during that period, but there was no way to do it, so I got the idea of composing poetry by memory. I started a new experiment, then. When I'd repeated the first line until I had memorized it completely, I'd go on to make up the second line. After I'd fixed those two in my mind, I went on to the third, and so on to the end of the verse, then to the end of the poem. I'd go over and over the poem, many times a day every day, until I had it engraved in my mind. (I recited all these poems to Fernando Arrabal in his apartment in Paris a few days after I'd left Cuba, and he insisted I let him record them on a tape recorder so I wouldn't forget them. Then we transcribed them. How right Arrabal was! Had we not done this, within just a few weeks I'd have lost them completely. These poems were published in a volume titled *Cavernas del silencio* [*Caverns of Silence*], by the Playor Press in Madrid.)

But while the Political Police were curing me, they continued to make my family suffer. Officers forced my mother, under threat of having my sister imprisoned, to write me a letter in which she said that I was an enemy of the people and deserved being shut up in isolation, and that there was no way I could ever thank the Revolution enough for what it had done for me. When Major Guido gave me the letter and I finished reading it, I knew it had been written under duress. Several times the letter said how kind and generous a man Colonel Blanco Fernández was; the Political Police relished the fact that my mother was forced to praise the man who had designed the repressive treatment I'd been receiving for years. They knew, too, how hurt I would be that my mother defended one of my torturers.

They often ordered my sister to come to Political Police Headquarters, then took advantage of my sister's being out of the house to terrorize my mother. One day my sister decided on the way to Political Police Headquarters that if they wanted to interrogate her, they could come and get her; she was going back home. When she got home and went into the house she surprised an officer dictating a letter to my mother. It was to be sent to Amnesty International. When my family and I were together at last in the

United States, my mother told me they made her write and sign many other letters and declarations, some to strangers they brought to the house, refuting my accusations and complaints.

When my sister refused to go to Political Police Headquarters, Colonel Blanco Fernández himself came to get her. He showed her a judgment against her, sentencing her to twelve years in prison. Of course, she'd never gone to trial. He made her get some personal items together and then took her off to the women's jail. She was forced to wait in a cell until that night, under the pretext that some paperwork still had to be done, and then they sent her home again, telling her they were going to come for her again the next day. They did this to her several times.

On one occasion Colonel Blanco Fernández and Captain Liar roughed her up to take her purse away from her and search her. One day Captain Liar came to the house and told my mother and sister they might as well forget about using their exit visa, there were just three avenues open to them: (1) become Communists, (2) conspire against the Revolution, or (3) try to escape Cuba on some little boat.

All these outrages were perpetrated against two perfectly defenseless women. Because of this psychological harassment my sister finally had to go into psychiatric therapy; today she is still under treatment.

53 / Freedom

didn't know until I left Cuba that Martha had taken a trip through Europe gathering support for my release.

Politicians, journalists, and intellectuals received her graciously and warmly in both Spain and France, where Fernando Arrabal wrote a letter to President François Mitterrand. He sent with it a letter from Martha asking for an interview with the French President. In Sweden, Martha met with Group 110 of Amnesty International. Per Rasmussen more than a year before had persuaded the nonsocialist coalition in Sweden to write letters requesting my release, offering me political asylum in Sweden along with a job in that country. Ranking members of the government of Sweden were also very kind and encouraging to Martha.

Per Rasmussen also somehow managed to persuade Pierr Schori, International Secretary of the Social-Democratic Party and current Undersecretary of Foreign Relations in Sweden, to meet with Martha. The interview was held very early in the morning in the Hotel Continental in Stockholm, since Pierr Schori didn't want to be seen with the wife of a Cuban political prisoner. He didn't allow Rasmussen or Humberto López Guerra, an expatriate Cuban filmmaker living in Stockholm, to attend the meeting. It was to be just he and Martha; he didn't want witnesses. It was all very cloak-and-dagger.

"Madame, if you want to do something for your husband I advise you not to continue your campaign of publicity and denunciations. You will never get him out of prison that way." Schori's suggestion exactly followed the Cuban authorities' advice. Régis Debray in France gave the same "advice" to Martha through a third party. "These things must be handled very quietly. . . ."

"However, Mr. Schori," Martha replied, "when a prisoner is mistreated in Chile or Argentina, socialists make a fuss. Do socialists still think Cuba is a paradise? Is that it?"

"No, no, of course not. Very few of us in Europe still think Cuba is a paradise," he said, looking at his two watches, one on each wrist.

"So if you know what's happening in Cuba, if you know there's an implacable dictatorship in Cuba, if you know all liberties have been suspended, why don't you speak out?"

"Because that would be giving the Americans a publicity weapon."

Martha could hardly insult the man by telling him she thought that attitude was immoral, dishonest, and unethical, so she remained silent for a moment. Then she returned to my specific case.

"It isn't intelligent to go on keeping my husband in prison. More and more people every day are becoming aware of his situation and joining the campaign to release him. That damages the image of himself and his government that Castro wants to present."

"Madame, intelligence and passionate anger are in conflict inside Castro," he said as he pointedly looked once more at his watches, "and passionate anger always prevails."

Martha could tell from the way he kept looking at his watches that her interview with Schori had come to an end, that he wanted her to leave. She stood up. Before she left, Schori warned her not to speak to the press about this interview. Perhaps he didn't want to provoke Fidel's passionate anger.

Ramón Ramudo, the Spanish-Swede, had been freed after the Political Police changed the charges against him—he was accused of smuggling silk handkerchiefs, which was a commonly used criminal charge in Cuba. Ramón managed to get the letters from my punishment cells through Cuban Security, and he arrived in Stockholm with them still in his possession.

That had been the last contact he'd had with me; neither he nor I knew that Martha was in Stockholm, yet by one of those divinely arranged coincidences Ramón learned that she was there. He was still terribly thin and yellow, the marks of prison and torture still apparent in his face and eyes, when Martha met him. Later he appeared on Swedish television and showed my letters. This TV appearance was extremely valuable for me, because the whole world picked up the story.

From Sweden Martha went on to Norway, where the extraordinary actress Liv Ullman and a group of journalists and intellectuals, stunned by what Martha told them, founded a committee in Oslo. So from frozen northern Europe, with its perpetual ice, the snowball was gathering size, strength, and velocity. It had become unstoppable, and it was about to squash Castro. He was learning what it meant to be the object of passionate anger. He would have to give in.

My treatment continued. As the months of daily exercises went on, I began to walk down the parallel bars without the aid of any orthopedic equipment, do knee bends and jog a little in place. How wonderful it was to take those first steps and to know I would probably be able to recover completely! I had conquered yet another obstacle!

Several bones in my foot had been dislocated during my escape attempt, now many years ago in 1961. They had knitted very badly, and when doctors examined my X-rays they always said I would never walk without a noticeable limp. But I wasn't limping. I forced myself not to—I would twist my foot around in the right direction, force my muscles to adjust, until I had compensated for the misaligned bones.

Curiously, in spite of being able to walk, do knee bends, and jog in place either between the parallel bars or in the bathroom before my daily shower, I couldn't walk in the relatively free space of the room without holding on to something. I was suffering that same lack of control I've mentioned as affecting me after being in the blackout cells. I zigzagged. And because of that I still often used the wheelchair. If I tried to walk from my bed to the bathroom I walked all over the room and as likely as not wound up at a wall 90 degrees from where I wanted to go. I needed real open space to recover perspective and the line of the horizon; four walls weren't enough. But I couldn't leave my room—the authorities had to protect the secret of my recuperation until the last minute.

One afternoon a new specialist came in to examine me. He tested my muscles and watched me do exercises. He then explained to me that all I needed was a few days in the open air to recover my balance for walking. A few days later Dr. Puente brought in a bicycle for more vigorous exercise.

The doctors were intensifying my treatment. I now was doing exercises and receiving therapy both morning and afternoon. The day of my release was approaching, though I had not the slightest inkling of that. And yet the torture of the lights, the silences of the doctors, the harassments continued. That duality was grotesque, maddening. The food was good and there was plenty of it, but I couldn't even get an aspirin for a headache. I had allergic welts and itching all over my body, but they wouldn't give me antihistamines.

One morning a group of colonels appeared and told me to get my things together.

"The general wants to see you," said the leader of the group.

The caravan of three cars left the prison and went to Villa Marista, the Headquarters of the Political Police, an enormous complex of buildings.

They kept me in one of the cells in a long, long hallway. Tens of thousands of Cubans had passed through those cells for "interrogations," really torture sessions meant to extract confessions real or imaginary. Many men couldn't withstand the torture and died. The Political Police always reported they had "committed suicide."

The cell I was in had a peephole through which the guard was constantly spying on me. That was so you'd always feel watched.

In a few hours a whole platoon of colonels and aides came to get me. They took me to a very luxurious office with carpets and red drapes, where a man some forty-eight years old was waiting for me. He was the general who headed the Political Police installation.

"Valladares, we've brought you here because we are going to release you . . . and possibly let you leave the country."

The news didn't produce the effect on me that they'd expected. The general was a bit taken aback. But I had known of many instances in which prisoners had been manipulated by having their hopes for freedom used against them.

"Doesn't that make you happy, Valladares?"

"Why are you releasing me, General?" I obviously didn't believe him very much. For years I had survived without that hope; I wasn't going to be overly eager to embrace it now.

"Because the Revolution is settling cases like yours now, in spite of your hostility while you've been in prison and your rejection of the Political Rehabilitation Program." He glanced at his watch, a Rolex, the watch which is a sure sign of Castro's favor. "It's late. You'd better get some rest."

He stood up and added, "We know you need some exercise in the open air. You're pale. Tomorrow Comrade Alvarez Cambra, your doctor, will come to see you. He's been directing your treatment, so he's kept abreast of your progress."

I couldn't sleep for the rest of the short night; the news that they were going to release me had come so unexpectedly, and I could really not afford to give it too much credence. I was afraid it was a new move in the Political Police game, and I tried desperately to figure out what strategy it obeyed. Maybe they wanted to build up my hopes and then make me agree to some condition, such as joining Political Rehabilitation. My experience with my enemies made me doubt their intentions until the last second—I just couldn't imagine they would release me without demanding something in return. I had no idea how strong the tide of public opinion in my favor had become; how could I imagine it would make Castro release me in spite of his arrogance and anger, his sworn word that as long as the campaign went on, I'd never leave Cuba?

The next afternoon Dr. Alvarez Cambra did come to see me. He very politely told me they were going to take me to a gym and let me out to walk through the athletic field.

First they had me walk through the halls, leaning on some officers. Then they took me to the gym, where the general was waiting for us. In the following days they made me walk up and down stairs, first slowly, then more quickly. I was becoming stronger and more fit day by day.

One morning Dr. Alvarez Cambra went with me out to the athletic field.

My first steps were a little unsteady; I had to lean on him and the general. An officer took films of me walking. Dr. Alvarez Cambra told me I'd quickly regain my ability to walk, and he was right. The first day I walked slowly, but the day after I was walking well, and by the third day I could jog slowly.

"When you can really run, we'll release you," the general told me. He had already told me that I was not only being released but also being permitted to leave the country. I told him that was fine, I was glad, but I'd only accept if my family could leave Cuba too. He'd said he'd have to check with his superiors (and I could guess what that meant). So on that third day I asked him again about my family's leaving. He said higher authorities had not seen fit to include my family in my release.

"Then I'm afraid I don't accept the exit visa, General. I'm not leaving without my family. They've been harassed and persecuted for years, held as hostages for my 'good behavior,' taken off the plane they were supposed to fly to Miami on, and all because you were taking reprisals against me. I'm not going away and leaving them here. They have everything ready—passports, visas, plane tickets, everything. It's not right that they go on suffering."

"You're mad, you don't know what you're saying—your family will leave later."

"No, General, I can't accept those conditions."

"Listen, tomorrow a man will come to see you who I'm sure will make you change your mind."

The next day I was on the athletic field doing exercises when the general came out with a tall, fair man wearing a moustache. He was Pierre Charasse, the interim French ambassador. It was my conversation with him that finally revealed to me the reason for my release. President Mitterrand had requested it of Castro, and Castro had agreed. M. Charasse showed me a copy of the telegram from the French President; he was awaiting my arrival in Paris in the next few days. The world's press was already publishing the news.

I had a sudden illumination. I realized the game had changed, that I now held the upper hand. I explained my family's situation to M. Charasse. I asked him to convey my thanks to the President of France, but, I added, "I'd rather stay here in a cell and eat cornmeal, with a clear conscience, than eat duck à l'orange at Maxim's and feel that I'd betrayed my family."

The ambassador was very kind. He told me to be reasonable. I'm sure that to him, my refusal to go with him to Paris, to my freedom, was nothing short of madness.

When he left I was filled with a feeling of great peace. I knew that the most important thing was to live in harmony with my conscience, doing what I believed I had to do, without regard for the consequences. That, the clearness of my conscience, was my true freedom, the God-given inner freedom which cannot be taken away from a man. I couldn't leave my family behind.

The general's reaction was predictable—he was furious. When he sent for me I could see that he was outraged. He told me once again, as they had been telling me for years, that they would not tolerate outside pressure and that Castro had found out what I was demanding and had said that as far as he was concerned, then, I could rot in jail.

"This is your last chance, Valladares."

"Thank you, General, but I'm not leaving without my family."

That night they returned me to prison. There was tremendous anger in the air. The same colonels who just days before had gone out of their way to be polite to me, as though in that way to erase from the books those years of torture and degradation, now refused to speak to me. Total silence reigned all the way back to jail.

Two days later the authorities brought my family and also M. Charasse to me. My mother and I finally embraced, after so many years without seeing each other; my sister kissed me in tears. They were both overcome with emotion—they hadn't known about the therapy I had received in secret. The authorities had wanted no leaks, so my family had never expected to see me walking. In fact, just months before when my mother had asked about me, officers had told her that I had refused all physical therapy. M. Charasse told me that the negotiations between the French government and Castro now included my family. I told him I didn't believe in Castro's word.

"Martha has waited for you for twenty-two years—neither one of you deserves having to wait any longer," my sister said firmly as she hugged me. "Go, Armando. At least we're not in prison. You've suffered too much to stay here anymore. You deserve a little happiness. Go, and be what God wants you to be."

"Armando, don't stay here for me," said my mother. "I've done nothing but pray that you'd be released. Now no matter what happens I can die in peace."

They took me back to Political Police Headquarters. The colonels were smiling and obsequious again. The day of my departure they took movies of me again, as I jogged around the athletic field.

When I was taken out of the cell for the last time the officer escorting me whistled loudly as a signal that he was bringing a prisoner down the hall. They always did that so two prisoners wouldn't see each other. Sometimes they even put a hood over the prisoner when they led him along the corridors.

Suddenly a prisoner ran out of a side entrance to the hallway, shoved the guard, made straight for the stairs, and jumped over the railing head first.

He screamed as he fell. Who was he? What had driven him mad? What tortures had he been through?

They issued me a suit, an overcoat, and a suitcase.

In my last conversation with the general, he gave me a veiled threat. My family was staying—their leaving depended on me. That meant if I spoke out against the Cuban government they'd never get off the island.

"The Revolution has long arms, Valladares—don't forget that. . . ."

I didn't reply. My mind was already far away, in Paris, where Martha, my real-life Penelope, was waiting for me. I had written a poem for her in 1979, which had ended on a note of hope after her anxious wait:

> *I will come to you*
> *this time there can be no doubt*
> *our meeting has been decided,*
> *defying hatred and abysses.*

The hour of my departure arrived. The procession of several cars headed down Rancho Boyeros Avenue toward José Martí International Airport. The plane was scheduled for seven in the evening. The setting sun dyed the afternoon pomegranate-red. My heart sent up a hymn of thanks to God, and I prayed for my family, who hadn't been allowed to come to say goodbye, and for my friends remaining behind in the eternal night of the Cuban political prisons.

As the cars sped along, a flood of memories rushed over me. Twenty-two years in jail. I recalled the two sergeants, Porfirio and Matanzas, plunging their bayonets into Ernesto Díaz Madruga's body; Roberto López Chávez dying in a cell, calling for water, the guards urinating over his face and in his gasping mouth; Boitel, denied water too, after more than fifty days on hunger strike, because Castro wanted him dead; Clara, Boitel's poor mother, beaten by Lieutenant Abad in a Political Police station just because she wanted to find out where her son was buried. I remembered Carrión, shot in the leg, telling Jagüey not to shoot, and Jagüey mercilessly, heartlessly, shooting him in the back; the officers who threatened family members if they cried at a funeral.

I remembered Estebita and Piri dying in blackout cells, the victims of biological experimentation; Diosdado Aquit, Chino Tan, Eddy Molina, and so many others murdered in the forced-labor fields, quarries, and camps. A legion of specters, naked, crippled, hobbling and crawling through my mind, and the hundreds of men wounded and mutilated in the horrifying searches. Dynamite. Drawer cells. Eduardo Capote's fingers chopped off by a machete. Concentration camps, tortures, women beaten, soldiers pushing prisoners' heads into a lake of shit, the beatings of Eloy and Izaguirre. Martín Pérez with his testicles destroyed by bullets. Robertico weeping for his mother.

And in the midst of that apocalyptic vision of the most dreadful and horrifying moments in my life, in the midst of the gray, ashy dust and the orgy of beatings and blood, prisoners beaten to the ground, a man emerged, the skeletal figure of a man wasted by hunger, with white hair, blazing blue eyes, and a heart overflowing with love, raising his arms to the invisible heaven and pleading for mercy for his executioners.

"Forgive them, Father, for they know not what they do." And a burst of machine-gun fire ripping open his breast.

Epilogue

"From our point of view, we have no human-rights problem—there have been no 'disappeareds' here, there have been no tortures here, there have been no murders here. In twenty-five years of revolution, in spite of the difficulties and dangers we have passed through, torture has never been committed, a crime has never been committed."

—Statements made by Fidel Castro to French and American journalists in the Palacio de la Revolución in Havana on July 28, 1983, and published in *Granma* on August 10 of the same year

A NOTE ON THE TYPE

The text of this book was set in Times Roman, a type face designed by Stanley Morison (1889–1967) for *The Times* (London) and first introduced by that newspaper in 1932.

Among typographers and designers of the twentieth century, Stanley Morison was a strong forming influence—as a typographical adviser to The Monotype Corporation, as a director of two distinguished English publishing houses, and as a writer of sensibility, erudition, and keen practical sense.

Composed by The Haddon Craftsmen, Inc.,
Scranton, Pennsylvania

Printed and bound by Murray Printing Company,
Westford, Massachusetts

Typography and binding design by
Tasha Hall